The Profession of City Planning

The Profession of
City Planning

Changes, Images, and Challenges
1950–2000

edited by
LLOYD RODWIN
and
BISHWAPRIYA SANYAL

CENTER FOR URBAN POLICY RESEARCH
Rutgers, The State University of New Jersey
New Brunswick, New Jersey

Published by the CENTER FOR URBAN POLICY RESEARCH
Civic Square • 33 Livingston Avenue • Suite 400
New Brunswick, New Jersey 08901–1982

Printed in the United States of America

Library of Congress Cataloging-in-Publication Data

The profession of city planning : changes, images, and challenges,
   1950–2000 / edited by Lloyd Rodwin and Bishwapriya Sanyal.
      p.   cm.
   Includes bibliographical references (p.   ) and index.
   ISBN 0-88285-165-9 (paper)
   ISBN 0-88285-166-7 (cloth)

      1. City planning—United States.   2. City planning—United States—
   History—20th century.   I. Rodwin, Lloyd.   II. Sanyal,
   Bishwapriya.
   HT167.P75   2000
   307.1'216'0973—dc21   99–33272
                                                                CIP

Cover design: Helene Berinsky

Interior design/typesetting: Arlene Pashman

In Memory of Lloyd Rodwin

1919–1999

About the Editors

LLOYD RODWIN, Ford International Professor Emeritus at MIT, was head of the Faculty Policy Committee of the Joint Center for Urban Studies of MIT and Harvard University (1959–69), organizer and director of the Guayana, Venezuela, planning and research program of the Joint Center (1959–64), and head of MIT's Department of Urban Studies and Planning from 1968 to 1972. President of the Regional Science Association in 1986–87, Dr. Rodwin served on the editorial boards of *Daedalus*, the *International Regional Science Review,* and other professional journals. He advised governments at all levels, international agencies, and nongovernmental and private organizations on issues relating to housing, urban policies, and regional development. His publications, which span nearly five decades, range from *The British New Towns Policy* (1956) to *Rethinking the Experience of Development: Essays Provoked by the Work of Albert O. Hirschman,* coedited with Donald A. Schön in 1994. Dr. Rodwin followed the progress of this volume through its completion before his death on December 7, 1999, as the book went to press.

BISHWAPRIYA SANYAL is Professor and Chair of the Department of Urban Studies and Planning at MIT. He has advised the Ford Foundation, World Bank, International Labour Organization, United Nations Center for Human Settlements, and United States Agency for International Development on development planning policies. Dr. Sanyal's research focuses on the economies, planning institutions, and planning processes of cities in developing countries. He is the former vice president of the International Division of the American Planning Association. His coedited book, *High Technology and Low-Income Communities: Prospects for the Positive Use of Advanced Information Technology* (with Donald Schön and William Mitchell), was published by MIT Press in 1999.

Contents

Part III

IMAGES OF CITY-PLANNING PRACTICE
Sectors

Part IV

THE PUBLIC IMAGE AND THE LEADERSHIP ROLE OF THE PROFESSION

Part V

WHAT ABOUT THE FUTURE?

APPENDICES

Preface

In its Winter 1997 issue, *Daedalus*, the Journal of the American Academy of Arts and Sciences, published evaluations of four disciplines—philosophy, economics, literary studies and political science. Prepared by leading figures in each of these fields, they were looked at as a unique way of portraying and interpreting American academic culture in transformation; and the editor suggested that such investigations were sufficiently promising to be worth pursuing in other fields and on a wider spectrum. "Change," he said, "has been a constant in the past century, but it is possible to argue that it has never been more rapid or more argued over than in the last fifty years." Of the many factors that account for the changes, he listed: the social, political and economic transformations of the past half century; the desire to deploy some of the more rigorous methods of the natural sciences; the subsequent "reactions" to the results including "a growing antipathy to what some saw as a failure to address certain of the more burning issues of the day." He added the sharpening political and ideological differences, "the vastly expanded and altered nature of the student bodies" and "the altered character of contemporary American society, and indeed of a changed international society."

Even before this issue of *Daedalus* appeared, the Department of Urban Studies and Planning (DUSP) at MIT decided to initiate a Faculty Seminar on "The Profession of City Planning" focused largely on the U.S. experience. The model was the first DUSP Faculty Seminar held at MIT in the fall of 1992, led by Lloyd Rodwin and Donald Schön. The subsequent book—*Rethinking the Development Experience*—was published jointly by the Brookings Institution and the Lincoln Institute of Land Policy in 1994.

For the February 1997 Faculty Seminar on the Profession of City Planning, a range of questions for exploration were raised. A few examples follow:

- How have the current assumptions, goals, values and practices of planners changed from those largely influencing the profession in the past?

- What do different types of planners report about the relative importance of the roles they are playing and the most critical problems they confront; their relationships with different interest groups and with top executives, public and private; about their experience with building a consensus or resolving conflicts; and about the relevance of their varying skills and perspectives—from design capabilities and environmental savvy to long- and intermediate-term perspectives and the pragmatics of implementation?

- In what ways have the roles, methods, and constraints changed over time in regard to environmental issues, transportation, and infrastructure?

- How persuasive is the evidence that land-use planning, physical design, and the three-dimensional environment are reemerging as critical components in the planner's kit of tools? If so, what accounts for it?

- Have the groups changed that urban planners have traditionally served? If so, how? How have class and ethnic issues changed over time? On which fronts do we have evidence of success or failure? What about group identity politics? How is this changing the previous controversies about interest groups and the public interest?

- How have the tools of planners changed? Have they been much affected by some of the current forces—for example, globalization, information technology, and identity politics? How do the changes in intergovernmental powers and roles affect the tools used, the groups served, and the effectiveness of policies? What's fresh or innovative in the current economic approaches?

- What about the alleged mismatch between planning theory and planning practice? Is this a new problem, and, in any case, what might be done about it?

- How concerned are planners about the ethical dilemmas often encountered in professional practice? What are the implications?

The chapters that follow sum up the responses of some of the leading figures in the field, with many MIT planning faculty serving as commentators. The differences of views, as well as the common denominators, point up the diverse, often conflicting, views of city planners and urban specialists on the professional practice of city planning. They underline as well what planners do and how well they do it, how and why their current activities differ from what was the case in the past, and how much and in what ways these efforts have or have not enhanced cities and the quality of urban life and made additions to the intellectual capital of the field.

We have, in effect, held up a mirror—or, rather, several different kinds of mirrors—for examining the changes in the roles, images, and practices, as well as the main claims and critiques of the profession.

Preliminary versions of all but six of the chapters in this book were discussed at the Faculty Seminar. The six exceptions are Lloyd Rodwin's examination of paths of change in economics, political science, philosophy, literature and city planning; Judith E. Innis's essay on post-modern planning; Donald A. Schön's chapter on the regulation process; Anthony Downs's examination of housing and planning; Ann Markusen's analysis of the craft and philosophy of planning; and Bishwapriya Sanyal's chapter on "Planning's Three Challenges."

To orient the discussion at the Faculty Seminar, two articles written by Michael Teitz and published in the journal *Urban Studies* were recommended to seminar participants as background reading:

Teitz, M. 1996. American planning in the 1990s: evolution, debate, and challenge. *Urban Studies* 33, 4–5: 649–71.

Teitz, M. 1997. American planning in the 1990s, Part II: the dilemma of the cities. *Urban Studies* 34, 5–6: 775–95.

A few of the authors of the chapters that follow refer to these articles or to Michael Teitz's remarks at the Faculty Seminar.

The book has five parts.

Part I is an historical overview. It contrasts the main changes in the United States over the past half-century in the profession of city planning, with the paths of change in the four fields noted above.

Part II is a collage of images about the ways city and regional planning is, has been, or should be practiced.

Part III provides sector images of the practice and effects of planning in housing, transportation, and the environment, as well as ways in which economic tools are, or have been, developed.

Part IV deals with the diverse public images and leadership roles of the profession.

Part V adds some positive and negative views on the direction of planning programs and practice, and on planning theory and philosophy, as well as some forebodings given the persistent problems of race and inequality. It presents an examination of three critical challenges the profession must confront in the future.

The appendix contains four sections. The first contains the chapter endnotes; the second, bibliographic references for all inclusive chapters; the third, brief biographical sketches of the contributors to this volume; and finally, the editors' acknowledgments, which record the various debts incurred in the wake of these efforts.

Summing up, the history of the planning profession in the United States is a record of efforts to improve the quality of the urban environment and to cope with or resolve conflicts between different interest groups, between values, aesthetics and egalitarian pressures, and about the processes to be followed and the ways decisions should be made. In the language of Holmes, it is one of those professions, like law, where one may well "wear one's heart out after the unattainable."

Part I

OVERVIEW

1

Images and Paths of Change in Economics, Political Science, Philosophy, Literature, and City Planning: 1950–2000

Lloyd Rodwin

Professions change. Not just in their ideas, tools and capabilities, or the problems they address and the services they render, but in the controversies that divide them, as well as the images others have of them or they have of themselves. In this book, we propose to examine these issues and changes in city planning practice. By way of context, we will first scan the changes and issues that have occurred over the past half-century in several other fields. We are in a particularly good position to do so because (as noted in the Preface) *Daedalus*, in its Winter 1997 issue, reviewed the changes and issues that have occurred during this period in the fields of economics, political science, philosophy, and literature. Leading figures in these fields depict some of the broader forces influencing the universities, as well as a portion of the American professional culture involved in this transformation.

In venturing this resume, three assumptions have been made: that the fields examined are more or less "professionalized"; that the *Daedalus* historical evaluations are reasonably accurate; and that there are common items in each of these fields that have not been sufficiently highlighted. These are the service functions, the role of research or scholarship (intellectual capital formation), and the ways of thinking in each of the fields about values in relation to professional behavior.

THE *DAEDALUS* STUDIES

Economics

Turning now to the investigations, all report a common denominator: that the fields are rife with controversy. However, theoretical economists such

3

as Robert M. Solow and David M. Kreps affirm a substantial consensus on methodology. They say a large part of the economics profession has opted for rigor over realism. To achieve this rigor, they devise models based on simplifying assumptions explored deductively, most of them designed to interpret data or to be tested by data. Using mathematical and econometric tools, economists take great pride in their quantitative approach. In the process, they have dropped or downplayed institutional subject matter and history, along with narrative and oral skills. These economists acknowledge that the literature in the field has become narrow and technical while calling attention to their "common methodological 'tongue'" and the reduction of "dialects" in their specialized subfields (Kreps 1997, 65–73). The bulk of the profession is still loathe to abandon its emphasis on general equilibrium theory or optimization studies. Keenly aware of the price paid to achieve this rigor, some are now trying to broaden their "canonical" assumptions and, hopefully, the relevance of their disciplines to the real world (Solow 1997).

The metaphor of the hourglass—Solow, Kreps, and others suggest—describes the path they have been forced, or deliberately chosen, to pursue: a drastic narrowing for a quarter of a century or more of the focus of the field, until the power and insights of their studies could increase and permit more flexibility. Now, many departments have added courses (for example, economic development and the economics of the environment), treating both market failures and successes. They make a greater effort to broaden assumptions, add and evaluate historical perspectives and data, and interact more frequently with specialists in law, psychology, sociology, and history. Recently, there has been an upsurge of interest in the work of the political and social economist Albert Hirschman; and Paul Krugman even suggests it would be fruitful to place greater emphasis on regions and cities. As yet, however, only a tiny minority of economists worry about issues of race, power, and the interests served by their colleagues. The latter are not even mentioned in the investigations discussed in *Daedalus*.

To many outsiders, both the rigor of, and the quest for, increased flexibility is admirable; but skeptics are legion. Whether the latter are right or wrong, issues are persistently raised about the price already paid. Graduate economics programs, it is reported, "are no longer attracting and retaining the ablest students from strong undergraduate programs"; even more that "economics, as presented at the graduate level, has become increasingly ill suited to the preparation of future members of the economics faculties in the undergraduate liberal arts setting" (Barber 1997, 96). A study by Oberlin College, in which nine liberal arts colleges participated, indicated:

> For the bulk of the twentieth century, the selective liberal arts colleges have nurtured notable recruits to the profession, on a scale disproportionate to their size. By the later 1980s it was abundantly clear that that

historic pattern no longer held. A study orchestrated at Oberlin College (in which nine of the country's most selective liberal arts colleges participated) indicated that the decade of the 1980s had witnessed a reduction in the flow of their graduates to Ph.D. programs in economics to merely 50 to 60 percent of the rate to which they had formerly been accustomed, despite the fact that the number of undergraduates majoring in economics at these institutions had grown considerably—most students come away from their experience in liberal arts colleges persuaded that economic analysis had payoffs in heightening the rationality of practical decision making, that it had relevance for public policy, and that it offered useful insights into the workings of an economy's institutions. . . . Those dimensions of "reality," however, were largely squeezed out of the standard first two years of graduate study. . . . The result was disaffection on the part of some promising talents. (Barber 1997, p. 97)

Then, too, there is a lot of brooding over the neglect of the *service* functions of economists: grumbling "about turning out idiot savants, skilled in technique, not with 'real world problem solving'" (Barber 1997, 98), plus protests on this score from general practitioners, business leaders, consulting firms, top educators, and administrative leaders of colleges; and from senior economists like Kenneth Arrow, established officers of the American Economics Association, dissident economists like Kenneth Galbraith, Raymond Vernon, and Albert Hirschman, not to mention faculty colleagues in other university fields, such as engineering, the sciences, and undergraduate faculty, requiring service inputs from their economics colleagues.

POLITICAL SCIENCE

So much for economics, regarded in many quarters as the most advanced of the social sciences. Let us turn now to Charles E. Lindblom's report about the situation in political science. At the outset, Lindblom—one of the more provocative and innovative figures in current political science—emphasizes that he is reporting, not lamenting, the characteristics of the field. Political science, he says, cannot compare with economics, let alone the sciences, either in new ideas or discoveries. Most of the advances in ideas (for example, information theory, game theory, structuralism, and systems analysis) come from other fields, such as economics, psychology, anthropology, and sociology and from specialists in other realms, such as Claude Shannon, Claude Levi-Strauss, Burrhus Frederic (B. F.) Skinner, and Norbert Wiener. There is no clear focus, Lindblom believes, on what to study; nor are there technical questions, as there are in science, that indisputably have to be solved before moving ahead to the next stage—as, for example, space exploration requiring work in physics or the control of communicable disease first requiring work in biology. At best, Lindblom suggests, studies in political science expand, refine, and correct subject matter, which, in the main, comes from lay thought: which is why, perhaps, there are few, if any, great discoveries or surprises (Lindblom 1997).

Also, if you do not discover and make findings, Lindblom asks, what does the field really do? Well, he suggests, it spends a lot of time "trying," but not very fruitfully. Political science also does a lot of historical studies—reporting, analyses, exploring new subject matter—while indulging in a great deal of inconclusive debate on a wide variety of themes, all of which provides much data, contextual information, empirical test of hypotheses, improvement of methodology, correction of previous views or errors, and sometimes perceptive evaluations of situations, variables, and various forms of political activity and behavior. Yet, in summing up, he concludes that very little done by specialists in political science—or for that matter, in any other branch of social science—can be shown to have been either unarguably or demonstrably necessary" (Lindblom 1997, 241).

In effect, Lindblom concludes that the significant findings or discoveries in political science (because of the subject matter and the limitations of existing tools) leave a great deal to be desired, however useful the more conventional activities and services of the profession are or have been in shaping and refining our thinking and general knowledge. A case in point he cites is the increasing interest in and development of teaching programs in the currently fashionable field of policy analysis, instead of public administration, with, as yet, no serious capability of coping effectively with the diverse, complex political variables that shape the more important of these decisions.

Lindblom and his colleague Roger M. Smith do note a bias among practitioners in the field toward helping democracy function, as well as efforts on behalf of racial, gender and immigration reform, activities with which he is in sympathy but which, he notes, produce explosive reactions in quarters less sympathetic to these views and which raise questions about the objectivity or adequacy of these investigations. He does, however, suggest a role (shall we call it a *service* role?) that the political as well as some other social scientists might reasonably pursue—a subject that "many laypeople care about but lack the skills to explore" (Roger M. Smith citing Lindblom 1997, 275–78): this would be the systematic identification and analysis of such serious social problems as equity and income distribution, which are distorted by disproportionate power or income, or structural and institutional defects. Perhaps by serving as intellectual gadflies, they might help redress the balance.

PHILOSOPHY

As is true of economics, the quest for clarity and rigor transformed the pre–World War II perspectives in philosophy. Perhaps the most influential voice then in the United States was John Dewey. Dewey's sense of philosophy and that of his followers—"essentially a public enterprise . . . directly involved in the formulation and solution of large-scale practical problems" (Nehemas 1997, 210)—was challenged by the analytical reformers: in the main, logical positivists who "held that all meaningful statements are either (1) verifiable statements about sense data or (2) analytic statements, such as the statements of logic and mathematics" (Putnam 1997). W. V. Quine, an eminent philosopher, even argued "that philosophy was continuous with science, a more abstract and general version of the natural investigation of the world" (Nehemas 1997, 214).

As in economics, many traditional subjects that did not meet these criteria were dropped: history, for example, and metaphysics and ethics. Over time, of course, the ideas of the analytical reformers were modified, and new fields and subject matter surfaced. Some examples are Noam Chomsky's explorations of language, work in cognitive science (now one of the most clearly interdisciplinary specialties within philosophy), and work on computational states or processes. Also, with the publication of John Rawls's *A Theory of Justice*, philosophy reentered "the public normative arena," with some joint efforts beginning to emerge in law, medicine, social science, and business. Even more intriguing, feminism introduced some of the ideas of Continental philosophy, work previously considered "paradigms of sloppy, disorganized and pretentious thought" (Nehemas 1997, 218). Stanley Cavell once facetiously observed that "Continental philosophers write as if they have read every philosophical work produced thus far, while analytical philosophers write as if they have read nothing" (Nehemas 1997, 219). Today, however, analytical philosophy is reported to be interested in the history of the discipline, and some philosophers "are even beginning to look at analytical philosophy itself as a historically situated movement, not simply as the revolution that for the first time stood philosophy right side up" (Nehemas 1997, 219).

The gulfs and conflicts, however, remain deep-seated. The situation is described as "calm, peaceful and rather detached," although there were attempts by groups opposed to analytical philosophy to take over the offices of the American Philosophical Association. Nonetheless, there is "a dangerous fragmentation in the field, with people who teach together in the same department having neither any idea of what their colleagues are doing, nor any interest in finding out" (Nehemas 1997, 251).

There is also said to be no canon today, no common ground, no set of works

> that members of a discipline would be ashamed to admit they have not read
> . . . and expected to have a view about them . . . and sometimes become
> almost enthusiastic about—no rudimentary set of problems common
> to the discipline, problems that even if not all philosophers consider

> them to be their own, they might believe will make their problems more
> tractable when they are resolved. (Nehemas 1997, 221–22)

The discipline is now "in a holding pattern, lacking a clear overall direction
and an explicit sense of unity and mission."

> A philosophy with a public—not a popular—voice can preserve some
> of the substantive concerns as well as some of the formal virtues of
> clarity and rigor that characterized analytical philosophy at its best. But
> it can also be an engaged and consequential enterprise envisaged by the
> American pragmatists as well as by most of the great figures in its his-
> tory. (Nehemas 1997, 223)

LITERATURE

If we now shift our attention to the field of literature, it becomes quickly
apparent that the changes here are more radical and the controversies even
more intractable than the other three fields. M. H. Abrams ironically observes that

> literary departments, which had hitherto represented themselves as the
> chief conservators, interpreters and propagators of the humanistic tra-
> dition and of the writings Mathew Arnold represented as "the best that
> has been thought and said" have become the major source of radical
> challenges both to the tradition and the inherited literary canon. (Abrams
> 1997, 116)

Sharp challenges, of course, are not novel in this field. Catherine Gallagher
reports that the various histories now available say that "literature professors
have always disagreed over the fundamental principles of their profession,
always engaged in theory wars, always been prompted by extra literary concerns . . ." (Gallagher 1997, 133). A leading example has been the shift from
a pre–World War I focus on language and history to literature and a redirection of skill from scholarship to criticism.

John Crow Ransom persuaded the profession that the usefulness and
justification of the departments of literature depended on their establishing
service roles which they and only they could perform. The task of these roles—
literary criticism and analysis of literary techniques—was to serve the writers of contemporary literature and the reading public at large (Ransom cited
by Gallagher 1997, 137).

Close reading of the text was the new shibboleth. It "marginalized all
studies of biographical, social and historical conditions and aspects of the
[work]" (Abrams 1997, 108). This approach—still popular, though somewhat deprecated today as formalism—was quite influential. Indeed, it has
been picked up "by the New Critics—including the American deconstructive

critics whose "closer reading" (in Paul de Man's term) shared the ahistorical formalism of their predecessors but replaced their disposition to discover coherence and a paradoxical unity of opposing meanings with a predisposition to discover incoherencies, "ruptures," and the undecidable gridlock of opposing meanings called "aporias" (Abrams 1997, 109).

To be sure, this was only one of many other insights or alternative ways of interpreting literary work. Other examples were concern with recurrent plot patterns and character types, diverse modes of representing reality, moral and aesthetic criticism, symbolic modes for encompassing experience, impressionistic essays, social, moral, psychoanalytic interpretations, broad-gauge synoptic historical studies—all of which provided "a vigorous, often mutually combative diversity in literary enterprises" (Putnam 1997, 110). After all, "the main ideal of literary criticism," Burke held, "is to use all there is to use" (cited by Abrams 1997, 110 [no source given]). But this was before "the Great Divide of the late 1960s and early 1970s, when the poststructural movement, by its radical challenges, brought to light the foundational assumptions that the earlier scholars and critics, under their differences, had implicitly shared" (Putnam 1997, 111).

The subsequent changes came about for several reasons: the cosmopolitanism of English departments, their interest in European and World literature, and "other currents of thought which were sometimes reinforced by the migration of intellectuals" so that "literature departments became the busiest academic ports of entry for European post-war intellectual movements" (Gallagher 1997, 140–41).

At the same time, departments in other fields appeared to be focusing on subject matter they could deal with effectively.

> In the wake of World War II, it seemed that students were being offered courses in philosophy that confined themselves to analyses of sentences, psychology seminars that preferred to study the simplified behavior of rodents, and political science courses bent on refining opinion polls. . . .
>
> Since one could not read Sartre in the philosophy department, Freud in the psychology department or Lukacs in the political science department, one read them in the literature departments. (Unfortunately or otherwise) the eclecticism . . . eventually came to include ideas that seemed corrosive to the bases of the program, ideas that discounted the foundational concepts of the "literary" as a particularly intricate and difficult kind of language and of "criticism" as the discipline of analyzing the literary. (Gallagher 1997, 141–42)

Over time, a series of challenges erupted, especially in the politicized 1960s. For example, Gallagher asks, doesn't the idea of the literary

> privilege an already privileged white, male, middle-class consciousness. . . ?
> And did not that restrictiveness relegate the more urgent, unambiguous and
> collectively conscious writings of minorities, proletarians and women to
> the category of the nonliterary? Could it not also be said to have eradi-
> cated all sign of historical specificity—from the works of past authors,
> creating a canon that narcissistically mirrored a narrow stratum of
> mid-twentieth century American experience? (Gallagher 1997, 144–
> 45)

In any case, "in giving up the claim to a unique subject matter—literary
analysis—these younger critics were irreverently and simultaneously laying
claim to a vastly expanded field of inquiry, e.g., Marxist humanism, structuralism, feminism, semiotics, cultural history" (Gallagher 1997, 146).

The change was massive and radical. New courses were added, existing
courses transformed, new criteria and assumptions introduced, and the concept of theories altered.

> So drastic is the change that a representative of once-normative modes
> of scholarly investigation and criticism is often at a loss to discover enough
> common ground in assumptions and vocabulary, and in the standards
> for what counts as evidence for an assertion to support profitable—or
> sometimes even mutually intelligible—discussions with an all-out ex-
> ponent of the new dispensation. (Putnam 1997, 113)

The curricula, in particular, have changed dramatically.

> There are courses in literature by and about women, in gender studies
> (that is, gay, lesbian and bisexual studies), in Afro-American, Asian
> American, Native American and post-colonial literature, as well as of-
> ferings in such topics as race and ethnicity, modes of "representations,"
> politics in literature and cultural studies. Prominent in a number of
> course titles is the stress on what is called "theory," thus: Postmodernism:
> Theories and Fictions; Current Questions in Feminist Theory. Even [for]
> courses that by their titles appear to be traditional offerings in periods,
> authors, and genres, the accompanying descriptions often indicate a
> decisive change in what they teach and the way they are taught . . . ; a
> course in Restoration Drama, for example, describes its subject as the
> major male and female playwrights . . . read through the lens of recent
> psychoanalytic, economic and performance theories. (Putnam 1997,
> 112)

The extremity of the changes is attributed to a variety of factors: the
entry of a new generation of faculty (including women and minorities) familiar with the Vietnam experience, anti-establishment in attitudes, persuaded
"that their group has been marginalized or ignored by the power structure

that has dominated the inherited culture" (Putnam 1997, 114). What this generation has to say is also fresh and publishable—or was. And the ideas of "four French writers—the deconstructive theory of Jacques Derrida, the power/knowledge theory of Michel Foucault, the revised Freudian theory of Jacques-Marie Lacan, and the neo-Marxist, ideological theory of Louis Althusser have provided the conceptual framework and methodology that spearheaded and reinforced the onslaught" (Putnam 1997, 114).

Not least, it is observed that

> Exponents of this rapidly expanding field dismantle the standard boundaries that distinguish cultural institutions, productions and artifacts; a number of them also delete the distinctions—attributed to the elitism of a dominant group—between high culture and popular culture and between major and lesser cultural products. Comic strips, film, television advertisements, pornography and industrial manufacturers thus become equal candidates for scholarly attention—a literary work, when it figures at all, is simply one among innumerable cultural products—and all these products are analyzed mainly by reference to the social structures and power processes that have brought them into being and endowed them with their meanings, their values and their relative social status. (Putnam 1997, 124)

Harold Bloom's mordant, pessimistic outlook is cited:

> I have very little confidence that literary education will survive its current malaise. . . . Finding myself now surrounded by professors of hip-hop; by clones of Gallic-Germanic theory; by ideologues of gender and of various sexual persuasions; by multiculturalists unlimited, I realize that the balkanization of literary studies is irreversible. (Bloom 1994, 117–18)

Others are more sanguine. M. H. Abrams thinks that, despite the current nihilism, we will profit from the challenges:

> Among the surviving changes, it seems certain, will be the study of writings by women and by racial, ethnic, and other groups that have been overlooked or marginalized by the limitations in perspective of scholars and shapers of culture, most of whom, as the proponents of these interests claim, were white European males. But such minority studies, having matured past the stage of militant advocacy, will be pursued more as an area to be studied and less as a political cause to be advanced. They will become much more discriminating in what, at present, is their wholesale critique of the Western intellectual tradition, in the recognition that the standards to which they themselves appeal—standards such as evenhanded justice, human equality and human rights—are ideals

that have been developed within the highly diversified tradition that many proponents of the new studies indict as monolithically and irredeemably patriarchal, logocentric, Eurocentric and sexist. (Abrams 1997, 128)

ANALYSIS OF THE STUDIES

The accounts of the big changes and issues in the four domains over the past half-century are by well-known, highly knowledgeable leaders in their fields. True, other rapporteurs might well tell quite different tales with other nuances or emphases. That's the clear risk in using these materials: but that said, what inferences might we draw from a comparison of these particular reports?

To begin with, in contemplating the changes and the issues about the services and capital formation in these domains, one is reminded of the observation of Alfred North Whitehead, that "The last thing we learn in a field is what it is all about. Men go on groping, sometimes for centuries, guided by a dim instinct and a puzzled curiosity until at last some great truth is unloosened" (Whitehead 1906, 223). None of these fields appear to be an exception to this aperçu. What is more, when these truths are unloosened, they shed light on the styles of intellectual capital formation, the attitudes to service functions, and the reflection of values in relation to both.

Let us review our examples. Take the way the economists in the top graduate schools developed their discipline by leaning on modeling while slighting *service* functions. That has produced strong, widespread, negative reactions—particularly concern about the lack of realism, narrowing of the field's scope, and neglect of functions (such as the education of undergraduates and the needs of professional practitioners working in the public and private sectors). Even though economists have long maintained that their models could accommodate different values, an articulate minority noted that the bulk of the profession worked for—and, in the main, served—the "establishment." Changes are in the offing, of course, but no one can say as yet whether the current efforts to broaden assumptions to take more account of institutions, history, and the realities of policy and decision making will produce a discipline that is more or less effective and respected.

If Charles Lindblom is right, all of the efforts in intellectual capital formation in political science have produced few substantive contributions, this due to the intractability of the subject matter and the limitations of existing tools. The same constraints may hold for perceptive innovations such as the substitution of policy analysis for public administration. We would do well, however, to note that Lindblom does draw attention to one possible, potentially important *service* function, one that many people care about but cannot themselves perform: the evaluation of systematic bias or flaws in the operation of the existing political system—bias and flaws that systematically disadvantage the poor, uneducated, and otherwise disadvantaged people. Such a *service,* Lindblom believes, may be a way to reinforce democratic values without producing explosive critiques from those on the right, regarding the loss of objectivity. Thus, in this field, too, the neglect of, and need for, a potentially valuable *service* function is underscored.

Philosophy, which took the same route as economics, appears to have fared less well. To achieve rigor and precision, philosophy also resorted to logic and mathematics in order to produce "meaningful" statements that could be explored or tested. To satisfy these criteria, it downgraded or jettisoned history, metaphysics, and ethics, as well as social pragmatism, evangelism, and any significant *service* functions. The end result is a technical, rigorous, narrow discipline with little communication or interaction either with other fields or with scientists whom positivists very much admired, or with the "attentive" public, or even with other specialists within the discipline. One of the field's great exceptions is John Rawls's *A Theory of Justice,* which reintroduced ethics and values, and even helped open the door to history and other issues. Here, too, there is stress on the need for a *service* function, a public (if not a popular) audience, and an effort to reduce, if not eliminate, the fragmentation between specializations and identification of critical common issues.

As for literature, its evolution, too, is instructive for our purposes. This is because the first great transformation of literature in the post-war period led not only to a shift in emphasis from philology and history to literature and literary analysis, but because this transformation was an effort to get away from a particularly nonpragmatic or nonutilitarian form of intellectual capital formation with the hope of producing a significant *service* function, i.e., addressing the need for general undergraduate education in contemporary literature, as well as the enhancement and reinforcement of the creative work now being done by contemporary writers. This highly touted *service* function, however, eventually led to the splintering of the field when the basic assumptions were challenged, especially the criteria used for the identification of canonical literature and literary works. In retrospect, it is not at all surprising that, sooner or later, these works would be examined and questioned by the subsequent antiestablishment generation, particularly women, blacks, Hispanics, and other new recruits to the profession. What is worth noting here is the role of values in the interaction of the capital formation and the functions, which, in turn, led to bitter dissent and the loss of consensus.

To sum up, some common (and, in many ways, interrelated) issues surfaced in all four fields during the first half of the century. These were: what the focus of the field ought to be; whether adequate attention was paid to the basic professional, or *service*, functions; the key interest groups served; and how to equilibrate professional skills and capital formation with ethics and values. What is striking is the way these same issues have surfaced in a similar guise in the field of city planning. This will be clear once we examine how planning, using Bob Solow's lingo, got to be the way it is.

CITY PLANNING

City planning, at least in the United States, evolved from a mixture of public and private surveying and real estate development activities, coupled with the ad hoc application of civil engineering skills to problems of transportation, utilities, and other challenges of infrastructure development. Then, too, city planning was romanticized as a civic art by the City Beautiful images of charismatic architects and landscape architects and by sympathetic business and elite reform groups. These dreams faded over time as the professionals grappled with the plan-making, regulatory, and development functions. Eventually, the recognition dawned that city planning, private as well as public, had become the chosen instrument and process for channeling, regulating, and sometimes even guiding the outcome of the countless economic, social, and political pressures, micro and macro, revolving around land use in different parts of the city. Hypothetically, optimization was the ideal, "satisficing" the pragmatic compromise. More often than not, however, personal leadership, power, and pressure politics turned out to be the ultimate realities.

IDENTITY ISSUES[1]

One way to interpret more specifically the conflicts and moods as this profession evolved is to recall the kinds of highs and lows, of exaltation and depression, associated with identity issues in adolescent human development and to relate those experiences to one of the most difficult tasks of a practitioner in a relatively new profession: understanding what the field is, what it has been and might yet be, and how the practitioner's role might change in the future.

Some of the clinical findings relating to the periods of childhood and adolescence do provide an intriguing metaphor. For example, according to Erik Erikson (1968), three major early periods in human development are, first, emergence from the womb to begin life as a separate personality; second, the semiautonomous phase of early childhood with great dreams of glory and achievement; and third, the shift to the socially and goal-directed adolescent phase. During this period there is a complex sequence that involves the discovery of new, deeper realities and more formidable constraints, interests, and demands, all of which challenge (and may frustrate) the adolescent's dreams.

Although the sequences for city planning can be no more than suggestive, it is possible to show a rough correspondence with Erikson's epigenesis of ego development. For example, pursuing the metaphor, it can be said that city planning first developed its independent "personality" when the various progeny emerged from the wombs of public health, civil engineering, architecture, landscape architecture, and surveying. In the semiautonomous phase that followed, city planners certainly prided themselves on their great dreams and potential for grandiose achievements. The subsequent shift of emphasis from master plans to the planning process then introduced the "socially and goal-directed phase"—adolescence. During this period, societal encounters of the profession disclosed a far more complicated reality than it had at first imagined. Time-honored ideas appeared superficial and inadequate. Cherished concepts like the neighborhood and the region turned out to oversimplify the melange of micro and macro areas relevant to planning and development. Faith in the capacity of planners to organize the physical environment was shaken by the discovery of complex economic, social, and political terrains they knew little about. Employment of city planners by local governments and the well-to-do client evidenced ties with the established interests. There was great pressure to be more rigorous in their thinking, more knowledgeable about research, more concerned with the underprivileged, more sophisticated about the realities of group bargaining, power politics, and participatory democracy. It would be surprising if this convergence of challenges and criticisms had *not* generated anxieties.

In the case of human development, Erikson characterizes such a situation as "a crisis of wholeness" because of the need to achieve at this time "a sense of inner identity":

> The young person, in order to experience wholeness, must feel a progressive continuity between that which he has come to be during the long years of childhood and that which he promises to become in the anticipated future; between that which he conceives himself to be and that which he perceives others to see in him and to expect of him. Individually speaking, identity includes, but is more than, the earlier years when the child wanted to be, and often was forced to become, like the people he depended on. . . . The search for a new and yet reliable identity can perhaps best be seen in the persistent adolescent endeavor to define, overdefine and redefine themselves and each other. (Erikson 1968, 84–85).

The young field of city planning experienced comparable identity problems. Its initial dream of comprehensive land-use planning turned out to be inadequate. City planning then sought to transform itself in line with its new perceptions, and with the perceptions and expectations of others. It tried to establish continuity between its old identity and its new needs, even to become like the people on which it depended. And so it was that funds were requested and became available for education and research programs that emphasized modeling, quantitative methods, urban and regional applications of the social sciences, and the human and managerial as well as the ecological concerns of city planning. Foundations, particularly the Ford Foundation, and university administrations monitored and tried to reinforce these trends in the universities.

The new horizons led to at least three identity problems. The first involved new skills and roles. City planners learned modeling and the uses of the computer, enthusiastically applying the techniques to problems of transportation, land use, housing, urban systems, and the management of these systems. Soon their bulky plans, previously spruced up with photographs, sketches, designs, and land-use maps, became even bulkier "scientific" studies replete with statistical and mathematical appendices and technocratic jargon. Other planners, however, rejected the emphasis on "scientism," efficiency, and rationality. Some mastered the arts of bureaucratic gamesmanship and political manipulation. Still others served as frank partisans of the poor and minorities, or as outright rebels dedicated to the transformation of the capitalist system and its urban subsystems while calling attention to the historic contingency of the latter—that is, the special forms urbanism assumed during this stage of capitalist development. Before long, it had become respectable to say that the planner could serve not only as a designer and coordinator but as advocate, negotiator, or coalition-builder. It was equally respectable to characterize the planner as knowledgeable not only about the problems of urban land use and environmental policy but as someone with generic skills in policy and analysis, the processes of communication and negotiation, as well as implementation and public management. The planner could also be an agent of "change" and a social reformer (liberal and radical), not merely a corrector of market imperfections. Increasingly, these multiple skills and roles were looked upon as ways of functioning within the field, either as a versatile generalist or as a specialist.

A second problem involved the dualism implicit in the term *city planning*. Were city planners essentially planners or urbanists? Because either alternative shifted the physical and design aspects of planning to the background, it was an easy next step to ask why one should hold fast to an urban (or regional) label if that is not the important modifier (Joint Center 1971). Why not be as free as possible to deal with all planning problems? This point of view was pressed especially by policy and planning specialists and by modelers, none of whom considered the physical environment, the city, or region, as the critical variables in their own work. For them, the terms *urban* and *regional* had become "null or a negative identity," whereas, to many practitioners, these views illustrated just how serious role confusion had become. To still others, the issue appeared ephemeral because, in their view, some focus is essential as long as resources are limited. One response—to emphasize policy analysis—still reflects a current wave of thought, but this emphasis offers no escape from identity problems. For, if the profession is centrally concerned with the problems of cities and regions, why not say so? If it is not, what is the emphasis to be? It is worth recalling that because the "Chicago School of Planning" (under the leadership of Rexford G. Tugwell in the late 1940s and early 1950s) focused on planning practice and theory, yet lacked an area of substantive specialization and comparative advantage, this general approach failed to take root anywhere; thus, most of the able members of this school sought, and eventually found, a haven in city planning and urban studies.

The third identity issue concerned the integration of professional and disciplinary elements. Early city planners emphasized the shaping of the physical and/or built environment. This emphasis, however, resulted in neglect of the societal aspects of cities and regions, in limited research, and in over-reliance on multidisciplinary, collaborative efforts. But, over time, city planners discovered that the social scientist had a limited interest in urban and regional problems, and that the architect, landscape architect, and engineer had only limited interest in macro design (as well as urban and regional) problems. This situation was not only unlikely to change; but as leading specialists in the field, city planners were being accused by the "attentive,"[2] as well as the general, public of being too narrow. Recognition of the inadequacy of their traditional role as land-use planners and of the inadequacy of the assistance likely to come from the social sciences has forced key planning schools to grasp the nettle and accept responsibility for building at least the relevant applied social science and macro design foundations of the field.

THEMATIC OR PARADIGM CHANGE

To compare city planning with the phases of human development is, at best, suggestive; but the comparisons are not likely to be persuasive to those skeptical of analogies in general and wary, in particular, of the oversimplifications and the determinism implicit in the concept of stages. The same questions can be examined from another perspective—that of *thematic* or *paradigm* change. There have been several studies of how the inadequacies of a ruling theme or paradigm[3] have generated challenge and crisis, as well as how the absence of a clear successor often exacerbates alternating attitudes of confrontation, confusion, frustration, even despair. We know, too, that an inadequate, and sometimes even wrong, hypothesis is often better for research and policy than no hypothesis at all. The same holds true for thematic positions or paradigms. That is why Gerald Holton has wryly observed that the attitude of past scientists has often been: "Let us not be misled by the evidence" (Holton 1974).

If problems persist, the normal approaches and values may become even more blurred and controversial, and the problems will be cited again and again as the key issue.[4] Their resolution may take a variety of forms. For example, Kuhn suggests three of the more obvious possibilities: adapt the old paradigm; set the problems aside as currently unsolvable; or achieve a combined conceptual and "gestalt" switch that will make it possible to attack all the problems afresh, yet within a different framework.

The process of adaptation to change in city planning has followed a similar course. As noted, until the end of the 1950s, the basic paradigm of the profession took for granted the need for a comprehensive organization of the physical environment in the form of a master, or general, urban land-use plan.[5] Urban designers, landscape architects, transportation planners, land developers, and still others were regarded as specialists, whereas city planners were expected to have a much broader concern for the urban physical environment. To produce this expertise, half to two-thirds of the training of city planners in leading programs was devoted to courses and workshops on land-use planning principles and practice.[6] To the extent that resources were available, additional instruction was offered in survey and research techniques, statistics, and applied social science (land economics, housing, urban sociology, and urban government and politics). These courses, along with some fieldwork, were expected to give students the knowledge necessary to enter the field; the rest was to be learned through practice. These were the ruling beliefs and approaches in city planning, at least in the United States and in many countries abroad.

Over time, a growing number of difficulties emerged which began to play havoc with these views. For one thing, technical studies, especially economic and social analyses for planning land use, often were superficial. Furthermore, master plans were inflexible or too flexible, a fault not corrected by comparing them to "impermanent constitutions" (Haar 1953). There were discrepancies between the aims and expectations of the comprehensive plans and the results of crucial decision-making processes that were generally political. Conflicts broke out, for example, between land-use planners and "housers" concerning the emphasis on economic development and physical renewal, and the frequent neglect of human problems, not to mention the sheer lack of understanding and often callous treatment of the poor and disadvantaged. Empirical studies of planning activities by social scientists made it clear that the doctrine of comprehensive planning was difficult to justify on the basis of descriptive or normative criteria. These studies showed most planning to be more ad hoc than comprehensive, and that most decisions involved the short term rather than the long term, multiple rather than single goals, and "satisficing" rather than optimizing. Planning behavior seemed to be interpreted better by political and game theory than by rational decision models. In brief, the basic premises of comprehensive land-use planning simply did not take adequate account of behavior in the real world—in particular, the bargaining and pressure groups and politics involved in influencing or making important development decisions (Lindblom 1959; Altshuler 1965a; Banfield and Wilson 1963).

RESPONSES AND ISSUES

Eventually there were three responses from the profession. The first was to push for a broader, more direct involvement on the part of the social sciences in urban and regional studies. (This was the main reason for the organization, in 1959, of the Joint Center for Urban Studies of MIT and Harvard University outside the city planning departments of either university.) Even in the mid-1960s, however, when interest in urban affairs peaked, urban and regional questions appeared, quite understandably, to have only a minor bearing on the central problems of the different social sciences, as well as law and civil engineering.[7] At best, social science departments might arrange for faculty appointments, and perhaps even disciplinary specializations, in urban economics, urban sociology, and urban politics. Also, one could expect cities and regions to serve as the occasional laboratory for illustrating or testing general problems of interest to these social scientists. This situation was much better than the egregious neglect of such questions in the past (all the more so in Europe); but it was most unlikely that the problems of the city and region would receive sustained attention except from programs with a central, long-term concern about these matters.[8]

The second response was the emergence of a more realistic view of what the planning profession could expect from the social science disciplines and a raising of sights as to the profession's own obligations. Specifically, MIT, Harvard, Berkeley, and other major university centers developed research, modeling, and relevant applied social science capabilities; improved their policymaking and implementation capabilities; and expanded the scope of city planning so that it might address problems not only *of* cities (for example, urban land use, urban renewal, urban design, and urban growth strategies at the urban, regional and national, as well as micro and neighborhood scale), but a number of related aspects of these problems *within* cities (such as race, poverty, crime, welfare, health, and education) (Rodwin 1972). Expansion in these directions—especially the apparent willingness to confront ways in which the work of the profession might help cope with problems *within* cities, was destined to be temporary. For the expansion, bound to raise questions of focus and of resource allocation, was unlikely to occur with competence and depth in all the new directions.

The current drive for a focus constitutes the third response. What the focus will be, and how it might change over time, is not yet agreed upon; but the odds are, city planners will not lose sight of their profession's comparative advantage. This is because the fate of a profession hinges on whether it has practical knowledge and skills and can therefore provide *services* people need, want, and will pay for, and which no other profession can or wishes to develop. In the past, we observed the special skills and services of city planners involved in making comprehensive land-use plans and organizing land-use planning and development processes. This remarkably influential paradigm held sway for about four decades before being seriously challenged.[9] Puncturing the paradigm's illusions was wholesome, albeit painful; and for this achievement, the profession owes social scientists a great debt (Gans 1962; Altshuler 1965a). In the years that followed, the scope of the profession's activities has expanded in other ways (though it must be acknowledged, as Phillip Herr reports, that comprehensive land-use planning is still highly valued in many smaller and medium-size cities). Nonetheless, an entire generation of young city planners takes pride in other technical skills—agenda setting, development, design, policymaking, research, entrepreneurship and implementation (including mediation and conflict resolution). Planners today also work on a wider variety of community and area development problems—the environment, conservation, preservation, redevelopment, and tourism. Also, where a need exists, they provide significant staff services working in roles and with skills that cut across traditional disciplinary boundaries:

> Across the U.S. civic groups—including community development corporations, not-for-profit housing developers, and neighborhood, social service, advocacy, environmental and a growing number of regional and statewide planning advocacy groups—are engaged in planning and advocacy work on issues that were once the exclusive domain of public-sector agencies. These include environmental and open space protection, land use, urban design and housing development, community and regional economic development, social services and related issues. A growing number of grant-making and operating foundations are also hiring program officers and staff with expertise in these areas. While the growth in the civic sector has been greatest in major metropolitan areas, even isolated rural areas now have a growing number of community development and environmental advocacy groups, supported by foundations and membership contributions. (Baxter 1997)

The upshot of the changes in thematic position or paradigm is likely to be an increased effort to integrate disciplinary and professional skills. Other perceptive leaders in the field share these expectations. William Alonso, for example, observed that, in the future, the demand will be not for multidisciplinary approaches, but increasingly for

professionals who are first and foremost scholars in the urban and regional problems and secondarily members of traditional disciplines,
[who] will bring to any particular situation a better sense of which problems can be tackled profitably and which cannot, and [who] will be
versed in the relevant academic and non-academic literature, the problems of government and the social realities, and [will] have developed a
sense of the possible and of the manner in which risks are taken. (Alonso
1971, 171–72)

A profession, like an individual, may be said to be in a healthier condition when it increases its ability and services to deal with felt needs; when it
achieves more realistic integration of its aims, subject matter, and tools; and
when it perceives itself and the world more accurately. Arguably, some of this
already holds for the profession of city planning. But there are some persistent issues being raised, underlined in the pages that follow, that point up the
considerable concerns prevalent on this score.

Perhaps the most ironic issue is that of outcome versus process. By
virtue of planning decisions becoming less technical, more democratic and
political, by working with groups, by engaging in mediation and conflict resolution, city planners now have less control over services and outcomes. Today,
instead of being charged with espousing wrong or inappropriate technical
notions, they are faulted in important quarters for being absent or less "visible," for the dearth of "big" ideas, and even for a dereliction in public or
charismatic leadership. Witold Rybcyznski confesses that he

> has nostalgia for a period when professionals did not listen to amateurs
> before making a decision. Decisions made by a majority vote will either
> be horrible because they must appeal to the lowest common denomina-
> tor or will result in no change. The only role for planners as profession-
> als with expertise will be in small homogeneous groups where values are
> similar. This means that planners will speak for different groups, not the
> common good. [10]

Alex Krieger, in his remarks at the 1997 MIT Faculty Seminar, concurred:

> The most damaging issue for planners is the loss of authority as the
> unanticipated flip side of the democratization of the planning process
> which leads to the dismissal of expertise. Planners . . . are perceived to
> have no greater insight into a particular matter than anyone else in a
> room. (Krieger 1997)

As a consequence, designers rather than city planners, he thinks, are
now in the vanguard of the profession. This leadership is reinforced by the
narrowness and clarity of their roles and their technical mastery of visualization.

Most planners, however, are loathe to retreat on this issue. At least in the American context, city planning involves more than technical skills. Bernard Frieden says that:

> The turn from professional-based to politically based planning was not a negative change. The past mistakes were made when planning was professionally driven. Politics stopped the bulldozers of urban redevelopment and politically based decisions are stopping many similar bad decisions from being made today. But a political process means planners no longer have the same authority they had in the past.
>
> Planners, however, are able to shape political movements in a positive direction. For example, they are often involved in preservation projects to revive historic neighborhoods. But they are not highly visible and certainly are less visible than when they were professionally driven. This is also true of the many development projects which are highly regarded by the public critics, including Battery Park City in New York, Pennsylvania Avenue development in Washington, D.C., and the Embarcardero in San Francisco. City planners were involved in these projects but received little credit. . . . [They] often operate under the motto "You can get a lot done if you don't take credit for it." (Frieden 1997)

And Lawrence Vale adds that the resurgence in physical planning is precisely because design is linked to other pressing planning issues. He cites two examples: the experiences of Cleveland, Ohio, and Washington, D.C.

> [T]he Herculean effort to re-image Cleveland in a post-Rust Belt context has taken more than the marshaling of economic statistics; it has also required the visual proof of new sports and museum facilities in formerly underused areas. The "Cleveland Tomorrow" campaign is equal parts development and public relations, and design and politics are conjoined in both parts. No one would suggest the NCPC plan [in Washington, D.C.] is a solution to the ever-mounting socioeconomic ills of Washington . . . [n]onetheless, it reveals important changes in physical planning practice, because it demonstrates that the pursuit of image entails more than the regularization of aesthetics. . . . Physical planning has returned *not as an alternative to economic planning but as an increasingly integrated component of urban development.* (Vale 2000)

Despite the great differences between architectural planners and city planners, they share a common concern for what is now called "place and form." It is the ethical interpretations of this concern that bid fair to haunt them. This emerges strikingly if we examine the stance of planners with regard to power and their reluctance—or inability, at least to date—to raise critical issues and to cope with moral imperatives.

Altshuler, for example, observes:

> Planners are trapped by the conservative institutions they work in. Also, big projects that attract federal and private money for development are run by deal makers like Robert Moses in New York, Ed Logue in New Haven, and Justin Herman in San Francisco. The deal makers pushed plan makers and plans aside to avoid public review which could impede a deal.
>
> Even more, political institutions and leaders and private developers pick among the elements of planning ideas and apply them in perverse ways. Zoning becomes a great force for racial and economic segregation. Urban renewal laws result in slum clearance with a vengeance, but little public housing despite provisions providing it. Yet, planners seldom dissent from these perversions. (Altshuler 1997)

There is also, he insists, a high price paid for consensus building. After all, an equally, perhaps even more important, challenge "is championing controversial values and addressing controversial issues. . . . Consensus building, an important skill for planners, fails to address planning's alliance with the powerful forces in society, which is detrimental to the less powerful" (Altshuler 1997).

Chester Hartman (1997) is even more scornful:

> If equity is a value of planners, where are the critiques of the nation's housing system and recommendations for changes which should be forthcoming from them. . . . Shouldn't they be leaders in the fight for decent, affordable housing for all?"

He adds that

> Power, equity, conflicting interests are being played out in cities around the intersection of race and poverty, changing demographics, and especially around housing policies and programs. Michael Teitz's decision not to discuss housing in his overview of planning "for lack of space" is additional evidence that poverty, race, and housing are not central to the history of the profession. (Hartman 1997)

To be sure, the city planner is not to blame for these tough social problems; nor can the profession, on its own, solve them. But neither can it turn its back.

Part II

IMAGES OF CITY-PLANNING PRACTICE

Collage

2

Planning Shapes Urban Growth and Development

Dennis Frenchman

From the viewpoint of a practitioner who reviews hundreds of requests for planning services each year, the profession of planning is not only *alive* but also increasingly important to shaping urban growth and development. In fact, over the past two decades we have witnessed an explosion in planning, with more plans being made now for more different kinds of situations than ever before. This changing scope of the profession demands a change in what—and how—we are teaching about it.

The growth in planning is a result of two converging forces: increasing competition for resources of all types and an explosion of information in the hands of consumers and constituents. The more information we have about the world, the more its workings and problems are revealed, and the more tools we need to tackle those problems. For example, it is easy to understand that increased knowledge of what is happening in the natural environment has fueled the growth of environmental planning. As the public has learned in ever greater detail, the effects of development on our air, water and land—and the number and scope of conservation agencies—have increased, along with the demand for planning tools to assess impacts, conserve open space, protect wetlands, site major facilities, and resolve environmental disputes. The accumulating effect of these interventions over the past twenty years is beginning to have a profound impact on the form of our cities.

Environmental awareness, however, is only one factor that has led to an explosion in planning. A similar phenomenon has occurred in a host of other areas that have emerged—heritage area planning, for example, along with cultural development strategies, tourism infrastructure, coastal zone management, new transportation networks involving bikeways, greenways, tour routes, urban rings, and neighborhood development programs. If one maps these planning efforts on a regional basis, a new mosaic emerges on the landscape, with different venues and roles for planning, along with new associations and alliances.

Within this emerging mosaic, we can see some real differences in these plans and planning efforts compared with those in the past. First of all, more and more plans are being prepared by private firms than by the public sector. There has been a shift away from in-house planning staff to the use of planning consultants of all types as resources have dwindled and planning has become detached from centralized state and federal funding programs. For better or worse, a side effect of this shift away from public agencies has been the loss of a centralized vision of planning. The result is a kind of rudderless free-for-all—in the absence of models or a professional compass, we see a modernist plan here, a fortress plan there, or a neotraditional plan. This diversity is not bad in itself, except that it results in a general level of mediocrity and vulnerability to the latest fad that will only accelerate as planning becomes more privatized and localized.

On the other hand, many of the plans that are being done are highly complex and multipurpose. They are not the simplistic land-use plans of the 1950s that many like to criticize but which aren't being made anymore. Land use remains a critical core, but current plans also address environmental issues, cultural resource protection, and economic development, and they often propose new organizations to implement what is proposed. Most all of them are being developed with a public process that is oriented to reaching consensus among constituencies. So all the lessons that planning schools have been preaching are being practiced.

The most interesting difference, however, is that many plans no longer try to fulfill an abstract vision of the ideal city. Rather, they seek to heighten the unique qualities and culture and individual identity of the places for which they are made. I think that this is because the *imageability* and uniqueness of a place have come to have great value and currency in the information marketplace. This is why cities—from Kansas City to Detroit—are trying so hard to differentiate themselves and celebrate their culture, along with making an interesting place.

Thus, we are moving from planning as a two-dimensional problem of how to best organize activities on the land to meet a universal ideal, to a three-dimensional problem by adding the element of *place*—How do these activities add up to a unique experience with cultural content and richness?— to even a four-dimensional problem, by adding the element of *time*—the new urbanists believe, for example, that we should be living in the Victorian era of cities. Kevin Lynch's question—"What time is this place?"—is more relevant than ever.

This situation poses several challenges to planning. First, we continue to operate within a public policy framework that seeks conformity, left over from the modernist, two-dimensional era of thinking. This is especially true not only in infrastructure planning for transportation and waterways management but also in other areas such as, for example, housing policy involving minimum property standards. How to change this structure to accept diversity and greater complexity is a daunting task. Second, some real experimentation is needed to explore new forms of urban living and identity and development, particularly in the face of major changes in lifestyle brought on by the information age.

On this point, it appears that the new urbanism is making some of the same mistakes of the old by preaching that one model fits all situations. In the absence of true creativity in designing forms of urban living, we are falling back on a new conformity based on old symbols and forms. I see this as a reaction against change rather than an embracing of diversity, and as a clear sign that we are desperate for new models.

Experimentation in new forms of urbanism should be *led by the schools of planning*, based on an understanding of the changes in community and social structure now underway.

And so, to come down to planning education and our core curriculum in the Department of Urban Studies and Planning at MIT, we now have a two-legged—or two-dimensional—core that includes both economics and institutional processes or organization-making. To these I would add a third dimension: the subject of *place-making*. By this, I mean creating environments that enhance the culture and meet the needs of those who inhabit them. This subject is much too important to the well-being of communities and their economic development to be left to architects, engineers, or real estate developers—although all of these groups should be involved. To the core skill of quantitative analysis that we require, I would add (or replace it with) a requirement for skill in *qualitative synthesis*. I think we need to be engaging students in the act of inventing new ways of making communities, ways that force students to resolve together emerging issues of urban economics, institutions, *and* place-making. This is not a call to develop a new ideal model of community, but rather one to explore the opportunities and to create options for communities to consider in seeking their own paths.

To participate in synthesizing options, we need to develop a *future orientation*. Right now, the profession is focused primarily on resolving problems of the present and developing solutions to current problems—inching forward into the future. I would argue that we need to extend our time horizon by studying where trends are leading and what kind of city may emerge. This is important not only because it is essential to be truly current but because we need to leap out ahead of current problems to conceive of communities that are consistent with the deeply held values of planning—such as equity, cultural diversity, and economic justice—that are constant and should never change.

If we don't, others will, and their models will become the options for local planning.

3

Challenge and Creativity in Post-Modern Planning

Judith E. Innes

Planners in the United States have never had it easy. Planning is barely accepted in some areas, and in dozens of states, cities and towns are under no obligation to have a plan nor to hire a person with planning education or experience. Planners work amid a confusing array of federal, state, and local public agencies with different missions and regulatory authority or funding responsibility, all of which affect what the planner must or can do. In only a handful of places does any regional authority help organize this maze of mandates and agencies. Regional environmental issues like air quality, management of limited water resources, and diminishing habitat for endangered species intersect with urban development, especially in growing states such as California. A planner has to know a great deal and be prepared to talk with many kinds of experts. She has to be on the front lines with the public, developers, and elected officials in hearings, workshops, and one on one. She has to live with a disjunction between what is expected of her and what she can actually accomplish (Innes 1994). She is part bureaucrat, part political player, and part professional with responsibility for independent judgment. Inevitably, because of this ambiguity, she has discretion but no clear guidelines for action. She faces difficult questions about what is ethical and to whom she answers—the public, her boss, elected officials (Howe 1994). The challenge for planners has grown in recent years as organized interests have increasingly become active players in planning decisions and as public trust in government has declined.

This chapter is reprinted from Judith E. Innes, "Challenge and Creativity in Post-Modern Planning," *Town Planning Review* 69, 2: v–ix (1998), with permission of the publisher.

This very challenge, however, has produced planners who are creating innovative ways of doing planning, taking on new roles, and designing new processes and institutions. They are doing things for which, for the most part, their formal education did not prepare them.[1] Academic research is just beginning to identify, document, and interpret this range of activities and to suggest how it is changing the basic nature of planning. While, of course, there are discouraged planners in many communities and agencies because of the unsupportive, ambiguous environment in which they work, there is much to be learned from those who have taken the challenges head on and who are carving out new ground, whether in the United States or elsewhere.

Planning in the United States is constantly reinventing itself. Even the most enduring of planning roles, that of local land-use planner, has evolved as such planners do more and more negotiation over development and more shuttle diplomacy among competing interests. New roles and institutional arrangements keep emerging. In the mid-1980s, for example, economic development offices sprouted up alongside land-use planning departments, typically staffed by planners who took a proactive stance toward development while doing little or no actual plan-making. More recently, other planners have helped invent an important new institutional form—the community sector—an interlinked network of community advocacy and nonprofit agencies that work together through flexibly associated informal networks to produce political power for disadvantaged groups over redevelopment and many other inner-city issues.[2] Still others have been instrumental in organizing innovative, stakeholder-based consensus-building efforts to address complex and controversial problems like the allocation of transportation funding or the creation of a statewide growth-management strategy.[3] They have invented these processes with little help from the literature, relying to some extent on the techniques of mediation and negotiation as they identify stakeholders and create missions and tasks for and with these groups. They serve as staff to the groups or even as stakeholder representatives themselves, working collaboratively instead of in a privileged setting of power.

In this context it is essential for the planning academy to try to understand actual planning practice and help planners to "see" this work in perspective.[4] Academics can pay attention to, and make comparisons among, a wider range of practices than can an individual practitioner, and they can track change over time. They can also search through a range of literatures and theories to develop interpretations to account for what works, and how, and what does not, and why. They can draw on insights that can make practice more effective. For example, the literature on business management and organizational development has much to offer in its accounts of innovation, leadership, and teamwork. The literature on use of language and metaphor can assist the understanding of how and why some planning discussions are productive and others are not. Finally, the literature on ethics and social theory can help uncover the dilemmas and fundamental challenges that planners face and offer alternative normative models for practice. The length of the list parallels the breadth and complexity of practice itself.

The planning academy must pay particular attention to cutting-edge practice—practice that is experimenting with new approaches and new kinds of interventions. Whereas academics clearly can make a contribution directly to practice by documenting this work, they need to pay attention to such innovations for more fundamental reasons. Practitioners have been on the front lines of a rapidly changing contemporary context. They operate at the interface of politics, bureaucracy, and public opinion. They are aware, if only tacitly, of changes the academy is just beginning to recognize, and they are independently inventing approaches academics have, in the main, neither proposed nor anticipated. Instead of the academy leading practice, it is the other way around. Academics have much to learn from these practitioners, not only about planning, but, more broadly, about change, institutions, group dynamics, and political processes, among other things. Ultimately, both practitioners and academics have the most to learn through a dialogue in which each can respond to the puzzles and surprises of the other with what they know best, while collectively piecing together a new way of seeing what planning can become in the twenty-first century.

Collaborative, communicative planning of the sort I see emerging stands in contrast to the modernist vision, usually referred to as "rational" planning and still widely taught in planning schools. The latter is an orderly (albeit hypothetical) process which assumes that meaningful collective goals can be defined, that expert neutrality is possible, that the best way to achieve a goal can be determined through formal analysis. Rational planning has discrete steps—goal-setting, alternative generation, evaluation, and decision. Planners, citizens, and elected officials have distinct roles, and they enter the process at different points. The planner's role is that of a neutral expert providing information and alternatives. Post-modern planning, however—planning designed to deal with the fragmentation, uncertainty, and rapid change of the early twenty-first century—merges the steps and mixes the roles. Participants do not accept the neutrality of any expertise, but accept as relevant, if not neutral, knowledge grounded in experience, intuition, and stories. They learn that communication is a form of action and that its form and content matter because it changes the participants. This planning is driven not by a search for the best way to achieve a goal, but by a package of actions that participants agree will improve on the situation. In these collaborative processes, decisions are only one product; along the way, many things happen that are not envisioned by the rational model.

For example, research to date suggests that post-modern planning is about making connections among ideas and among people and that this connection process sets in motion a whole series of changes. Joint learning changes both accepted ideas and attitudes, and it can produce innovative approaches. This planning bridges and coordinates among organizations and jurisdictions. Its most important contribution may be the flexible links it creates among important players so a city, region, or agency can be rapidly responsive to change (Dodge 1996). This planning is about finding continuity and commonality in a fragmented social and political environment where subgroups celebrate their differences. It entails negotiating new ways of framing public problems and new roles and relationships for public and private actors to get around dilemmas and find ways out of seemingly intractable controversies. It involves creating ways for players to continuously monitor events and get feedback on the workings of an environmental or urban system so they can adjust their own actions. Post-modern planning confronts the challenge of continuous change, not by creating blueprints or rigid regulatory regimes, but by trying to influence the direction of change and preparing to meet uncertainty. Because such collaborative processes engage the emotions and imagination of the stakeholders whose actions produce and reproduce cities and regions, they can have powerful practical consequences. They can also provide an antidote to declining trust in government and the sense of loss of civic community.

While there is much still to be learned, the research on planning practice has already provided a fertile array of intellectual resources. It has told us, for example, that much planning is not just *through* but *about* communication.[5] It suggests that we, as educators, may not have paid enough attention to the conceptual, practical, and ethical dimensions of communication as we focused instead on analytic tools or pragmatic and procedural issues. It has told us that planners' work is centrally about making collective meanings and bringing coherence to a complex and changing world (Marris 1996). The important part of planning is not deciding what must be done for the next 20 years, but being adaptive and creative as the future unfolds, being prepared to shape that future in ways we cannot now anticipate. The research has told us that processes matter and that citizens have real knowledge that is central to successful planning. Indeed, citizens and all the players who make up a city or region are part of the complex system that constitutes the city, and all must therefore be part of the solution.

Planning theory itself has changed in the past decade or two, as it has become more and more grounded in the realities of practice, and more and more relevant to practice. Ironically, as it grows more linked to practice, it less often purports to say how planning ought to be done. It more often tells us in a nuanced way how practice of various kinds has worked, permitting each reader to draw her own lessons for her own situation. Planning theory is much more about helping planners see themselves and what they do than it is about providing prescriptions. Planning theory today tells planners that they may not be able to shape places into the forms they choose, nor predict the specific results of actions; but it does affirm that they are key participants who assist the many other players in urban development to help to ensure that cities are more workable, efficient, livable, sustainable places.

4

Merging Place-Making and Process in Local Practice

Terry S. Szold

Two separate streams of practice have been flowing in the field of local planning. The streams have meandered close together in recent years but have not combined or reached a confluence. One stream relates to "place-making," community design, and the facilitation of alternative development outcomes; the other relates to the process of planning itself and how communities seek to organize themselves around the creation of plans and related interventions. Although issues related to the first stream will be my principal focus, unless we attempt to harness both streams and nurture their concurrent development, the results of planning will, at best, be amorphous, and, at worst, potentially irrelevant to shaping the form and function of the American landscape. Because so much is at stake for the profession and the communities we seek to serve, both practice and education share major responsibilities in relation to merging the streams.

Planners have been playing the game of the last Phantom Spirit in Dickens' *A Christmas Carol*. In essence, we wish to show (and frighten citizens with) the specter of the future yet to come, particularly if we collectively fail to intervene. As Scrooge states to the last spirit: "You are about to show me shadows of the things that have not happened, but will happen in the time before us." Can we prove to communities that if collective development behavior is modified or dramatically changed, a different, more desirable outcome will result? What process will we employ to steer communities toward this alternative future? The profession of planning, if it is to remain a robust and effective field, will be required to answer these questions.

THE TWO STREAMS

For the purpose of discussion, it is useful to illustrate some of the characteristics of, and distinctions between, the two streams noted.

PLACE-MAKING

The place-making stream relates to planning endeavors focused on spatial development, urban design and city form, public realm, streetscapes and related infrastructure, and the general imaging and re-imaging of places. The characteristics, competencies, and skills of the place-making players are *design and graphic skills*, *spatial lens and perspective*, *artistic*, *strategic*, and *synthesizer*.

PROCESS

The process stream relates to planning endeavors focused on citizen participation, equity, inclusiveness, and the organization and anticipated benefits of the process itself. Concerns involve the following questions:

1. Who gets to have a say?
2. How are issues debated?
3. What is the framework for resolving disagreements?

The timeliness of a plan and the type of plan to be prepared, given available resources and time constraints, are also anchored within this stream. The characteristics, competencies, and skills of the process players are *highly articulate*, *organized*, *consensus builders*, *instigators*, *synthesizers*, *leaders*, and *enablers*.

While the streams share common attributes, there are some clear distinctions between them. Some may argue that the distinctions represented by the polarity are exaggerated. Even if the distinctions are exaggerated, they still exist, within both professional practice and the curriculum of planning programs that credential future practitioners.

LAND-USE AND COMPREHENSIVE PLANS

Michael Teitz (1996) states that land-use planning is the "traditional core" of the field. Despite the growing national consensus about the need for regional solutions and interventions related to growth, as evidenced in a wide body of recent literature from the field (DeGrove 1992), and the American Planning Association's "Growing Smart" initiative (1996), I believe that the arena for most practitioners in the United States will remain closely focused on local space—its control and evolution. If the shaping of local space does remain a central feature of planning practice, professionals will need to have a clear idea about how interventions and plans can ensure better development outcomes. We will also need to be able to articulate and illustrate to our primary constituency—the public—why we should be trusted to shape the future of our communities. Comprehensive and general plans, and how they evolve in the future, may provide a pathway to merging these streams.

A recent study of twentieth-century land-use planning (Kaiser and Godschalk 1995) evaluates the different plan types that have evolved in practice and been used by cities to plan for their physical evolution. Plan types were reviewed and grouped in a "family tree" of distinct types and hybrids: the General Plan, representing the main trunk and genealogy of the tree, and further areas or branches such as the Verbal Policy Plan, Land Use Design Plan, Land Classification Plan, and Development Management Plan. The branches eventually are combined into the hybrid plans of contemporary practice, which involve the integration of the various parts of the prototype plans. Kaiser and Godschalk have effectively summarized and illuminated the evolving land-use planning template for communities. They are optimistic about the continuing usefulness and importance of land-use planning, primarily because of its ability to "adapt," and perhaps because it works better than the alternative—no planning at all.

Most of my experience in professional planning practice in the past fifteen years has been in this traditional core, planning for small and medium-sized communities with populations of 15,000 to 80,000 in the New England region. A review of plans in this region over the past decade would yield a categorization similar to the grouping provided by Kaiser and Godschalk. The town of Carlisle, Massachusetts, for example, chose a Verbal Policy Plan to guide its recent growth management program. This suburb of Boston chose the goal of "rurality" as the central theme of its plan. Burlington, Massachusetts, one of Garreau's "Edge Cities," used a hybrid planning approach for its master plan, focusing its efforts on a series of development strategies represented in the Land Use Element of the plan, which involved nurturing the physical form and development qualities of various town gateways. Primary goals of the plan involved discouraging big box retail uses, strengthening the town's existing economic base, creating a town center–based development strategy for the community's traditional retail corridor, and planning for high-technology uses on properties with significant redevelopment potential.

Moving south from suburb and edge city to the metropolis, Boston inaugurated a new master plan in 1997, dubbing the plan "Boston 400" to coincide with the city's 400th anniversary in the year 2030. The city's current residents are being asked to envision the future of their city, three decades from today. Officials at the Boston Redevelopment Authority have spoken about the plan in a manner that departs from the parlance used to describe traditional master and urban renewal plans from the 1960s. The person overseeing the development of the plan has stated, among other things, that the plan is about "connections to neighborhood" and "public realm" (Lupo 1997). She has also discussed the future of the city in spatial and physical terms, and raised questions in a series of neighborhood meetings designed to elicit from residents their desires for the city's future form.

At a minimum, each plan and initiative cited above has the power of being used as a "guidance document" and/or as inspirational devices for the municipalities involved. The plans can also be used to shape regulatory interventions and the programming infrastructure. To the extent that plan recommendations become institutionalized through the creation of new zoning provisions, some certainty about scale, density, and use can be expected. Many plans, however (including those of recent vintage), provide little guarantee of development quality, nor do they provide clear examples or images of what developers should actually build—although they are clearer about what should not be built. The plans are weak in terms of the process that should be used to ensure meaningful implementation.

Comprehensive plans fell out of fashion for a time. The time and expense involved in producing such plans may have been a factor related to their temporary loss of currency. Other factors were also influential. Planners and citizens alike feared that, upon completion, plan recommendations would be too dated to be useful. Another fear, perhaps lurking beneath the surface, is a practical worry about Daniel Burnham's admonition—large plans, while having "magic," defy realistic odds of implementation. Although comprehensive planning has rebounded, at least in New England, planners still worry that plan recommendations not be overly prescriptive. By avoiding the subject of prescriptions, however, critics of the profession were able to question the value of the products that planners produce, in addition to providing an opening for questioning the very purpose of the regulatory power exerted by planners or their agencies.

In 1996, the National Conference of the American Planning Association highlighted the "Form-Based Planning" approach. This approach to planning provides specific examples of the types of development that are encouraged and discouraged in various areas of the community. The pitch of roofs, building elevations, materials, facades, and shape of building and building alignment—all are conceptually rendered in the form desired, for both commercial and residential areas. The proponents of this concept highlighted their approach as an example of "New Directions in Land Use Regulation." Louisville and Jefferson County in Kentucky, for example, have embraced this form-based approach and made their concept readily available to other jurisdictions. Adams Township and Pittsburgh, Pennsylvania, along with Eagle, Colorado, are utilizing a "character- and context-based" approach to regulating development (Duerksen 1996). In some of these communities, development models are incorporated within zoning districts. Some of the development models emphasize compact, mixed-use development—a strategy that until recently was the antithesis of past and contemporary zoning practice.

Some may argue that these communities have simply incorporated the approach of design review into a basic set of development guidelines and regulations. A less cynical observer, however, should conclude that this approach provides further evidence that the Euclidean paradigm, while not breaking apart, is changing. Development outcome—and not simply a linear form of use or density classification—is becoming a pursuit of land-use planning. Even if the approach is not evident in most forms of master planning, it is nevertheless becoming a more common feature of recent planning and regulatory endeavors. Therefore, whether through the side door or the back door, place-making may be finding its way back to the core.

STRONG CURRENTS IN THE STREAMS

The tension that exists between the new urbanists and others in the planning community is, at least in part, emblematic of the separately flowing streams and currents in the practice of planning. The almost religious fervor exhibited by some proponents of this movement has led to colorful and interesting public and private debates. The new urbanists have gained attention not only because they advance distinct alternatives to conventional development, but because they represent a movement that seeks to reestablish what they claim are the fundamental aspects and physical connections of communities. They believe that the physical connections of people and place are made nearly impossible because of our rigid and ubiquitous adherence to the tenets of Euclidean zoning.

Will the new urbanism offer something genuinely different beyond the veneer of a more attractive kind of urbanism, or even suburbanism? It may be too early to draw a firm conclusion about this question, as Michael Teitz wisely counsels (1996). It is not too early, however, to conclude that the movement and its literature, at least to date, have left it to others, perhaps by default, to address the redistributive and equity questions associated with the physical and social evolution of our collective landscape. If function does not follow form, planners, who are the target of scathing reviews by some proponents of this movement, will clearly be left to wrestle with the issues that design theory alone can neither grasp nor adequately address. Will rigid adherence to the new urbanism, instead of Euclidean zoning, trap us in the nineteenth century, as Dennis Frenchman observes? The search for new models of development will and must continue.

Nonetheless, the new urbanists have, at least temporarily, captured the flag of place-making back from land-use planners. They have shown us some models and examples of alternative futures for the American landscape, while also racing downstream in a powerful and highly visible way. Unfortunately, as they race in the place-making stream, they offer little in the way of process to help the profession navigate the challenges left in their wake. There are hopeful signs, but the confluence still lies ahead.

A "WANTED LANDSCAPE"

In an article about negotiating agreements related to affordable housing development, Noah Dorius (1993) asks us to think about the challenge of planning as a quest for "wanted land uses." This question is likely to continue to resonate in the field for some time, particularly since the creation of plans and alternative development scenarios will consume much of practitioners' time. At the same time, additional questions deserve to be asked, especially in communities that have remaining open spaces or that are subject to major redevelopment activity. What, qualitatively, should the emerging built and natural landscape be like? How can it be envisioned and effectively described? If words such as *density*, *use*, *bulk*, and *height* were deleted from the lexicon of terms planners use, could we make a compelling case to the public that the anticipated results of a strategic or comprehensive plan justify the laborious process of preparing and implementing the plan? How many planners wish to have this assignment?

Planners in the future will have to take up this challenge. Information technology is already available to demonstrate, at least in the aggregate, what the development pattern will be like if trends are simply extended. But, if it is the intervention of planners and planning that can change the built and natural landscape, we will have to demonstrate it, at least hypothetically, with models that are realistic and tactile. Colors and shading, representing density or use, will not suffice.

THE INFLUENCE OF EDUCATION ON PRACTICE

It is remarkable that many students today can pass through a master's in city planning program and not be able to articulate or illustrate preferred development outcomes. American planning may have evolved from traditions of architecture and landscape architecture, but today's planning students can avoid courses in land use and physical planning altogether. Both the field and education in general are rapidly embracing different fluencies and specialties, even though these specialties continue to wrap themselves around the title and discipline of planning. There is a danger in too much specialization, however. As specialties and distinctions grow, a separate kind of vocabulary results for each area. If we are not careful, our field, already addicted to acronyms, will require the use of translators.

A real opportunity exists to nurture and train planners to envision and portray potential alternatives for the physical and social evolution of society, and to fashion appropriate interventions that merge the considerations of process, place, and development outcome. In addition to the core curriculum offered in planning programs, contemporary courses challenge the traditional boundaries of the field itself. Courses that focus on equity and fairness, the effectiveness of public process, dispute resolution and consensus building have gained highly visible seats at the table of the profession and in academe. Planners are becoming more comprehensive in the scope and breadth of their knowledge. Since the very nature of planning and practice itself is an invitation to comprehensive thinking, schools of planning should nurture diversity and the growth of specialties. At the same time, they should maintain a commitment to training the generalist planner—that special individual who can embrace multiple considerations when evaluating the merits of a particular intervention or strategy. New information and communication technologies, along with the inexpensive array of imaging software that is available, will help us further merge the streams.

There is encouraging new evidence that the streams of process and place-making are meandering closer together—seeking a complementary integration. Forging the various streams and currents flowing within our field should be a mission that transcends any boundaries that exist between practice and education. It is an obligation that rests equally on all those connected to the profession of planning; but the initial burden of the obligation rests squarely on the shoulders of education. It is likely that students who will become the practitioners of tomorrow will not need to worry about any lack of integration between place-making and process. Optimism on this front is grounded in what appears to be two clear trends evident in our discipline: the availability of information technology to help planners represent alternative futures spatially, and, as this collection and the 1997 MIT Faculty Seminar demonstrate, the profession's willingness to look at itself critically and, where necessary, reinvent itself.

5

City Planning in Small and Medium-Size Cities

PHILIP B. HERR

The statistical rule of thumb is that one should base projection on history two to three times as long as the term of the projection. Daniel Burnham's plan for Chicago was new at the start of the twentieth century. A third of this century went by before MIT began producing planning professionals. T. J. Kent's *The Urban General Plan* (1964) was published after the midpoint of the century. Obviously, over the full century, there has been enormous change in the profession. Planning as a distinct profession did not exist at the beginning of the century, and it has been fundamentally transformed at least twice over its history. Taking that long perspective, five changes in small-city planning over the century seem evident, especially in the latter half.

PLANNING IN SMALLER CITIES: CHANGE

First, in smaller communities, the use of professionals in planning has been greatly increased. Except in California, professional planners were virtually nonexistent on small-community staffs until the final third of the twentieth century. That source of practice for planners has grown fairly robustly since then, despite the growth in conservative ideology, trends toward deregulation, and takings concerns, among other impediments to planning in this era, as cited by Teitz (1996, 1997). Those impediments are indeed evident in both small and large communities.

Second, there has been a drift toward "community development," rather than planning, as what planners do in smaller cities. Planning in smaller communities might be characterized as being dominantly concerned with guiding investment—the business of regulatory planning—rather than managing disinvestment, which is essentially the business of community development and larger, older places. True, this generalization is dangerous both across communities and over time in a single community. Cambridge, a large, older city, until recently predictably following the "manage divestment" mode, is now struggling with growth, which imposes a need for guiding investment through regulation. Los Angeles, for decades similarly struggling to manage growth, has, according to Con Howe (see chapter 7 in this volume), seen its dominant planning needs reverse mode into community development designed to manage divestment. In both cases, the modal shift has been difficult to accommodate quickly. Despite that, I believe, the small-community professional role more commonly centers on community development efforts: getting grants, no matter for what; making deals; luring investment. There are lots of reasons, including the increasingly entrepreneurial posture of communities. More important, however, are the credits planners earn for tangible community benefits from concrete grants and investments.

Third, and despite the above, there is greater comprehensiveness in small-community local planning now than there was in the past. True, in many of these communities narrowly focused zoning remains synonymous with planning. However, long-range comprehensive plans are more and more widely supported by enthusiastic citizens, at the same time that professional confidence in that device has faded. Note the direction of the "Growing Smart" initiative of the American Planning Association (APA), framing "new" directions for American planning. Indicative of the APA constituency, that initiative advocates a return to the classic model of Kent's *Urban General Plan* (1964).

Fourth, in smaller communities there has been agonizingly slow acceptance of strategic, flexible, dynamic approaches whether to planning, regulation, or community development. Perhaps that slowness reflects the dominance of amateurs and modestly skilled professionals in small-community planning.

Fifth, and again despite everything said above, over the course of the twentieth century there has been large growth in small-city reliance on police-power controls. That growth continues, despite takings concern, popular support for the concept of deregulation, and conservative ideology. Local regulation is proving to be a monotonic process, almost never abandoning prior regulatory territory but constantly adding to it, for political and pragmatic reasons that are not very obscure.

SUCCESSES IN SMALLER CITIES

Small-community planning has helped America get what it wants:

- Homogeneous communities, as articulated by Robert Wood's *Suburbia* (Wood 1958);

- "Towers in the Park," as promoted by Le Corbusier and the modernist school;

- "Spread City," much as advocated by Frank Lloyd Wright.

Looking back at that history is a reminder of the adage that one best be careful about what one wishes for, since the wish might be granted. Sprawling suburbia and eroding rural qualities are much less a failure of planning's influence or power than a failure of vision by both public and planners. The evidence is clear: planners helped America get what it got. Big-city planners gave us urban renewal; small-city planners gave us homogeneous-use, low-density zoning. Our profession, with notable exceptions, embraced both. We "succeeded" at what we sought, deniable only through a revisionist lens.

FAILURES OF PLANNING IN SMALLER CITIES

Two failures seem important. First, planners have failed to promote a superior alternative to what the public uncritically wanted. There were many prophetic warnings: Benton MacKaye, Lewis Mumford, Clarence Stein, Thomas Adams, and many others led, but few actually followed. The prophets' message was not internalized in the small-community context, even by most of the professionals practicing there.

Second, the profession failed to produce a body of professionals who understood how to manage processes that both respect citizen understanding and creativity and give professional insights genuine standing. The dominant professional view remains — that professionals know best, and that they will "educate" the people as necessary to get their proposals adopted. Too few accept the view that the citizens of their communities really can contribute creatively to the community's planning in ways that professionals simply cannot. Too many of those who do accept that view abdicate full professional responsibility; they passively make plans out of citizen views inadequately informed by insights that professionals are uniquely qualified to contribute. Academic literature is rich in describing the creative synergies between citizen and planner. Practice is discouragingly poor at actually creating that synergy, although it is getting better.

SUMMING UP

In his retrospective perspective, Bishwapriya Sanyal discussed theory regarding the substance of planning, the procedures of planning, and normative theory (Sanyal 1997, 2000). Certainly, there is little evidence of important gains in substantive theory for the smaller-city context. The dominant substantive insight of this era seems to be a return to the patterns of an earlier time. Similarly, any gains in procedural theory seem modest. The rhetoric of procedural theory moves in small cyclical waves: the need for big ideas is evident.

The ethical framework for planning in smaller communities has certainly experienced change. A half-century ago, and for some time thereafter, planning in smaller communities was the domain of consultant planners, who come closest in our field to having professional independence from constraints imposed by either market or state. Today, however, planning even in smaller communities is dominantly a state function executed by servants of the state. That is our normative reality. An observation often repeated at the 1997 MIT Faculty Seminar was that the only cited "new idea" of our time is neotraditionalism. That "new idea" comes not from market- and state-bound professional planners but almost exclusively from relatively independent architects.

I can conclude optimistically: our planning skills *have* improved. Information technology helps substantially; our understanding of dispute resolution and, even better, dispute avoidance, gradually grows; and team approaches become more and more common and effective, at least in the small-community context.

6

Notes on Planning Practice and Education

Allan B. Jacobs

The city-planning function in local government is well established. As often as not, plans and planning are mandated: cities, urban areas, special districts are required to do "planning." The private sector engages in planning just as government does. Depending on the scale at which the private sector operates, the plans it produces have elements similar to those produced by the public.

At one level, we are concerned here with a straightforward question: What does it take to do the job? The "job" will differ depending on the nature of the place involved. The nature of the places varies according to size, geography, people, economic well-being, and history. It might follow, then, that different places require different expertise in order to do planning for them.

The reality of city planning as an accepted part of government does not necessarily mean that it is done well or effectively. Before getting to the dual questions of the specialization required to do urban planning and to construct a planning core—here, thought of as a central core of knowledge, information, and skills that everyone in a field might be expected to master, and thought of in an academic context—I find it useful to look, albeit briefly, at the state of professional urban planning as I have experienced it in recent years and to look, again briefly, at the mandates to do urban planning, as found in city charters and the legislation that set up the departments where city planning occurs.

RECENT EXPERIENCE

I want to start with recent experience in planning departments. These are the encounters that tell me, as much as anything, how urban planners approach

47

their jobs, how they are perceived, how important the role of urban planning is or is not, and, by extension, how well prepared the professionals may be for the tasks at hand.

As little as seven years ago, the City Planning Department of San Francisco was central to development in the city: land-use policy and land-use law, economic development, project development, physical form and design, redevelopment, and so on. Today the department is considered largely a rubber stamp agency, a costly hurdle to be bypassed whenever possible by special legislation and an elite group of pragmatic doers in the mayor's office. Part of the problem stems from a reorganization of government that diminishes the role and position of city planning, giving more power to the mayor. One can ask at the start, why was it deemed desirable to diminish planning, and why isn't planning as important to this mayor as it is to others? It's a complex question, and the answer to it has many facets, not the least of which is the nature of the mayor. A good part of the answer, however, stems from an agency that for years has increasingly concentrated on the permit and development *process*, at the expense of ideas and plans. The simplest of development proposals can take forever to decide; it is costly, and it goes through the Planning Department. At the time of the recent governmental changes, there was a modest debate as to whether the Planning Department should continue to exist.

Years ago, in the late 1960s or early 1970s, a small group of professionals had a bumper-sticker-type sign that read "The Process Is the Plan." I remember telling them that could not be so in my office, but that the plan would be the plan. There is process to everything. Getting up in the morning is part of a process, and so is using the toilet. But there has to be a point—a priority—to it all, not just getting through the day.

Not too many years ago, I was called by the director of the Los Angeles City Planning Department and asked what urban design was. After telling him as best I could in three or four minutes, he said that maybe his department should have some of that.

I have been paid good money to teach the staff of a city planning department how to do land-use planning. The director did not object to my presentation; he even invited me. He didn't know how to do it either. Staff members, after being questioned, admitted that they had been trained in policy determination—"making policy," they said.

When I act as a consultant in cities around the country, regardless of the client, I always ask about the city planning department: Why aren't they doing this work? What do their plans say? Is the planning department an important force here? Is it a source of ideas? How important is it? Is the director an important leader? Does the development community, or the environmental community or design community, look to someone on the staff as an expert or a leader? More often that not, the answers are negative, which is not to say that they are *always* negative. Too often, when I *do* find substantive expertise on a staff, it is hidden or silent. How many times in recent years have I heard that someone wanted to talk to me in private but could not state publicly their findings or conclusions.

These days, I ask students if they would want to work directly in the public realm, for the public. More often than not, the answer is no.

Regularly, I find that people called city planners are masters of process, but not of substance.

Too often, I find that while city planning has been mandated and accepted, the institution (and, by extension, the people who do it) are frowned upon. The planners are the "bureaucracy," in the negative sense of the word.

Making most development decisions one by one—with the focus on process, without benefit of something called a plan—is to forget why the field exists. My experience suggests that the field has long since gone too far down that path, and that is in part why it is often held in low esteem.

MANDATES TO DO CITY PLANNING AS FOUND IN CHARTERS AND LEGISLATIVE ACTS THAT CREATE CITY PLANNING DEPARTMENTS

Perhaps my experience is not representative. I'd like to hope it is not but suspect it is. It is against this experiential background that I read Mike Teitz's two essays in *Urban Studies* (Teitz 1996, 1997), from which his chapter (ch. 32) in this volume is drawn. They are truly elegant pieces of academic review and organization. I have had some minor quarrels with them—there's not much here on physical changes in cities or design—but they *are* elegant. Mike does note the absence of planners in the 1997 paper that deals more with current times. At the same time, those papers aren't helpful to me as a practitioner. They leave me nowhere in terms of direction or purpose. Autobiographically, I was reminded of the mid-1960s when, after ten years of practice, I was teaching at Penn, a minor member of an esteemed and renowned faculty. Those were troubled times, the late 1960s. "Long, hot summers" did not necessarily refer to the weather, but to riots and arson. I soon became aware that the elegant academic language and debates I heard had little to do with professional experience. Nothing rang true. Urban planning was something different than what I was hearing. It was better that I leave, so I went to San Francisco.

I have always found it useful to be clear about what the client wants before I offer my services and before I start to work. For public planners, a crucial starting point is in the legislation that establishes city planning, either a charter voted on by the people or a legislative act. A good look at those acts may well produce the answer to a central question raised: Why the fresh interest in land-use plans and three-dimensional environments?

When people or their representatives put down on paper what they want city planners to do, overwhelmingly, in my reading, they say they want plans (and policies) that deal with the physical development of their communities: land uses, open space, transportation, public works, commerce, industry, and the like. They talk about the long range, about coordination; they talk about the interface with neighboring cities. They are often concerned with physical form. They may talk of zoning. They are not unconcerned about health, efficiency, or housing. But, if there is a focus to anything, it is the physical environment where people live. If these concerns are not central issues for professionals in the field, it may well be because they have not been trained that way—that is, not to perceive them as issues.

During the 1960s—earlier in some places, later in others—a lot of urban planning became mandated (as opposed to permitted) by state and federal legislation. I would make an observation about plans that are mandated by some level of government above the level where the planning gets done. When someone tells you that you have to do something you don't want to do, or that you think is less important than something else, or that might cost you a lot of money, or the case for which is poorly made, you will often do as little as you can to get by. This is true at a basic employment level, for example, or at the state level when the state tells the city what it must do. It is best if the local community decides it wants something; then there is a better chance of forceful, clear plans with which to start, as well as concrete actions that implement them.

SPECIALIZATION

The so-called profession of city planning in this country started with the getting together, toward the end of the nineteenth century, of specialists from many different, largely distinct professions and fields: architects, engineers, public health specialists, social welfare advocates, lawyers, landscape architects (and more, I am sure)—with a common concern for the conditions in cities and their people. They understood that each discipline or field had a legitimate role to play in solving urban problems and reaching urban potentials. There was a logic to these interests coming together, to do comprehensively what they could not do alone. It made sense, as well, to establish, in local governments (and in universities), departments to do comprehensively what each discipline would or could not do.

Today, a case can be made that the field has become so complex that we need specialties within the field. Probably we do; my experience would indicate as much. But we also need generalists.

Turning, for a moment, to the academies, what might happen if there were no departments of urban planning such as the one at MIT or Berkeley? Would other disciplines have evolved so as to create, within themselves, specialists in urban planning? Haven't some done that in reality—for example, in law, public health, transportation engineering, architecture, real estate, and landscape architecture? Which of these, however, takes a comprehensive, long-range look at cities? Would there be anyone to challenge the transportation engineers? Why not? Today's "skinny streets" and "cheap streets" programs in Portland, Oregon, for example, come from engineers. In Canada, Ontario's "new street" options come from architects and engineers. Arguably, natural scientists have had more to do with environmental awareness and standards than have urban planners. Maybe the long range would be considered if there were no planning departments.

Without departments of city planning at universities, would there be city-planning departments in cities? Probably so. Take a look, as I have suggested, at their charters.

Addressing the question of specialization, I look to what urban planning is supposed to do, as defined largely by public clients and what they have asked for (collectively, in their various mandates), but also to what private clients expect and need, and certainly to my own biases as to what the field ought to be doing. I note the following, briefly:

- Specialists in natural factors as determinants, constraints, and opportunities for the locations, development, and uses of urban land
- Specialists in urban design: the arrangement of built form in relation to the land itself and to the legitimate needs of those who inhabit urban areas
- Transportation–land-use specialists: transit, roads, pedestrians, bicycles, and so on
- Housing specialists (maybe a part of economics)
- Land-use and environmental law specialists
- Social dynamics specialists
- Data development and management: GIS mapping
- Building conservation and preservation
- The city-planning generalist as a specialist

There is, and will be, a need for urban planners who know something about most of these specializations.

To make a list is certainly not to suggest that any one city or office should have all these specialists at its beck and call, or that any one school should teach all of them.

EVOLUTION OF A CORE:
THE BERKELEY EXPERIENCE

With the expansion of the urban planning field and the development of concentrations, it was perhaps inevitable that the question of a core of courses, or knowledge, should arise. A case can be made that any specialist working in the field should have a central core of knowledge, information, and skills shared by those in the field. A specialist would do well, also, to have some knowledge about some area of expertise other than his or hers, knowledge that is brought to bear on the planning of urban environments (carry this very far and it becomes circular, with everyone being a generalist again). My view is that any specialist working in the field should have some knowledge and understanding of natural factors, urban design, land/development economics, transportation planning, public infrastructure, housing, and how government works, and should know law as it relates to urban planning.

At Berkeley, the core has, over the years, evolved from no core to the one we now have. For many years, there was no core of required courses. There was, apparently, an "understanding" of what the most essential courses were, one that was passed on to students by other students and by faculty advisers. Department lore has it that "everyone" took one or two or three particular courses, but I can't attest to that. Neither was a specific core of courses required during the department's first era of specialization—land use, housing, regional planning—that emerged in the late 1960s. Again, each specialization had an informal, "understood" core, but there were no requirements.

The first required core of courses came in the early 1980s and was not universally accepted by the faculty. It took about a year to start undermining the program. As an example, a studio course was required. It didn't take long for inventive faculty to develop all kinds of new courses and call them "studios." Indeed, in those days, it was next to impossible to get agreement on what a "studio" was—which, if it weren't so sad as a documentary about common language, would be humorous.

A required core has reemerged, but one that permits choices, with one exception. Everyone at Berkeley must take the History of City Planning course. All students must take two methods courses, from a menu of five. The other requirements are an institutions course (from a choice of four), an economics course (from a choice of three or four), and at least one studio course.

Essentially, then, there is a core of six courses that must be taken, but only one course that all students must take.

Beyond this central core of courses, Berkeley has seven areas of concentration and each of these has its own core, which amounts to as many as four courses:

- Housing and project development
- Transportation
- Metropolitan regional planning
- Land-use planning
- Urban design
- Community development
- Environmental planning

Students have an option that permits them to develop their own concentration, but this is rarely invoked. They are required to select a concentration by the end of the first semester. At the same time, many students change from one concentration to another. There are enough electives in any student's program to permit this kind of flexibility.

CONCLUSION

How to conclude? I am on my department's admissions committee. I read what would-be students want to do, what they want to concentrate on, and I read their reasons for wanting to do city planning. Probably these are the same people who apply to MIT. The largest single group say they want to concentrate on what we call "community development." Reading more closely, community development comes down to local, comprehensive planning that includes land use, housing (particularly for low-income people), transportation, and economic development. "Local" can be anything from a neighborhood to a whole local community to a city. There is much concern for low-income people and people of color. The statements are utopian in nature; their authors want to be part of building wonderful communities. So do the authors of statements directed toward urban design, transportation, environmental planning, and planning for developing areas.

Much of what students want to do sounds naive, and much is old-fashioned. Then again, maybe it's not. Maybe, instead of telling students the possible concentrations, we should spend time listening and hearing what they want to do, then concentrate on helping them achieve it. And, finally, maybe we should begin to understand the limitations of *process* and concentrate more on substance—singular and plural.

7

Planning Practice in America's Largest Cities

Con Howe

If the state of municipal planning departments in America's largest cities reflects the state of the planning profession, then the profession is in trouble. The first half of the 1990s was particularly traumatic for big-city planning departments. In the face of a national recession and local budget crises, planning departments in large municipalities disappeared altogether or were drastically downsized. In cities such as San Diego and St. Louis, where traditional departments have disappeared, planning staff and functions have been merged with permitting and economic development agencies. Where planning departments continue, their downsizing has been by as much as one-third; this has been the case in the largest departments in New York City and Los Angeles. While staff size and independent identity are hardly the only measures of planning departments, no practitioner would argue that today's planning agencies are at the zenith of influence or effectiveness with the planning problems of our largest cities.

Should the profession care? Arguably, "planning" is being done in an increasing number of ways, and municipal departments have represented a decreasing percentage of the overall market for planners for years. Certainly, it is hard for the profession to ignore a part of its practice that has historical ties to its inception. It is also hard to shortchange a part of the practice with such potential for addressing major urban issues. More important, however, the changes that have affected municipal planning have parallels that affect the entire profession, and many of the responses and hopeful directions have relevance throughout the field.

THE REGULATORY MIND-SET

One of the most basic changes confronting municipal planners is that of the antiregulation, antigovernment mood that has swept all levels of government.

The typical municipal planning department has spent decades developing increasingly complex and controlling zoning regulations. To earlier generations of municipal planners who had drafted "toothless" plans, these regulations must have seemed the epitome of power for planning departments. The environmental and open-meeting law requirements of the 1970s and 1980s added detailed procedural requirements. For a time during the high-growth 1980s, the regulatory approach won friends for planning departments among neighborhood groups still smarting from the past excesses of development. But too many regulations seemed divorced from longer-range plans, rather than implementing them; in the worst examples, regulations were tools for an ism known as "NIMBY" (Not In My Backyard). The administrative and procedural requirements of regulations were so demanding that the other planning functions and missions atrophied. By the beginning of the 1990s, the typical large-city planning department would have been more aptly titled a zoning or permitting department.

The advent of the national real estate debacle of the early 1990s pulled the rug from under these "permitting departments." With development in even previously hot markets at a standstill, what possible use did city governments have for regulators when there was nothing to regulate?

Underlying this practical reality was the antiregulatory, antigovernment mood that had been gaining momentum since the "Reagan Revolution." Elected city officials, who at one time had championed "slow growth" and the planners who had assisted them, now demanded "permit streamlining" and economic development. As Michael Teitz says in his *Urban Studies* article series, "American Planning in the 1990's" (Teitz 1996, 1997), municipal planning departments were simply "out of step" in this new environment.

A parallel, reinforcing trend has been the increasing interest in public–private partnerships and in "market-based planning." Earlier attitudes that plans were implemented solely through regulation and direct government action have been replaced by the approach that partnerships with private-sector and nonprofit entities are the proactive, effective way to address urban problems.

In the past decade, there has been an explosion of partnerships in varied forms: nonprofit, community-based developers; quasi-public corporations; designated developers; business improvement districts; and contracted-out services. From one perspective, these have all been supplements to ongoing city agencies—whether they are planning, housing, redevelopment, or public works departments. Yet, from another perspective, these partnerships are alternatives, filling voids left by bureaucratic and regulatory departments. The philosophy of market-based planning is that, in our economic system, sustainable changes occur only in concurrence with market forces, and that planners better understand and utilize the economics of the marketplace. Summarizing this view, Alexander Garvin defines successful planning as "public action that generates desirable, widespread, and sustained private market re-action" (Garvin 1996). Generations of planners (and developers) imbued with an "us versus them" mentality have found market-based planning hard to understand or accept.

THE LOSS OF CONSTITUENCIES

Planning departments have lost traditional constituencies and, in a well-intentioned effort to serve many clients, have lost the unswerving support of any one client. Since the beginning of professional practice in this country, high-minded civic organizations have been loyal advocates of city planning and the municipal departments that would carry it out. The very creation of planning commissions and departments was a triumph of their advocacy. Whereas Burnham's plan for Chicago was sponsored not by the city but by the private Commercial Club of Chicago, by the 1930s all major American cities had municipal planning departments to undertake such work.

Today, for a host of social and economic reasons, such broad civic organizations are fewer in number and influence. Where they do exist, they are as likely to be critics of municipal planning departments as they are to be supporters.

The "advocacy planning" of the 1960s helped awaken municipal planners to all the constituencies that they were not serving. This accelerated planning departments' earnest efforts to broaden their clientele, sometimes in the role of honest broker, sometimes in the role of outright advocate. More than a few municipal planners were caught in a cross fire between newfound community clients and their official clients, elected or appointed officeholders. Efforts to serve everyone led to confusion over who is the client, and the erosion of support from any one client. Ultimately, previously underserved groups, as well as other interest groups, seek their own representative or advocate—a role often filled by a planner, not just a municipal staff member.

At the same time, few planning departments have maintained consistent support or patronage from their city's chief executive or city council. While some of this may be due to the fickleness of term-limited elected officials, to a great extent municipal planners have only themselves to blame. Their regulatory approach may stop an unwanted project, but at the same time it produces few immediately visible results. Budget offices and redevelopment and economic development agencies are perceived as delivering the kind of visible products that elected officials crave. Typical planning research that leads to no clear next step will hardly command the attention of crisis-driven big-city mayors.

In summary, by the latter part of the 1990s, the typical big-city planning department had lost its way. As a result both of trends outside their control and of their own shortcomings, municipal planning departments are unpopular and sometimes irrelevant. Their regulatory mind-set and bureaucratic constraints have led them to be perceived as impediments to change rather than instigators of positive results.

POSITIVE TRENDS

This current, discouraging state of municipal planning is balanced by several positive trends that affect the entire profession but which are especially relevant to big-city planners. First of all, as Teitz points out, the social and economic problems of our central cities are broadly accepted as major issues confronting the nation. No one disputes that the kind of problems planners address remain critical problems. Planners have not worked their way out of a job.

The potential role of municipal planners is heightened by the trend of devolution for federal responsibilities to local government. As Washington has eschewed the role of solving urban problems, expectations are increasingly placed on city government. Possibly not since the time of John Lindsay have big-city mayors been seen as such important and visible public figures. These mayors, traditional clients of planning departments, need the useful products of good planning departments as never before.

As another positive trend, the traditional gulf between planners and developers is evaporating—in part as a result of the experience with, and demand for, public–private partnerships. For their part, professional planning schools have incorporated economics, real estate, and development into their programs, turning out professionals who are, in effect, "market-based planners." There is a new generation of developers knowledgeable and supportive of planning practice coming out of real estate centers established in the 1980s at schools such as MIT, Penn, Columbia, Berkeley, and the University of Southern California. As the skills and experience of their staff change, municipal planning departments will be better able to move from a regulatory mind-set to one of partnering.

The increased application of technology in big-city planning departments—especially the advent of Geographic Information Systems (GIS)—is giving them a new opportunity. GIS has the ability to make huge amounts of data understandable—and therefore influential—to decision makers. It blends two traditional responsibilities of planning departments: data research and mapping. At a minimum, GIS enhances a planning department's reputation for public information, and, depending on how it is used, heightens its analytical capacity and influence on public policy.

Another new opportunity for municipal planners is the increasing demand for transportation planning in relationship to land use. This is best evidenced by the requirements and resources provided by the federal ISTEA program. Transportation issues, too often the exclusive domain of traffic and public works departments, require the capacities and attention of planning departments. This parallels the way earlier environmental laws gave new responsibilities to planning departments.

PRESCRIPTION

While the trends discussed above hold promise for municipal planning departments, these departments must reorient themselves to take advantage of the opportunities and reestablish themselves as a vital part of professional planning practice. Many of the prescriptions for their revitalization hold true for planning practice and education as a whole.

Possibly the most important role planners can play in big-city government is the role of integrator. Planners' skill at integrating across disciplines and areas of practice becomes more critical as urban problems become more multidimensional. Effective planning departments can and do integrate the work of housing, transportation, public works, redevelopment, and economic development departments to produce products and programs responsive to urban problems. In some cities, and under some mayors, planning takes as central a role in the administration and policy development of government as budgeting.

The typical planning department that has been pigeonholed as a "zoning department" must regain opportunistic roles in policy analysis, capital programming, information technology, and implementation. The imprecise definition of *planning* allows municipal departments to earn a more expansive role in their governments. The skills of planners as integrators complement their skills as negotiators and consensus builders.

PRODUCT AND CLIENT ORIENTED

In order for municipal planning departments to build (or rebuild) a more central role, they must become both more product oriented and more client oriented. It is no wonder that departments that undertook unfocused research or unresponsive studies were downsized to a core zoning and permit-processing staff. Each zoning decision and each permit processed was a product. Mayors and city councils have the right to expect research to lead to application and for plans and policies to lead to results. Training planners to be product and results oriented is greatly enhanced by their interaction with the staff of implementing agencies and with the community.

Another key ingredient to the planner's revitalization is increased client orientation. The earlier discussion of the multiplicity of clients will remain true, but for planning departments in city government, in a very real way, their clients are the elected officials—typically the chief executive or mayor. This fact should not be met with hand wringing, however. In a democracy, elected officials are the lens through which public issues are identified and solutions enacted. The instances where planners have achieved the most results have been when and where they have attached themselves to enlightened and proactive mayors.

Being client oriented, especially in the eyes of a chief executive, does not mean passively waiting for the client to bring the planner a problem. In the best reformist tradition of the profession, planners should be identifying problems and bringing them and their possible solutions to the attention of decision makers. For the planners' agenda to become the chief executive's agenda is possibly the ultimate evidence of a department's utility.

Having the elected official as dedicated client does not replace the need for the municipal planner to build—and serve—many constituencies. Any elected official reflects and responds to a wide variety of constituents—from neighborhood groups to the development community to environmental advocates to racial and ethnic minorities. A planning department's service to all these constituencies says much about how it is perceived and its effectiveness. "Serving" need not be the same as "advocating." Every community group that participated in what it thought was a fair process, every nonprofit organization that got useful and objective information, every citizen seeking a permit who was treated as a customer—all walk away with a positive view of the planning department.

The care and development of these constituencies, though time-consuming, is essential input to the planner. An important means of communicating to these constituencies is the media, and municipal planners should learn how to make their products understandable and reportable.

Another key prescription to building the credibility of a planning department lies in its role as a provider of information. So many policy decisions are made with so little information, and a few well-chosen facts can have such an impact on public debate, that this role cannot be underestimated. New applications of systems and GIS technology can be a powerful tool to planning departments in effectively fulfilling this role. Being the consistent source of relevant, objective information to all parties and raising the level of public dialogue makes a planning department essential ("information

is power"). Good information underpins the planner's analytic and diagnos-
tic roles. The challenge to planning departments is to make relevant information available in clear and useful ways.

A final prescription is to infuse municipal planners with a better understanding of the private market. The implementation of their plans—whether
through regulation, incentive, or public investment—will depend on that
private market. Thus it becomes crucial that we understand how to effect it
and use it.

PLANNING EDUCATION

The trends currently confronting big-city planning departments, and the suggested responses, are relevant to the professional planning schools and programs in American universities. First, although municipal agencies, as employers, are not as large as they used to be, they remain a visible, historic part
of the profession. Second, there are parallels between how a municipal planning department and a planning school can react to changes in their field.
Both are institutions with the advantages and disadvantages of being somewhat insulated from change. Both have protections—civil service and tenure—
that make rapid changes in staffing impossible.

Ultimately, however, neither need exist. Indeed, in the last decade, planning schools and programs alike have disappeared or been dismembered.
The prescription for municipal planners to be integrative suggests that planning schools should continue to explore joint programs and interdisciplinary
initiatives. They should ensure that their curriculum is inclusive—even given
the time constraints—and that students learn the skills of integrating specializations and disciplines.

Product and client orientation leads planning schools to consider their
students and their graduates' employers as their customers and clients. This,
in turn, leads to an assessment of whether a school is competitive in attracting students and meeting the needs of the professional practice. Preparing
students to be product and client oriented thus becomes a part of the curriculum.

Other recommendations for curriculum include competency with systems and GIS technology and understanding of real estate development and
the private market. Already, the increased technological capacity of municipal
planning departments is largely due to the skills of a new generation of staff,
many of whom are planning school graduates. Similarly, skills in market-based
planning are coming out of those schools that have created real estate programs or other means of training in economics. At those universities where
real estate programs are intended to turn out developers but not potential

municipal planners, a closer integration of the real estate and planning programs should be considered.

In summary, planning departments in big cities throughout the nation are confronted with trends that alter the need and demand for their services. Typically, planning departments have not responded effectively to these changes; nor have they taken advantage of them. To be relevant to the urban issues of their cities, they will need to undertake reorientation and entrepreneurial initiatives. Schools educating future planners will have to undertake parallel efforts to meet the needs of this changing professional practice.

8

Town Planning: Limits to Reflection-in-Action

Donald A. Schön

THE EVOLVING CONTEXT OF PLANNING PRACTICE

Town planning has a charter membership in Glazer's society of minor professions. The institutional context of planning practice is notoriously unstable, and there are many contending views of the profession, each of which carries a different image of the planning role and a different picture of the body of useful knowledge. At the present time, for example, planners function variously as designers, plan makers, critics, advocates of special interests, regulators, managers, evaluators, and intermediaries. In planning as in other professions, each role tends to be associated with characteristic values, strategies, techniques, and bodies of relevant information. But in the planning profession, images of role have evolved significantly in relatively brief periods of time. The profession, which came into being around the turn of the century, moved in succeeding decades through different ideas in good currency about planning theory and practice, partly in response to changes in context shaped by planners themselves. The history of the evolution of planning roles can be understood as a global conversation between the planning profession and its situation.

With the development of the city planning movement in the early years of the century, planners first gained visibility, power, and professional status. The growth of comprehensive and master planning and the widespread establishment of local planning commissions in the United States paralleled the formation of the coalition supportive of town planning in Britain.[1] Following World War II, probably as a result of military and economic planning in wartime America, the idea of central planning extended its scope from comprehensive

---

This chapter is reprinted from Donald A. Schön, *The Reflective Practitioner: How Professionals Think In Action*. Copyright ©1983 by Basic Books, Inc. Reprinted by permission of Basic Books, a member of Perseus Books, L.L.C.

and master planning for towns to such fields as urban renewal, urban and regional transportation, health services, public education, mental health, and criminal justice.

In these domains, among many others, the centralist planner operated from the base of institutions created and legitimized through legislation brought into being by a coalition of political forces. The planner framed his role at the center of a system for which he planned, in relation to agencies which would implement his plans and clienteles who would benefit from them. His system of knowledge-in-practice dealt with the framing of objectives and goals, the imagining of a desirable future, the description of baseline conditions, the identification of alternative strategies of action, the description of constraints to be circumvented or removed, the mapping of the system to be influenced, and the prediction of the consequences of action. Later, planners also came to be concerned with the feasibility of implementing plans and the political problems of "selling" them.

Through the mid-1960s, centralist planning proceeded in this mode. Its operations were based on two main assumptions:

1. There is a working consensus about the content of the public interest, sufficient for the setting of planning goals and objectives, and

2. There is a system of knowledge adequate for the conduct of central planning.

It does not matter that these assumptions may never have been true. They were widely believed to be true, and they set the terms of reference for the planning profession. But by the mid-1960s, both assumptions were in trouble.

The public at large, and planners themselves, were becoming increasingly aware of the counterintuitive consequences, the harmful side effects, and the unwanted by-products of implemented plans. Plans designed to solve problems either failed to solve them or created problems worse than the problems they had been designed to solve. Some of the phenomena planners were most anxious to influence—poverty, crime, urban congestion and decay—seemed tenaciously resistant to intervention. The most broadly believed predictions (those relating to school enrollment, for example) turned out to be mistaken. Attempts to build formal, quantitative models of social phenomena foundered in complexity. Attempts to conduct social experiments were confounded by unanticipated and uncontrollable changes in the experimental context. Planners were found sometimes deliberately, sometimes unintentionally, to be serving interests incongruent with their espoused values. Social critics and angry political pressure groups demonstrated that plans had meanings and consequences well beyond those envisioned by urban planners. And as the perceived scope and complexity of planning increased, planners found that their techniques and models were inadequate to the tasks of analysis, diagnosis, and prediction. Planning "problems" came to seem more like dilemmas made up of conflicts of values, interests, and ideologies unresolvable by recourse to the facts.

By the mid-1960s, the apparent consensus about the content of the public interest—perhaps even about the feasibility of establishing such a consensus—had faded away. As the harmful consequences of centralist planning and governmental action were discovered, special interest groups formed around issues of injustice, hazard, and neglect. By the late 1970s, it was clear that there was no national consensus about the public interest. There was rather a field of special interests: minority groups, women's groups, environmentalists, consumers' groups, advocates of health and safety at work, the handicapped, the protagonists of special education and basic education, neighborhood conservationists, advocates for neighborhood schools, energy conservationists, advocates of zero population growth, advocates for and antagonists of abortion, moral and religious fundamentalists, advocates for guns or gun control, advocates for crime prevention, and advocates for deinstitutionalization of prisons and mental hospitals. These constituencies had learned to organize themselves, enter into public debate, and take political action in order to bring their concerns to legislative and judicial reality.

In some cases, special interest groups took positions which were in direct and explicit conflict with one another. In other cases, conflicts of interest became clear only as the success of one movement led to consequences contrary to the interests of another. In still other cases, conflict became evident as the different movements found themselves competing in hard times for scarce resources.

Throughout the 1960s, a new breed of social planners began to criticize established institutions because they rode roughshod over the less powerful. Herbert Gans, Jane Jacobs, Francis Piven, and Mark Fried, among other students of urban renewal, showed how planners acting ostensibly in the public interest actually served the interests of real estate developers and large corporations by displacing the poor and ethnic minorities.[2] The social critics and advocate planners operated in a social field made up of the constituents they sought to protect, the established institutions they fought, the media they tried to influence, the courts through which they often sought redress of grievances, and the legislatures through which they tried to shape laws that would regulate the behavior of established interests. Their knowledge-in-practice had to do with issues such as these: expressing the interests of the dispossessed, or empowering the dispossessed to express their own interests; demystifying the professional personas of the centralist planners, showing up their intended or unintended alliance with established interests; explaining how the actions of government and business affect the less powerful; formulating policies and programs to protect the less powerful and identifying the practices of established interest groups which needed most to be watched and controlled; figuring out how to gain visibility and political voice for the dispossessed; building connections to legislators, regulators, and executive agencies.

As these critics, advocates, and organizers were able to bring their ideas into good currency, they succeeded in influencing the legislative process either to regulate the actions of established institutions or to establish programs of service or income support for special interest groups. As a partial consequence of their success, the present social context of planning has become a field of institutions organized around contending interests. Regulatory systems have been established by law to monitor and control the actions of agencies such as businesses, schools, hospitals, universities, and real estate developers. The courts play a large and increasing role as adjudicators of doubtful cases, interpreters of the law, dispensers of sanctions for violation of the law, and sometimes as direct monitors or managers of systems in default.

Within these institutional fields, planners no longer follow the centralist planning model. They practice in relation to a growing variety of special interest groups and regulatory systems, and they have developed a variety of new or modified roles. They may function as spokesmen, strategists, or technical staff for parties to the regulatory process. They may perform watchdog functions, reviewing, for example, the environmental impact statements of developers or the affirmative action plans of government agencies. They may position themselves in the neutral space between regulators and regulated, functioning as mediators who convene interested parties, helping them to understand one another's position, to identify common interests, or to fashion an acceptable compromise.

In these intermediary roles, more like the traditional roles of the lawyer than the sometime centralist planner, knowledge must be developed and brought to bear on issues such as these: understanding the field of actors and interests with its potentials for satisfaction, frustration, mutual constraint or mutual enhancement; formulating issue-specific targets for negotiation, mediation, or inquiry; creating conditions for effective control or evasion of control, for successful negotiation, or for productive inquiry; designing intermediary interventions and assessing their effectiveness; maintaining the conditions of credibility and legitimacy on which the intermediary roles depend.

In the case that follows, I shall consider an example of this most recent form of planning practice, showing how one intermediary planner has evolved knowing-in-practice which enables him to address issues such as those listed above. In this case study, however, I shall explore several more general features of professional knowledge.[3]

A professional role places skeletal demands on a practitioner's behavior, but within these constraints, each individual develops his own way of framing his role. Whether he chooses his role frame from the profession's repertoire, or fashions it for himself, his professional knowledge takes on the character of a system. The problems he sets, the strategies he employs, the facts he treats as relevant, and his interpersonal theories of action are bound up with his way of framing his role. In the case that follows, I shall describe such a system of knowing-in-practice.

Further, a system of this sort tends to be self-reinforcing. Depending on the kind of role frame he has constructed and on the kind of interpersonal theory of action he has evolved, a practitioner's reflection-in-action may be more or less limited in scope and depth. In the case that follows, I shall try to show how limits to reflection-in-action are set and maintained.

SOME OF WHAT ONE PLANNER KNOWS

The individual whose practice we will be examining in this chapter is a town planner concerned primarily with the physical development of the town he serves. Yet he makes no comprehensive plans and prepares no designs for neighborhoods or regions. He has defined his job as one of reviewing proposals submitted by private developers to local regulatory bodies, and has positioned himself as an intermediary between these two parties. He seeks, by advising and negotiating with developers, to influence the direction and quality of physical development in the town. Substituting these functions for the more traditional preparation of plans, he plans by proxy.

Given his way of framing his role in the town and his image of the dilemmas associated with that role, the planner has learned to treat his practice as a balancing act in which he tries continually to advise and negotiate with developers while at the same time preserving his credibility with all the parties on whom his role depends.

In the following protocol, a transcript of a videotape at one of the meetings recorded in the planner's office, a developer presents drawings and plans for remodeling an apartment building which he and his uncle own in the town. Under the town's development bylaws, the planner must review such plans before submitting them to the Zoning Board of Appeals which has authority to grant or withhold variances.

As the tape begins, the planner rolls up his sleeves, consults his notes, and leans across the table to look at the developer and his architect.

> *Planner:*   I'll give you a review here. I think we ought to base some of the discussion we had a couple of weeks ago. You've got plans, and what I suggested is that we go over the zoning bylaw to see

exactly how they conform. The building plans, the structure itself, is no problem, but I think that within the zoning bylaws we've got to have some areas that we have to look at very closely in the site plan. Okay? Now, uh, and as far as the building is concerned, I think we can work out the details with the building inspector about the code requirements.

Architect: Right.

Planner: . . . which you work with all the time anyway . . .

The planner has defined the meeting's purpose, which is to review the developer's plans to see "exactly how they conform" to the zoning bylaw. He divides this plan into two parts, one that he finds acceptable ("the structure itself") and one that he finds problematic ("the site plan"). From here on, he will review elements of the site plan which he has listed for comment.

First, however, he checks to see whether the developer is familiar with the bylaws.

Planner: . . . but, Tom, have you had a chance to look at the development bylaws?

(Developer looks at architect).

Architect: Well, I've gone through it roughly.

Planner: Why don't we look at the lot?

Developer: We've blown the plans up quite a bit for you . . .

Architect: They were real small, you couldn't see 'em.

Now the planner zones in on the first item on his list, the question of lot size.

Planner: All right, now. Under the new apartment controls in our town, before the new bylaw enactor, you had to have 20,000 square feet of lot area; you had only 14,341. As you know, it's apparently impossible to get any more.

Developer: Uh-hum.

Planner: Now, what you wanna do is add a couple apartment units to this building. That is gonna require a variance . . . because . . . you are . . . adding to a multifamily building in an apartment zone where the lots aren't large enough. So you're gonna need a variance on lot size. . . . At the same time, you'll need a special permit because you are dealing with an apartment structure, but that can be handled. As I look at it, without seeing a more detailed site plan (but that can be put together eventually), the only variance you need is on lot area. Everything else is all right.

The developer, still preoccupied with the visibility of his plans (as though that might remove the difficulty), questions whether he is really in violation of the bylaw.

Developer: I don't know. I think I have something a little bit larger for us to look at. I don't know that we violate too much of the thing, especially if we get involved in taking down that little thing up front there.

The planner explains how the developer may be able to justify a variance on lot size, ignoring the latter's hint that there may be no need for it.

Planner: Obviously you have no problem with the floor area.
Developer: We don't.
Planner: You have no problem with land area per dwelling unit, and when you go to the Zoning Board of Appeals, obviously that's gonna be one thing you want to play out. Even though you don't have the 20,000 square feet of land, you're not even approaching the zoning limit, because you're dealing with existing buildings.

Without pausing to sound out the developer's reaction to these suggestions, the planner goes on to point out additional requirements in the bylaw.

Planner: The new zoning bylaw does have two open-space requirements, and they're slightly different from other bylaws you may have worked with. You must have a landscaped area, which is 10 percent of the gross floor area of the buildings on the lot, not 10 percent of the lot area, unless you have a usable open-space area of 25 percent of the building. Now look closely at the definitions of the bylaw: What constitutes landscape? What constitutes usable?
Developer: Uh-hum.
Planner: Essentially, the section of your landscaped area can be met perhaps here, or along part of the site.

The developer checks out what is included under the term "usable open space."

Developer: When they say usable, are they referring to space that's been paved for parking?
Architect: No.
Developer: No, so that's over and above that.
Planner: So it's unpaved.

Architect: Unpaved.
Developer: Unpaved.
Planner: Unpaved.

With this chorus of "unpaved"s confirming the existence of the problem, the architect moves to suggest how the problem could be solved:

Architect: You take that door down, that's how you could solve this very easily.

But the developer does not show much interest in this idea. His attention has shifted to a new consideration which leads him to depart from the planner's carefully prepared list of possible violations of the bylaw:

Developer: You know, when I went back after our last meeting I discussed [it] with my uncle, who is the other owner of the building. He said something and he made a lot of sense. Well, look, he said, if we've got to take down the store, he said, and if we violate (and it appears to me that the biggest thing in the 20,000 flipper rule that we don't violate too badly from what I can see—but you're the planner, you know better than I). If we're violating only that anyway, he says, why don't we ask for a couple more apartments? Why are we settling for eleven? Because then we'd be able to do other things, even with maybe keeping the same structure. And I have no answer for that.

If there is only one variance needed on lot size, what about the possibility of increasing the number of apartments on the lot? To which the planner responds:

Planner: Now, I'm not going to say yes or no.
Developer: All right.
Planner: Because I think there's only so much you can put on this land.
Developer: Right.
Architect: Legally.
Planner: That's the criterion. Now, I don't know if it's nine, ten, eleven, twenty, or fifty. But I do know that as long as you're dealing with existing buildings, you know, 14,000 square feet of land is not, I think, going to be a serious problem. But I'm not the Zoning Board of Appeals. That's their decision. If you then begin to overbuild on the land, you have to have variances for open space.
Developer: We don't want that.
Planner: Right. Now all you have to worry about is one variance.

Having disposed of the developer's question, the planner proceeds to the next item on his list:

Planner: The other thing I think you want to look at very carefully is the article on parking. The parking requirements are slightly different than they used to be. In an apartment house, you have to have one parking space for each efficiency, one and a half for each two-bedroom, two for each three- or four-bedroom. I'm not sure exactly how much parking you have provided here now.

Developer: Right, I think we have seventeen there.

But the parking requirement is complicated by two further provisions of the bylaw:

Planner: Also in the parking section, I want you to look at Section 812, there are setback requirements for parking areas. We want to keep them off the lot line. Now that's gonna limit your area a little bit.

Architect: You mean side and rear.

Planner: Once again, I'm not urging you to lay it out. Now, this is just a simple layout here. There are other ways, I'm sure, to do it.

Architect: Oh, every one that you eliminate, the better off you are, there's no question about it. Now if it comes down to the 20,000 square feet variance, and even the parking variance, that's still not too bad.

Planner: Okay, but it's gonna take some layouts to determine what you can and can't do. These parking spaces were thrown in without looking at the new ratios. Because we looked at them very carefully, and I think we found that you have four extra spaces.

Developer: Yes.

The planner now turns to his concluding piece of advice:

Planner: When you go down the road and actually apply for the variance and go to the public hearing, make sure you're prepared to answer these questions. Now, uh, I don't want to prejudge, but the one question they're going to ask is, what hardship do you have with this particular piece of property? Why do you need the variance to do what you want to do?

Developer: Well, based on what I told you, is that a sufficient hardship?

Planner: As I say, I don't prejudge.

Developer: No.

Planner: There are certainly economic considerations. Generally, you know, you've got a situation where you've owned a piece of property for a long time. In order to do something in these times when costs are different, you need to increase the income potential of the building.

Developer: Exactly.

Planner: But they're gonna want to know specifics, and I think that's the kind of thinking you ought to work on. Okay?

And here the architect raises a new possibility:

Architect: With regard to the fact that he has to go for a variance anyway, what's the possibility of going for a new building?

Planner: I think then you're gonna run into difficulties, because you're asking for a new variance. Now, if you're asking for a new building to replace the eight units that you have there, then I seriously doubt that a variance will be granted. The town has made it very clear that in order to build new apartments you've got to have 20,000 square feet of land. And I know of no case where they're granted a variance for a new building on a lot under 20,000 square feet.

In the remaining few minutes of the meeting, the developer agrees that he had "pretty much ruled out that route."

What happens in the protocol. Most of the planner's behavior in this meeting can be understood as an attempt to follow rigorously an agenda which he establishes at the outset: to review the developer's plans in order to see exactly how they conform to the zoning bylaw. Hence the planner takes up, in turn, the factors of lot size, open space, and parking. The developer and his architect respond by questioning the meanings of such terms as "open space," by suggesting how the various problems might be solved. On two separate occasions, however, the developer or his architect makes a proposal and the planner responds to it in a way that suggests a kind of bargaining. Early in the meeting, the developer quotes his uncle's suggestion that as long as they need a variance because of the "20,000 feet flipper rule," why shouldn't they go for a couple more apartments? The planner responds with "Now, I'm not going to say yes or no . . . ," but he goes on to spell out the factors that will govern the board's response, all the while setting limits to his own authority to give such an answer ("I'm not the Zoning Board of Appeals"). At the very end of the protocol the architect raises the question of going for a new building, and here the planner answers firmly, "I know of no case where they've granted a variance for a new building on a lot under 20,000 square feet."

Elsewhere the planner prepares the developer for a future meeting with the Zoning Board of Appeals, rather as though he were preparing a student for an exam. He signals questions to be asked, answers that will be acceptable, and homework to be done. (". . . they're going to ask what hardship do you have . . ? Why do you need the variance to do what you want to do? . . . think about that.") At the same time, he tries to avoid giving the impression that he can make such decisions himself. ("As I say, I don't prejudge.")

Thus the planner undertakes three main tasks. As he *reviews the plans* and notes possible violations of the zoning bylaw, he *advises* the developer about the need for variances. He *prepares him for the examination* he can expect when he puts his case before the Zoning Board of Appeals. And he *bargains with the developer*, responding guardedly to proposals the developer uses, apparently to discover how much he will be allowed to get away with.

The planner's conduct of his meeting with the developer can be understood in terms of his attempt to solve problems he has framed around these three main tasks.

In his review of the plans, he is meticulous. He takes pains to document his evaluations ("Don't forget these items . . . When you work on the site plan, I'll give you a copy of this if you want"). At the same time, he continually exhibits a concern with the limits of his own authority, announcing frequently that he can only anticipate the board's actions and can make no decisions by himself. He behaves, in other words, as though he must conduct a rigorous preliminary review of plans which is in constant danger of being misconstrued as final.

Occasionally he calls attention to a possible violation of the bylaw, communicating information he appears to think the developer may regard as negative. At each such point, he behaves as though he wishes to avoid discouraging the developer:

> As I look at it, without seeing a more detailed site plan (but that can be put together eventually), the only variance you need is on lot area.

Here he stresses that only *one* variance will be necessary, pointing out that he has not yet seen the final site plan, but plays down the difficulty of preparing such a plan. When he points out a potential problem, he makes the remedy seem easy:

> Now, this is just a simple layout here. There are other ways, I'm sure, to do it.

And he tries to make the negative information palatable by surrounding it with "good news":

> The building plans, the structure itself, is no problem, but I think that, within the zoning bylaws, we've got to . . . look at very closely in the site plan. Okay? Now, uh, and as far as the building is concerned, I think we can work out the details with the building inspector about the code requirements . . . something you work with all the time anyway.

The planner deals with negative information by minimizing it, making the remedy seem easy, and surrounding it with good news.

As he preps the developer, he suggests the form of an acceptable answer but makes clear that someone else will finally grade the exam:

> Now, uh, I don't want to prejudge, but the one question they're going to ask is, what hardship do you have with this particular piece of property?

He is careful to say that the developer will have to work out the details by himself:

> *Planner:*   In order to do something in these times when costs are different, you need to increase the income potential of the building, and in order to do that, you need to rehabilitate the building.
>
> *Developer:* Exactly.
>
> *Planner:*   But they're gonna want to know specifics, and I think that's the kind of thinking you ought to work on. Okay?

The planner's problem seems to be this: without usurping the board's evaluative role or doing the developer's work for him, he must make sure that the developer will be able to give the right answers.

When he responds to proposals for a few more apartments or a new building, he behaves again as though he had to meet conflicting requirements. He tries to prevent the developer from putting forward proposals the board will reject:

> . . . there's only so much you can put on this land . . . That's the criterion.

But he also tries to avoid discouraging proposals the board may accept:

> . . . as long as you're dealing with existing buildings, you know, 14,000 square feet of land is not, I think, going to be a serious problem.

Having thus conveyed the impression that he can predict or influence the board's behavior, he ends by setting a limit to his own authority.

> . . . I'm not going to say yes or no. . . .
> . . . I'm not the Zoning Board of Appeals. . . . That's their decision.

Thus as he reviews the developer's plans, prepares him for his forthcoming session with the Board of Appeals, and bargains with him, the planner performs a balancing act. He tries to criticize the developer's plans without discouraging him. He tries to be stringent in his review of plans and at the same time permissive. He tries to lead the developer along the right lines without reducing the developer's responsibility for his own proposal. And he behaves authoritatively while presenting himself as devoid of authority.

Framing the role and the situation. Just as we can understand the planner's behavior in terms of the problems he has set for himself, so we can see these problems, and the resulting balancing act, as a consequence of the way he has chosen to frame his role.

When the planner began to work for the town, he knew that several roles were open to him. Like his predecessor, he could have made himself into a writer of plans, covering the walls of his office with maps and charts. Or he could have become a community organizer and advocate. He chose, instead, the intermediary role.

He seeks to bring to reality his image of what is good for the town, but he cannot initiate anything. Like a labor mediator, marriage counselor, coordinator, or broker, he must solicit and respond to the initiatives of others. He can only plan by proxy, through his influence on the plans of others. In this intermediate function, he is interdependent with those who initiate and with those who have regulatory authority. Without the planner's advice and help, the developers cannot understand and negotiate the hurdles they must jump in order to gain permission to build in the town. Without their proposals, the planner cannot realize his image of what is good for the town. Without the Zoning Board of Appeals, the planner has no function. Without the planner's screening and tailoring of development projects, the board could not do its regulatory job.

These interdependencies are essential conditions for the "review game" which the planner plays with the developers. The developers come to the planner for advice and review of plans, and he uses this to bargain with them. In return for their concessions to his image of what is good for the town, he will help them get what they want from the board. As he remarks in an interview,

> When a person gets in a variance case or a special zoning case, I immediately see an opportunity for negotiation and an opportunity for us to lend some assistance, and maybe give away a little within bounds, but also extract something for the town.

The planner tries to win the review game by wringing concessions from the developer, while at the same time helping him to pass the board's review. The developer tries to win by getting concessions from the planner without paying too great a price for them. The planner can lose the game in two ways: by allowing bad projects to get through, or by discouraging good ones. The developer can also lose in two ways: by failing to get his project through, or by paying too high a price for getting it through.

In order to be able to play the review game, the planner must maintain his credibility both with the developers and with the Zoning Board of Appeals. With both groups, he has worked hard to shape the attitudes and expectations which are essential to his intermediary functions. At the beginning, he had to create the institutional arrangements which legitimize his role. As he explained,

> Under the old zoning bylaws, there was no requirement that we file a report. We took it upon ourselves to file. Under the new zoning bylaws, which we wrote, there are more stringent standards. We will continue our same policy, but by addressing specific items in various cases. These are now in the bylaws.

He had also to create, in developers and board members, a network of expectations. Board members had to learn to respect his expertise; developers, to respect his influence with and knowledge about the board. These expectations had to become routine and, once routinized, they had to be continually reinforced.

Thus the planner has a dual objective. In order to improve the town he must win the review game, but he must also maintain the credibility on which his role depends. In these two requirements, which turn out to conflict with one another, lie the origins of his balancing act.

As the planner reviews the developer's plans, he must search out mismatches between the plan and the pertinent rules. For each mismatch, he must estimate the likelihood that the board will grant or withhold an exception to the rule. He must invest ways of circumventing their negative responses, and he must predict their reactions to such efforts at circumvention. His knowledge-in-practice must be adequate to all of these activities. But in addition, he must avoid being perceived a usurper of the board's regulatory function. For if he is so perceived, both members of the board and developers will cease to regard him as an intermediary. On the other hand, if he is perceived as lacking in knowledge or influence, he will be unable to bargain successfully. Similarly, he must be tough enough to screen out unacceptable projects, or he will lose his credibility with the board. Yet he must not exclude acceptable projects, or he will shut off the flow of proposals.

As he preps the developer, the planner must anticipate the board's questions, distinguish the less from the more important of these, and determine the direction of acceptable answers. He must also gauge the developer's understanding of the problems, distinguish what he can and cannot do for himself, and motivate him to do the necessary homework. At the same time, he must avoid becoming identified with the developer's proposals or he will cease to be regarded as an intermediary.

The planner's bargaining with the developer follows a familiar schema. There are two parties, each of whom has a stake in the outcomes of interaction. Each must communicate his own wants, learn what the other wants, formulate proposals, and learn the other's responses to them. Each gives something in order to get something, trying to get as much as he can while giving as little as possible, and the process continues until each party gets what he is willing to settle for, or until one party decides to stop. In order to bargain effectively, the planner must know a great deal about costs and benefits of interests to the developer, and he must know a great deal about the board's likely responses to proposed concessions and about the effects of such concessions on the quality of building in the town. But the planner must conduct his bargaining without appearing to usurp the board's role.

The problems the planner sets for himself are the problems of balancing these several constraints. In order to review effectively while preserving his credibility as an intermediary, he strives for thoroughness and clarity but also insists on presenting his review as preliminary. In order to insure that acceptable projects will be approved while at the same time protecting his intermediate status, he tries to make sure that the developer understands how to answer the board's questions while at the same time distancing himself from the developer's proposal. In order to bargain effectively without discouraging the flow of proposals, he tries to convey negative information and also to make it palatable, and he tries to convey his ability to make or withhold concessions while at the same time remaining within the bounds of his legitimate authority.

In the bargaining process, especially, the planner's balancing act leads to strange effects. Clearly, planner and developer bargain with one another. Privately, the planner states explicitly that they do so. Yet in their public meeting, they give the impression of attempting to conceal what they are doing.

When the developer makes a bid for concessions, he does so indirectly, by referring to a conversation with his uncle. And when the planner responds, he says,

> [I don't think it's] going to be a serious problem. But I'm not the Zoning Board of Appeals.

The developer bids indirectly, by appearing to transmit his uncle's request for a clarification of the rules, and the planner responds indirectly, by guardedly predicting the board's reaction.

Why this indirectness, as though the success of the game depended on appearing not to play it? In the planner's case, the explanation lies in the conflicting requirements that flow from his dual objective. He must negotiate with developers, and in order to do so, he must claim, at least implicitly, to be able to make or influence the board's decision on requests for variances. But this claim makes him vulnerable to the danger that developers will put him in place of the board. The board might resent this usurpation of their authority, and developers might take it as a cue for increased pressure or even, perhaps, for bribery. Hence the planner's frequent "I'm not the Zoning Board of Appeals!", uttered just when he has made an implicit claim to authority.

In the developer's case, he acts as though he were colluding with the planner by appearing to share the assumption that the latter has no authority. If the planner is to appear to have no authority, the developer must appear to make no bids for concessions.

But this collusion, which makes the review game into an "open secret," adds a new layer of ambiguity to a process that is already ambiguous. In the review game, each possible violation of the bylaw is also a possible bargaining point. When the planner brings up such an item, he may or may not be communicating an invitation to negotiation. If, in addition to this, the planner and the developer cannot admit to the game they are playing, then ambiguous invitations and ambiguous responses can never be publicly clarified.

The self-reinforcing system of knowing-in-practice. The planner's balancing act flows from the particular way in which he has framed his intermediary role. It is true that his twofold objective is inherently conflictual, requiring that he negotiate with developers without infringing on the board's authority, but this is not by itself sufficient to create the conditions for the balancing act. These follow from the theory of action he uses to set and solve the problems of his interactions with developers and members of the board.

The planner's interpersonal theory of action conforms to a model that Chris Argyris and I have called Model I.[4] An individual who conforms to Model I behaves according to characteristic values and strategies of action. His values include the following:

- Achieve the task, as I define it.
- In win/lose interactions with others, try to win and avoid losing.
- Avoid negative feelings, such as anger or resentment.
- Be rational, in the sense of "Keep cool, be persuasive, use rational argument."

Among the strategies by which he tries to satisfy these values, there are the following:

◻ Control the task unilaterally.

◻ Protect yourself unilaterally, without testing to see whether you need to do so.

◻ Protect the other unilaterally, without testing to see whether he wishes to be protected.

When the several parties to an interaction behave according to Model I, there are predictable consequences. The behavioral world—the world of experienced interpersonal interaction—tends to be win/lose. The participants in it act defensively and are perceived as doing so. Attributions to others tend to be tested privately, not publicly, for public testing accrues a perceived risk of vulnerability. Hence, attributions tend to become self-sealing; the individual cannot get the data that would disconfirm them. And individuals tend to employ strategies of mystery and mastery, seeking to master the situation while keeping their own thoughts and feelings mysterious.

The planner in our protocol frames the problems of his meeting with the developer in a Model I way and brings a Model I theory of action to their solution. He perceives the review game, which he plays with the developer, as a win/lose game. He sets and tries to solve problems by a strategy of mystery and mastery.

He has decided ahead of time, for example, what the developer needs to know. In order to make sure that the developer gets the right message, he sets up the meeting in his own office and asks the architect to be present, because he believes the architect will help the developer to pay closer attention to what is going on. He introduces his agenda at the beginning of the meeting and follows it rigorously throughout. He stamps in the messages he regards as important, and uses his expertise (as in the matter of parking spaces) to reinforce his strategy of control.

In order to keep the developer from reacting defensively to negative information, he uses a variety of techniques to soften or mask the impact of his criticisms of the plans. He preps the developer for his presentation to the Zoning Board of Appeals, while indicating to the developer that he must treat the proposal as his own. And he negotiates with the developer, exhibiting the authority he denies, and induces the developer to collude with him in appearing not to be negotiating.

The intermediary role, by itself, requires none of these strategies of action. But the planner's framing of the intermediary role does require them. The balancing act follows from the fact that the planner keeps the conflicting demands of the intermediary role to himself and attempts to manage them by unilaterally controlling the impressions he creates in the minds of others.

Thus his framing of the role, his setting of the problems of the meeting, and his Model I theory of action, make up a self-reinforcing system. One could say either that he has framed role and problems to suit his theory of action, or that he has evolved a theory of action suited to the role and problems he has framed.

LIMITS TO REFLECTION-IN-ACTION

The planner is an individual who likes to reflect on his practice. Indeed, his willingness to participate in our research grew out of this interest. But he limits his reflection to his *strategies* of unilateral control. He mentioned in an interview, for example, that he spends time experimenting with such rhetorical devices as delivery, intonation, and eye contact. He reflects on the strategies by which he tries to create the desired impressions in others, but he does not reflect on the role frame, problem setting, or theory of action which lead him to try to create one impression rather than another.

Indeed, his balancing act and his strategy of mystery and mastery are bound together in a system of knowing-in-practice which tends, in several ways, to make itself immune to reflection. Since the planner is doing one thing while appearing to do another, he cannot easily make his assumptions public or subject them to public testing. His sense of vulnerability discourages reflection. And he is so busy managing the balancing act, manipulating the impressions he makes on others and defending against vulnerability to exposure, that he has little opportunity to reflect on the problem settings that drive his performance. Moreover, for the same reason, he is unlikely to detect errors of interpretation which might provoke broader and deeper reflection.

Our protocol contains, as it turns out, an example of just such an error.

In an interview following his meeting with the planner, the developer revealed that he had decided against going forward with his project *because he would have to apply for a single variance.* He had other opportunities for investment, he explained, and he did not want to spend his energies on what he thought would be a long and cumbersome process of appeal. He had made this decision during his meeting with the planner, but he had chosen not to reveal it.

When he learned of the developer's decision, the planner was shocked. He had based his strategy on minimizing variances, but he had assumed that a single, easily obtainable variance on lot size would not stand in the project's way.

Nevertheless, to the developer, the need for a single variance had loomed large. And he had responded with a strategy of mystery and mastery similar to the planner's. He had run a private test of project feasibility, and when it produced negative results, he had decided unilaterally to abandon the project.

The planner's and developer's theories of action had combined to produce a behavioral world in which each withheld negative information, tested assumptions privately, and sought to maintain unilateral control over the other. In this sort of climate, the developer was unlikely to reveal his negative decision. To do so would have violated the "open secret" of the review game into which the planner had drawn him, and it would also have called for a degree of trust unlikely within a Model I behavioral world. For similar reasons, the planner was unlikely to make a public test of his assumptions about the developer's decisions.

As a result, the planner was unaware that his efforts had been futile from the moment the developer learned of the need for a single variance. The planner had no access to information that might have put this pivotal assumption in doubt.

It is of interest, nevertheless, to ask what *might* have happened if, contrary to fact, the planner had become aware of his mistake. In what directions might his inquiry then have taken him?

This is a peculiar sort of question because, in order to have become aware of this information, the planner would have had to behave according to a very different theory of action, one conducive to the public testing of private assumptions. Argyris and I have proposed a model of such a theory of action, which we call Model II. The question stated above then becomes the following: What might have happened if the planner had operated on a Model II theory of action?

An individual who conforms to Model II tries to satisfy the following values:

- Give and get valid information.

- Seek out and provide others with directly observable data and correct reports, so that valid attributions can be made.

- Create the conditions for free and informed choice.

- Try to create, for oneself and for others, awareness of the values at stake in decision, awareness of the limits of one's capacities, and awareness of the zones of experience free of defense mechanisms beyond one's control.

- Increase the likelihood of internal commitment to decisions made.

- Try to create conditions, for oneself and for others, in which the individual is committed to an action because it is intrinsically satisfying—not, as in the case of Model I, because it is accompanied by external rewards or punishments.

These three values are interconnected in several ways. Valid information is essential to informed choice. Freedom of choice depends on one's ability to select objectives that challenge one's capacities within a tolerable range, which again depends on valid information. An individual is more likely to feel internally committed to a freely made decision.

Among the strategies for achieving these values, there are the following:

❑ Make designing and managing the environment a bilateral task, so that the several parties to the situation can work toward freedom of choice and internal commitment.

❑ Make protection of self or others a joint operation, so that one does not withhold negative information from the other without testing the attribution that underlies the decision to withhold.

❑ Speak in directly observable categories, providing the data from which one's inferences are drawn and thereby opening them to disconfirmation.

❑ Surface private dilemmas, so as to encourage the public testing of the assumptions on which such dilemmas depend.

When the several parties to an interaction behave according to Model II, they tend to be seen by others as minimally defensive and open to learning. They tend to be seen as firmly committed to their positions but equally committed to having them confronted and tested. Discussions tend then to be open to the reciprocal exploration of risky ideas. Assumptions are more likely to be subjected to public test and are less likely to become self-sealing. Learning cycles—not only with respect to the means for achieving one's goals but with respect to the desirability of the goals—tend to be set in motion.

If the planner had been operating on a Model II theory of action, he would not have devoted his energies to maintaining unilateral control of his own agenda, but would also have tried to elicit the developer's agenda. He would have tested for the developer's responses to the information that a variance would be required, and he would therefore increase the likelihood of discovering that for the developer the need for a single variance was enough to make the project unattractive.

Had he become aware of this negative information, the planner might have gone on to reflect on his approach to the conflicting demands of his intermediate role. He might ask, for example, why he finds himself in the position of having to bargain with the developer without appearing to do so—a condition that exacerbates the problem of getting access to crucial information about the developer's intentions. This condition grows out of the planner's balancing act which depends, in turn, on his attempt to manage the conflicting demands of his role by a strategy of mystery and mastery—that is, by keeping his conflicting objectives private while controlling the impressions he creates in the minds of developers and members of the board.

If he were operating on a Model II theory of action, the planner might ask himself, "What if I were to make my dilemma public?" This would have implications for his conduct both with board members and with developers. It would carry risks, but it would offer the possibility of important benefits.

In a more open discussion of his role in the town, the planner might describe to the board his strategy of using "review of plans" to seek out opportunities for negotiation with developers. He might point out that he cannot negotiate effectively unless he can exercise some authority of his own, without fearing that the board will later reverse his decisions. At the same time, he might indicate his recognition of the fact that final decisions do remain with the board. He might invite the board to monitor his negotiations, working with him to keep the lines of authority clear and at the same time flexible. By surfacing these issues, it is true, he might irritate some members of the board; but he might also confirm publicly what many of them had already privately suspected.

With developers, the planner might admit that, while his actions are subject to the board's final approval, he does have some discretionary freedom to decide on requests for variances. In doing this, he might open himself to more vigorous attempts on the part of developers to subject him to pressure or persuasion. It is hard to see how this would be a very great risk, however. Since the developers already bargain with him, they must believe that he has some freedom to carry out his end of the bargain.

Under these conditions, the planner would have reframed his balancing act. The central conflict of his intermediary role would remain but it would be a public conflict. There would be no need to bargain while appearing not do so. The planner would be less likely to make undetected errors. At the same time, he would experience new demands for Model II behavior. He would no longer measure his effectiveness in terms of the successful performance of his balancing act but in terms of his ability to bargain openly, to share control of the interaction, to advocate his own goals firmly while inquiring effectively into the goals of others. He would also reduce some of the impediments to his further reflection-in-action.

CONCLUSION

The case of the town planner illustrates, in one small episode drawn from the practice of one planner, how and with what sorts of consequences planning roles are framed. I have tried to show how planning roles have evolved in a global conversation with the planning situation which has led, at various times over the past decades, to the salience of centralist planning, advocacy, regulatory and intermediary roles. But I have also tried to show, in the case of a practitioner of intermediary planning, how knowing-in-practice consists of a self-reinforcing system in which role frame, strategies of action, relevant facts, and interpersonal theories of action are bound up together.

The intermediary role, in which a practitioner places himself between those who propose and those who dispose, carries inherent potentials for conflict. Nevertheless, the meaning of this conflict for practice varies greatly with the way in which each practitioner frames his role. Role frame is interdependent with interpersonal theory of action, and the resulting system of knowing-in-practice has consequences both for the practitioner's ability to detect crucial errors and for the scope and direction of his reflection-in-action. In our example, the planner's balancing act is tied to his Model I theory-in-use. In the alternative that I have outlined, a Model II theory-in-use would be linked to a framing of the intermediary role in which private dilemmas would be made public and private assumptions would be subjected to public test. In the first case, attributions tend to become self-sealing, and reflection-in-action tends to be limited to consideration of the effectiveness of strategies of unilateral control. In the second case, errors of attribution are more likely to surface and reflection-in-action is more likely to extend in scope to the entire system of knowing-in-practice, including the framing of the role itself.

So long as a practitioner chooses to play an intermediary role, he cannot avoid the conflicts inherent in the role. But within these constraints, he has considerable freedom to choose the role frame he will adopt and the theory of action according to which he will behave. Depending on these interdependent choices, he will increase or constrict his capacity for reflection-in-action.

9

Planning Education for an Expanding Civic Sector

Robert D. Yaro

Across the United States, civic groups—including community development corporations, not-for-profit housing developers, and neighborhood, social service, environmental, and a growing number of regional and state-wide planning advocacy groups—are engaged in planning and advocacy work on issues once considered the exclusive domain of public-sector agencies. These include environmental and open-space protection, land use, urban design and housing development, community and regional economic development, and social services. A growing number of grant-making and operating foundations are hiring program officers and staff with expertise in these areas. Although growth in the civic sector has been greatest in major metropolitan areas, even isolated rural areas now have a growing number of community development and environmental advocacy groups, supported by foundations and member contributions.

Though complex, the reasons for these trends reflect the extension of the American tradition of civic activism on important community issues noted by observers as far back as de Tocqueville. Robert Putnam and others have emphasized that a healthy civic sector is necessary for the success of whole societies (Putnam 1992). But Putnam's assertion that there has been a withering of this sector in the United States in recent years simply does not appear to be true in these environmental, community development, and planning-related fields. The growth in the number of civic groups in these areas since 1980 and the breadth of their concerns represent a reaction to the disengagement of the federal government since the Reagan administration from many of these issues. These changes are also indicative of a more general decline in public-sector leadership at the state and local levels. Civic groups have moved into the resulting vacuum and are seeking to provide the leadership no longer being provided by public officials and agencies.

In addition, a greater number of foundations now support these activities. Experts in philanthropy expect a major period of growth in the number of foundations and the size of their endowments in the first decades of the twenty-first century. This will occur as wealth is transferred to the baby boom generation, and as wealthy baby boomers who have made fortunes in financial services, software, media, and high-technology areas reach retirement age. Several large or newly established foundations—including Ted Turner, Doris Duke, David and Lucile Packard, William and Flora Hewlett—are focusing their giving on growth management, environmental protection, inner-city revitalization, and similar planning-related fields. Since the raison d'être of these foundations is the promotion of civic activism and advocacy in these fields, they have focused their grantmaking almost exclusively on established and new civic groups. This trend bodes well for continued growth in the civic sector.

While many civic groups began as ad hoc groups with small volunteer staffs, the overall trend is toward increasing budgets and full-time professional staffs, often including professional planners. Although overall employment trends are positive, planners appear not to be benefiting from the resulting opportunities as professionals trained in related fields, such as public policy and administration, urban design, law, and environmental sciences, continue to fill most of these jobs.

Potentially contradicting my arguments here are the American Planning Association's biennial surveys of employment characteristics of professional planners (APA 1996). A look at the survey results over the decade from 1985 to 1995 shows that the share of APA members working in the civic sector is a tiny, and declining, percentage of APA's membership. The share dropped from 3.1 percent in 1985 to 2.0 percent in 1995 (APA 1996). This survey finding could be the result of one or more of several different factors, such as:

- Planners are not participating in the growth of civic-sector employment.

- Civic-sector planners do not identify with the traditional goals and concerns of APA's membership, and therefore do not belong to APA, or their employers do not pay for membership in APA (as most public-sector employers do), thus discouraging membership and participation in the survey.

- Civic-sector employment growth is not occurring to the extent suggested here.

Determining which of these factors is driving APA's results would require additional research beyond the scope of this discussion.

Changes in planning education programs might be considered in order to give planners the skills needed to gain access to and succeed in the civic sector. Planning curricula could be modified to include courses in advocacy and political action, not-for-profit management, and fund-raising and development. It should be noted that some public policy programs are modifying their curricula to give their students the skills needed to gain access to civic-sector jobs, in a time of continuing public-sector retrenchment and civic-sector growth.

Two case studies, one national and one regional, illustrate the growth in civic-sector activity, as well as the extent to which professional planners are underrepresented in this growth. Both case studies are based on the personal experience of the author and do not reflect an authoritative survey of employment in these two areas. In this sense, these observations are subjective rather than empirical. The national case study is the Growth Management Leadership Alliance, a nationwide association of chief executives of state and regional growth management advocacy groups. The regional case study focuses on the growing civic sector in the New York metropolitan region.

THE GROWTH MANAGEMENT
LEADERSHIP ALLIANCE

The organization 1000 Friends of Oregon established the National Growth Management Leadership Project (now called the Growth Management Leadership Alliance [GMLA]) in 1990 to create a mutual support and information-sharing forum for the nation's expanding statewide and regional growth management groups. Today, more than 25 states and regions are represented in GMLA's membership. 1000 Friends of Oregon was established in 1975 to provide advocacy for successful implementation of the state's growth management program (Senate Bill 100). It has played a crucial role in building public understanding and support for the law, in building broad civic, business, and community coalitions for its implementation, and in successfully opposing a number of legislative and voter initiatives that might have undercut the program.

Since the establishment of Oregon's law, thirteen other states have adopted state growth management systems (Delaware, Florida, Georgia, Maine, Maryland, Minnesota, New Jersey, Rhode Island, Tennessee, Utah, Vermont, Washington, and Wisconsin; in addition, Hawaii's law was adopted in 1961). Nearly all of these states have a civic group that helped pass the law or that was established to support its implementation. These groups are the core of GMLA membership. Other groups promoting passage of state growth management laws (representing Colorado, Massachusetts, Michigan, Pennsylvania, and other states) are also members. In addition, GMLA includes regional planning advocacy groups representing several metropolitan regions (including New York, Chicago, Cleveland, and San Francisco) and several natural resource areas (the Chesapeake Bay, the South Carolina coastline, the Yellowstone bioregion, and others).

Despite the fact that all of these groups are dealing with the creation or implementation of state growth management programs—an issue well within the purview of the planning profession—only one of GMLA's 25 participating executives (the author) holds a graduate degree in planning (Lawrence 1998; Liberty 1998). None are AICP members. Most have backgrounds in law, public policy, or the environmental fields. And the staffs of GMLA organizations contain only a handful of professionally trained planners.

Both of GMLA's past presidents, Robert Liberty (president of 1000 Friends of Oregon) and Barbara Lawrence (president of New Jersey Future), have posited that planners may not seek out civic-sector jobs because the skills and temperament required of planning advocacy leaders may differ from those required for conventional planning positions (Lawrence 1998; Liberty 1998). While most planners see themselves as agents of change, successful planners in the civic sector must be entrepreneurial and innovative as well as willing to confront and change the status quo, not work within it. Prospective graduate students with this entrepreneurial and confrontational outlook may seek out public policy and law degree programs, rather than graduate planning programs.

CIVIC-SECTOR PLANNING IN THE NEW YORK METROPOLITAN REGION

The tristate metropolitan region surrounding New York City contains parts of Connecticut and New Jersey as well as southeastern New York State. With 20 million residents and an estimated $700-billion economy, it is the largest urban region in the United States.

The Regional Plan Association is the oldest civic-sector planning group in the region, having been established as an ad hoc group in 1922 and incorporated in 1929. Until 40 years ago, RPA was essentially the only civic group in the region engaged in land use, transportation, environmental planning, and urban design issues. Then, in the 1960s, a new generation of community-based planning organizations and community development corporations emerged, encouraged by the Great Society and the civil rights movement. In the early 1970s, dozens of environmental groups emerged as the environmental movement burgeoned in the years following the first Earth Day (in 1970). In the 1980s, nonprofit housing developers as well as neighborhood, environmental justice, and other groups emerged, and foundation funding for their activities expanded rapidly in response to the Reagan administration's abandonment of urban programs.

The region's civic sector now includes an estimated 50,000 not-for-profit groups (Yaro and Hiss 1996), and employment growth in this sector is expected to be strong into the first decade of the twenty-first century. While most of these groups are engaged in traditional civic areas—including the needs of youth, the poor, and the elderly, and religious or educational concerns—a growing number are shifting their focus to issues once the exclusive domain of urban and regional planning commissions and planning consultants—including community development corporations, environmental and neighborhood organizations, and urban and regional planning and advocacy groups.

Environmental advocacy groups such as the Environmental Defense Fund (EDF) or the Connecticut Fund for the Environment, for example, were established to deal with issues of air and water quality. In the 1990s, these groups expanded their activities to include a major focus on transportation and land-use concerns, including growth management planning and brownfields redevelopment. In recent years, EDF has led the Tri-State Transportation Campaign (TSTC), which advocates for transit investments and opposes the construction of new highways. Among TSTC's coalition members, only the Regional Plan Association is led and staffed by professional planners; the remaining 11 groups are all led by lawyers, environmentalists, or public relations professionals. EDF is also active in efforts to protect major open spaces, such as Sterling Forest and the Long Island Pine Barrens, both in New York.

Another civic coalition, Connecticut's Coastal Corridor Coalition, has successfully developed a strategy for transportation demand management in the I-95 corridor, stretching from New Haven to Greenwich. This program was recently adopted by the Connecticut Department of Transportation and endorsed by the governor. The corridor's 11 members include business, environmental, and civic groups, but a professional planner leads only one of them (again, RPA), and the professional staffs of these groups include no planners.

TRAINING PROFESSIONAL PLANNERS FOR THE GROWING CIVIC SECTOR

How can professional planners become more active in civic-sector planning activities? And how can planning educators adapt graduate planning curricula to provide planners with the skills and attitudes required to participate in and gain entrée to this growing sector?

Students in graduate planning programs have already gained a broad range of technical skills that equip them for civic-sector planning; many also take courses in advocacy planning. Few programs, however, provide coursework in not-for-profit management, fund-raising and development, entrepreneurship and leadership, advanced land-use and environmental law, and other skills needed to succeed in the civic sector. Many of these courses are already being offered in business, law, and public policy schools, and that is where the next generation of civic-sector leaders will be trained.

Planning programs could easily create new concentrations in civic-sector planning by allowing planning students to cross-register for these courses (where they exist) in law, business, and public policy schools. They could also bring in executive directors of civic groups as adjunct faculty to lead seminars that focus on these concerns. Planning faculty could strengthen their offerings in advocacy planning and use their networks to promote internships and career placements in civic groups. Guest lecturers from civic groups could be invited to speak to planning students, both to introduce students to the opportunities in the field and to introduce civic leaders to the interests and skills of planning students wishing to pursue careers in the civic sector. Planning programs should actively promote these new offerings to undergraduates interested in civic-sector careers.

As noted above, successful civic-sector planners require a more entrepreneurial and confrontational approach to their work than is ordinarily required of public-sector or consulting planners. For this reason, planning schools must seek out students with these attitudes, as well as create studios, internships, and other vehicles to promote these views.

MISSED OPPORTUNITIES

Planning programs are missing an obvious opportunity to train the next generation of civic-sector leaders, and planning students are missing the growing employment and career opportunities in this sector. Planning curricula could easily be adapted to open this new and growing sector to graduates of professional planning degree programs.

10

Nonprofits: New Settings for City Planners

Christie I. Baxter

The growing significance of nonprofits is evident from the numbers. According to a survey by the Independent Sector (Hodgkinson et al. 1993a, 133, 357), revenue-producing charitable nonprofits (registered with the Internal Revenue Service as 501(c)(3) organizations), as well as 290,000 religious congregations (not required to register with the IRS), raised almost as much money in 1990 and 1991 as the federal government raised in personal income taxes and state and local government raised from all forms of taxation. Charitable organizations raised more than 90 percent of these revenues, and well over half of these organizations were founded after 1970.[1]

With the mushrooming of nonprofits between the public and private sectors have come questions about the roles these organizations play. Are nonprofits more like public organizations or private organizations? Does having a charitable mission mean these organizations act in the public interest, or do nonprofits advance more private interests? Also, given the growing activity by nonprofits in addressing the development problems of cities, what happens when nonprofits take on city planning?

In a study for the Urban Institute, Salamon and Abramson (1982) proposed that government and nonprofits at the start of the Reagan administration were partners. In a kind of "nonprofit federalism," nonprofits delivered social, community development, education and research, health care, and arts and culture services that government had determined, through the political process, as desirable but that government itself could not deliver directly.[2]

Conservative sociologist Robert Nisbet (1962) suggested that government and nonprofits were more competitive. He argued that too much government action had weakened such traditional institutions as families, churches, neighborhoods, and voluntary associations, resulting in the "decline of community" in the modern world. Government needed to "get out of the way" and free up the voluntary and private sectors to act.

The Reagan administration espoused this theory of competition between government and the private voluntary sector when it proposed in 1980 that reducing government funding would be a first step in reviving voluntary action. Reagan's successor, George Bush, later underscored this theory in his "1000 Points of Light" speech. Salamon saw it otherwise; according to him, in withdrawing from the partnership, Reagan was "ignoring or misunderstanding the consensus" that a partnership between government and nonprofits was a good thing (Salamon and Abramson 1982, 22).

Increasingly, scholars and practitioners see nonprofits as mirrors of neither the public nor the private sector but as a sector in their own right.[3] Organizations such as the Independent Sector, the Association of Research on Nonprofit Organizations and Voluntary Action, and university-based research centers across the country are building our understanding of the special characteristics of this sector.

CITY PLANNING IN NONPROFITS

Nonprofits plan, finance, and implement a wide range of social programs in areas ranging from education to the environment to economic development. In addressing the problems of cities, nonprofits tend to focus more on building institutions capable of changing patterns of behavior than on creating plans for physical change. Yet, changes in the physical patterns of settlement often are the consequence of institution building. Thus, as nonprofits acquire the power to change settlement patterns, their agents become city planners.

For example, following Robert Kennedy's visit to the nonprofit Bedford Stuyvesant Restoration Corporation in 1962, the Ford Foundation, a leading nonprofit funder, began what became a 20-year program of support to community development corporations (CDCs) as vehicles of neighborhood change. CDCs, in turn, have undertaken redevelopment projects for neighborhood constituents across the nation, building houses, shopping centers, office buildings, parks, and businesses. Nonprofit hospitals, universities, and churches have also undertaken revitalization and other targeted multiyear, multiproject development projects of the kind that used to be supported by government. In urban communities across the country, local nonprofit institutions have taken the lead from city planners in shaping the future of their neighborhoods.

The growing role nonprofits play in city redevelopment raises several questions about the nature of city planning in the context of a three-sector economy. Do nonprofits act as partners to government, helping it plan? Are nonprofits more like private entities, implementing the plans laid down by government? Or do nonprofits approach redevelopment in a way that changes entirely our notions of planning and implementation? Four examples of planned redevelopment initiated by nonprofits suggest some answers. In each case, the discussion focuses on the following questions:

- ◻ Who were the planners' constituents? What happened to the "public interest"?

- ◻ What did plans consist of?

- ◻ What did the planning process look like?

- ◻ How did these planners address the problem of implementation?

In the first example, in Boston's Dudley Street Neighborhood Initiative (DSNI), planning occurred within the context of a "collaborative" neighborhood revitalization program. The subsequent success of DSNI prompted foundations to support similar initiatives in cities around the country. In the second example, an African-American church and a historically black university initiated neighborhood revitalization efforts in Jamaica, New York, and in Charlotte, North Carolina. The third example involves redevelopment by a private family foundation of the historic Wilson District in downtown Dallas. In the final example, the Hyams Foundation pursued its historic mission of social reform by helping build a new institution for neighborhood investment in Boston.

The Dudley Street Neighborhood Initiative[†]

Dudley Street straddles Dorchester and Roxbury, two of Boston's most impoverished neighborhoods. It is a multiracial, multi-ethnic neighborhood. Most of Dudley Street's residents are of African, Hispanic, and Portuguese descent. During the 1960s and 1970s, residents and leaders of nonprofit organizations working in these neighborhoods watched with alarm the progress of urban renewal in neighboring Roxbury; and in the early 1980s, the Boston Redevelopment Authority turned its attention to Dudley Street. To avoid the fate of their neighbors, leaders of various nonprofit organizations working in the Dudley Street neighborhood, plus students from Roxbury Community College, joined with residents to initiate their own revitalization process. Participating organizations included La Alianza Hispania, the Roxbury Multi-Service Center, St. Patrick's Church, the Orchard Park Tenants Association, WAITT House (an agency linked to the Sisters of Charity and St. Patrick's Church), the Mt. Pleasant Neighborhood Association, and Nuestra Comunidad Development Corporation. In 1984, the Riley Foundation, a private

---

[†] This section is derived from *Streets of Hope* (Medoff and Sklar 1994).

foundation in Boston, decided to provide long-term support to the initiative, becoming the neighborhood's "deep pocket."

In an earlier era, residents of Dudley Street might have become participants in a government-led, top-down planning process focused on solving the neighborhood's problems. Instead, as participants put it, planning was "flipped on its head." Focusing first on institution building, the participants crafted an organizational arrangement that could guide the revitalization process over time. Key to this was the creation of a neighborhood-led governing board. Its decision-making structure, developed through extensive negotiations within the community, placed residents first and government last. Of the 31 seats on the board, 12 were reserved for residents, 11 for representatives of nonprofit organizations (including 2 religious organizations), 4 for business, 1 for city government, and 1 for state government; 2 seats were undesignated.

DSNI then began to create its own "bottom-up" plan (Medoff and Sklar 1994). Following strategies originally put forth by John McKnight of the Center for Urban Affairs and Policy Research at Northwestern University, DSNI based its plan on the assets of the community. Such an approach was radically different from the medical/surgical approach of government planning.[4] Similarly, DSNI's vision of the neighborhood's physical form differed in important ways from the vision of government planners. The Boston Redevelopment Authority's planners had proposed the development of a new town with a $750 million complex of office towers, hotels, housing, and historic parks. Boston's commercial development market was beginning to boom, and the plan provided significant opportunities for implementation by the private sector. DSNI developed an alternative plan: stakeholders in the neighborhood, assisted by planning consultants, envisioned an "urban village," to be developed through a series of discrete projects undertaken over time.[5]

Most important, strategies for implementation by DSNI were integral components of the planning process. For example, a key function of the planning consultants hired by the DSNI governing board was to educate residents. As these consultants put it, "in our view, community participation is a means to an end. It is the vehicle for community residents to become informed decision-makers with the staying power and resources to move from decision-making to implementation" (Medoff and Sklar 1994, 97). Later, in a pathbreaking achievement, DSNI received from the city its power of eminent domain in the neighborhood. In 1992, the Ford Foundation loaned DSNI $2 million to help carry out its new power. The loan allowed DSNI to create a nonprofit organization called Dudley Neighbors, Inc., to acquire and hold neighborhood land in perpetuity and lease it to developers. Nonprofit developers, including Nuestra Community Development Corporation and the Boston Metropolitan Housing Partnership, developed housing for sale to residents; funding came in part from the Riley and Hyams foundations. Groundbreaking for the first homes took place in 1993.

The DSNI experience was one of the earliest of many similar initiatives sponsored by foundations around the country. The Annie E. Casey Foundation initiated a program called New Futures in Bridgeport, Dayton, Little Rock, Pittsburgh, and Savannah, along with a follow-up program called Rebuilding Communities in Boston, Denver, Detroit, Philadelphia, and Washington, D.C. The Ford Foundation funded what it called the Neighborhood and Family Initiatives in Detroit, Hartford, Memphis, and Milwaukee. The Rockefeller Foundation funded Community Planning and Action Programs in Boston, Cleveland, Denver, Oakland, San Antonio, and Washington, D.C. Asset-based planning from the bottom up was a central feature of all of these efforts.

AFRICAN-AMERICAN INSTITUTIONS

A number of educational and faith-based organizations, many from the African-American community, have also entered the arena of city redevelopment, broadening their missions to include changing conditions in the neighborhoods in which these institutions are located. For example, in the mid-1980s, the new president of Johnson C. Smith University, a historically black university, decided to sponsor the redevelopment of an area adjacent to the school. As a starting point, he asked the Cambridge planning and design firm of Lane Frenchman to help create a plan. In 1991, the school decided to sponsor the creation of a community development corporation, known as the Northwest Corridor CDC, which began its own planning and development process. By 1995, the university, through the CDC and other vehicles, had developed a new supermarket for the neighborhood, along with an office building and housing; it had also prompted the city to invest in street reconstruction and a new branch library and to initiate a community policing program. In 1998, a conference in Baltimore attracted 30 similarly motivated, historically black colleges and universities and their affiliated community-based organizations to discuss ways in which their institutions could contribute to positive neighborhood change (Seedco 1998).

Several African-American churches have become active in neighborhood development. In Jamaica, New York, the Allen African Methodist Episcopal Church undertook redevelopment of the neighborhood adjacent to the church. To do this, the church created a series of subsidiary nonprofit corporations: credit union, housing development corporation, school, home care agency, women's resource center, and senior citizens' organization. By the early 1990s, Allen's housing corporation had produced more than 320 units of housing; it was managing 17,400 square feet of commercial real estate; and the New York State Department of Housing and Community Renewal had designated it a neighborhood preservation agency. In addition, Allen owned and operated a multiservice center housing city and state social service agencies, including a city health clinic. In 1987, church revenues exceeded $1.7 million; revenues of its subsidiary corporations were over $12 million. Initial financing came from the collection plate. The church continues to set aside one-third of its annual collections for development (Byrd 1990).

THE WILSON DISTRICT

Nonprofit redevelopment is not limited to residential use, as the example of the Wilson District shows. In 1981, the Meadows Foundation, in Dallas, began to acquire property in a downtown area known as the Wilson District. At the start, the foundation had the rather narrow goal of finding new offices for itself. This goal quickly merged with the foundation's interest in providing space for the various nonprofit organizations it supported. Meadows decided to purchase more space than it needed itself and to create a center for its nonprofit grantees.

Wilson District was a residential neighborhood in the nineteenth century. Like many of the downtown development projects studied by Frieden and Sagalyn (1989), the district had been a city redevelopment project in the late 1960s. The city had offered incentives to private developers who undertook land clearance. Developers had purchased and demolished a number of buildings, but when their efforts to market the land failed, they left. Warehouses and low-grade commercial structures were later built next to the few remaining nineteenth-century residences. By the late 1970s, according to the foundation's president, these residences were vacant and dilapidated. Little paint was left, most of the wood was rotting at the edges, window screens were hanging, shutters were dangling, and signs said KEEP OUT. Drug dealing, prostitution, and vagrancy were the activities most visible to the public (Ordorica 1995).

In 1981, the Meadows Foundation purchased one block; by 1994, it owned 20 acres in the district, acquired and redeveloped at a cost of $41 million. In area, the foundation's holdings were on the same order of magnitude as the government's urban renewal projects of the 1960s (Government Center, in Boston, totaled 44 acres), and they exceeded the size of most downtown redevelopment projects of the 1970s and 1980s, such as Pike Place Market in Seattle (7 acres), Fanueil Hall Marketplace in Boston (6.5 acres), or Town Square in St. Paul (4 acres) (Frieden and Sagalyn 1989).

Like DSNI, Meadows began by focusing on institution-building. In this case, the foundation wanted to find a way to support the activities of its nonprofit grantees. All tenants in Meadows-owned properties are nonprofit organizations that occupy their space rent-free. Meadows has also developed an organizational support system designed to encourage the growth and development of these organizations through management training and technical assistance. In addition, Meadows wanted to demonstrate that preservation could be an economic revitalization tool. To ensure that the preservation activities would stabilize and improve the local economy, the foundation required that contractors solicit bids from businesses within a two-mile radius of the district; such businesses have done about 35 percent of the restoration work.

Meadows tailored its development activities to match specific opportunities. The first block the foundation acquired contained one vacant parcel, which the foundation filled by moving a house from another part of the city. On the second block, house moving became a major theme. The foundation later turned the process around and donated to the Dallas County sheriff's office a metal warehouse building for use as a substation. The donation was accompanied by a $50,000 grant for use in the building's reconstruction at another site.

The city has played a traditional regulatory role, controlling the development through a historic preservation ordinance. As of the mid-1990s, Meadows was trying to get the city to renovate a nearby city park.

The Hyams Foundation

In the early part of the twentieth century, Isabel Hyams, a wealthy Boston woman, decided to support a settlement house in the Italian community of East Boston. The settlement house, like many others around the country, sought to improve living conditions for immigrants and to build individual citizenship. In the 1930s, Isabel Hyams decided to leave her wealth in trust after her death, to continue the work she had begun, and she convinced her brother, Godfrey, to do the same. As part of its grantmaking throughout the 1970s, the Hyams Foundation supported a number of neighborhood organizations.

In the 1980s, Hyams decided it could carry out its neighborhood development mission by helping finance housing and commercial development projects undertaken by community development corporations. Like other nonprofits, Hyams focused on institution-building. The Local Initiatives Support Corporation (LISC), a nonprofit organization created by the Ford Foundation to provide financial and technical assistance to CDCs around the country, had invested in a number of projects undertaken by Boston CDCs, but LISC resources were limited. The corporation suggested that if Hyams were to purchase some of LISC's existing loans, LISC could use the proceeds to invest in new neighborhood projects. Hyams agreed. The purchase provided LISC with liquidity, and it set a precedent for the purchase of LISC loans by other buyers. Subsequently, LISC created a formal secondary market institution, the Local Initiatives Managed Assets Corporation, to regularly recapitalize itself (Baxter et al. 1991).

Hyams, LISC, and LIMAC are now part of a network of institutions that provide the investment capital to support the implementation of projects planned by nonprofits, such as DSNI, Johnson C. Smith University, and the Allen African Methodist Episcopal Church (Baxter 1996).

PLANNING IN THESE EXAMPLES

In each of these examples, the planning process differed significantly from the "traditional" process of the government-planning era. Key factors included how the planners in each organization defined their constituency, how they understood the process of change, and what they anticipated would be the process of implementation.

First, the nonprofits defined their constituencies in specific terms— residents of Dudley Street, members of the Allen AME church, or the non-profit grantees of the Meadows Foundation. Each nonprofit then broadly defined the areas a development plan might cover. For example, DSNI participants sought a common vision that encompassed "all aspects of the life of a community, from economic development to education, from the natural environment to the built environment, from culture to recreation to sports, from human needs to race relations, from youth to senior citizens" (Shiffman 1992). Meadows wanted to provide its grantees with low-cost space, but at the same time it wanted to provide management assistance, education, and other support its grantees might need to be effective. Traditional government planning does the opposite: defining a broad constituency—the public—but addressing only those elements government can regulate, such as physical land use or density.

Next, like the highway planners in Alan Altshuler's study of highway planning in the Twin Cities in the 1960s (Altshuler 1965a), or planners for private development companies today, the nonprofit planners' study focused on helping their own organizations achieve their missions. The planners were inside the development organization, and the development plan thus became an element of the organization's strategic plan. In a sense, nonprofit planners addressed head-on the "implementation problem" often faced by government planners, by making the plan part of the implementation strategy.[6]

The nonprofits studied also focused on the process of community change and defined institution-building as their starting point. Participants expected that specific visions of the future would change; their strategy for ensuring good future outcomes was to enable people to change by changing the systems that support them. In the case of DSNI, a central aspect of the plan involved strategies for advocacy, constituent organizing, and education that enabled stakeholders to make the key planning decisions. Hyams decided to support neighborhood development by helping LISC to change the flow of capital to neighborhood projects. The integration of planning and implementation may explain the tendency on the part of nonprofits to focus on ways to institutionalize change. In any event, nonprofits in these cases paid attention to the systems and processes of change traditional planners seldom consider.

Finally, the planning process in these cases tended to be interactive and organic. Plans often involved interactive descriptions of goals, strategies, and potential projects that looked appropriate at different times. When the Meadows Foundation began acquiring property in downtown Dallas in 1982, it had no intention of creating a 20-acre district. Its actions were incremental, but they accumulated over time to become a whole. As the organization tested its plans against real opportunities, its planners shifted directions, responded to new opportunities for development, tested mechanisms for change, fed the information back to the organization, and used it in the next round of planning. Although planning was incremental, in the Meadows case, it was guided by a consistent mission: support the nonprofits in their work, preserve the district's architecture, and distribute the benefits of the economic activity to the neighborhood. Inherent in this approach is the emergence over time of the physical projects that will comprise the redevelopment. In contrast, a traditional plan, like an architect's drawing, describes the desired outcome for a particular locale.

DILEMMAS FOR PLANNING

As these examples suggest, nonprofit planning differs from government planning, and the differences raise questions for planning practice. Is what we old-fashioned city planners have learned about changing settlement patterns relevant and useful in this new setting? If so, how can we help ensure that nonprofits avoid our past mistakes and achieve greater success in reforming our cities?

To traditional city planners, what nonprofits are doing may look less like planning than merely groping along. The process is decentralized and organic, as is the knowledge necessary to support it. We no longer have a cadre of professionals, known for their expertise and the boldness of their personal visions, to mentor younger professionals. If we search for the Ed Logues or the Ed Bacons of the 1990s, we won't find them. Is there a need for broader visions, and can city planners help nonprofits articulate them?

A second issue is that nonprofits serve individual constituencies whose interests do not necessarily aggregate to a broader public interest. Nor is the activity of a nonprofit subject to public debate. Can city planners help ensure that the broader public interests are served in the process?

A third issue concerns research. In the era of government planning, government-funded academic institutions do "basic research" in the interests of informing the practice of planners. Today, these general research funds are much less available. Instead, most research is closely associated with direct program applications and is done by consultants, industry-based groups, and university-based research centers associated with specific organizations and constituencies. For example, the Center for Community Development Research at New School University (formerly the New School) in Manhattan is closely connected to the nonprofit housing network and to LISC, and the research agenda is defined by the center's clients: CDCs, LISC, and other "industry partners." Research centers within the industry networks, such as the Urban Land Institute, the Foundation Center, and the Independent Sector, do research in a similar client-responsive way. In other fields, this type of "contract research" is faulted for producing findings that meet the short-term needs of clients but fail to probe more fundamental and important issues. Can planners contribute to broadening the perspective of development-related nonprofit research?

One thing is clear. The center of initiative for neighborhood redevelopment has shifted from city hall to the offices of nonprofit organizations and their bankers—foundations. This opens new opportunities for planning practitioners committed to reforming our communities and revitalizing our cities.

11

Looking Back, Looking Forward

Israel Stollman

We opened a century of planning with the basic inventions in place for an urbanizing, industrializing country: safe elevators, steel skeleton buildings, mass transit, automobiles, and aircraft; typewriters, telegraphy, telephones, and radio; and electricity generation to power it all. It remained for the 1940s to invent the electronic digital computer and, especially, the transistor. These are the more tangible among the ingredients in the socialeconomicpoliticaltechnologicalculturalecological stew that moved us from a rural country of 75 million in 1900 to an urban country of 150 million in 1950, to, say, 275 million in 2000. Planners influenced this growth in some measure, with some success and some failure. Glimpses of our earlier evolution may adjust perceptions of where we are and how planning is evolving.

THE COMPREHENSIVE PLAN

Comprehensive planning emerged from the work of park planners, sanitary engineers, and others in the nineteenth century. A 1901 example, following these precedents, was the McMillan Commission Plan for Washington. A Senate committee took the responsibility for designing the area of the mall away from the U.S. Corps of Engineers and chose a comprehensive approach led by planners of their day. Alfred Bettman pursued the spirit of progressive reform when he wrote that the comprehensive plan is necessary if coordination of development "is to be brought about by anything approaching a scientific method." The more we learned, the less positive we became about the thoroughgoing science of our methods, but we did not lose a belief in the need to coordinate development comprehensively.

The comprehensive plan has survived internal critics and external critics. The Lindblom view that it is incrementalism that succeeds, or the Karl

Popper view that only "piecemeal engineering" can protect us from deterministic comprehensiveness, both focus on the immediacy of implementation. Both assume a rigid comprehensiveness that does not translate into current programs and policies; neither does it evaluate results or learn and make changes. Michael Teitz (1996, 1997), as well as Kaiser and Godschalk (1995), are right to emphasize that the ongoing strength of comprehensive planning lies in continuous adaptation to needs and challenges.

The growth of specialization and specialized knowledge among planners has produced a counterpressure and a fragmentation of planning work. The American Institute of Certified Planners (AICP) reinforces comprehensiveness in requiring professional planning experience as a qualification for membership. The definition of that experience continues to include "employing an appropriately comprehensive point of view." Without this view, specialty planners may seek to optimize results for one function that neglects links to others; they may choose an immediate benefit that neglects long-range consequences. The specialized technical divisions of the American Planning Association (APA) provide similar reinforcement by focusing intense interest on specialties within a comprehensive planning community. Other currents run in the same direction. There is a fresh realization that problems of transportation, poverty, housing, economic development, and environment cannot be solved in isolation from each other; yet, as the character of planning products becomes more complex, some clearer test of what is "appropriately comprehensive" would be useful, something more explicit than I-know-it-when-I-see-it, yet ambiguous enough to fit diverse cases.

LAND-USE REGULATION

It is hardly surprising that, in an era of deregulation and a return to market forces to achieve public objectives, there remains broad support for maintaining the public regulation of land use. This broad support stems from the origins of zoning in New York City, when it was supported both by business protective of commercial interests and by reformers concerned with dwelling congestion, light, and air. Over the years, zoning evolved from timorous rigidities to venturesome flexibility, from cookbook formulas to negotiated permits. Land is a refuge: home and neighborhood are to be protected. Land is a livelihood as well: profits and jobs are to be protected. It is the localism of regulation that attracts support.

Earlier development found protection too constraining. Clarence Stein was happy that the site for Radburn had no zoning. Developers saw a zoning classification as a temporary hold on land to be released in response to their proposals. Today, growth management has become a synonym for planning with its long menu of techniques that fit regulations to diverse local objectives. Some communities choose the objective of no growth, designing tight controls to maintain development as established.

Departures from the uniformities of the standard acts of the 1920s have only recently been adopted in some of the states. APA's *Growing Smart* project will contribute to the diversification of state law within a set of common general objectives. The project, active through the 1990s, was slated for completion by the end of 1999. It is producing a legislative guidebook for the executive and legislative branches and providing a national clearinghouse and database for planning statutes. The guidebook deals with the wide array of subject matter within the new range of planning issues; it presents alternative statutory proposals that address the different situations among the states, and that will be in a format that contemplates continuing revision. Representatives of public officials at state and local levels who will be responsible for adopting and administering new laws helped guide the project. Department of Housing and Urban Development (HUD) and other federal agencies support it. Portions of the guide recommend procedures for integrating state environmental policy acts with local planning. *Growing Smart* has begun to produce "smart growth." Maryland has adopted policies under that name which direct growth to places with existing investment in infrastructure. A continuing issue will be the balance between state directive and local choice. What policies should be mandatory in the state interest? What policies may be chosen at the option of a community? What policies are only suggested, but with the footnote that there will be keen disappointment if they are not adopted?

Michael Teitz (1996) is rightly concerned about the threat to planning that would stretch the concept of *taking* to cover much of governmental intervention. The threat is greater from the political than from the judicial direction. The self-advertised property rights movement is a consortium of mining interests, some land developers, in-holders, conservative anarchists, and others who are building antiregulatory grievances into a basis for radical individualism in the use of land. Their communications have ranged from a video that caricatures the National Park Service as a sadistic Gestapo to an apology for Adam Smith's lapse in proposing that government has a role in building highways. While these battles continue, environmental values are finding broader political support. More people are extending their sense of neighborhood as a refuge for the wider landscape, airscape, and waterscape.

Pushed by the property rights debates, the rights themselves may evolve in the other direction, to the point where public interests are explicitly recognized. The de facto reality is that the buying and selling of real property is the buying and selling of a license to use land, subject to public conditions.

Courts may clarify in what ways the "investment-backed expectations" of landowners require treatment that differs from investment-backed expectations in other business ventures. The evaluation of takings may be paralleled by the evaluation of givings: the public investments that create and maintain land values.

HOUSING AND SOCIAL POLICY

The group of people who came together early to form the planning profession included many who were concerned with social issues of housing, public health, and working conditions of the poor. Lawrence Veiller, prime mover of tenement house regulation, was one. He put his faith in regulating low-priced housing rather than providing public subsidies as the path to social improvement. He dissented on the adoption of New York's first zoning ordinance, believing it gave too much away to commercial interests. Leaders of the settlement house movement were among the founders of modern planning. Lillian Wald, of the Henry Street Settlement, was one of the general advisers, in 1922, in organizing the Plan of New York and Its Environs. At that meeting, Wald hoped that "organized, cooperative plans. . . will make impossible the further growth of segregated, ugly quarters for racial groups or economic classes."

Social emphases diminished in planning as prime attention was given to physical development. The Great Depression returned interest to the city social, but most planners saw issues of poverty and race as lying beyond their knowledge, experience, or professional expertness. Not until 1967 did the American Institute of Planners vote to eliminate references to land use in delimiting the scope of the profession's interests.

Teitz (1997) refers to the "disasters of public housing and urban renewal of the 1950s and 1960s" as failures of social planning. More accurately—insofar as there were disasters—they may be seen as programs in which good policies were often overwhelmed by stronger forces. Planners knew that public housing should not be located on slummy, industrial sites; they knew that it would be better scattered in small clusters. They knew that rehabilitated older houses would make good public housing, that tenants should not be moved out when their earnings went up, that good design doesn't cost more, that housing should be racially integrated, that omitting toilet seat covers is a stupid economy, and that you should not tear down a decrepit unit for every new one built. The miracle was that any public housing was funded at all. Opponents kept the number of public housing units built low for authorizations and lower for appropriations. They wrote in the self-defeating requirements, and they called Senator Robert Taft—otherwise known as Mr. Conservative—a communist for supporting public housing.

One may wonder about the future of equity planning as a new emphasis of social planning following concerns about exclusionary zoning and housing practices and efforts at advocacy planning. Krumholz adopted the principle of creating more choices for those who have few choices. This guided a choice of issues and their analysis. He credits much of his effectiveness to running a solid, professional planning department. He accepted requests for information and advice on the wide spectrum of planning issues and responded completely and promptly. Equity planning was a part of constituent service.

Tragedies can catalyze frustrations and turn them into riots, and urban riots focus attention on the inner city. It did once again in Los Angeles in 1992. Planners reacted with a flurry of task forces and agendas for change. Continuing discussions looked more deeply into planning responsibilities and inner-city problems and concluded that there should not be an equity planning world that parallels an establishment planning world. Issues of equity are entwined with planning issues of general application. All planning procedures may create a distributional tilt. APA then had a collection of essays prepared. In 1994, *Planning and Community Equity* was published, which illustrated how solutions to inner-city problems can be integrated in general proposals that address transportation, housing, environment, and other standard topics. This direction should lead not to equity planners but to equity in planning.

Two other developments will sharpen debates on how American values affect the distribution of public and private goods: gated communities and business improvement districts. Both have older antecedents. The New York co-op apartment building with a doorman is a gated community. The Fifth Avenue Merchants' Association was a business improvement district. Each privatized community wants its private assessment for services to add to services supplied publicly. Some community associations are lobbying for exemptions from taxes they see as paying for duplicate or unused services.

The issues are illustrated by court mandates in several states to reform public school finance where unequal tax bases produce unequal schools. Affluent parents wonder about the dividing lines between money spent at home for books or PCs and money pooled informally in a donation to supplement school programs and money "pooled" formally through the happenstance of higher taxes.

The shopping mall is a variation of a business improvement district; with private policing, it is, figuratively, gated. It has also opened questions of freedom to picket, pamphleteer, or roister in the new-style town square. As with the other variations, we will be some time balancing all the permutations of public taxation, private assessment, public service delivery, and private delivery.

THE PROFESSION

Professional city planning grew quietly and slowly. In 1940, total membership of the American Institute of Planners was 171. The category of "full member" required planning experience and education generally comparable to the requirements of AICP today. There were 91 full members in 1940; there are about 11,000 members in AICP today. Those who held a planning degree in 1950 are outnumbered by those who teach planning today. Growth was steep enough in the 1950s to lead the planning schools to organize their own association.

The key to the profession's growth was the acquisition of official responsibilities: zoning and subdivision regulations in the 1920s in accordance with a comprehensive plan; public works programs in the 1930s, in accordance with a comprehensive plan; urban renewal in the 1950s, in accordance with a comprehensive plan. Then planning became "whatever there are grants-in-aid of " in accordance with a comprehensive plan. The expansion of responsibilities was paralleled by closer ties with political decision makers. When federal planning supports contracted in the early 1980s, planning staff scrambled to keep programs going, and many agencies found strong local support for their emphases on growth management and environmental protection.

There continues to be the hazard of divergence between practice and theory. When the APA was established in 1978, many planners urged eliminating the *Journal of AIP*, as it was known then, as incomprehensible and irrelevant to planning practice. A staff proposal to continue it as a journal of the AICP, delivered to all AICP members as its core audience, was narrowly defeated. Instead, the journal was turned into an optional subscription service of APA. It has a minority readership of 11,000, including non-APA members (APA has about 30,000 members). The divergence has continued despite strong efforts by successive *Journal* editors to provide a bridge between academics and practitioners.

Peter Hall believes the gulf between practice and theory is increasing. He has strongly disparaged contemporary planning theory as it is presented in the literature. His view was challenged by theorists who investigate communicative action. Teitz (1996) believes that communicative action is here to stay as the guiding planning theory. There are reasons for skepticism.

Communicative action, which derives from the thought of Habermas, has the advantage of offering a grounding in the empirical study of practice. It seems odd to stress that the strength of a theory is its rediscovery of practice. How else would a theory be tested? There seems to have been introduced a new style of pragmatism that is deductive and top-down rather than bottom-up, fitting findings to the theory. It invites the squib by Carl Schorske that "in the dissonance between the political reality and the claims of the traditional theorist, it is the given reality that must be corrected, not necessarily the theory by which it is understood."

Communicative action may be skeptical about the positive tradition of science, but it seems also to be skeptical about the *provisional* tradition of science, provisional knowledge growing out of inductive pragmatism. As reformers, we like to think that a new approach will empower those who are unheard in the planning and decision process, but we assume that we will hear from, and empower, the good, the true, and the beautiful. Property rights extremists, antitaxers, and survivalists (assuming they do not fall among the good, true, and beautiful) also want to be heard better, also have their intuitions and stories to tell, their wish to be part of the consensus, and an eagerness to speak their truths to power.

Communicative action as applied to planning is a hortatory rationale for choosing sides rather than an explanatory guide to address the clash of values. It is useful in urging a transparency in the decision making of planners, in giving high scrutiny to the unexpressed consequences of decisions, in representing submerged values, and perhaps in doing the journalist's work of translating the spin of the politicians. As a currently dominant theme among academic researchers, however, it carries a high opportunity cost. Several other theoretical investigations that may benefit the field go unexplored. The complexity notions of the Santa Fe Institute people, for example, have high potential applicability to planning. John Holland, an Institute scholar, suggests interesting possibilities in his book, *Hidden Order* (Holland 1995). Theories as yet unnamed will undertake to explain the peculiar relations of constraint, contingency, and intervention that derive from the practice of planning.

What new lines of evolution lie ahead? As a small profession with a large mission and a large ambition, we must consider how to invest our collective time over the next decades. Our influence was substantial early on. Secretary of Commerce Herbert Hoover appointed his first committee on zoning entirely from among the 52 members of the National Conference on City Planning who had transformed themselves in 1917 into the American City Planning Institute. In the 1930s, the growing band of zoning administrators was co-opted into the planning field when ASPO offered them the best source of information and advice. Once ASPO had them in the fold, they were scolded for not following planning principles. To this day, no separate national association of zoning officials has been formed. This combination of people who know and who can exercise official responsibilities effectively in response to public problems has propelled the profession's growth and evolution.

Two of our larger failures over the century point to responsibilities that should be picked up again. Both failures involve national programs born in the 1930s and killed in the early 1940s: the national planning associated with the National Resources Planning Board (NRPB) and the regional planning for which the TVA was an experimental prototype. National planning was not permanently rooted despite the NRPB's extensive and excellent work. Regional planning was not extended, as proposed, to other regions throughout the country. Their history was complex, but a fair simplification would emphasize the failure to develop a constituency and cultivate political support.

A revival of national and regional planning will not likely take place through omnibus legislation, but the multiplication of programs in its separate components should one day call for their necessary coordination. One component that may be ripe to add to national planning is capital improvement programming. The federal budget does not now distinguish long-term capital investments from current operating expenses. Our ability to plan long term, to weight priorities, and to finance projects soundly is restricted. The Federal Reserve chairman, Alan Greenspan, appreciates the potential benefits of a capital budget but is more concerned about its potentially distorting effects on the definition of deficits. Long-run capital debt would be removed from expenditures except for debt service producing instant budget balance (and more truly reflecting the way families balance their budgets). If the federal budget were to stay in balance for several years, this concern might be removed. A capital budget, incorporating pork-barrel projects as honest priorities, would be a tool far superior to line-item vetoes. It would also strengthen the coordinating and planning capacities of the Office of Management and Budget.

It may seem a paradox, but as it is desirable to separate our capital expenditures from operating, it will be desirable to detach some operating costs and attach them to the capital budget. It is more than rhetoric to point out that some expenditures with the effect of developing the long-term capacities of people—human infrastructure—are as significant to productivity and growth as physical infrastructure. The G.I. Bill, spending more than $14 billion on veterans' education from 1946 through 1952, was just such a capital investment. Its positive effects in transforming the country are far-reaching. It would be a hugely complex step to take at each level of government. Yet the social/physical capital improvement program would be a more mature, effective way to achieve the next phase of national development.

Regional planning (defining *regional* at the level of natural resources, not of the metropolitan area) has been reviving with the establishment of environmental and conservation programs, with official probing to find policies of sustainable development, and even with some formal activity by Congressional caucuses based on region. There is still an Appalachian Regional Commission and a TVA, as well as scattered one-function and interstate agencies.

The likeliest path to more comprehensive planning for development issues that sweep across large regions will follow the coordination of water policies. This is a major need that interlaces other regional issues and is bubbling up more vigorously with the competition for water. At the federal level alone, more than 40 agencies separately decide or affect the use and quality of water.

Planning has changed and will continue to change. We once regulated smoky industries with a Ringelmann chart that simply graded the lightness or darkness of smoke. In 1951, we urged that planners move from such specification standards to performance standards. Today, we administer the complexities of the Clean Air Act. One hundred years ago, we were concerned "how the other half lives," and later, for "one-third of a nation." Now we find one-eighth of the people below the poverty line. Respecting the differences of measures and standards over the years, the actual number of poorer people about whom we must concern ourselves has remained at 30 to 40 million.

The planning profession began as a collection of diverse professionals sharing an interest in better communities, then decided that it is a distinct profession, specialists having found a communion. Then, following Harvey Perloff, we became generalists-with-a-specialty. Now, the demands of specialization make us specialists within a planning culture.

The next 50 years will increase the country's population by some 120 million people, using the middle projection of the U.S. Census. That will occupy a considerable additional country of homes, workplaces, travel paths, and play spaces. Yet, much of the landscape will be changed only lightly. Planners who are young today will wander through inner-city streets in 2050 with the mental maps of today and not get lost. The ambition of planners in dealing with massive development and conservation is not limited to a role as the shepherd of permits but to embrace responsibility as a guide to the evolving reach of community aspirations.

A school in Chicago founded on the ideas of John Dewey is naming its newsletter *The Live Creature* to recall Dewey's thought that "what the live creature retains from the past and what it expects from the future operate as directions in the present." For all our future-mindedness, planners must remember the test of the present good. It is in the present, only this year, that a six-year-old can enjoy the pleasures of being six.

12

Equity Planning: Problems and Roles

PHILLIP L. CLAY

An important question to ask in the context of the goals of equity planning is how the interests of poor and minority residents can be framed in a more politically powerful way. In cities, the emerging stakeholders—investors, nonfamily households, and region-serving interests—are gaining, while attention to the poor is not.

In addition, cities play a critical role in shaping the physical environment and the application of technology to that environment. They build road systems, transit systems, install water and other utilities in ways that shape the physical city, and, as a result, shape social opportunities. The nature of the infrastructure shapes the ability of residents to move about the city and take advantage of the local array of opportunities and services. More than distance, the availability of infrastructure determines whether young people are isolated, whether there are public facilities, and whether the common wealth is available to make up for a lack of family resources.

The maintenance of public buildings—schools, libraries, public hospitals—is important because they are located at the neighborhood level and provide public resources for those who cannot avail themselves of private options. Their presence defines the ability of the neighborhood to be helpful to the social development of its young.

A major issue today facing the implementation of welfare reform and its success in promoting self-sufficiency is the provision of empowering services. In the creation of day-care services, the lack of appropriate and affordable space in which to offer child care constitutes a major obstacle. Neighborhoods where the physical infrastructure is in place find it easier to focus resources and attention on programming and outreach. A neighborhood that possesses physical assets it can use is empowered by these resources. To lack the facilities needed to achieve social goals that help define a neighborhood does not support the development of opportunity.

This is all the more important because, in recent decades, there have been major inflows of people to central cities—blacks from the South until the early 1970s; Puerto Ricans and Mexican Americans, Asians, and Central Americans more recently. Nearly all these groups settled in cities, where they face challenges in becoming part of their new communities. Young blacks who moved to the big cities in the 1940s found industrial jobs that, even taking into account their unequal opportunity, were better than what they had left in the South. Opportunities for these workers would, in fact, expand. They became industrial workers in numbers sufficient to create a solid working class and in the next generation a growing middle class. Good jobs that helped the sons of postwar black migrants had disappeared by the time their grandchildren and great grandchildren reached adulthood in the 1980s and 1990s.

Not least, the social fabric is important as a resource because neither the market nor the government has the will or capacity to initiate and implement social change. Even though we cannot define or offer rigorous proof, there are some indicators to be found in the literature and in practice. A neighborhood has social fabric when:

- There are shared values among members of the community on such matters as childrearing and the value of education, individual responsibility, mutual obligation, "family values," and so on.

- Informal and voluntary associations enjoy broad participation.

- Children are considered a community resource, and their development is at the heart of how communities set priorities and assess themselves.

- Informal institutions emerge to address community problems.

- Community institutions and standards are understood and respected by community members and outsiders.

- There is a dense network of associations and obligation that cuts across generations and other types of segmentation, such as race and class.

- Community members celebrate successes that members experience, viewing the success of residents as a community asset and source of pride.

- Loss, failure, and suffering in the community stimulate support, renewal, and recommitment.

- Community institutions nurture and support the development of leaders, as well as framing and enforcing accountability of leaders and members.

Of course, having all these features is a high, perhaps impossible, standard. Few places can boast of having all these features all the time. The extreme, and perfect, case of social fabric is probably the small village. The real-world urban neighborhood that comes closest is probably the ethnic working-class neighborhood. Some immigrant and minority communities are able to have some other features as well, although they are more likely to be sub-communities rather than larger concentrations. The point is, social fabric and social capital are generated by a community; only then are they supported by that community.

Planners played some role in each of these processes as they have unfolded in recent decades. There are ways the planning profession helped advance opportunity, as well as other ways in which we contribute to inequality and isolation.

THE ROLES WE PLAY

As scholars of the city, we have an interest in the processes, systems, markets, and so on that explain how cities grow and change, how the population and shape of the physical environment are transformed over time, and the consequences of these transformations for city form and quality of life.

We are, in addition, scholars of urban practice who focus on the roles and institutions by which cities are shaped and their development is influenced. We seek to learn from past experience and offer these lessons to future planners and current practitioners. We seek to understand what defines competence and effectiveness for individual practitioners and to build this understanding into our curriculum. It is important to stress that we have been notoriously negligent in addressing the second of these roles.

As interdisciplinary scholars, we have done considerable work on understanding the ways cities work. Our colleagues have explored urban history, markets, institutions, demographics, and the physical environment. We have drawn lessons from all these to inform planning, and in so doing, to present a more holistic view of the city than is shown by economists, social scientists, or design professionals. One can debate how good a job we have done, but clearly this was the focus of much planning scholarship.

In the area of research in practice, our late colleague, Donald Schön, as a leader in this area, helped draw our attention to it in ways that go well beyond the mechanics of public administration or traditional city planning pedagogy. It would be a lasting tribute to him if more of us would devote some of our research time to this issue. If this issue were consistently reflected in our courses—in particular, more advanced courses on urban institutions that would look at, for example, the increasing complexity of institutions and markets in which planners operate—we could make a major contribution to the field and to the education of our students.

In some ways, the issues we face in cities today have less to do with what represents a good idea than how we can implement a good item, given the competing institutional pressures and configurations of interests in American cities.

The third area of challenge has to do with professional competence and effectiveness—how individuals, given their own personal demographic class and other features, operate in the field. We have a long history of promoting internships, studios in nondesign areas, extended summer projects, and so forth. We have not, however, consistently taken the challenge of addressing how we can help students operate, given their background in a multicultural, multiethnic, and complex environment such that the organizations and projects in which they are involved can be effective settings for designing and implementing the changes. While students leave our program well armed with analytical tools, not all of us can boost their personal effectiveness and confidence. Students have asked for help; we have yet to find a way of learning what to teach them and then effectively incorporating it into our curriculum.

13

The Planning Profession and Reform

CHESTER HARTMAN

I am struck by the point Michael Teitz makes about how small a role our profession played, and plays, in some of the most important current policy and political issues having to do with cities—issues such as reform of the welfare system and devolution—even though it is at the state and local levels that what we do as planners ought to have the greatest impact. Maybe that's because Teitz (1997) is correct in his observation that "planning's dominant concerns are elsewhere [than cities]." The central issues focused on in the 1997 MIT Faculty Seminar—power, equity, conflicting interests—relate primarily to cities and their populations, the intersection of race and poverty, the rapidly changing demographics of the United States, the impact of all this on our economy, political life, and urban/metropolitan patterns. Back in 1994, the *APA Journal* conducted a forum entitled "Paul Davidoff and Advocacy Planning in Retrospect," my contribution to which was "On Poverty and Racism, We Have Had Little to Say." Sadly, that dismal observation continues to be true a half-decade later.

I am also struck by Teitz's passing comment that, for lack of space, he omits discussion of housing policy (Teitz 1997). Partly, it's personal pique, since housing, along with the race–poverty intersection, is what I have devoted my entire professional life to. More to the point, however, is the centrality of housing to the problem of conflicting interests: it is where the issues of class and race manifest themselves most clearly in our society, where planning seemed previously to have done little to affect the deeply ingrained class and race segregation (now hypersegregation) that characterizes our metropolitan areas. Housing policy has to be central to what planners do. Housing is central to access to education, resources, and jobs, as well as the largest expenditure for most lower-income households. Housing equity is also the principal source of wealth generation for most households, and the discriminatory housing market is primarily responsible for the vast wealth disparities between black and white households. If equity is to be a strongly held value in our professional work, then profound critiques of our housing system and proposals for its radical restructuring need to be written, proposed, and worked for.

In the same vein, what is very much needed—if power and equity are to be kept at the forefront of the planning profession, and the profession is to play a significant role in twenty-first–century America—is to keep the utopian tradition alive, not necessarily in the physical planning sense but in terms of policies and programs that lead us toward greater equity, as opposed to the opposite direction our society is headed in today, as measured by growing income and wealth gaps, a two-tiered job structure, educational tracking, the workings of our criminal justice system, immigrant-bashing, the mean, nasty, self-indulgent political climate that prevails—all in a context where race is a pervasive but unacknowledged subtext.

Some basic rethinking is required about the role of government as well. Planners are government-oriented, and must be, for many of the tools they need. But I would label myself, as Barbara Ehrenreich did recently, as something of a "recovering statist." That is, progressives should not be knee-jerk defenders of government. There are some things only government can do, and does well: provide needed resources, set and enforce standards. But administration of various programs designed to assist in creating social and economic justice is most effective if it is small-scale in nature, as close to the need and the needy as possible, with maximum involvement of community-based organizations and the entire nonprofit sector.

If all this sounds like a 1960s redux, so be it. That was a time when there was a real sense that at least a segment of the planning profession was an integral part of the movement for social and economic justice. Sadly, I do not see such a movement today—either in the profession or the society at large.

Part III

IMAGES OF CITY-PLANNING PRACTICE

Sectors

14

How City-Planning Practices Affect Metropolitan-Area Housing Markets, and Vice Versa

Anthony Downs

What are the key ways in which the real forces operating in metropolitan-area housing markets affect city-planning practices, and how do real city-planning practices affect those housing markets? The first step in understanding these mutually causative forces is to properly conceive of the way metropolitan-area housing markets actually operate. The existing housing stock, the new housing development process, the housing renovation process, and the aging of housing within an entire metropolitan area together form a *single integrated dynamic social system*. This system can be fully comprehended only when viewed from two aspects.

First, *it must be considered as whole*, without regard for municipal and other boundaries. Yet, city-planning processes in each metropolitan area are fragmented into different plans and policies for each local government. Moreover, most such plans are drawn up and modified in each locality with little regard to what is happening in the rest of the metropolitan area.

Second, *this system must be viewed as a dynamic process that changes over time*, and in ways that are, in part, predictable. Nevertheless, the city-planning processes in each locality tend to view the housing therein as a fixed (and therefore static) construct, because they focus on its characteristics at that moment. The tensions between these two realities, and the way they are ignored in most real-world city planning, form the basis for the discussion in this chapter.

Author's Note

The views in this article are solely those of the author and not necessarily the views of The Brookings Institution, its trustees, or its other staff members.

WHY HOUSING MARKETS FORM A DYNAMIC
REGIONAL SOCIAL SYSTEM

The aspects of housing markets that make them a dynamic, metropolitan-wide social system are set forth below.

Housing markets are subdivided into neighborhoods, and households react to neighborhoods as relatively homogeneous spatial units. A neighborhood is a spatially compact area usually considered by the overall community to contain relatively homogeneous housing units and households of similar socio-economic status. Neighborhoods are not abstract concepts; in fact, neighborhood boundaries are always defined by local residents in concrete terms. Moreover, not all neighborhoods are homogeneous. Some contain both single-family and multifamily units and commercial properties; yet they are treated by local markets as distinct entities. In other words, neighborhoods are what the residents say they are.

Neighborhoods are dynamic entities in constant flux—more closely resembling processes than static conditions or states—because of household movements. On the average, about 30 percent of all American renter households, and 10 percent of all American owner-occupant households, move each year. These ratios differ by region; they are higher in the West and Southwest and lowest in the Northeast. Therefore, flows of people into and out of neighborhoods are a vital part of housing markets and cities in general.

To remain demographically stable, any neighborhood requires constant in-movements of residents like those who are leaving. Any divergence between newcomers and existing residents causes a longer-run change in the neighborhood's composition. Similarly, if their physical condition is to remain stable, neighborhoods require constant inputs of capital to offset the physical decay, aging, and deterioration of housing and other structures therein. To put it another way, a neighborhood can remain stable in composition and condition only if its amenities are attractive enough to entice constant inflows of new residents and new investments, to replace those "leaving" through outmigration, death, and decay.

Neighborhoods also represent bundles of multiple traits that are evaluated by those considering moving into or remaining in them. Such traits include the physical condition of local structures; the location of the neighborhood in relation to key urban facilities such as downtown and major universities, hospitals, and shopping areas; the type of transportation serving the area; the ethnic composition of the residents; the socioeconomic status of the residents; the quality of public schools serving the neighborhood; and the quality of other public services available. Research is ambiguous about how much these neighborhood traits affect the behavior or nature of individual residents or resident households. Such traits, however, certainly affect the willingness of households to move into or remain in a neighborhood. These attitudes of households about neighborhood acceptability tend to influence who will move into them, thereby influencing their long-run composition. Attitudes such as these involve the acceptability of each area's socioeconomic status, its ethnic and nationality composition, and the quality of its schools and other public services.

Residential neighborhoods typically go through a multistage life cycle from initial development through maturity to aging and decay, to possible renovation and resurrection. This cycle arises because of the long life of the physical capital invested in housing and the dynamic growth of U.S. metropolitan areas over time. Most residential neighborhoods are initially created at the periphery of urban settlement, because metropolitan areas the world over expand from the inside outward. Because of American policies established by local governments, housing in new neighborhoods of the United States is required to meet high-quality standards at its inception—standards that most poor households cannot afford. Thus, new neighborhoods initially are occupied primarily by households in the upper third of the income distribution, unless housing subsidies are involved. Because U.S. housing policies have kept the total volume of subsidies for low-income households relatively low, most poor households cannot afford to live in newly built dwellings.

As neighborhoods age, certain of their initial basic traits nearly always change in predictable ways. Their relative geographic position shifts from being on the periphery to being farther and farther inside the periphery, because newer neighborhoods are built farther out. Therefore, the older neighborhoods are, the more likely they are to be located in the inner core of the area. Their physical capital deteriorates with time and use, and the design of the housing in them tends to become more functionally obsolete, in comparison with newer housing. Thus, the housing in them becomes relatively less desirable than newer units. However, this process of relative deterioration can be offset by constant high-level investment in repairs and renovation if a neighborhood has some unusually strong attractions that keep it relatively desirable despite its age.

Another way neighborhoods typically change over time is that their residents tend to become lower-ranked in the socioeconomic hierarchy of the overall metropolitan-area society, since their housing becomes relatively less desirable over time. This process can also be offset by the same high-level investment described above.

Once the physical deterioration of a neighborhood becomes advanced, and its relative socioeconomic status becomes low, it tends to attract only residents too poor to maintain it in good condition. This creates a self-aggravating downward cycle into destitution, unless such a decline is checked by a reversal of demand for its housing.

Unlike humans, such a "dead or dying" neighborhood can be resurrected from further downward movement in its life cycle to upward movement through the above stages, or directly into one of the higher stages. This requires some change in conditions, which greatly increases the demand for housing in that area because its relative attractiveness has risen compared to the level of attractiveness in the past. Examples include major urban renewal investments in an area, the founding of a new major university or hospital there or nearby or the expansion of existing ones, creation of a new shopping center nearby, construction of a nearby highway that increases the general accessibility of the neighborhood, and an "invasion" of a formerly poor area by more affluent households seeking homes closer to downtown or other key amenities.

The extent to which older residential neighborhoods experience this life cycle depends greatly on the overall balance of supply and demand in the entire metropolitan-area housing market. This, in turn, depends on population growth—especially immigration—on the one hand and new housing construction on the other. In periods of rapid metropolitan-area population growth, the demand for housing often rises faster than the supply. This leads to rising housing prices and a tendency to overcrowding at the low-income end of the housing market. An example is the period from 1940 to 1960 in U.S. metropolitan areas. Under these circumstances, the life-cycle process slows down. Even the oldest, most dilapidated neighborhoods become intensively used and often overcrowded.

In periods of rapid housing construction, the overall supply of housing in a metropolitan area may rise faster than the demand for it. Even if most of the newly built housing is in outlying suburbs, the resulting increase in overall housing supply can affect neighborhoods throughout the metropolitan area. This is true because each newly built, newly occupied home starts a "chain of moves" that affects up to four households. One moves into the new unit, leaving an existing unit behind which becomes occupied by a second household. The movement of the latter out of an older unit frees that unit for occupancy by yet another household. Research shows that up to four households thus improve their dwellings for every newly built unit that becomes occupied. This leads to stable or falling housing prices throughout the area, as well as a tendency to rising vacancy or even abandonment in the poorest parts of the area's overall inventory. An example is the period from about 1960 to 1980 in most U.S. metropolitan areas. Under these circumstances, the life-cycle process speeds up. Older areas deteriorate faster and may become abandoned because even the poorest households can find alternative quarters.

There is nothing inevitable, however, about this neighborhood life-cycle process. Its manifestation in any neighborhood can be greatly changed by both market forces and public policies.

Neighborhoods throughout a metropolitan area tend to form a socioeconomic and ethnic hierarchy, with easily identified tops and bottoms, and fewer distinguishable middles. The individual neighborhoods in this hierarchy are only roughly homogeneous. This hierarchy arises in part because of the dynamic life cycle experienced by an individual neighborhood. As most neighborhoods age, they move downward in relative desirability, thereby moving downward in the hierarchy as well; but a few neighborhoods with outstanding amenities remain at the top of the hierarchy. Their residents constantly invest in maintaining and renovating their housing units, and demand for those units remains high. Residents may also use exclusionary policies to prevent negative forces from affecting their housing inventories.

Creation of such a hierarchy is facilitated by fragmented governments and exclusionary zoning policies. Individual localities try to resist declining in status and quality in the hierarchy by excluding both physical and social forces likely to reduce their relative desirability. Generally, localities that contain unusual amenities—such as lakefront locations, major universities or hospitals, and close proximity to regional downtowns—are the most successful in keeping up high demand for their housing. They seek to bolster those amenities by adopting policies that require initial construction of only expensive new units, high-level ongoing housing maintenance, and exclusion of housing types likely to be occupied by relatively low-income households, specifically multifamily and subsidized housing.

The socioeconomic hierarchy of neighborhoods in each metropolitan area extends across local borders, encompassing the entire area. Some high-end and some low-end neighborhoods may have borders that coincide with local municipalities; but the overall hierarchy spans the entire metropolitan area.

Local residents the world over tend to be against major neighborhood change of any type. Such change almost always disconcerts people who have come to terms with the existing conditions where they live. Hence, there is a conservative bias in citizens that expresses itself if they have strong influence over local conditions or decisions concerning such conditions. This bias against improving conditions is found even in poor areas, since such improvement might make it more costly to live there—so-called gentrification.

THE SOCIAL COSTS THAT ARISE

Many widespread city-planning policies and behaviors are not based on a realistic response to this large-scale housing system in each metropolitan area. This results in various dysfunctions of city-planning systems that reduce their effectiveness. Some of the most important of these are now discussed.

Failure to coordinate local land-use plans. The most obvious such dysfunctionality is that each locality develops its own comprehensive plan without rationally coordinating its creation or its management with the plans of all the other localities nearby. In fact, city planners, like all elected local politicians, are motivated to maximize the perceived welfare of their local constituents and to shift as many social costs as possible onto residents of other localities. This results in widespread adoption of inconsistent policies among adjacent communities, and sometimes of "beggar-thy-neighbor" policies. Both types of policies preclude any rational overall response to the regional nature of the entire housing system.

Widespread use of "fiscal zoning." A nearly universal example is the adoption of "fiscal zoning" by local governments. Each government tries to attract or retain within its borders those land uses that will yield a "surplus" of property and other tax revenues over the costs to the local government of serving those uses. Examples of such "profitable" land uses are regional shopping centers, office parks, and very low-density, high-cost single-family neighborhoods. Conversely, each local government tries to repel or expel from within its borders those land uses that impose higher service costs on the local government than it collects in taxes from them. Example of such "loser" land uses are multifamily housing and single-family neighborhoods occupied by low- or moderate-income households with several children.

In reality, local governments are not philosophically identical to profit-maximizing or tax-minimizing private enterprises; hence, they need not adopt policies that assume that is the case. On the other hand, they must balance their total revenues and total costs over the long run, because they cannot sustain fiscal deficits for long. Therefore, significant pressure exists for them to engage in such "fiscal zoning," even though, in practice, this means weighting the political value of potential resident households differently, depending on their incomes. Since fiscal zoning awards higher intrinsic value to wealthy households than to poor ones, it is essentially "undemocratic" in its treatment of residents, both existing and potential.

The result is intensive competition among local governments to attract "surplus-producing" land uses that can be located in many different places. This causes local government to compete in offering tax breaks and other benefits to the developers who control such uses, thereby reducing the benefits of the "surpluses" to all governments concerned. Conversely, all local governments try to prevent "loser" land uses from locating within their boundaries by restricting the amount of land zoned for those uses. Hence, developers of multifamily housing have a hard time finding sites for their units, and the overall supply of such housing is lower than it would otherwise be in the absence of such policies. This set of programs penalizes low-income households and benefits commercial developers.

Fiscal disparities and inequities. Another important result of these policies is a disproportionate bearing of the social and governmental costs of responding to poverty by localities in the older inner-core portions of each metropolitan area. They contain concentrated-poverty neighborhoods and much higher overall fractions of poor residents than most newer, more outlying areas. These poor residents generate lower tax revenues per household than wealthier residents, while at the same time giving rise to higher public service costs per household, especially for schools and police. This situation results in fiscal disparities that prevent local governments from offering equal public service qualities and other opportunities across the entire metropolitan area—especially when it comes to the quality of public education provided to residents.

Certain dynamic metropolitan area–wide demographic forces, such as high-level immigration of low-income households from abroad or from rural areas, also result in disproportionate impacts on different neighborhoods and localities across the entire metropolitan area. Those localities that contain the "entry-port" neighborhoods for such movements have their housing much more adversely affected than do those localities with no such "entry ports." Poor newcomers tend to overcrowd older units because they cannot afford to pay market rents for units that conform to occupancy laws. At the other extreme, wealthy suburbs rigorously enforce their zoning codes to prevent any such overcrowding, thereby reducing the burdens of dealing with poverty that their governments must bear. This aggravates the fiscal disparities already noted.

Inability to deal with actual neighborhood differentiation explicitly and effectively. Another dysfunctional outcome arises because it is politically difficult for public officials, including planners, to openly take notice of neighborhood differentiation by income and race or ethnicity, or even social and economic status. If planners explicitly take such differences into account, or even admit that such differences exist, they can easily be accused of illegitimate biases or behavior that is "undemocratic" because it does not assume that all residents are completely equal. Yet, actual inequalities of conditions— which exist throughout the world and within every metropolitan area—are vitally important in affecting household behavior, and therefore in affecting the proper public policies to adopt in dealing with that behavior. For example, in every large city, police departments that assign resources among neighborhoods in relation to the demands for service originating therein always assign more resources per capita to low-income neighborhoods than to high-income neighborhoods, since per capita demands for services are much higher in poor areas than in wealthier ones. This is "undemocratic" in the sense of not treating every group equally, because it sacrifices such equality to achieving more efficient use of scarce resources. Police departments are able to engage in such "undemocratic" behavior because their need to do so, in order to improve overall security, is obvious to all.

The political bias against city planners' recognizing inequalities among neighborhoods tends to prevent planners from explicitly taking into account the life-cycle positions of individual neighborhoods within their communities. They cannot label a given area as "seriously decaying" without being attacked by residents there as insensitive or as discouraging of additional investment. Nor can they assign scarce renovation and investment resources among neighborhoods so as to maximize the overall impact of those resources. Doing so tends to concentrate those resources in neighborhoods with the best chance of improving their overall conditions per dollar invested. That is normally not the case in the most deteriorated and destitute areas, where overall improvements per dollar invested are likely to be low. Yet, for planners to recognize this reality exposes them to the charge of "favoring the rich" or at least "discriminating against the poorest neighborhoods." In fact, city planners are under great pressure to divide available neighborhood improvement resources equally among political districts, each represented by one elected official, regardless of the economic sense of doing so. This "fair share" allocation diverges from what any purely economical, rational allocation scheme would indicate, thereby, from a purely economic point of view, wasting resources.

Recognizing racial or ethnic changes within or among neighborhoods is particularly difficult politically. Still, the failure to do so causes policymakers to avoid adopting policies that might ameliorate some undesirable impacts of such changes. For example, in the massive change from all-white to all-black neighborhoods that occurred in many large northeastern and midwestern cities in the 1950s and 1960s, explicit recognition of what was happening might have led to stronger policies to "open up" more outlying areas to occupancy by blacks and other minority groups. This could have taken some of the pressure for rapid racial change off the white neighborhoods immediately adjacent to mainly black areas, at least slowing the process of transition from all-white to all-black occupancy there.

Unequal enforcement of building and housing codes in different types of neighborhoods. Another dysfunctional result of this problem is that large cities cannot enforce building and housing codes in all parts of their housing inventories to the same degree if they are experiencing large-scale immigration of poor households. Many of those households cannot afford to live in housing that meets the quality standards required by local ordinances; hence, they double and triple up, with multiple households occupying units legally designed for a single household. If local governments enforced their housing codes rigorously under such circumstances, they would eject thousands of households into homelessness on city streets. For obvious and sound reasons, they do not want to do this. Hence, they are forced to overlook massive code violations in some neighborhoods while rigorously enforcing codes in other, more affluent neighborhoods—as the residents there want them to. This apparent duplicity—which is, in practice, nearly inescapable—could be remedied by adopting explicitly different quality standards in different areas. This more honest approach, however, is rejected as politically unacceptable and "undemocratic" because it appears not to treat all citizens alike. Yet, they are certainly not all alike in reality, in terms of their ability to pay housing costs; and the city government does not, in reality, treat them all alike because to do so would invite disaster.

In reality, failure to explicitly recognize the need to house poor people at standards different from those enforced for nonpoor people conceals the extent to which many poor households live in undesirable conditions. This deflects public consciousness toward other issues—mainly local crime, which is so heavily covered by local media that its extent becomes grossly exaggerated.

Not taking advantage of mixed-use potentials. City-planning practices usually involve creating land-use zones that segregate different types of uses from each other. Specifically, they segregate residential uses from commercial uses. This can—though it need not—make it impossible to achieve a socially optimal spatial mix of retail facilities and residences that would minimize resident trips in cars by making local walking trips for shopping convenient. Locating many small food and other convenience stores in the midst of residential areas might induce more walking shopping trips, as it does within residential areas of large cities. On the other hand, when advocates of this "new urbanism" tactic have tried to put it into practice in the suburbs, retail firms often refuse to operate the small local outlets thus called for, arguing that these small outlets do not achieve the high sales volumes required for maximum efficiency and lowest prices.

The basic conflict between maximizing existing housing values and making shelter accessible to newcomers and renters. City planners and local elected officials are under strong political pressure from homeowners within their jurisdictions to adopt policies that maximize the market values of owner-occupied homes already existing there. This pressure is powerful even in cities that contain sizable fractions of renting citizens, because homeowners tend to be more locally active politically than renters. The former tend to remain in their present neighborhoods much longer than the latter, and they have a much greater economic stake in seeing home values rise.

The most effective way to respond positively to this pressure is to create a greater shortage of housing within the locality in relation to the demand for it, thereby putting upward pressure on the prices of existing homes. Of course, no planners or politicians ever admit publicly (or, perhaps, even to themselves) that intensifying whatever local housing shortage now exists, or creating one, is the means they are pursuing to improve home values. Nevertheless, this is the truth, whether they admit it or not. This strategy can best be implemented by (1) increasing the minimum sizes of lots for detached or attached dwellings, thereby reducing the number of units that can be built in the locality; (2) reducing the amount of land zoned for multifamily dwellings, or eliminating such zoning altogether; (3) limiting the number of new units permitted each year, thereby postponing really large increases in supply; (4) charging higher fees per new dwelling for community services, schools, utility hookups, traffic mitigation, and so on; and (5) reducing the proportion and amount of land within the community zoned for *any* residential uses by increasing zoning for commercial use, parks, roads, and so forth.

Although these tactics benefit homeowners already living in the locality, they impose higher costs on those trying to buy homes there, and on renters both living there and trying to enter. These higher costs emerge because housing prices are higher than they would be without such tactics, thereby making it more expensive for these groups to enter the community or, if they are renters already present, to remain there. In general, this political pressure tends to benefit more affluent groups in society while penalizing poorer ones.

This is natural, since it is existing homeowners—who are, on average, much more affluent than existing renters—who press for this strategy and benefit from it; and renters and potential entrants who lose. Hence, this strategy creates an economically regressive redistribution of wealth in both the overall metropolitan area and society as a whole.

The tendency for local growth management planning to expand overall "sprawl" into larger total territories. Most local growth management planning involves one or more of the tactics described above, which limit increases in a locality's housing supply, either annually or permanently. In particular, local growth management policies tend to reduce overall population densities, rather than raise them, through a process known as "downzoning." But when many individual communities engage in downzoning, a given total increase in a metropolitan area's population during a year or a decade must be spread over a larger total territory. This occurs because new construction takes place at lower densities, and existing built-up areas absorb fewer new housing units on infill sites than would happen if no such downzoning occurred, or if it were less widespread. Therefore, one consequence of both the fragmentation of zoning powers among many localities and pressures within those localities to restrict housing supply is the extension of more low-density "suburban sprawl" development farther out from the original center of each metropolitan area. (This conclusion assumes that the metropolitan areas involved are growing in total population.) Thus, ironically, uncoordinated attempts by individual localities to respond to the perceived ills generated by "suburban sprawl" can aggravate those ills, rather than reduce them.

CITY PLANNING AND MARKET REALITIES

Relationships between city planning practices and the realities of metropolitan-area housing markets are complex, sometimes even counterintuitive. They can be fully understood only if housing markets themselves are perceived as ongoing, dynamic processes operating across entire metropolitan regions, rather than static constructs operating within individual localities. Such an understanding may help city planners recognize the many dysfunctional behavior patterns they currently undertake as part of their "normal" activities and try to change those behavior patterns to avoid the socially undesirable results.

15

Education for Transportation Planning in a New Century

Martin Wachs

One of the most important defining characteristics of American society is mobility. Our social and economic mobility continues to be dramatic compared to most other nations. Children of immigrants attain status and achieve successes their parents could only have dreamed of. Mobility is central to American ideals, and to a great extent our social and economic mobility is dependent on physical mobility. If we understand physical or geographic mobility to be the ability to traverse space safely and quickly, increasing physical mobility has been a defining trend in American life, one of the greatest areas of social and economic change over time, and one of the principal concerns of urban planners.

Our physical mobility today is greater than it has ever been. At the turn of the twentieth century, most Americans still lived on the land; farmers left their property for business, pleasure, or family reasons relatively infrequently. People shopped at general stores near where they lived, attended small rural schools offering few classes, rarely saw doctors, and attended tiny local churches. The coming of the automobile brought opportunities to leave the farm for business, social, and recreational reasons, as well as opportunities to shop at chain stores having greater variety and lower prices than local general stores. Similarly, small one-room schoolhouses quickly gave way to larger centralized schools, and tiny churches were consolidated into larger and more substantial ones. Medical care became far more accessible, and doctors made house calls. The first national and regional parks were founded in this era of new mobility.

In cities, prior to the coming of public transit systems and the automobile, densities reached unhealthful levels because people had to rely on physical proximity, and most walked to work. Wooden walk-up tenement buildings in the shadows of soot-belching factories were firetraps and health hazards. The construction of transit routes and the replacement of distance-based fares by the flat fare in the early years of the twentieth century were seen as salvation from crowded, disease-ridden inner cities. Poor people using the subways could live much farther from where they worked than they could in earlier years, and the flat fare made distance less of a barrier. In other words, the transportation system was in earlier days explicitly designed to be an instrument of social and economic policy, and I believe that planners in the twenty-first century should again be explicit in their use of transportation policy for such purposes.

There are some defining dimensions of transportation planning that are enduring and that have defined the practice of transportation planning for decades. These are the context of transportation planning as it is done today and as it has changed over time. After discussing these contexts, I will go on to enumerate changes that I think have been underway for several decades, and how these ongoing changes relate to professional education for planners. Taken together, the enduring themes and the evolving transitions suggest the following recommendations for strengthening the education of transportation planners.

TRANSPORTATION PLANNING CANNOT BE LEFT TO ENGINEERS

The vast majority of transportation practitioners in the United States are trained as civil engineers, and I expect many future transportation specialists to be engineers. But transportation is, more than ever, a social and economic system as well as a physical system that is linked to land use, energy policy and environmental concerns, and housing and economic development. Therefore, it is essential to maintain a prominent place in the urban planning curriculum for transportation studies. I believe, too, that many important innovations in transportation education and research will emerge from planning and social science inquiries, as well as from the more technological approaches of engineers. Increasingly, the university is being characterized by interdisciplinary studies, and transportation is one of the areas of scholarship that lends itself most readily to research and teaching across disciplinary boundaries. The leading university programs in transportation will surely involve contributions from both fields, urban planning and engineering.

STRENGTHENING TECHNICAL EDUCATION
IN A POLICY CONTEXT

Because of the continuing, and growing, complexity of technical analysis in transportation planning, there is a need to incorporate into the education of transportation planners new approaches to data analysis, geographic information systems, survey techniques, and modeling methods. Because of the complex socioeconomic setting within which transportation planning is practiced, however, it is critical that the technical elements of the specialist's preparation be embedded in a context that provides them with an understanding of policymaking. While technical expertise is needed today as much as ever, good preparation for transportation planning practice must also incorporate an understanding of the concepts of equity, the tools for consensus building and dispute resolution, and a deep understanding of the political context within which transportation policy is made.

This is another way of saying that transportation planning must be embedded within the institutions, trends, and patterns that characterize urban planning more generally.

LINKS BETWEEN TRANSPORTATION AND OTHER SECTORS

Without sacrificing sectoral knowledge within transportation, there is a need to prepare students for the practice of transportation planning in a world that increasingly acknowledges the interrelatedness of this field with other subfields of urban planning. To become successful transportation planners, students need greater exposure to the processes of urban growth and to principles, laws, and methods of land-use planning. Neophyte transportation planners must also understand the basic principles of urban economics and public finance. It probably is equally true that students who plan to focus on housing, the environment, or urban development should develop a broader understanding of transportation policy and planning than was the case in planning education in the past.

INCORPORATING TELECOMMUNICATIONS AND INFORMATION FLOWS

In the same way that urban transportation systems transformed urban life and urban form at the turn of the twentieth century, it would appear that the turn of the twenty-first century will be characterized by the information revolution. All planning students, especially those concerned with transportation policy and planning, need to develop an understanding of the ways in which computers and information flows are changing the very nature of urban form, function, and process. We are already well along the path to the information society, but our planning institutions and the curricula by which we impart professional education to the next generation of planners do not sufficiently recognize, and are not incorporating, the fundamental ways in which urban life and planning are being changed by information technology.

EDUCATION FOR PRACTICE

Because the complex interaction between technical analysis and political context always complicates the practice of transportation planning, and because transportation planning is always done in a context of interaction with other sectors, such as land use, economic development, and housing, transportation planning education, to be effective, must be in close contact with the real world. This may be achieved by including in the curriculum some project classes or studios in which students work on real-world problems, by frequently including practitioners as guest speakers in lecture classes, by requiring students to pursue internships as part of their educational experience, and by encouraging theses or professional reports that address current policy problems in environments where real-world clients seek products that are immediately useful.

In support of these recommendations, in the next sections I review some of the ongoing or continuing themes in transportation policy and planning that I believe have endured for decades; then I examine some of the ways in which I believe the field has been changing in recent years.

LONG-TERM TRENDS

TRANSPORTATION PLANNING

Planning to meet transportation needs, like planning for some other infrastructure systems such as power and water and waste treatment, has long been inherently regional in scope rather than highly localized. In fact, transportation is one of the elements that led planning into regionalism as long ago as the 1920s and 1930s, and transportation has been one of the prime motivators for what some have called the new regionalism of the 1980s and 1990s.

In 1912, officials in Cleveland, Ohio, sought federal financial support for a study of transportation alternatives to alleviate the growing traffic congestion in their city. They wrote a proposal to the U.S. Secretary of Commerce, seeking support for a planned effort to hire consultants who would help them develop a transportation plan. The Secretary responded that the national government was indeed interested in supporting Cleveland's effort to plan a solution to its transportation problems. But, the Secretary wrote, if they accepted financial help, the local authorities would have to develop a plan that was regional in scope and that would ignore the political boundaries between Cleveland and surrounding jurisdictions. Interestingly, the Secretary made reference to the fact that planners in Boston had already made great progress toward the development of a regional transportation plan prior to that date.

Transportation concerns were among the most pressing factors leading to the widely studied regional problems of the New York metropolitan area and to the development of a regional plan for the improvement of conditions there in the 1920s and 1930s. The conduct of transportation studies at the regional level was reinforced by a series of federal laws enacted between the 1950s and 1990s, all of which made federal funds available to transportation planning activities that were comprehensive, coordinated, and continuing. Most of these activities were carried out at the regional level by councils of government or other forms of multijurisdictional study organizations that have emerged as today's metropolitan planning organizations.

The Intermodal Surface Transportation Efficiency Act (ISTEA) that was passed in 1991, and the 1998 Transportation Efficiency Act for the 21st Century (TEA-21), reinforced the long commitment to regionalism in transportation planning by giving regional agencies far more flexibility and far more authority over the expenditure of federal transportation funds than they had ever had before.

Transportation Is Fiscally Independent

Whereas local county roads and neighborhood streets in urban areas are financed primarily by local property taxes, major capital investments in transportation at the regional or interregional scale have largely been funded since before 1920 by user fees deposited in "trust funds" separate from other government accounts. Tolls have financed many highways and bridges, while gasoline taxes—along with excise taxes on vehicles, tires, batteries, and car parts, and truck fees that vary with vehicle weight—have financed most capital investments and maintenance costs of highways. Similarly, fares have borne a substantial—though over time a decreasing proportion—of transit operating expenses. This long-standing financial arrangement means that transportation projects are generally not in competition with other government expenditures such as health care, national security, and education. Because of dramatically improved automobile fuel economy, in recent years transportation funding has failed to keep pace with inflation and certainly has lagged behind transportation construction and operating costs. New construction has slowed, and the condition of the existing system is deteriorating as experts debate the best way to augment current funding. Nevertheless, the trust fund arrangement has, by and large, protected transportation investment programs, resulting in a far more extensive transportation network than exists in most other industrialized nations. The politics of transportation expenditures is strongly influenced by the existence of trust funds and by the dependence of transportation programs on fees paid by the users of the systems themselves.

THE INFLUENCE OF PORK BARREL POLITICS

In part because the user financing system provides a secure and continuing financial base for transportation projects, this sector has long been one that has been subjected to what has traditionally been called "pork barrel politics." Very often, the principal motivation for spending money on transportation projects is the delivery of money to particular constituencies, to fulfill political obligations rather than primarily to improve transportation efficiency or to maximize system performance, although, of course, these different purposes are not necessarily mutually exclusive. There is a tendency to respond to political pressure by using transportation funds to support large-scale, capital-intensive projects rather than more modest improvements in transport operations. From my perspective as a transportation planner and analyst, solutions to congested arteries and strategies for urban traffic management that could be extremely cost-effective often are passed over in favor of approaches that are much more expensive, flashy, and rewarding in the sense that they provide large contracts to political supporters.

INTERACTIONS BETWEEN LAND USE AND TRANSPORTATION

People don't travel for the sake of traveling, but because they wish to benefit from activities located on parcels of land that are separated in space. Planners, therefore, have a broad understanding that land-use patterns determine traffic patterns. Consequently, many believe that land use and transportation should be planned and managed in concert, and to a certain extent this is successfully done in some countries outside the United States. Yet, the American tradition is for land use to be governed and managed at the local level, and there is little willingness to cede this authority to regional or state bodies. Local authorities are also unwilling to accept traffic problems at the regional level as a basis for local land-use decisions. The obvious conflict between regional transportation concerns and local land-use policies leads to the perception (and, in some cases, the reality) that transportation planners can do relatively little either to prevent or to accommodate growing traffic congestion. The perception that more highways beget only more traffic congestion is largely the result of our unwillingness to control land use and transportation jointly. There are examples of specific efforts to overcome this "disconnect," such as Portland, Oregon, which is gaining international attention. Nevertheless, the absence of connection between land use and transportation policy is a pervasive, persistent theme.

Transportation Planning Is Technocratic

Transportation planning has long been dominated by quantitative analysis, mathematical models, and the increasingly complex use of computers for data analysis, forecasts, and evaluation of alternative investments. After World War II, some of the first civil applications of electronic computing involved the processing of data describing traffic flows and person-trip patterns; and the urban freeways constructed in the 1960s and 1970s were among the first large civil systems that were planned using complex computerized analysis. Transportation planning continues to be highly technocratic. Recently, for example, standard methods of transportation planning have been broadened to incorporate the regular use of Geographic Information Systems (GIS). The federal government is currently sponsoring a Travel Model Improvement Program, an extensive effort to improve our capability to "microsimulate" travel on urban transportation networks. A major portion of the research in support of the development of these new travel-forecasting capabilities is being conducted at Los Alamos National Laboratory and is employing the most powerful computers in the nation.

The emphasis on quantitative analysis in transportation planning is increasing over time, as sophisticated comparisons of alternative investments and their environmental impacts are required by a variety of federal and state regulations. To become an effective transportation planner, a graduate student must learn statistics, data analysis, modeling, and computer techniques. It is ironic that transportation analysis is so complex, while many of the decisions regarding the funding of particular projects are based primarily on political considerations. In many instances, we train our students to be deeply competent with respect to technical analysis; when they begin to practice professionally they quickly discover that years of analysis, costing millions of dollars, is given less attention than blatantly political concerns when it comes to making the most important transportation decisions. On the other hand, good analysis does sometimes influence the political debates, certainly contributing to our understanding of the social and economic phenomena that cause, and result from, travel and from the operation of transportation systems.

TRENDS AND CHANGES
IN TRANSPORTATION PLANNING

While the enduring characteristics of transportation planning described in the introduction to this chapter give definition and continuity to the field, it is also true that there have been changes in the nature of transportation systems and policy that also influence the nature of current practice. In this section, I highlight some of the most salient recent changes in transportation planning that are influencing the careers of recent graduates and that should be carefully considered as revisions are made in transportation planning curricula.

THE SHIFT FROM SYSTEM DEVELOPMENT TO MAINTENANCE AND MANAGEMENT

The American transportation system has matured. For well over a hundred years we have built railroads, transit systems, highways, ports, and airports in a developmental, instrumental way—creating economic, social, and educational opportunities, providing regions with competitive advantages, and lowering the cost of doing business. Today, in the United States but certainly not in developing nations, the emphasis is rapidly shifting to maintenance, rehabilitation, refurbishment, and a more efficiently managed existing system. Precious few new airports or ports will be built in the United States; numerous urban areas are building few or no major additions to their highway systems; and the recent spurt of rail transit system construction is slowing considerably. Incremental adjustments continue as we close gaps in highway networks, upgrade air terminals, modernize container ports, and widen highways and bridges. Even major, multibillion-dollar initiatives—for example, the development of "Intelligent Transportation Systems"—involve applications of automation and telecommunications to dramatically increase the capacity of existing highways rather than expand them.

The nature of the planning process associated with system management, renewal, and adjustment differs considerably from the process followed in designing new transportation systems from scratch, and it seems appropriate to expect that neophyte professionals in this field will require different analytical tools and practical skills than did transportation planners in previous decades. As a reflection of the changing nature of transportation analysis, the latest transportation faculty appointment at Berkeley is someone (educated at MIT) who specializes in infrastructure management, optimum pavement-replacement cycles, and statistical studies of the aging of physical facilities. Similarly, more and more of my graduates are finding employment dealing with system performance measurement, the provision of management services, and the scheduling of maintenance and replacement, while fewer are involved in planning or designing new systems.

Students preparing for careers in transportation planning in developing nations may still require skills more closely related to the planning and design of new capital systems than do students preparing for domestic careers in transportation. On the other hand, many students do not know at the time they enter graduate schools whether their practice will eventually be domestic or international. This may place an extra burden on planning schools to broaden the curriculum in transportation at exactly the same time that there are pressures to expand in other directions.

TRANSPORTATION AND ENVIRONMENTAL PRESERVATION AND ENHANCEMENT

Transportation systems are the source of a substantial proportion of urban air pollution and are among the major users of energy in urban areas. Recently, we have come to understand that transportation systems are also significant contributors to the production of greenhouse gases that affect global warming, and that they contribute substantially to water pollution by changing watercourses and drainage patterns, and through the deposition of polluting chemicals on and near roadways and railways. Since 1970, there has been a truly significant shift in transportation planning and management, elevating environmental concerns and analysis of environmental impacts to an increasingly central position. While transportation planners continue to be concerned with mobility, their work at times appears to be dominated by concerns for the mitigation of air and water quality problems, noise, and the visual intrusion of transportation facilities. In some communities, for example, the programming and construction of sound walls is among the largest capital construction programs associated with transportation, and highway agencies today often build systems for collecting and treating water that runs off highways. A surprisingly large proportion of the transportation workforce at regional and state agencies is engaged in environmental monitoring, impact analysis, and mitigation. This, of course, adds to the cost of transportation, a cost that constitutes part of the reason we are engaged in relatively little new construction or expansion of transportation systems. It may well be that this shift in emphasis will be beneficial to the quality of life in the United States, even though the process is a source of resentment and tension among transportation agencies, which, after all, conceive of their missions in different terms. Nevertheless, it is certain that training for modern transportation planning must involve far more attention to the concept of sustainability and to environmental science and policy than was ever the case previously.

THE INCREASING IMPORTANCE OF TECHNOLOGY

With the passage of time, transportation systems have, more and more, become characterized by advanced (and complex) technology. Whereas some observers note that there have been few revolutionary changes in engines or propulsion systems over a very long period of time, and that today's cars, buses, and trains are basically similar to those of 40 or 50 years ago, the constant progression of evolutionary changes is both impressive and significant. It would appear that the major direction of technological change in transportation systems is the melding of the technologies of transportation and telecommunications.

Telecommuting has the potential to change the temporal and spatial distribution of travel, and gradually the introduction of innovations in telecommunications into transportation systems is changing the nature of urban travel. Yet I doubt that our growing ability to communicate via telephone, computer, and fax will reduce or eliminate the need to travel; on the other hand, it would appear that these capabilities are gradually changing the temporal and spatial *distribution* of travel.

In addition, the monitoring of transportation systems performance for congestion levels, accidents, and weather-related incidents enables transportation agencies to respond quickly to changes and relay information to travelers in time to influence their choice of route, mode, and departure time. The simple radio traffic report is merely the precursor of "smart" transportation systems that include instantaneous information about the current location of the bus you intend to catch at the corner near your house, or the appearance on a screen located on the dashboard of your car of a map showing the "optimal" route between your origin and destination, given current traffic conditions. Gradually, such innovations, coupled with automated braking and steering systems, are leading toward the reality of the automated highway.

This is an area where technological change is accelerating, leading to questions about the capacity of our institutions to provide the necessary decision-making capacity and management skill to keep up with the possibilities. How will automated highways, for example, influence automobile insurance, and how will we cope with societal transitions to automated highways when some drivers are too old to cope with the new technology and others are too poor to acquire it? While electrical engineers and control theory specialists are today at the forefront of transportation research, there are many questions that must be addressed by social scientists, planners, and experts in public policy; and we must prepare our graduates to play a role in the transition to the emerging technology.

GROWING INEQUALITIES IN ACCESSIBILITY

Despite the fact that transportation policy is made at the regional level, and despite the increasingly sophisticated databases available to transportation planners and our increasing capabilities to analyze travel patterns and socioeconomic data, transportation planners and policymakers have been able to contribute little to the resolution of the growing disparities within regions between haves and have-nots, between the wealth of the suburbs and the growing poverty of the inner cities. In many regions, new rail systems are being built that increase the number of commute choices available to car-owning suburban residents who work downtown, while reducing inner-city local bus services and raising fares for the poor, the carless, and the recent immigrant. A lawsuit in Los Angeles, for example, following an effort to dramatically increase inner-city bus fares while reducing inner-city bus services and expanding suburban rail lines, alleged that the planning process was discriminatory and that the regional agency's distribution of funds was in violation of the 1964 Civil Rights Act.

Such problems result from the fact that the regional transportation decision-making process is increasingly dominated by an alliance of middle- and upper-income suburban residential communities and central-city businesses and landowners. Similarly, in transportation planning, like other planning sectors, the needs of the poor have little influence and are receiving little attention or resources.

Welfare reform has called special attention to problems of inequality in the allocation of transportation resources. Some believe that transportation problems will be among the most important barriers preventing current welfare recipients from entry into the paid workforce. Whether through increasing car ownership, by strengthening traditional transit routes, or by establishing special transportation services to link inner-city welfare recipients with suburban employment sites, the transportation needs of welfare recipients are forcing us to refocus our attention on transportation planning for the benefit of needy populations, as well as calling attention to the fact that, for too long and in too many ways, transportation planning has served the haves to a far greater extent than the have-nots. Transportation issues are becoming a focus for the environmental justice movement—a theme I expect to remain a major concern in transportation policymaking in the coming years.

Transportation as Multimodal

Universities have concentrated their transportation studies on the movements of people, especially at rush hours, between residence and workplace. Slowly we have broadened the study of transportation to include nonwork travel—for example, for shopping, social and recreational purposes, and personal business. Urban transportation planners have given surprisingly little attention to the movement of urban goods. Trucking contributes greatly to the urban economy, and truck movement directly affects the quality of urban life. Goods movement contributes disproportionately to urban congestion and environmental problems. Ports, airports, railroad yards, and other terminal facilities comprise a surprisingly large proportion of urban land and are the source of a large and growing proportion of urban trips. The task of the urban transportation planner is certainly evolving to include much greater concern for intermodal goods movement, as well as intercity and international passenger movement. Unfortunately, the state of our knowledge is much weaker with respect to these increasingly important components of urban transportation than it is to the more traditional subject of peak-hour commuting.

FAILURE TO REACH CONSENSUS

In the 1950s and 1960s there was widespread consensus that urban areas needed to expand highway networks, that the growing suburban population had to be served by new highways. Federal, state, and local resources were applied to the solution of this widely perceived problem, and the pace of highway construction was at an all-time high. Planners played an important role in the layout, design, sizing, and financing of the growing network of highways. Today, the sense of mission and the clarity of the commitment of transportation planners has given way to contention, argument, disagreement, and far less clarity as to what the professional transportation planner should be trying to achieve. Some still believe that system expansion is needed, that mobility is the overriding goal of the transportation planning enterprise. Others favor transit expansion as environmentally sensitive and acceptable, while opposing highway expansion. Still others believe the emphasis should be on maintenance of existing systems, but that expansion should be avoided. Further, many environmentalists argue that the principal goal of transportation planning should be energy conservation and reduction of air pollution and greenhouse gases. The lack of consensus among transportation planners and elected officials has led both to long, contentious debates and to a malaise that permeates the profession. One of the factors leading to limited productivity of new transportation innovations is the inability of decision-making bodies to concur on just what types of innovation are most needed at any particular place and time.

CONCLUSION

Nearly 50 years have passed since Harvey Perloff (1957) urged planning educators to think of the purpose of our field as "doing good . . . competently"—to aim, through graduate education in planning, at producing "generalists with a specialty." While I did not at first think of Perloff's early writings on planning education, it now seems to me that they are as timely today as they ever were. In my talk at MIT, I urged planning educators to consider transportation as an essential topic within planning education, but not to separate considerations of transportation from planning in general. To be an effective transportation planner, one must know a great deal about the specifics of transport technologies and programs in modern society, but at the same time be well versed in planning theory and methods. In addition, what clearly distinguishes a planning education for a career in transportation from approaches taken elsewhere in the university, including civil engineering, is the emphasis in the field of planning on making social and economic changes in the world. This also requires a curriculum that links knowledge and tools specific to the field of transportation with those generally applicable to the entire profession of planning.

16

Urban Transportation Planning

RALPH GAKENHEIMER

This is an exciting time for transportation planning from the viewpoint of the urban planning profession because the relationships between planning and transportation have increased dramatically in number and intensity during recent years.

Before this decade, those relationships tended to be limited and transient. The formulation of the land use/transportation equilibrium relationship in the 1950s was a moment of initial enthusiasm about the planning–transportation relationship, but the actual work had evolved into a technical activity dominated by a cadre of systems engineers. During the period of emphasis on the major U.S. urban transportation studies, the 1960s, there actually was little participation of urban planners in those studies and little transport planning taught in university planning departments. Also, for planners during the 1960s, the policy spotlight tended to shift toward pressing urban social problems and away from problems of physical mobility. During the 1970s, with the indications of poor performance of the land use–transportation equilibrium in planning by then well observed, there was a tendency in major studies to abandon the land-use dimension. At the same time, during that decade, there was the arrival of the perception of a transit or highway alternative; there was also a realization that not all the demand for auto mobility could be served, and there arose a more genuine commitment to public participation than earlier. These realities made the field considerably more complicated. During the 1980s, the gradual maturation of the environmental movement continued to bind transportation to urban planning in several ways. At each phase, the basic problem of travel forecasting has remained fundamental, but it has become only one function among many.

During the 1990s, one unexpected turn was that the land-use dimension reappeared on the agenda. After years of abandonment as an effort not productive in balancing travel demand with the intensity of land use, the more recent perspectives arose from the gradual strengthening of land development planning in the hands of actors concerned with growth management and attending to ecological hot spots. These have made for more compelling reasons in dealing with the transport/land relationship than the earlier, more abstract concern for equilibrium—which was hard to focus for implementation and never of great concern to the electorate at large, dear though it was to the hearts of planners. At this stage, the land-use dimension is engaged at the small scale by planners concerned with compact city and neotraditional planning objectives, as well as at the large scale by growth management and access management.

Now, the planning–transportation relationship is bound together by numerous ties—land development, social equity, land and water conservation, air quality, energy consumption, telecommunication impact on space, the greenhouse effect, even, once again, the ambition of metropolitan transportation and land-use equilibrium—which looks suspiciously like what was tried before with so little success. The challenge is up, and the opportunities for contribution are numerous.

Martin Wachs has arrayed ways that transportation planning has remained the same, and ways it has changed, during the last decades. He has shown that the pattern is quite different from other sectors of planning. I would like to respond by digging a bit deeper into some of these points.

It is remarkable how the basic elements of transportation planning have remained the same across time. Note, however, that it is especially the analytics of the field that have remained the same. The fundamental job of enhancing access has remained similar throughout, though several new perspectives have arisen in addition.

The continuity is partly attributable to the fact that the fundamental access objectives of transportation are fairly simple and have, for the most part, been achieved by adding facility capacity. Wachs adds the additional, important point that the financing is reasonably stable and independent. That is, of course, very important. We need only consider the path of housing as a planning sector under circumstances of great change in financial and programmatic backing to see a very different profile. Housing has, in some periods, dominated the planning field, but at other times, been nearly absent because of shifts in political commitment and financial support. Note that, while financial support for transportation has been stable (largely because of the major authorization legislation), public and political interest in transportation planning actually is quite variable. It tends to be the residual of the focus on currently topical planning issues. During the issue-free 1950s, transportation was politically important; during the socially committed 1960s, it was much less so.

Another stabilizing factor is that transport decisions usually are "lumpy"; that is, the scale of change is large for each decision. Unlike land-use policy, which is implemented parcel by parcel, transport project objectives are difficult to change in midstream. You cannot build a half-mile of highway and abandon it if plans change—which leads to a conservative tendency in the field. The current interest in automated highways, for example, is unlikely to take hold, simply because the magnitude of change all at once would be nearly impossible to achieve—equipping an entire corridor lane, plus equipping thousands of vehicles to use it. The consequence is that, as long as transportation planning is concerned only with the planning of large-scale facilities, it tends to be characterized by a different perspective which sometimes is unfriendly to urban planning. When transportation planning moves toward including more incremental elements, somewhat greater closure occurs between the fields.

For better or worse, the stability conveyed by the unitary leadership of the field should not be overlooked. The Transportation Research Board has convened the field and dominated its literature for more than 75 years (fully back to the beginning of any serious public planning). For almost 30 years, the U.S. Department of Transportation has set requirements for planning methods in considerable detail and largely fixed the field's research agenda.

Note that this unity of leadership is not characteristic of other countries. It is dramatically absent in the developing world, where the influence of various northern national engineering and planning guilds come and go— with the result that there is little tendency for any single perspective to mature over time. Rather, there is a tendency for each wave of new initiative to displace the previous one. But U.S.-style unitary leadership is also absent in Europe, where there has been considerably less focus on the modeling of demand as a basis for study, and more interest in trying innovative solutions. Liberation for the same measure of dominance by a national intellectual collegium can lead to more experimentation. In France, where most transportation research is done by employees of the national government, it is, nonetheless, more liberated from national policy than in the United States. This is suggested by the contrasting transportation vocabularies in French and English to describe roughly the same concepts. In the United States, terms often are from a government public relations–based vocabulary that suggests more what we wish the phenomena *were* than what they *are*. In French, it is often a simple statement of what it is, or sometimes an ideologically loaded assertion of what it ought to be. There is no real translation for the American phrase "community participation"; here, it is more likely to be called a "stakeholder movement." The French would not use *congestion pricing* to mean selling HOV space to paying users!

Transportation decision making has become extremely complicated. Under the circumstance of concern for mobility, environment, equity, employment, and urban economic development—all at the same time—there will likely be no majoritarian position on transportation. The result is to make urban projects very difficult to pursue. There have been virtually no major highways built in U.S. cities, except in the South and Southwest, since 1970. Even Boston's artery depression, which might have been easy as a kind of highway removal project, has had a hard time. For agreement of transportation actions of any kind, it is noticeable that the creation of a local culture is essential. Houston has become perhaps the most successful American city in the use of new telecommunications-based traffic management. It hasn't gone unnoticed there that success has been built on a high level of consensus on a planning style that agrees on crucial issues such as the role of public transport, the centrality of traffic operations in system planning, and the virtual exclusion of land-use planning. Similar coherence, based on an entirely different perspective, is evident in Portland, Oregon, where a highly focused concern for the environment has resulted in a remarkable degree of commitment to land development as a means of enhancing access and mobility. Few cities can marshal such civic cultures.

The result has been to turn the spotlight on traffic management—lately in the form of intelligent transportation systems—as an option. That may very well be a good thing, but in American transportation planning, there are grounds for saying it has been a refuge rather than an attraction, as is evident from its modest achievements.

Since all transportation planning is, in some sense, ultimately based on demand analysis, Wachs's comment on the increasing difficulty of demand forecast is both interesting and important. Lifestyle change and new telecommunications are at the root of it. Households are more cooperative now, with fewer traditional gender roles, while increasingly lean work environments enable workers to fill more functions, many of them requiring trips outside the workplace. Work trips are only 18 percent of the total because they are linked, both outbound and inbound, to several more service trips, but we still cannot deny that work trips are the defining ones (of destination and timing.) To put the package into a projection system, however, is very difficult. New telecommunications technologies also have a difficult path to track. Many trips will be replaced by communications, but for every one of them, new trips will be created—because communications are also used to make appointments! Internet shopping reduces trips to stores but increases the need for freight delivery.

As a result, it is more important than ever to balance quantitative with conceptual methodological skills. This is now an era of innovation on all sides. It is a challenging time to be a transportation planner.

17

U.S. Urban Environmental Planning

LEONARD ORTOLANO

A s late as 1960, the term environmental planning was little used. Even though the term is now used widely, no standard definition exists. For my purposes here, it involves actions that can restore or maintain environmental quality by controlling pollution, conserving resources, and guiding land use.[1] This encompasses much of what is taught in university courses on environmental planning,[2] although the content of these courses is highly variable.[3]

The field of environmental planning is highly fragmented. Environmental planners lack a professional organization bearing the name *environmental planning*, and there are no professional licensing requirements for practitioners in the United States. Many people engaged in environmental planning identify more closely with a traditional academic discipline or with their employment position than they do with environmental planning as a profession (Petulla 1987, 133–34). Although some university programs in urban planning and natural resources management have "concentrations" in environmental planning, many individuals who do environmental planning work were trained in other disciplines such as city planning, landscape architecture, biology, economics, and law. The following account of the evolution of environmental planning in U.S. urban areas helps explain why professionals engaged in environmental planning often do not identify with either the environmental planning profession or the city planning profession.

ENVIRONMENTAL REGULATION AND IMPACT ASSESSMENT

In the last half of the nineteenth century, efforts to improve public health in American cities centered on the implementation of engineering works.[4] Four

144

factors came together during that half-century to signal the beginning of sanitary engineering practice:

- ◻ *Public health surveys.* Beginning in 1850 with Lemuel Shattuck's survey of sanitary conditions in Massachusetts, public health specialists conducted systematic surveys that disclosed environmental conditions contributing to the spread of disease.[5]

- ◻ *Scientific breakthroughs.* Medical authorities and scientists demonstrated that drinking water can convey cholera, typhoid fever, and other diseases and that sewage often contains organisms that cause these diseases.

- ◻ *Water carriage sewerage.* During the 1850s, engineers (later called "sanitary engineers") began installing what was termed *water carriage sewerage*, sewers "sloped to facilitate gravity flow of waterborne wastes [and stormwater runoff] to outfall points located beyond the immediate environment of the urban dweller" (Peterson 1983, 15).[6]

- ◻ *Advances in water treatment.* Sanitary engineers demonstrated the efficacy of water filtration and other procedures designed to enhance the safety of public water supplies.

REGULATING WATER POLLUTION

With the creation of the Massachusetts Board of Health in 1869, efforts to control water pollution began in earnest. Physicians and sanitary engineers working at state and local boards of health played key roles in drafting water pollution control regulations. By 1910, only 4 percent of the nation's population had its wastewater treated.[7] The management strategy preferred by sanitary engineers was to rely on the ability of natural waters to assimilate organic waste. The operative phrase was "dilution is the solution to pollution." This dilution approach often proved ineffective, and the need for wastewater treatment became increasingly apparent. By 1939, about half the nation's municipal wastewater was treated. The locus of water pollution control activity remained at the state and local levels until 1956, when major federal water quality laws were first enacted.[8] Between 1956 and 1987, federal water quality laws established (among other things) subsidies for municipal treatment works, requirements for states to set standards for natural waterways, federally imposed standards governing the release of municipal and industrial wastewater, and a national wastewater discharge permit system. Since 1956, the responsibility for regulating water pollution has been shared by federal, state, and local governments; and by the 1990s, after nearly a half-century of major investment and effort, great progress had been made in reducing water pollution from point sources, such as wastewater release from municipalities and factories.

Much less success has resulted from efforts to control *non-point* (or diffuse) sources of water pollution, such as stormwater from urban and industrial areas, as well as runoff from construction sites, farms, mining operations, and logging areas. Slow progress in controlling non-point sources has resulted in part because non-point source pollution can be managed most efficiently at the watershed level; but agencies and governments with pollution control authorities typically operate at the city, county, state, and federal levels. Coordination among agencies on non–point-source water pollution control often is a massive problem because the agencies involved frequently have conflicting agendas and priorities.[9] Some attempts to improve the handling of non–point-source problems have involved *watershed planning*. The central idea here is to conduct planning at the level of a watershed (as opposed to a city or a county) so as to improve coordination and enhance the efficiency of non–point-source control efforts.[10]

Cities contribute to the non-point source water pollution problem, in that urban runoff, which often is heavily contaminated, passes untreated into local bodies of water. A modest step toward managing pollution from urban runoff was taken with passage of the 1987 amendments to the federal Clean Water Act. These amendments require cities to obtain national discharge permits for releases from storm drains. Many older cities contribute to the non-point source water pollution problem in a second way. In an estimated 1,100 communities, both stormwater and wastewater flow in the same sewer network. During a heavy rainfall, flow in these sewer systems can overload the capacity of municipal treatment plants and degrade water quality significantly.[11]

AIR QUALITY MANAGEMENT

The history of air quality management in the United States dates back to the late nineteenth and early twentieth centuries when industrial cities such as Chicago and Pittsburgh passed local ordinances to control discharges of smoke and soot.[12] The locus of air quality management responsibilities remained at the municipal level until well after World War II. With passage of the Clean Air Act of 1963, the federal government entered as a significant force in regulating air emissions from smokestacks. Later in the 1960s, the federal government began regulating emissions from motor vehicles. Since then, the federal government has shared air quality management responsibilities with state and local governments. By the early 1990s, the regulatory focus had expanded to include regional and global air quality problems such as acid rain and stratospheric ozone depletion.[13]

In recent years, the federal government has introduced *market-based schemes* to complement traditional methods for regulating air quality. The most ambitious of these is the tradable permit system used as a centerpiece of the acid rain provisions in the Clean Air Act Amendments of 1990. In this system, electric utility companies with coal-fired power plants receive tradable sulfur dioxide (SO_2) emission allowances each year. An SO_2 emission allowance grants a utility permission to emit one ton of SO_2 during one year. A utility that cuts SO_2 emissions below the level permitted by its allowances can sell its excess allowances. The market forces put in motion by this trading scheme have led to dramatic reductions in the cost of meeting SO_2 reduction targets in the Clean Air Act Amendments of 1990. Moreover, the success of the program has led to numerous applications of tradable permits and other market-based pollution control programs.[14]

Many air pollution problems involve the relationship between land use, transportation, and air quality. For example, land-use plans that separate housing by long distances from workplaces frequently lead to increased air pollution. This is illustrated by the "jobs–housing imbalance," a term used to describe a city with a housing stock that does not come close to accommodating the number of people who work there. For example, cities in Silicon Valley in California suffer from a significant jobs–housing imbalance, and many workers have little choice but to commute long distances. Most of these commuters go to and from work by driving alone, and their collective contribution to air pollution is significant. Moreover, low-density housing developments that contain few retail services within walking distance compel many Silicon Valley residents to rely on motor vehicles for practically all their shopping needs.[15]

As a consequence of links between land-use plans and motor vehicle emissions, many regional air quality agencies have implemented regulations that are de facto land-use controls. This is illustrated by programs of the South Coast Air Quality Management District (SCAQMD), which operates in California's Los Angeles, Orange, and Riverside counties. SCAQMD's programs involving "emission reduction credits" and tradable pollution permits influence firms' decisions regarding the location, expansion, and closure of their facilities.[16] In addition, links between land use, transportation, and air quality have led air quality management agencies to implement programs encouraging people to cut back on their auto usage—for example, by carpooling or by using public transit.

REGULATING SOLID AND HAZARDOUS WASTE

The regulation of hazardous waste in the United States began only recently. Although some guidelines from the 1940s cautioned that municipal landfills could be a source of groundwater contamination,[17] it was not until the 1970s that contamination of groundwater by hazardous substances received wide attention. Key sources of contamination included municipal landfills; pits, ponds, and lagoons used by industry to dispose of hazardous waste; and leaking tanks storing chemicals and liquid wastes. The public outcry over contamination from these sources led Congress to develop an elaborate system for managing hazardous waste.[18]

The history of federal hazardous waste management began with the U.S. Resource Conservation and Recovery Act (RCRA), which was enacted in 1976.[19] Until passage of the Act, the collection, transport, and disposal of solid and hazardous waste in the United States had been managed by local authorities. Even though federal air and water quality laws of the early 1970s contained provisions governing toxic substances, those provisions were not implemented effectively. The pre-RCRA federal legislation pertaining to solid waste— the Solid Waste Disposal Act of 1965—did not directly regulate hazardous waste.

RCRA (and its amendments) regulates currently active hazardous waste storage, treatment and disposal sites, and current solid and hazardous waste streams. The law also restricts the types of materials that can be deposited at municipal waste disposal sites. Four years after enacting RCRA, Congress passed the Comprehensive Environmental Responsibility, Compensation and Liability Act of 1980 (CERCLA), which contains rules governing liability for cleaning up hazardous material from contaminated sites. CERCLA also provides for federal cleanups at selected sites using money from a trust fund (the "Superfund"). Many states have followed the federal lead by establishing counterparts to federal laws regulating hazardous materials.

As a result of widespread public concern over adverse health effects linked to solid and hazardous waste, the siting of new waste disposal facilities has become extraordinarily difficult. The "not in my backyard" (NIMBY) syndrome results from citizens who oppose having hazardous waste facilities located near their homes and workplaces. (More generally, the syndrome applies to many "locally unwanted land uses," or "LULUs," including nuclear power plants, airports, and drug rehabilitation centers.) Many states have responded to NIMBY problems by enacting siting laws to cope with public opposition to hazardous waste facilities (for example, measures to compensate "host communities"). Some of these laws try to overcome the NIMBY syndrome by requiring use of mediation and related dispute-resolution procedures to help proponents of waste disposal projects and affected parties reach consensus on proposals for siting facilities.

The increased public scrutiny of decisions on the siting of hazardous waste facilities was accompanied by widespread recognition that communities of racial and ethnic minorities contain a disproportionate share of these facilities. During the 1980s, the focus on this inequitable facility-siting inspired a grassroots movement aimed at securing environmental justice. The movement's concerns included (in addition to the above-noted siting issue) the disproportionate exposure of low-income and minority communities to toxics and the poor enforcement of environmental laws in those communities.[20] In response to charges of environmental injustice, environmental agencies have conducted numerous studies such as the comparative risk assessments organized by the U.S. Environmental Protection Agency (1992). Despite the increased attention given to equity issues by environmental agencies, concerns over the fairness of hazardous waste siting decisions have persisted and fueled grassroots opposition to proposed hazardous waste facilities.

An unintended outcome of the federal laws regulating hazardous waste is "the brownfields issue." *Brownfields* have been defined as

> abandoned, idled, or underused industrial and commercial sites where expansion or redevelopment is complicated by real or perceived environmental contamination that can add cost, time, or uncertainty to a redevelopment project. (Region 5 of the U.S. Environmental Protection Agency, as quoted by Davis and Margolis 1997, 5)

Brownfields are closely linked to CERCLA because potential developers of brownfield sites fear that they can be held liable for cleaning up those sites. Banks and other lending institutions share this concern. As a consequence, great numbers of contaminated commercial and industrial sites—many in central cities and inner suburbs—are underutilized.[21]

The brownfields issue is especially pertinent to inner-city areas where the presence of brownfields has stymied urban redevelopment efforts. Costs extend beyond the loss of new jobs and tax revenues for cities. The existence of brownfields also encourages urban sprawl, as developers bypass brownfield sites in urban areas in favor of uncontaminated ("greenfield") sites on the outskirts of cities.

ENVIRONMENTAL IMPACT ASSESSMENT

Although careful, empirically based arguments for assessing the environmental effects of proposed development projects were made in 1864 by George Perkins Marsh, a pioneering physical geographer, such assessments were not required until passage of the U.S. National Environmental Policy Act of 1969 (NEPA).[22]

While this act contains numerous provisions, it is best known for stipulating that when a federal agency makes a decision that can significantly affect "the quality of the human environment," that agency must prepare preliminary environmental impact studies (referred to in regulations implementing

NEPA as "environmental assessments").[23] Based on results from these pre-liminary studies, the agency may need to develop a full "environmental im-pact statement" and circulate it for comment by citizens, agencies and other parties affected by the agency's action. This process has expanded public access to information about environmental impacts of proposed federal ac-tions and provided interested parties with new ways to influence agency deci-sion making.

Because NEPA concerns actions by federal agencies, its influence on projects in urban areas is limited. NEPA does not apply to projects initiated by private developers or nonfederal agencies unless there is a "federal handle," such as a federal grant, loan, license, or permit. For example, NEPA has influenced urban highways subsidized by federal funds, urban housing projects that received federal loans, and airports that required federal approval.

The National Environmental Policy Act has inspired many state-level versions of NEPA, several of which apply to decisions by state and local gov-ernments. In California, for example, the state NEPA extends to actions by city and county governments (for example, zoning changes) and thus requires environmental impact assessments for private development projects that have a significant impact.

Despite their nearly 30 years of history, environmental impact assess-ment requirements remain controversial. Critics argue that many assessments for individual projects are inconsequential because they are conducted long after key project decisions are made, and because recommendations in envi-ronmental impact statements (such as recommendations for impact mitiga-tion measures) are often ignored without penalty.

In addition to institutionalizing procedures for conducting environmental impact assessments, NEPA and the state NEPAs have caused many public and private organizations responding to assessment requirements to reorganize their planning procedures, hire environmental professionals, increase citizen participation in their planning, and incorporate environmental values in their decision making. Such changes in the structure and processes of organiza-tions may be as important as the environmental impact assessment docu-ments produced for particular projects.[24]

RESOURCES CONSERVATION

Any examination of the resources conservation dimension of environmental planning must consider the ideas promoted by Gifford Pinchot, head of the U.S. Forest Service in Theodore Roosevelt's administration and a key figure in the history of natural resource conservation. For Pinchot, resource con-servation meant both the efficient use of natural resources and the prevention of waste. His development-oriented perspective represented the only conception of conservation within many federal and state resource management agencies before 1960.

During the 1960s, public opinion was much affected by Rachel Carson's widely read book, *Silent Spring*, which warned of the damage to ecosystems from pesticide use. The public was also much influenced by extensive media coverage of environmental disasters such as the Santa Barbara oil spill. Many citizens came to believe that the natural environment was more than a resource to be placed at the disposal of economic development.

By the early 1970s, the public had become frustrated with the lack of action by government to improve environmental quality. Indeed, the government itself—with its new highways, power plants, and other infrastructure projects—was widely viewed as part of the problem. As a result of the change in public sentiment that occurred in the 1960s and 1970s, many Americans embraced environmentalism as a core value, and Pinchot's conception of conservation as the wise and efficient use of resources was no longer the only widely held view of conservation.[25] Indeed, many people were influenced by books such as *Limits to Growth* and *Small Is Beautiful*, which argue that the earth's finite resources impose natural bounds on population growth and economic development.[26] Instruction on the importance of preserving natural systems and the value of recycling even began to be widely promoted in schools (kindergarten through high school), as well as in colleges and universities.

Efforts to conserve resources in the urban context are illustrated by the numerous municipal recycling programs implemented since the 1970s. Shortages in the space available to accommodate solid waste have led many municipalities to implement curbside collection of newspaper, glass, and other recyclables. Some cities have arranged to collect lawn clippings and other organic yard waste from households for transport to municipal compost centers. Citizen participation in municipal recycling programs (which is voluntary) has been strong because many people have accepted the view that recycling and reuse of materials is an important, socially valued activity.

Short-term shortages of resources have prompted the establishment of many resource conservation programs. Consider, for example, actions taken during the oil crisis of 1973. Long lines at gasoline pumps, increased gas prices, and public awareness of the nation's vulnerability to actions by oil-rich nations led to the demand (albeit short-lived) for energy-efficient motor vehicles. In addition, much attention was given to alternative forms of energy (for example, solar energy), and to "superinsulated" homes and energy-efficient home appliances. Many architects have responded to energy conservation pressures by incorporating solar energy in structures they design. In addition, several communities have adopted "solar access zoning, which prevents structures or trees from being placed in such a position that they block the direct access of other buildings to the sun" (Levy 1997, 280).

Other short-term resource shortages have led to major conservation efforts. For instance, severe droughts typically have caused water agencies to promote water conservation measures such as leak prevention and the use of drought-tolerant landscaping, low-flow shower heads, and low-flush toilets. Similarly, farmers and companies using large quantities of water have responded to droughts by implementing water-saving measures.

In some states, the importance of resource conservation has been recognized by legislation that mandates planning for resource conservation. For example, the California legislature passed the Urban Water Management Planning Act in 1983, a law requiring cities to create plans for evaluating options for water conservation and reclamation. A decade later, California enacted the Water Conservation in Landscaping Act, which requires local agencies to prepare ordinances that promote efficient water use in landscaping. Cities and counties throughout the state have responded to these laws (and others) by implementing programs to use highly treated municipal wastewater for landscaping, agricultural crop irrigation, and some industrial processes.[27]

Since the 1980s, resource conservation has been practiced extensively in the private sector. These practices, often grouped under the label "pollution prevention" (or "cleaner production"), include reducing the amount of waste generated by redesigning products or production processes. As an example, electroplating factories can reduce the chemical wastes they generate simply by collecting plating chemicals that drip off metal parts before they are transferred to rinsing baths. Pollution prevention includes materials recycling and reuse, as well as water and energy conservation.

For a number of reasons, companies have been motivated to embrace pollution prevention as a corporate goal: the high cost of dealing with increasingly stringent regulations, fear of liability for the remediation of sites contaminated with hazardous waste, the problem of finding reasonably priced ways of disposing of hazardous waste, and the recognition that profits can be enhanced by conserving water and energy and by recovering and reusing materials. The potential to enhance profits is even explicit in the name of one of the most widely known corporate programs: "Pollution Prevention Pays" (the 3M Company). Many firms have conducted environmental audits to identify opportunities for pollution prevention and to assess and improve their compliance with environmental regulations. In addition to conducting environmental audits, firms are engaging in a variety of related activities, including risk assessments, product life-cycle assessments, and environmentally sensitive product design. ISO 14000, a series of voluntary environmental management standards issued by the International Standards Organization in the mid-1990s, have guided many such private-sector activities.

Planners can play an important role in promoting pollution prevention and other environmentally friendly business practices. The work done in Oregon by Portland's energy office, in creating the program "Business for an Environmentally Sustainable Tomorrow" (BEST), is an example. Its activities include "providing educational and technical services; . . . serving as a broker between businesses and other agencies and offices with relevant expertise . . . [providing] free energy efficiency design analysis; [and] helping companies set up recycling programs. . . ." (Beatley 1995, 386).

LAND USE

The land-use dimension of environmental planning includes several distinct elements: land-use control, urban open space, environmentally based land-use planning, neotraditional planning, and transit-oriented development.

CONTROLS

Since the 1920s, local zoning ordinances have been used extensively to control the use of private land in the United States. For decades, however, zoning ordinances failed to restrict development in environmentally sensitive natural areas. During the 1950s, geographers and other environmental professionals began documenting the adverse effects of building in floodplains and wetlands.[28] Although the case against building in floodplains related largely to the mounting toll of flood losses (despite massive investments in flood-control projects), arguments for limiting development in wetlands centered on their value as ecological resources. Initial efforts by local governments to regulate development in floodplains and wetlands often were challenged in court; but, by the 1980s, the constitutionality of these regulations was widely accepted.

Controls on private development took on new forms in the 1960s, when communities as diverse as Petaluma (California), Boulder (Colorado), and Boca Raton (Florida) established programs for controlling the *timing* of development, not just its location. While these local growth-management programs embraced traditional objectives, such as maintaining a balanced housing supply, some programs included environmental objectives such as preserving prime agricultural land and open space. Growth-management techniques used by communities included such innovations as a limit on the number of residential units constructed each year and the requirement that a new development be within prescribed "urban limit lines."

Government attempts to regulate private land were extended when regional organizations were created with the power to restrict land use based on environmental grounds. For example, the California legislature created the San Francisco Bay Conservation and Development Commission (BCDC) in 1965 to control development along the edge of San Francisco Bay. The BCDC soon began blocking projects that involved filling in wetlands along the Bay. As another example, the Tahoe Regional Planning Agency (TRPA) was formed in 1969 to control development in cities and counties within the Lake Tahoe basin on the California–Nevada border. The TRPA developed an ordinance restricting the fraction of a land parcel that could be covered based on a number of environmental factors, including landslide hazard, water table elevation, soil erodibility, and the fragility of flora and fauna. Planning studies used as a basis for regulating development in the Lake Tahoe basin were widely cited for their innovative applications of land-suitability studies and carrying-capacity analysis.

The 1970s also witnessed the emergence of a "quiet revolution in land use control" as states created new institutions to cope with urban sprawl and the loss of environmental amenities outside densely settled areas.[29] States enacted laws creating statewide planning programs. Examples include Vermont's Environmental Control Act (1970), which established a statewide permit program for major land development projects, and the California Coastal Zone Conservation Act (1972), which called for plans to conserve the coastal zone and imposed new building permit requirements. Statewide land-use legislation continued into the 1980s, with passage of Florida's Local Government Comprehensive Planning and Land Development Regulation Act (1985), among others.[30]

Governments' ability to control the use of private land has increasingly come under scrutiny since the 1980s. Many jurisdictions have been sued by property owners who claimed their constitutional rights under the Fifth Amendment had been violated by regulatory action. A clause in the Fifth Amendment to the U.S. Constitution reads: ". . . nor shall private property be taken for public use without just compensation." The "regulatory taking issue" involves cases in which environmental and land-use regulations that provided public benefits are alleged to constitute the de facto taking of private property, which requires compensation under the Fifth Amendment. Although the legitimacy of governments' ability to restrict land use without compensating owners had not been debated extensively in decades, the U.S. Supreme Court revisited the issue in 1978, in *Penn Central Transportation Company v. New York City*. Since then, the Court and U.S. Congress have struggled to work out an acceptable balance between regulating land use to satisfy public needs and allowing landowners to exercise their property rights.[31]

OPEN SPACE

American cities have a long history of preserving open space, as demonstrated by the many colonial-era town squares and village greens in New

England. Three aspects of urban open space planning are notable because of their strong link to environmental quality issues: creation of parks and parkways in metropolitan areas, private efforts to preserve public open space, and the rehabilitation of ecosystems within cities.

Many of the most famous parks in American cities were created during the second half of the nineteenth century, a time when park planning was linked to the broader movement to improve sanitary conditions in urban areas. At that time, large vegetated expanses in cities were thought to improve public health, in addition to uplifting people's spirits. The link between urban parks and the health of city dwellers was promoted by Frederick Law Olmsted, Sr., one of the leading figures in the history of landscape architecture in the United States. Although Olmsted's arguments for urban parks included other elements (for example, the value of parks in providing businessmen with refreshment from the rigors of commerce), he emphasized the public health benefits of parks. His position is illustrated by the following excerpt from a presentation to the American Social Science Association in 1870:

> Air is disinfected by sunlight and foliage. Foliage also acts mechanically to purify the air by screening it. Opportunity and inducement to escape at frequent intervals from the confined and vitiated air of the commercial quarter, and to supply the lungs with air screened and purified by trees, and recently acted upon by sunlight. . . . [I]f these could be supplied economically, our problem would be solved. (Olmsted, as reprinted in Le Gates and Stout 1996, 339)

Working with his partner, the English-born architect Calvert Vaux, Olmsted laid out a series of parks and parkways that have inspired generations of landscape architects and city planners. Olmsted is most widely known for his work in creating New York's Central Park, but his contributions to the park systems of Boston, Chicago, Louisville, and other American cities are also widely celebrated.

During the early twentieth century, the emphasis shifted away from parks on the grand scale of Central Park to neighborhood-level parks and playgrounds.[32] In addition, greenbelts along roadways (sometimes called "parkways") became an important element of park systems within urban areas. Starting in the 1950s, parklike settings were created within the context of new office developments in metropolitan areas.[33] The pacesetter—Research Triangle Park, in North Carolina—was created in 1953. Each leaseholder in the park was required to develop its site to satisfy constraints on open space, drainage, and slope. In addition, lessees were required to meet performance standards that limited noise, vibrations, and odors, as well as air and water pollution.

As American suburbs multiplied during the 1950s and 1960s, loss of open space within metropolitan areas took on new political significance. A number of influential organizations—for example, Resources for the Future, and the Urban Land Institute—prepared reports characterizing the growing loss of urban open space.[34] In addition, in 1958, Congress created the Outdoor Recreation Resources Review Commission (ORRRC), and in the 1960s, Congress established funding programs designed to help governments at all levels acquire open space. During the 1960s, many local and regional organizations—conservation commissions and regional park and open-space districts—were formed to acquire open space in metropolitan areas.

Private organizations often play a key role in conserving open space in metropolitan areas.[35] In recent decades, hundreds of local and regional land trusts have been formed to create conservation easements and acquire private land for public purposes.[36] The number of local and regional land trusts grew from about 130 in the mid-1960s to nearly 1,100 in 1994.[37] These organizations have purchased land varying in type from riparian corridors and ecologically significant habitats to farm and ranch lands.

Land trusts have also been advocates for environmentally sensitive land-use planning. For example, the Brunswick–Topsham Land Trust in Maine played a leading role in causing the local town council to adopt a conservation-oriented land-use plan. And the Hillside Trust in Cincinnati conducted sophisticated planning studies to advise local government and developers on how development could proceed in sensitive hillside areas.

In addition to preserving open space, many groups have been working to restore or "rehabilitate" ecosystems within cities and suburbs. For example, Urban Ecology, a nongovernmental organization founded during the 1970s in Berkeley, California, has worked to bring back part of a creek that had been culverted and covered for more than 80 years. Rather than return ecosystems to a natural baseline condition in which people are, in a sense, excluded from nature, many ecosystem rehabilitation projects accommodate people and consider management of ecosystems for multiple uses as a more appropriate goal than restoration to a historic benchmark condition. For example, some communities have converted garbage dumps into local parks, and many grassroots organizations have rehabilitated local streams and wetlands in ways that accommodate multiple uses.[38]

ENVIRONMENTALLY BASED LAND-USE PLANNING

Frederick Law Olmsted is best known for his design of urban parks and park systems, but his design of communities that take advantage of natural features is also notable. The Chicago suburb of Riverside, designed by Olmsted and Vaux, has curvilinear street patterns, is sensitive to the local topography, and includes extensive areas of open space. It was admired by Ebenezer Howard, whose 1898 book, *Garden Cities of To-morrow,* had an enormous impact on later efforts to integrate nature into cities, to create greenbelts around cities, and to develop self-contained "garden cities" outside of central cities.

Another key figure in the history of environmentally based land-use planning is Patrick Geddes, a Scot trained in biology whose *Cities in Evolution* and other writings (early in this century) continue to influence urban and regional planners. Following World War II, the ideas of Geddes and others led some landscape architects to integrate ecological parameters into their plans for both small parcels and large tracts of land.[39] The cause of integrating ecology into landscape design was advanced considerably with the publication of landscape architect Ian McHarg's *Design with Nature.* McHarg (1969) argues that a study of the geophysical and biological properties of a land area can reveal the most suitable uses for a particular parcel (in this context, "suitability" is based largely on geophysical and biological criteria).

McHarg's study procedure—which he calls "the ecological planning method"—involves the following steps:

❑ Preparation of spatial inventories, in which the slope, soil type, vegetation, and other attributes of different parcels are mapped, with a separate map created for each attribute

❑ Delineation of land-suitability criteria (criteria indicating the geophysical and biological attributes that could best accommodate different types of land uses)

❑ Superimposition of inventory maps for the various attributes to obtain a composite map

❑ Analysis of the composite map, using the land-suitability criteria[40]

McHarg and his associates at Wallace, McHarg, Roberts and Todd, employed this planning strategy in studies for numerous urban areas, including Staten Island, lower Manhattan, and the inner harbor area of Baltimore. The strategy was also used in the creation of The Woodlands, a new town outside Houston, Texas. Similar planning strategies undertaken under various names—for example, "land suitability analysis"—have been applied by many others.[41]

Technologies created during the past few decades have made it easier to perform the kinds of studies detailed in *Design with Nature.* In particular, advances in the use of satellite imagery and other remote-sensing techniques have made it simpler to compile data on physical and biological parameters. In addition, the widespread use of Geographic Information Systems has made it possible to superimpose maps conveniently by computer.

THE NEW URBANISM AND
TRANSIT-ORIENTED DEVELOPMENT

In 1990, the average American urban dweller traveled more than 11,000 kilometers by automobile.[42] For urbanites on other continents, the comparable figures are as follows: Australia, 6,600 kilometers; Europe, 4,500 km.; and Asia, 1,500 km. At the same time, the average urban dweller in the United States traveled only 475 kilometers by mass transit in 1990, compared to 882 km. in Australia, and more than 1,900 km. traveled by city dwellers in Europe and Asia. The environmental damage from this dependence on autos includes problems such as urban sprawl and its destruction of prime farming land and natural landscapes, photochemical smog that can be primarily attributable to auto emissions, and many other traffic-related impacts such as noise, neighborhood severance, and visual intrusion (Kenworthy and Laube 1996, 280).

Recently, some architects and city planners have promoted styles of development that recognize the intimate relationship between land use, transportation, and environmental quality. For example, Peter Calthorpe has advocated (and built) development projects that he refers to as "pedestrian pockets," mixed-use developments within a short distance of a transit station. These 50- to 100-acre zones include housing, offices, retail services, day-care centers, recreation, and parks (Calthorpe 1989).

Pedestrian pockets are an example of "transit-oriented development"; and Bernick and Cervero (1996) provide numerous others. Pedestrian pockets are also illustrative of what has recently been referred to as the "New Urbanism" or "neotraditional planning." Spokespersons for the new urbanism include Andres Duany and Elizabeth Plater-Zybeck. A widely cited example of the neotraditional planning approach is a Duany and Plater-Zyberk project begun in 1982: the Traditional New Development of Seaside, Florida. The project involves about 200 homes as well as civic and commercial buildings on 80 acres of coastland. Like Calthorpe's pedestrian pockets, the emphasis at Seaside is on encouraging residents to reduce their dependence on autos.

CHALLENGES FACED BY
ENVIRONMENTAL PLANNERS

Despite notable progress in improving urban environmental quality, significant challenges remain, especially in the context of efforts to create sustainable cities. Since the 1980s, the word sustainable has been used widely as part of an international discourse on "sustainable" development, but there is little agreement on the meaning of *sustainable*.[43] The one thing most definitions of sustainable development have in common is the obligation to avoid "compromising the ability of future generations to meet their own needs."[44] The discourse on sustainable development—which often centers on the development programs of nations, regions, or particular economic sectors—has been extended to cities. In the urban context, the term *sustainable communities* (or synonyms such as *eco-cities*) is often used. According to Beatley,[45]

> *Sustainable communities* . . . strive to reduce resource consumption (e.g., energy, water) and the generation of wastes (e.g., air pollution, solid waste) and seek to promote, as well, greater liveability and social equity. The concept of sustainable communities lends support for a number of specific urban and regional policies and programs, including these: promoting more efficient compact and contiguous development patterns; reducing dependence on the automobile and promoting greater use of mass transit and other alternative modes of transportation; and promoting mixed-use development and infill growth. (Beatley 1994, 44; emphasis added)

Environmental planners face the challenge of making sustainable cities more than a concept. Measures (or indexes) of sustainability need to be created, and analysis methods and planning strategies need to be developed to operationalize the sustainable cities idea. William Rees and Mathis Wackernagel,[46] for example, recast the question posed in analyzing the *carrying capacity* of cities by asking, "How large an area of productive land is needed to sustain a defined population indefinitely, *wherever on earth that land is located?*" (Rees and Wackernagel 1996a, 227; emphasis in original). They answer this question by estimating "the area of land/water required to produce sustainably the quantity of any resource or ecological service used by a defined population or economy at a given level of technology" (Rees and Wackernagel 1996a, 227). This area is called the *ecological footprint.*

Results from an analysis of Vancouver, Canada, illustrate the ecological footprint concept. Rees and Wackernagel (1996a, 233) estimate, conservatively, that the 472,000 people living in Vancouver (as of 1991) require about 2 million hectares of land for their exclusive use to maintain their consumption pattern. Since Vancouver occupies only about 11,400 hectares, the city requires a land area nearly 180 times its size to support its activities. The authors maintain:

> Cities necessarily "appropriate" the ecological output and life support functions of distant regions all over the world through commercial trade and natural biogeochemical cycles. . . . *No city or urban region can achieve sustainability on its own.* (Rees and Wackernagel 1996a, 236; emphasis in original)

In other words, any analysis of sustainable cities must investigate how cities rely on hinterlands as sources of material, energy, and water, and as sinks for the waste products of urban activities. While recognizing that sustainability analysis includes socioeconomic issues unrelated to the natural environment per se, Rees and Wackernagel (1996b, 134) argue that ecological footprint analysis can be used to measure progress in achieving *ecological sustainability*, which they take to mean living "within the means of nature."

The challenges to the city-planning profession represent opportunities for planning educators. Currently, many graduate programs in urban and regional planning offer courses in environmental planning for planning students who choose to specialize in that field. To the extent that these programs can strengthen their offerings in environmental planning, their graduates will be better able to meet the sorts of challenges outlined above. Graduate programs in urban planning would provide a notable public service by making environmental planning a core component of the education of *all* their students, not just those specializing in environmental planning.

18

Environmental Planning:
The Changing Demands of Effective Practice

Lawrence Susskind

There is substantial overlap between the work of environmental engineers and environmental planners. They both must know how to inventory natural resources, although historically planners have focused more on the use of land, while civil (now environmental) engineers have focused on managing water supply and quality. Both have, for almost 30 years, been involved in assessing the environmental impacts of development, although the planners usually have an added responsibility for social impact assessment as required under various federal and state impact assessment statutes. Planners, it seems to me, have taken more responsibility, especially in the past 10 years, for finding ways to reduce or manage the risks associated with development (particularly the siting of new facilities) and for encouraging sustainability; whereas engineers have emphasized the assessment of risk. This difference gets to the heart of the dichotomy between environmental planners and environmental engineers: planners are more comfortable dealing with the politics of environmental decision making and helping groups deal with their disagreements when trade-offs have to be made.

These distinctions have consequences for what planners (as opposed to engineers) need to know, although there probably will continue to be overlap between the two.

INVENTORYING NATURAL RESOURCES

These days, most planning schools invest substantial class time (and a disproportionate share of their financial resources) in teaching Geographic Information Systems (GIS). Computer-based techniques for natural resource mapping and multimedia tools for tracking changes in the physical environment are expanding rapidly. Environmental planners need to know how to use both the hardware and the software associated with GIS, particularly as they relate to land-based inventories.

Of course, merely displaying and tracking changes in natural systems is not sufficient. Planners also will be expected to interpret these changes as well as to forecast the direction in which the changes are likely to move in the future. Ecological or landscape analysis has evolved rapidly since the early days of McHargian manually prepared overlays. Now, planners must be able to use sophisticated image enhancement and projection techniques to present easy-to-read representations of complex changes in the natural environment that local, regional, state, and even global decision makers can use in making policy.

Environmental planners also need to know how to calculate the economic value of environmental "costs" and "benefits." This is no easy task. Resource economists are still debating the best techniques to use. The emergence of ecological economics—a different technique entirely—has further confused matters. While the debate goes on, a number of states are enacting legislation requiring various petitioners to assess the economic value of the environmental damage that cannot be mitigated at various contaminated sites. Thus, even though the theoretical and methodological issues are as yet unresolved, planners must be able to move forward. This requires an understanding of the debates and an ability to apply classical microeconomic concepts at the heart of cost-benefit analysis.

Environmental planners need to know a great deal about the changing natural resource base available to various kinds of communities and how to appraise the asset value of these endowments. They do not, however, need to be ecologists, aquatic biologists, or landscape architects. They do not have to become economists. They do not need programming skills sufficient to design new GIS software (although some will pick these up along the way). Instead, they need to be informed consumers of these specialized skills and tools.

ASSESSING THE IMPACTS OF DEVELOPMENT

Since the adoption of the National Environmental Policy Act in the United States and its state and international "offspring," planners have been involved in preparing environmental impact assessments. These extensive efforts to forecast and avoid the adverse impacts of development are a formidable representation of the institutionalization of environmental planning. Not only do EIA requirements stipulate that planning for all large-scale development and infrastructure projects that receive any federal or state money must consider alternatives (including a "no build" option), they also require careful analysis of a wide range of environmental and social impacts (and ways of mitigating them)—along with the involvement of all relevant stakeholders in the scoping of such analyses and the interpretation of findings. On the other hand, the fact that most EIAs are used to justify decisions already made, rather than to look closely at genuine alternatives, contributes to the sense of powerlessness that many planning professionals tend to feel.

Along with impact assessment has come growth in risk assessment. While there is no parallel piece of legislation requiring that risk assessments be prepared before federal, state, and local environmental policies can be adopted, risk-based approaches to the formulation of regulation and the consideration of policy options are increasingly prominent. Today, risk assessment must also incorporate consideration of risk perception. As it turns out, the way various segments of society view risk is as important as the mathematical calculation of the level of danger or hazard involved.

More traditionally, municipal planning still entails a review of the likely impacts of land development. Whether under the banner of growth management or as part of a system for calculating exactions, local developers increasingly are required to present forecasts of the impacts (usually meaning costs) associated with projects or changes in land use that they propose.

Preparing such forecasts involves more than merely modeling the trends involved. Assumptions have to be made about the counterintuitive impacts of complex systems and the interaction of multiple levels of activity—from local to global.

FINDING WAYS TO MANAGE THE RISKS

Having produced the various analyses described above, environmental planners are expected to be able to formulate and help implement strategies for managing the risks associated with new development, particularly those mitigating the toxic impact of residuals of various kinds. This involves designing regulatory regimes and implementing institutional arrangements that will ensure adequate monitoring and compliance.

Regulatory action still includes the preparation of plans of various kinds (that is, land-use and zoning ordinances), but it also covers the setting of a wide range of public health and environmental protection standards, including guidelines for the use and cleanup of different types of toxins. Old regulatory strategies that rely on command-and-control are being supplemented by more elaborate "market-oriented" techniques for shaping corporate and individual behavior. With each approach, however, the setting and enforcement of standards remains central to the tasks of environmental planning.

ASSISTING GROUPS, COMMUNITIES, AND NETWORKS

The three tasks just described must often be undertaken in a highly charged political context. Indeed, one of the unavoidable realities of environmental planning at the beginning of the twenty-first century is that it nearly always involves brokering agreements among contending interests with agendas in conflict, as well as very different interpretations of the science and acceptability of the risks involved. Thus, effective environmental planning hinges as much on the planner's ability to broker consensus as it does on anything else.

In an earlier time, this would have been described in terms of promoting public involvement or public participation. Traditionally, it involved organizing public hearings or staffing blue ribbon advisory committees. Today, it is characterized by multi-stakeholder dialogue, consensus building, and what is usually called "mediation" or "conflict resolution." It is concerned with achieving informed agreement more than with educating the public or allowing complaining groups to have their say. This transition was stimulated, in large part, by changes in America's legal and regulatory climate. In an effort to ensure greater fairness and accountability, the United States, as well as other western democracies, has expanded the "rules of standing," empowering groups with only a tangential stake in a particular environmental-planning decision to use the courts to challenge political and technical decisions of various kinds. In addition, given the rise in litigation (as well as adding to it), courts have expanded the "rights" not only of environmental advocacy groups, but of the environment itself. Thus, as standing to sue and the right to a clean environment have expanded, procedural requirements (public notice, recordkeeping, open meeting requirements, tests of reasonableness, and so on) have multiplied. All of this means that public decisions not to the liking of even a single politically powerless group can be delayed, or even blocked, through litigation.

Environmental planners must be conversant with these legal developments and all the procedural requirements involved. They must be able to design consensus-building processes and mediate conflict if called on by the contending parties to do so. Above all, environmental planners must be able to negotiate their way through risk controversies of all kinds.

THE REAL WORK OF ENVIRONMENTAL PLANNERS

While Leonard Ortolano has written about urban environmental planning, professional schools today are as focused on global and regional planning as they are on city-scale problems. Not only that, but planning schools in the

United States are training a substantial number of professionals from other countries. Indeed, by one estimate, fully one-third of the students enrolled in master's-level study in urban and regional planning are from outside the United States.[1] That means educational programs in environmental planning must be comparative in their perspective, and they must stress transnational ideas such as sustainability, which apply in every culture and context; if not, they will lose their market. It is no longer tenable to suggest that students from other countries learn "the American way" of doing planning and then import those ideas back to their country. Instead, the internationalization of the student body has encouraged environmental planners trained in American schools to think of themselves as multinational practitioners—able and willing to work for extended periods of time almost anywhere in the world. Moreover, internationalization has forced them to become comparative in their perspective, thereby engendering an increasing sensitivity to the importance of cultural variation and cross-cultural communication.

Suppose we look further at four "generic" descriptions of environmental planning that seek to capture the changing scope and scale of contemporary practice. The first description focuses on a municipal-level planner in the United States working on the open-space portion of a traditional master plan. The second, also in an American context, looks at the tasks associated with preparing and implementing a state-level recycling plan. The third, while presented in an American context, could just as well be in any other country's national environmental protection agency. The fourth description depicts the work of an environmental planner in a multilateral bank, like the World Bank, and hints at the fact that there is a wide range of multilateral institutions with an increasing need for environmental planning professionals.

PREPARING A LOCAL OPEN SPACE PLAN

The prototypical image of a professional planner is as the preparer of a master plan; that is, a land-use map, accompanied by a zoning ordinance and a statement of development goals and objectives, that spells out the direction in which a community expects to grow. Historically, master plans have been primarily blueprints for new development, but increasingly master plans now include statements of environmental protection objectives and commitments to promote sustainable development.

Preparing a local open space plan (and embodying the goals of conservation, preservation, and sustainable development in relevant land-use control ordinances) now requires both a sophisticated inventory of open space (including agricultural and recreational) resources and an assessment of their environmental asset value. Local land-use planners must also be familiar with the ways in which nongovernmental organizations (such as land trusts) come into play when a municipality is thinking about preserving open space. Indeed, if local planners want to meet their open space objectives, they must be able to catalyze elaborate regional, state, and national networks of advocacy organizations. It is these organizations, not municipalities, that will meet with private landowners to discuss the legal and tax implications of "saving" land deemed high priority for conservation. An open space plan is no longer merely a description of what the municipality intends to do with land that is publicly owned. Local zoning ordinances are, in some respects, less important than they used to be; private initiatives are now central to the protection of open space. The coordination of extraregulatory action (an almost entrepreneurial responsibility) is very much on the shoulders of the local environmental planner.

All local planners need to be savvy environmental planners who know when and how to call on specialists with skill and knowledge that transcend their own. Environmental planning specialists in municipal planning agencies (as well as other environmentally relevant departments such as transportation, energy, and water) also need to be able to understand and react to opportunities and crises that arise unexpectedly. The task of preparing or updating the open space element of a master plan (every five to ten years) is relatively less important than being able to mobilize political support for a private-land purchase no one expected would ever have been possible at the moment the opportunity arises. This kind of work requires someone who is both politically nimble and committed to superior environmental performance.

A State Recycling Plan

There are a great many more environmental planning positions open at the state level than there were just a few years ago. State environmental agencies have increased the scope of their responsibilities as new federal and state laws were added to respond to public pressure to ensure environmental protection. In addition, state public health, agriculture, transportation, housing, and energy departments have seen their mandates expanded in ways that require them to draw on the skills of environmental planners.

Recycling is an example of a new environmental requirement at the state level. Preparing and implementing a state recycling plan is a demanding assignment, both technically and politically. First, recycling targets have to be set. Cities that fall short of their annual recycling targets will, of course, complain that the targets are unrealistically high. Cities that meet the targets will complain that those that have not achieved their goals are not working hard enough to meet them. Strategies for supporting public and private efforts to meet recycling goals need to be developed; these can range from subsidies for demonstrations of new recycling technologies to permitting requirements making it harder to rely on traditional landfill disposal methods. State purchasing and tax policies can also be used to create markets for recycled materials of all kinds. Nevertheless, finding the right blend of incentives, controls, and public educational strategies is not easy.

We are at a moment in the evolution of environmental regulation in which traditional command-and-control methods are seen as heavy-handed and often inefficient (because they do not take into account the needs and constraints of each situation). More market-oriented approaches sound appealing, but it is not yet clear what form these should take or how they must be linked to the setting of state- or federal-level standards. Furthermore, market-oriented approaches require monitoring and compliance mechanisms that are much more expensive. The person designing and implementing a state recycling program will be pressed by numerous lobbyists (scrap resellers, trade associations, environmental organizations, business associations, and others) to do things "their way." Legislators will be divided between those who think the state has no role in recycling ("let the market take care of it") and those who believe the state should take the lead in building and operating regionalized recycling facilities—even if this requires a heavy subsidy. Dealing with the media to ensure public awareness of the need for and benefits of recycling is yet another responsibility of the recycling manager.

The need for a sophisticated analysis of the economics and technological options involved will have to be handled either by the program manager or that person's staff or consultants. In any case, detailed studies will be required to justify whatever policy directions the state government chooses. After-the-fact assessments are also certain to be controversial as various interest groups try to prove, using their own "expert" analysis, that they were right and the program should be changed in some way. It is most unlikely that a state program manager with no specialized training in environmental planning could handle this job.

NATIONAL AIR QUALITY REGULATIONS

National-level environmental planning responsibilities are increasing in almost every country. Professionals working at this level need as much political, legal, economic, and technological sophistication as their local and state counterparts. In addition, they must be able to "read" the larger political forces at work. Inside the bureaucracy, environmental planners must deal with a complex intergovernmental dynamic as regional offices contend with national headquarters and different parts of the country demanding special attention for their supposedly unique situations. The ability to cope with the bureaucratic games that determine how much of an agency's budget will be allocated to each subdepartment, and who will rise in the ranks of the central administration, is crucial to the success of a national environmental agency staff member.

Regulating air quality is a growing specialty in environmental planning. The ability to design an ambient monitoring system and interpret the results typically involves a great deal of engineering input; however, the overall task of managing a permitting program involves far more than what a narrow engineering perspective has to offer. Being able to explain in a public setting why standards are the way they are—why certain risks to highly sensitive populations are viewed as "acceptable" and how in the face of increasing scientific uncertainty costly regulations can be justified—demands that a federal-level air quality program manager be able to call on a surprising range of skills and a broad menu of technical insights. Environmental planners working at the national level are usually expected to be both more technically specialized and more adept politically.

ADVISING THE WORLD BANK

Multilateral development banks around the world are adding to their environmental staffs. They need professionals with a background in the financial realities of banking and investment (these institutions are, after all, banks that want to get their money back, but they also have an increasingly "green" mandate). New environmental departments have been added at some of these institutions to entrepreneur "greener" projects that will respond to new political mandates. In other instances, although new departments have not been added, environmental planners have joined the technical ranks to help assess the potential environmental impacts of proposed projects before funding decisions are made.

Over the past 15 years, the World Bank (in Washington, D.C.) has added more than 150 environmental specialists to its staff. Many of these professionals have an environmental planning background. Several are assigned to geographically (that is, regional) specialized departments, where they are called on to help diversify the portfolios of their banking units. This may mean traveling quite a bit to meet with private organizations or state-run agencies to encourage them to apply for loans for cleaner energy production. It may mean working with applicants to strengthen the environmental evidence included in their applications. Or, finally, it may require meeting inside the World Bank with financial analysts who do not understand why "greener" projects are often more costly in the short run and perhaps less financially sound.

Environmental staff at the Bank are expected to be as well versed in economic analysis as the rest of their professional peers *and* to be knowledgeable in the field of environmental analysis.

These four descriptions are intended to highlight the changing scope and character of the work of environmental planners. They also have dramatic implications for what it will mean to university departments to do a good job preparing the next generation of environmental planners.

PREPARING THE NEXT GENERATION OF ENVIRONMENTAL PLANNERS

Working backward from the four descriptions above, it should be obvious that it matters who does the teaching, how the curriculum is structured, what skills are emphasized, the relative importance of research (as compared to practice), and the centrality of cross-cultural and multinational perspectives. Summed up below are some suggestions on each of these issues, with a concluding note on the importance of sustainability as an organizing precept in the education of environmental planners.

What Kinds of Faculty?

It is impossible for faculty members not involved in practice to train effective practitioners. While not every member of an academic department needs to be a practitioner, in a small academic unit in particular, most faculty members need to be involved in, or at least conversant with, the problems graduates will be facing. Adjunct appointments can add balance to a more research-oriented faculty. In addition, students need to learn how to view environmental problems from a variety of disciplinary and professional perspectives. Thus, it helps if faculty are broadly representative of different academic and professional backgrounds.

In the final analysis, it is extremely difficult to organize a complete environmental planning curriculum within a single academic department or professional school. Students need access to faculty from a panoply of fields. But these faculty members need to work together (as opposed to putting all the burden on students to move among them), in order to model the collaboration that the students will be expected to emulate in their practice. Finally, a faculty that is engaged internationally is likely to be far better prepared to explain the dilemmas of working cross-culturally and demonstrate the steps involved in adapting the experience of one country to the needs of others.

The MIT Environmental Policy Group consists of six faculty members, two of whom divide their time with other program groups in the department, such as environmental design and international development. Four are regular members of the tenured or tenure track faculty; two are adjunct faculty with well-established credentials as innovative practitioners. These six include faculty with advanced degrees in law, public policy, planning, industrial engineering, and public health. All but one are engaged as international consultants and advisors. Even with such a rich array of resources, the two dozen MCP and 15 doctoral students enrolled at any time take more than half their coursework outside the department.

Organizing the Curriculum

A professional degree in planning requires a two-year curriculum. At MIT, slightly more than one-third of this time is spent meeting departmental core requirements, including the preparation of a thesis. Another third is taken up with a recommended sequence of subjects offered by the environmental policy group. The final third involves electives taken anywhere at MIT or Harvard, including fieldwork.

Although every planning department has its own version of a core curriculum (for example, many departments substitute a project or a capstone studio for the thesis requirement), most expect their students to master the basics of planning theory and history, applied microeconomics, quantitative reasoning, and public management (including computer applications). Beyond that, there is much less agreement on what is essential in the environmental policy and planning sequence. The MIT group suggests courses that cover environmental policymaking, including the tools of policy analysis; environmental management, including the legal and ethical dilemmas that arise in practice; international environmental planning, with a focus on the emergence of global issues; and scientific and engineering perspectives, including the techniques of risk assessment, life-cycle analysis, impact assessment, and industrial ecology. Students, however, are free to propose a different package. Most choose an environmental economics elective and a theme, such as air quality or climate change, which leads them to courses in other departments in order to achieve greater technical depth in that area.

Most students, especially those with only a few years of field-based experience, sign up for an internship with a public agency, private consulting firm, or not-for-profit advocacy group. Recently, the department has developed a practicum which allows students to work as a team to provide advice on a current policy problem facing an agency or municipal client.

Students from other planning specializations depend on our group to offer an overview of environmental planning. Likewise, for students in our area interested in computer applications—such as the design of Geographic Information Systems and the application of multimedia tools for representation and on-line dialogue—other departmental specializations offer additional coursework.

What Skills Will Be Needed?

Candidates for a professional degree tend to think in terms of the job they will take when they graduate in two years; academic departments, however, need a 10- to 15-year time horizon. As educators try to anticipate the demands on environmental planners a decade hence, a half-dozen trends seem worth noting. The shift away from command-and-control approaches to environmental regulation is likely to continue, especially in the United States, where that approach probably has achieved most of what it was designed to accomplish. Whereas some policy analysts think a more market-oriented approach—involving emissions trading, information-forcing strategies, and the like—is the direction to take, my own sense is that we will see a shift to "strategic alliances." We will rely on neither the heavy hand of government nor the free market, but will look for more efficient ways to catalyze private action to achieve the goals set by government. Moreover, this is a worldwide trend. Environmental planners will have to figure out how to meet environmental protection standards, for example, by meshing those objectives with attempts to meet other needs. Open space or conservation goals, for instance, will have to be achieved, at least in part, by building on what is done to meet the objectives of agricultural production. Recreational goals will have to be met within the framework of economic development and environmental protection objectives. More careful integration of multiple objectives in overlapping sectors of the economy will require the negotiation of detailed alliances among groups which traditionally have operated in separate policy arenas.

To craft such agreements, environmental planners will need to sharpen their negotiation skills. They will need to be attentive to the work of increasingly globalized networks that blur the distinctions among the public, private, and voluntary sectors. They will need to draw on elaborate data resources and tap communication links that exceed anything known today. Their focus will be more anticipatory (that is, pollution prevention) than it has been, thus requiring new forecasting skills. Ultimately, informal and opportunistic interaction involving boundary spanning and entrepreneurship will be at a premium.

How can university departments better prepare their graduates to operate in this new context? Primarily by abandoning traditional teaching methods (such as lectures) in favor of problem-focused, team-oriented, client-centered assignments that teach second-order (learning-to-learn) skills rather than knowledge acquisition.

The Importance of Research

As academic departments offering professional training become increasingly practice oriented, they should not abandon their research orientation.

The continued development of intellectual capital in environmental planning is crucial. One way to improve both theory and practice is to assign the former to doctoral-level studies and the latter to professional education. To do so would probably be a mistake, however. For knowledge to be useful, scholarly studies must be practice-linked; for practice education to be truly instructive, it must be informed by careful reflection. Thus, a better way to link theory and practice is to ensure that master's- and doctoral-level studies are fully integrated.

Environmental planning needs a research agenda, particularly one that looks at the relative effectiveness of different techniques and strategies for implementing environmental policy. We also need systematic studies of the effectiveness of various analytic tools. For instance, even though environmental impact assessment has been used around the world for several decades, there are fewer than a dozen documented efforts to go back, after the fact, and review the accuracy of the forecasts and forecasting tools on which decisions were based. The research community has spent far too much time debating esoteric frameworks for problem classification, and not nearly enough time on the review of risk-management efforts.

Many professional degree candidates find that some involvement in faculty-led research activities is a useful component of graduate study (that is why MIT maintains a thesis requirement). If a practitioner has never been involved in scholarly research or theory building, he or she is likely to have much less appreciation of the usefulness and limitations of ideas "in good currency." Also, practitioners are often called on to "purchase" needed research. Firsthand experience increases consumer awareness! Finally, part of the task of strengthening professional education is to reflect carefully on the experience of thoughtful practitioners. Graduate students can play a helpful role (and learn exactly how hard it is to reflect on their own experience) by participating directly in efforts to document the experience of other practitioners. These materials can be valuable additions to the stock of new teaching tools.

THE CULTURAL CONTEXT

Having impressed on students the need to be sensitive to cultural differences and the difficulties of cross-cultural communication, it is not clear what prescriptions ought to follow. Obviously, the American educational establishment believes that what it teaches professionals in every field, including environmental planning, is relevant to the rest of the world. Exactly what transformations are required, however, and how to make them, are rarely discussed.

At MIT, we assume that the cultural context in which a planner works is paramount. We also assume that it is possible to make adjustments that will allow a professional to move successfully from context to context. These adjustments hinge on being able to "read" each situation and to have both the confidence and the humility to alter ways of doing things. Learning to distinguish *interesting* from *essential* differences as one moves from setting to setting requires heightened sensitivity, an ability to frame pertinent questions, and sufficient mastery of concepts and techniques to be able to alter the way they are employed in each situation. The goal of professional education must be to teach this sensitivity, to offer the right framework of questions, and to build such mastery.

SUSTAINABILITY AS AN ENVIRONMENTAL PLANNING CONCERN

For many years, comprehensiveness was the byword of professional planning practice. Planners offered a commitment to completeness and a willingness to wrestle with complexity that distinguished them from other professionals. Over time, though, comprehensiveness was attacked from within the profession and without, and eventually fell into disrepute. Other guiding precepts as well—like community control and quality of life—have come and gone. It is hard to distinguish a fad from an enduring insight, except with the benefit of hindsight.

At the moment, the practice of environmental planning seems to be coalescing around the notion of sustainable development. Both locally and globally, environmental advocates feel comfortable pushing for a commitment to sustainability, because it draws attention to at least three things that are very important to them—the idea of limits, a commitment to future generations, and (once again) the interconnectedness of all our actions and of "man"-made and natural systems. Indicators of sustainability are emerging[2] that will allow us to measure how ecologically sustainable the various development strategies are.

While it is too soon to say whether sustainability will last as a unifying measure of the work of environmental planning, there is a good chance it will. Because sustainability seeks to balance social, economic, and environmental needs, it encourages dialogue rather than confrontation. Because it is possible to measure the changing "ecological footprint" of a city, the results of environmental planning efforts can be assessed. For now, I would argue that graduate training in environmental planning should address the idea of sustainability and, perhaps, even organize around it.

19

Economic Base Studies for Urban and Regional Planning

Andrew M. Isserman

One cannot plan for a place until one understands it. Comprehensive regional plans, economic development plans, land-use plans, transportation plans, and other planning efforts are shaped by a mental image of economic and demographic conditions and change. An understanding of what is—combined with values and views regarding what ought to be—form the context and motivation for professional planning.

First-rate economic and demographic analyses meet several goals. They respond to basic human quests for an understanding of the present, a grasp of the future, and the perspective on the present and future that only an appreciation of the past can provide. Successful economic and demographic analyses tell a convincing story. Doing that requires not only technical and computing skills in using quantitative methods, but also writing and communication skills in interpreting and presenting information. Good planning analyses avoid the nearly mindless, pro forma presentation of compendia of data. They draw on those data but transcend them, to create a coherent mental picture of present, past, and future. The old adage, part science and part art, is particularly true of planning analysis. When all is said and done, the ultimate goal is to create a credible, clear image of a place and its prospects, to get to understand a place as never before.

In this dual role of quantitative analyst and storyteller, the planner must develop unique professional competencies. They are related yet different from the core competencies of other professions or disciplines. Economic and demographic analyses for planning draw on methods of economics and demography, but the professional planner must demand more of these methods and extend them in ways unknown to the economist or demographer. The economic and demographic analysis needed for planning is rarely taught in economics or demography degree programs. Planning also requires skills of synthesis similar to those of a historian or trial lawyer. Both marshal facts in an attempt to tell a convincing story. So, too, the planner must reconstruct the past and draw believable inferences about the future.

This chapter reviews the history and state of economic base analysis. The methods of the 1950s and even the 1930s have proven surprisingly durable despite new theories of economic development, different expectations and attitudes toward government, and changing roles of experts and citizens in the planning process. These new emphases, as well as new technologies, should bring forth a new mind-set for conducting economic base analyses. The old methods can and should be used in new ways.

A HALF-CENTURY OF HANDBOOKS

> The project of an economic and industrial survey was ambitious in scope and novel in character. No general agreement existed as to the facts which were essential and pertinent for an analysis of the operation of economic forces under conditions of collective action such as those contemplated by a regional plan. . . . It was necessary to break new ground. (Haig 1928, 114)

Thus, more than 70 years ago in New York, the study of economic forces was incorporated into the making of regional plans. It occurred almost simultaneously with federal attempts under President Herbert Hoover to create a social science understanding of the nation's economic and social condition (Wilson 1975). The President's Research Committee on Recent Social Trends—appointed in 1929 to study education, unemployment, health, race, and urban sprawl, among other topics—was a pioneering effort in the government's enlistment of social science research to inform and shape public policy. Part of the very same movement was planners' search for "facts which were essential and pertinent" to create better and more livable cities and regions.

Land-Use Planning

Two strands of economic base analysis have merged. One originated in land-use planning, the other in economic development and comprehensive regional planning. Quite possibly, Frederick Law Olmsted himself first brought the economic base concept into the planning process. In a letter dated February 21, 1921, he wrote:

Productive occupations may roughly be divided into those which can be called primary . . . manufacturing goods for the general use (i.e., not confined to use within the community itself) and those occupations which may be called auxiliary, such as are devoted directly or indirectly to the services and convenience of the people engaged in the primary occupations. (included in Haig 1928, 43)

The economic historian Frederick Nussbaum (1933, 36, quoted in Andrews 1953) succinctly described these two components of the economy as "town builders" and "town fillers." Town builders "command a means of subsistence from elsewhere," while town fillers serve the needs of the town builders.

"The essential outlines of the economic base idea as we now know it" were developed by Homer Hoyt while working for the Federal Housing Administration in the late 1930s (Andrews 1953). His textbook, *Principles of Urban Real Estate*, written with Arthur Weimer and published in 1939, made economic base analysis a formal, systematic part of land-use planning. It provided "a method for estimating future population trends and the potential demand for various types of land uses in the city" (reprinted in Pfouts 1960, 36). In Hoyt's lexicon, town-building activities became "basic" employment that determines the extent of growth, and town-filling employment became "service" employment.

Hoyt's method entails multiplying a sequence of key ratios. Its 12 steps follow (with some changes in his wording):

1. Ascertain the number of urban growth or basic employees in each industry or trade.

2. Subtract the number of urban growth or basic employees from each industry or trade to determine its service employment.

3. Calculate the ratio between basic and service employment.

4. Calculate the ratio of total employment to the total population.

5. Estimate the probable future total number of basic employees by interviewing the managers of principal basic industries or by taking into account past trends.

6. Estimate future total employment by applying the current ratio of basic employment to total employment or an adjusted ratio.

7. Estimate the future population of the area by applying the current population-to-employment ratio or some other appropriate ratio.

8. Estimate the potential need for housing by dividing the estimated population increase by the average family size, or that size adjusted for fertility trends.

9. Calculate the amount of land needed for new residential growth by estimating the proportion of added families that will live in apartments, row houses, detached single-family houses, and small estates, and the amount of land required for each type of residence.

10. Estimate the amount of land required for new commercial centers by calculating the square feet of floor area required in department stores, variety stores, supermarkets, apparel stores, and all other types of stores to handle the volume of sales created by the added population, and also allow a four-to-one ratio between parking and selling areas.

11. Estimate the amount of industrial space required for new growth by multiplying the number of added employees by the average number of square feet of factory and yard space used by each employee in modern factories.

12. Allocate shares of the growth within the metropolitan area on the basis of new highways, new sewer and water extensions, new industries, vacant land suitable for residential use, trends of growth, and prestige of the area.

Almost six decades since its inception, Hoyt's system remains intact in contemporary planning practice and textbooks. For example, in their definitive work, *Urban Land Use Planning*, Kaiser et al. (1995, 151) write:

> The first step is to identify which industries or proportions of industries are classified as basic, and which as nonbasic. . . . The next step is to compute the base ratio and base multiplier. . . . Finally, that base multiplier is applied in answering a planning question . . . [such as] projecting future total employment based on projections of future basic employment. Employment projections are then used to estimate demand for land; environmental resources (e.g., water supply or air quality); and public infrastructure (e.g. waste-water treatment or transportation).

Similarly, Hoyt's echo resonates in their instructions for urban land-use design:

1. Determine the number of employees to be accommodated.

2. Develop future employment density standards, that is, employees per gross acre of employment center area.

3. Divide the number of employees by density standards to estimate the number of acres that will be required. (Kaiser et al. 1995, 327)

A spatial extension of the economic base concept produced another enduring effect on land-use planning practice. The Lowry model (1964) followed the by then standard procedure of generating service employment and population from estimates of basic employment. In the economist's jargon, basic employment is exogenous to the model; that is, it is determined outside the region and is external to the model, whereas service employment and population are endogenous—determined internally by the model and affected by the exogenous factors. Lowry extended this thinking to land-use design and transportation modeling. Basic employment, being oriented toward market demand from outside the region, can take place on sites independent of the location of the local population. Hence, sites for these activities are selected outside the Lowry model, often based on the judgment of local planners, as in Hoyt's twelfth step. On the other hand, service activity is located endogenously by the model based on residential location. Service employment is "assumed to be *both* generated purely by final demand within the region *and* locationally oriented toward that final demand (population)" (Massey 1973).

Thus, the bifurcation of economic space into activities producing for demand originating outside or inside the area leads to a parallel distinction in land use between activities that need access to local markets and those that do not. This distinction persists today: "Economic base activities are not primarily oriented to local consumers and are thus less constrained in site selection by required access to local markets" (Kaiser et al. 1995, 317).

REGIONAL PLANNING AND ECONOMIC DEVELOPMENT

Although "the concept of the economic base has been developed largely in the works of city planners and other researchers interested in urban problems" (Tiebout 1956, 160), it also attracted considerable attention in leading scholarly journals. Writing in the *American Economic Review*, Rutledge Vining (1949, 90) observed that "a community seems to be organized around its 'export' industries." Furthermore, "part of the [region's] employment produces goods and services sold only or primarily to the inhabitants of this region. This employment is called the 'residentiary' or passive employment. . . . The rest of the employment produces primarily for export to other regions. This employment is called the 'primary' or 'active' employment" (p.93). Writing in the *Review of Economics and Statistics*, Hildebrand and Mace (1950) preferred the terms *nonlocalized* (export) and *localized* and used monthly employment estimates for Los Angeles to calculate the multiplier relationship between them. Writing in *Economic Geography*, John Alexander (1954) pointed out that "The composition of a city's or region's basic activities may be quite different from that of its total economic structure. Since it is the basic activity which is important to the economic existence and growth of the city or region, the explicit identification of such activity is significant for analysis and for distinguishing between types of regions." Between 1953 and 1956, *Land Economics* published a set of 12 papers by Richard Andrews on "the mechanics of the urban economic base." The debate in the *Journal of Political Economy* between Nobel laureate Douglas North (1955, 1956) and Charles Tiebout (1956) over economic base theory and regional development is still widely read. The *Journal of the American Institute of Planners* itself published numerous economic base articles between 1955 and 1958, many written by highly influential scholars, including Homer Hoyt (1945), Stuart Chapin (1954), Hans Blumenfeld (1955), Sue Moyerman and Britton Harris (1955), James Gilles and William Grigsby (1956), Morgan Thomas (1957), Charles Tiebout (1957), Richard Pfouts (1957), Britton Harris (1958), and Richard Andrews (1958). The economic base concept remains so enmeshed in planning practice today that the American Planning Association's Web page designates Blumenfeld's 1955 article as "required reading for those who want to understand what the field of planning is all about" (www.planning.org/info/).

By the 1960s, the economic base study had become established in its own right, not merely as a step in land-use planning. Walter Isard's *Methods of Regional Analysis* devotes 11 pages to technical and conceptual "difficulties" in estimating the basic-service ratio (Hoyt's step three) and its use in forecasting (Hoyt's step six). Nevertheless, Isard et al. (1960, 199) conclude,

> A careful economic base study contributes to an understanding of the functions of the various economic components of a city or region. In particular, it identifies and highlights the export activities, which to a greater or lesser extent are necessary for the existence of the city or region.

"As an instrument for projection," they caution, "it can be used only under certain ideal conditions" (p.204).

Economic base studies have attracted noteworthy private-sector support, becoming an essential part of economic development planning and policy. The Committee for Economic Development (CED), a national organization of business leaders founded in 1942 to bring the nation out of World War II without a depression, took an interest in area development and economic base studies. In 1960, CED stated that "the first step toward meeting the public problems of an area is a detailed knowledge of its economic base." It noted that many economic base studies had been conducted since the 1930s and that there was a "need for a single small volume which brings together the best thinking on the logic of base studies and emphasizes methods which are within the financial and technical means of most communities." With this goal in mind, CED commissioned and published *The Community Economic Base Study* by Charles Tiebout.

Tiebout tied the economic base concept securely to Keynesian multiplier models and the associated concepts of propensities to consume, import, and invest; yet the parallels with Keynesian theory had little effect on analytical practices. Tiebout's succinct statement of the logic of the economic base study parallels Hoyt's steps one through three, and six:

> Economic base studies divide the economy into two segments: (1) firms and individuals serving markets outside the community; and (2) firms and individuals serving markets within the community. . . . Export markets are considered the prime mover of the local economy. If employment serving this market rises or falls, employment serving the local market is presumed to move in the same direction. . . . The simplest assumption is that over the long run the proportion of basic and nonbasic jobs will remain about the same. Hence, an increase in the number of basic jobs will eventually produce a proportionate increase in nonbasic jobs. (Tiebout 1962, 13)

Tiebout recognized as export activities local purchases by tourists and other nonresidents, employment by the federal government, pension spending by retired persons, and other activities that bring funds into an area (pp. 40–42).

Principles and Practices of Urban Planning, the famous "Green Bible" edited by William Goodman and Eric Freund (1968), made the economic base concept canon law. The chapter "Economic Studies," by Richard Andrews, discusses its application and limitations and reviews the various shortcut methods for estimating export employment, including the location quotient and minimum requirements approaches. As chapter 4 of 20, its position reflects the status of economic base analysis among the "basic studies for urban planning" and its place early in the planning process (as illustrated also by Hoyt's steps).

A marked change is found in *The Practice of Local Government Planning*, a successor volume to *Principles and Practices*. Economic base studies are discussed only briefly within the chapter on economic development. Praful Shah (1979, 610–11) charges that "historically, most economic base studies have been ground out according to fairly prosaic formulas," and planning schools and planning journals have "been overly preoccupied with the techniques of statistical manipulation, data classification, and definitions of economic activities for the purpose of forecasting." Furthermore, "most economic base studies have had only limited policy orientation" because they have been oriented toward "the metropolitan region through which few governmental actions are exercised." They do not give sufficient guidance for local governments "to take necessary steps to provide a favorable investment or reinvestment climate" and to determine over what private economic decisions local government policy can "exercise a decisive leverage." Nevertheless, Shah concluded, "regional economic base studies have achieved a new level of understanding of the regional economic system and how it works. Certainly, the regional planner has made good use of economic base studies in his or her forecasting and overview activities" (p. 611). Yet, *The Practice of State and Regional Planning*, published in 1986, includes only a one-page discussion of the economic base model and forecasts.

The economic base study quickly regained any lost prominence. A popular textbook, *Community Analysis and Planning Techniques*, by Richard Klosterman (1990), devotes almost 100 pages to detailed instructions for economic base studies and forecasts. *Understanding Your Economy*, published by the American Planning Association in 1992, gives economic base analysis a major role in a new context—"support of community 'strategic planning,' a consensus-building process that involves key segments of a community in joint planning for the area's economic future" (McLean and Voytek 1992, xi). This handbook combines the export base concept, the location quotient measure, and another persistent method, shift-share analysis, into "industry targeting analysis," to evaluate the performance and prospects of local industries. It does so within the traditional, fundamental axiom of economic base analysis that the "industries that are most crucial to local economic growth are those that produce goods and services sold outside the local economy, generating an inflow of income" (p. 60).

Written with the support of the U.S. Economic Development Administration, *Understanding Your Economy* is a contemporary answer to Robert Haig's quest for agreement on the facts that are essential when analyzing the local economy. A striking aspect of today's answer is the persistence of methods and concepts that had been largely thought through by the late 1950s and early 1960s.

THE TRIUMPH OF PRAGMATISM

From a methodological standpoint, the practice of economic base analysis has three defining characteristics: (1) its pragmatic blend of ratios and judgment, (2) its limited reliance on theory, and (3) its effective use of comparisons across places. Measurement, comparison, and extrapolation form the essence of most economic base analysis—with a good deal of professional judgment included, whether explicitly or implicitly.

Take the Hoyt-derived approach to land-use planning as an example. The 12 steps are a chain of measured ratios, with some judgment decisions interspersed. After interviewing managers of principal basic industries and/or considering past trends, a decision is made regarding the future level of basic employment (judgment). Then the ratios take over. Basic employment times the observed (measurement) or adjusted (judgment) ratio of total to basic employment yields future total employment (extrapolation). The ratios continue with a population-to-employment ratio (measurement) times employment, to yield future population (extrapolation), and so on, through square feet per employee for factory and yard space. Planning standards (judgment) today provide another form of ratio, such as the acres of neighborhood park or playground per 1,000 population (Kaiser et al. 1995, 390).

Very little economic theory is embedded in such planning analysis. Only one link in the ratio chain has attracted the attention of mainstream economists—namely, the ratio of total to basic activity, also commonly called the economic base multiplier. Tiebout (1962), among others, demonstrated that this ratio is a simplified form of the Keynesian multiplier. In the 1960s, macroeconomic Keynesian multipliers were the cornerstone of fiscal management of the national economy, and economic base analysis was seen as a simplified regional variant of an idea in good currency. The simplification was necessary, indeed clever, because regional accounts or data analogous to the national ones did not exist. The key idea—that exogenous forces or exports drive economic growth and development—was very much in the mainstream of economic thought.

The relative paucity of data led to an emphasis on comparative techniques to provide a measure or benchmark. For example, in the absence of actual trade data, exports from a region were measured by identifying economic specialization, using data on the location of employment. The logic is simple: If a region has proportionately more coal miners than the nation, it probably is exporting coal to other places. From this kind of logic were born the location quotient and minimum requirement approaches to estimating exports (Isserman 1980). Embedded in each are strong theoretical assumptions regarding consumption, productivity, and international trade. Yet, the key operational idea is the comparative notion: The nation or other regions can usefully serve as a benchmark against which specialization—and, thus, the export base—can be measured.

The use of theory in conventional economic base analysis is much more similar to the use of theory in demography than in economics. Demographers, too, devote considerable effort to measurement—to identifying key ratios (for example, fertility and mortality rates) and to creating projections by extrapolating the ratios into the future. They also use a comparative approach when extrapolating the ratios by adapting data from other places. For example, model life tables reflect the mortality experience of countries that have already passed through a similar transition.

Debate has focused on the stability of the economic base multiplier over time, whether it is long-term or short-term, its relationship to input–output multipliers, and the accuracy of the various estimation techniques. There have been chicken-and-egg disputes over whether exports are the engine of a place's growth or whether service industries that make a place a competitive exporter are the true engine. There have been convincing demonstrations that places can flourish by exporting services—be they banking, computing, health, or tourism—and that equating exports with only manufacturing, farming, and mining is no longer valid, if it ever was. There have been reminders to recognize import substitution as well as export development as potential sources of economic growth. Whatever the state of these debates, planning practice has adhered pragmatically to the basic methodology of measurement, comparison, and extrapolation, combined with professional judgment.

NEW CONTEXTS AND USES

Much has changed in the social and political context of urban and regional planning over the past half-century. This section briefly notes three sets of ideas that affect planning, as well as demonstrates how elements of economic base analysis can be reoriented to the new ideas. First, the theory of economic change has focused or refocused on agglomerations, clusters and networks of firms, industrial districts, industrial organization, external economies, cumulative causation, and the globalization of the economy. The tools of economic base analysis offer a useful empirical foundation for measuring and understanding some of the phenomena being discussed. Second, interest in strategic planning and reinventing government has produced an emphasis on accountability and evaluation. The comparative dimension of economic base analysis can be extremely useful in creating benchmarks and measuring planning outcomes. Third, the roles of expert and citizen have changed markedly since the 1950s. Economic base analysis can serve a useful role in a citizen-oriented process to create the employment and population forecasts that are central to planning.

DETECTING CLUSTERS

More than three decades after MIT Press launched Walter Isard's book series in regional science, Cambridge is again the font of stimulating books in regional economics (Isserman 1995, 1996). Michael Porter (1990) argues that the competitiveness of nations depends on the competitiveness of regions, which often translates into a cluster of related industries and supporting institutions within the region. Earlier, Michael Piore and Charles Sabel (1984) drew attention to the industrial districts of Italy and the capacity of small, interdependent firms to create strong local economies. Paul Krugman (1991) focuses on increasing returns, agglomerations, and the "new economic geography," and Edward Glaeser and colleagues (1992) on innovation and the growth of cities.

This emphasis on industrial districts, clusters of industries, innovation, and competitive advantage has affected the vanguard of planning practice in economic base analysis. The third regional plan for the New York region, *A Region at Risk* by Robert Yaro and Tony Hiss (1996), merges the cluster concept with the export base idea. It identifies "eight clusters of export industries, along with their networks of local suppliers" that "represent the industries driving the region as a global center of capital markets, corporate management, information production, trade and goods production, and the arts and popular culture" (p.35).

Two other aspects of this part of the New York plan are noteworthy. First, the authors succeed in communicating an image of the region. Creating a succinct, accurate image of the economic base of a region is a necessary part of a successful economic base study. It reflects an understanding of a place, and an essential step toward that understanding is identifying a region's specialization. The new analytical step, if it is indeed a new step, is to attempt to identify the functional clusters among the region's industries. Second, the Regional Plan Association proceeded from the technical identification of those clusters to discussions with leaders in each industry to identify "priority challenges" facing each, and to "strategic investments and collaborative activities by the private and public sectors." The economic base analysis provided a way of understanding the organization of the economy, which was then used to organize part of the planning process and produce specific planning recommendations.

To demonstrate how some simple economic base data can help in understanding an economy and its clusters, this chapter compares and contrasts the main manufacturing and service exporters in the home counties of the nation's three leading engineering schools. They are, from east to west, the Massachusetts Institute of Technology, the University of Illinois at Urbana-Champaign, and Stanford University. The analysis marries 1950s-vintage economic base concepts with today's computer technology and federal databases, to provide a level of detail impossible when the methods were first introduced. The methods themselves are simple comparative statistics. The location quotient measures the relative importance of an industry in a place and the nation by dividing the industry's share of jobs locally by its share of jobs nationally. Thus, the location quotient of 4.99 for the manufacture of semiconductors in Middlesex County, Massachusetts, means that semiconductors have a fivefold larger share of the Middlesex economy than of the

TABLE 19.1
Manufacturing and Service Specialization of Middlesex County, Massachusetts (1995)

SIC	Industry	Firms	>1,000 Jobs	Total Jobs	Location Quotient	Surplus
	Manufacturing Sector					
399	Administrative and auxiliary	146	5	16,719	1.92	8,010
3679	Electronic components	99	2	8,613	6.66	7,319
3674	Semiconductors and related devices	36	1	5,871	4.99	4,696
3841	Surgical and medical instruments	36	1	4,233	6.38	3,570
3810	Search and navigation equipment	18	1	4,251	3.28	2,955
3860	Photographic equipment and supplies	11	1	3,211	6.68	2,731
3571	Electronic computers	22	1	3,235	5.14	2,606
3661	Telephone and telegraph apparatus	13	1	2,998	5.57	2,460
3826	Analytical instruments	33	0	2,635	10.93	2,394
3825	Instruments to measure electricity	30	0	1,968	4.80	1,558
	Service Sector					
8220	Colleges and universities	31	7	49,689	6.05	41,479
7372	Prepackaged software	313	1	13,954	13.10	12,889
8711	Engineering services	473	3	14,619	3.24	10,105
8731	Commercial physical research	196	2	9,632	8.31	8,473
7363	Help supply services	221	3	23,539	1.50	7,802
7371	Computer programming services	463	0	8,606	4.22	6,565
8742	Management consulting services	697	1	8,023	3.47	5,714
7374	Data processing and preparation	99	2	7,038	3.97	5,265
899	Administrative and auxiliary	105	2	8,120	2.59	4,987
7349	Building maintenance services	317	2	9,808	1.82	4,418
8080	Home health care services	105	0	8,494	1.73	3,576
7373	Computer-integrated systems design	123	0	4,055	5.57	3,327
8712	Architectural services	213	0	4,115	4.66	3,232
8732	Commercial nonphysical research	96	0	2,929	3.63	2,121
7378	Computer maintenance and repair	59	0	2,210	5.32	1,795

Source: Author's calculations from 1994 and 1995 *County Business Patterns* data (Washington, DC: U.S. Department of Commerce, Bureau of the Census, 1997).

national economy. Middlesex's relative specialization in semiconductor manufacture amounts to 4,696 additional jobs. These extra, or surplus, jobs are sometimes called "export jobs," on the assumption that specialization in employment indicates production sold elsewhere (Isserman 1980).

MIT's home county is host to numerous high-technology manufacturing establishments, 36 in semiconductors and related devices alone, one of which has more than 1,000 employees (table 19.1). It is also the home to administrative units (as opposed to producing ones) of 146 firms. The highest location quotient, 10.93, testifies to its leadership in the production of

TABLE 19.2
Manufacturing and Service Specialization of Champaign County, Illinois (1995)

SIC	Industry	Firms	>1,000 Jobs	Total Jobs	Location Quotient	Surplus
	Manufacturing Sector					
2035	Pickles, sauces, and salad dressings	1	1	1,963	124.09	1,947
3089	Plastics products	5	0	1,210	3.21	833
2431	Millwork	1	0	673	9.35	601
3714	Motor vehicle parts and accessories	2	0	821	2.2	448
2752	Commercial printing, lithographic	16	0	778	2.26	434
2710	Newspapers	5	0	730	2.32	415
3949	Sporting and athletic goods	3	0	429	7.54	372
2079	Edible fats and oils	1	0	354	22.15	338
3085	Plastics bottles	1	0	339	13.14	313
2731	Book publishing	9	0	355	5.54	291
	Service Sector					
8010	Offices and clinics of medical doctors	39	1	2,628	2.04	1,339
7513	Truck rental and leasing, no drivers	4	0	261	8.97	232
7040	Membership-basis organization hotels	34	0	159	18.54	150
7372	Prepackaged software	6	0	256	2.04	130
8640	Civic and social associations	48	0	407	1.36	108
8690	Membership organizations	8	0	187	2.37	108
7020	Rooming and boarding houses	5	0	93	13.87	86
8350	Child day-care services	37	0	499	1.2	84
7371	Computer programming services	27	0	308	1.28	67
8620	Professional organizations	9	0	107	2.29	60
7291	Tax return preparation services	6	0	171	1.5	57
7336	Commercial art and graphic design	8	0	86	1.88	40
8049	Offices of health practitioners	9	0	145	1.32	35
7549	Automotive services	7	0	99	1.49	33
7334	Photocopying and duplicating services	6	0	87	1.41	25

Source: Author's calculations from 1994 and 1995 *County Business Patterns* data (Washington, DC: U.S. Department of Commerce, Bureau of the Census, 1997).

analytical instruments. The service sector of Middlesex County is specialized in education, research, and business services. Here, the highest location quotient is for prepackaged software, again illustrating the synergy between the county's manufacturing and service industries. A nice picture of a well-integrated, high-technology, knowledge economy emerges from the data.

The University of Illinois's home county fails to show such technology and knowledge clusters. Champaign County's manufacturing specialization is decidedly more traditional. Its 10 major manufacturing exporters range from pickles, sauces, and salad dressing to book publishing (table 19.2). Printing and publishing suggest a cluster, with 25 establishments combined, or even 30, if newspapers are included. Six establishments in plastics might be another cluster. Perhaps these clusters rely on engineering and technology breakthroughs and a link to the engineering and science research, but the case is not certain. The four highest location quotients are between 9 and 124 (!), but each reflects only one establishment. A Kraft branch plant with more than 1,000 employees accounts for the location quotient of 124. The service sector also is less research- and business-oriented than that of Middlesex. Prepackaged software has a location quotient of 2, compared to 13 in Middlesex, despite the fact that what are now Netscape and Eudora were both invented at the University of Illinois. In all, the data reveal relatively few local employment spinoffs of the knowledge created at the university. (The university itself does not appear in the data because, unlike MIT and Stanford, it is a public institution listed under state government and not in the services sector.)

Santa Clara County, home of Stanford University and Silicon Valley, is the high-technology manufacturing center par excellence. Its location quotient for semiconductors is 23, compared to 5 for Middlesex, with 165 establishments compared to 36 in Middlesex (table 19.3). It has strong, complementary specializations in education, research, and business services. Its prepackaged software industry has 251 establishments, a location quotient of 10, and 12,000 employees, making it somewhat smaller in absolute and relative terms than Middlesex. The 113 establishments manufacturing circuit boards, 59 producing computers, 89 making instruments to measure electricity, and 224 doing commercial physical research, to cite just a few, are what make Silicon Valley the textbook example of a modern industrial cluster preeminent in the science and technology economy (see Saxenian 1994). And its nature comes screaming out of the economic base data.

EVALUATING OUTCOMES

Two interrelated forces have contributed to greater emphasis on accountability and evaluation within the public sector. First is a general suspicion of government programs and bureaucracies and the desire to cut expenditures and reduce taxes. Second is the growing emphasis on strategic planning in the corporate world. Strategic planning has spilled into the public sector, bringing with it discussions of strengths, weaknesses, opportunities, and threats to the local economy, local quality of life, and other planning concerns. Along with reinventing government, greater responsiveness to clients, and organizational mission statements has come a search for increased program effectiveness and appropriate outcome measures (Osborne and Gaebler 1992).

TABLE 19.3

Manufacturing and Service Specialization of Santa Clara County, California (1995)

SIC	Industry	Firms	>1,000 Jobs	Total Jobs	Location Quotient	Surplus
	Manufacturing Sector					
3674	Semiconductors and related devices	165	7	30,305	23.40	29,010
399	Administrative and auxiliary	113	8	28,948	3.02	19,351
3679	Electronic components	179	5	20,209	14.17	18,783
3571	Electronic computers	51	3	14,894	21.49	14,201
3761	Guided missiles and space vehicles	2	1	13,129	29.53	12,684
3661	Telephone and telegraph apparatus	39	3	9,908	16.70	9,315
3572	Computer storage devices	27	2	9,552	33.91	9,270
3672	Printed circuit boards	113	1	8,755	15.30	8,183
3559	Special industry machinery	63	1	7,733	11.01	7,031
3825	Instruments to measure electricity	89	1	7,101	15.71	6,649
	Service Sector					
7363	Help supply services	220	4	30,276	1.75	12,933
7372	Prepackaged software	251	1	12,310	10.49	11,136
8220	Colleges and universities	26	2	19,819	2.19	10,772
7371	Computer programming services	713	2	10,676	4.75	8,427
8731	Commercial physical research	224	2	9,389	7.35	8,112
8711	Engineering services	618	1	8,310	1.67	3,335
7378	Computer maintenance and repair	80	1	3,440	7.51	2,982
7996	Amusement parks	4	1	3,205	4.60	2,508
7334	Photocopying and duplicating services	84	0	2,851	4.96	2,276
7379	Computer-related services	355	0	2,966	3.56	2,134
7381	Detectives and armored car services	81	1	5,805	1.50	1,945
8020	Offices and clinics of dentists	1,054	0	6,373	1.43	1,921
7349	Building maintenance services	365	0	7,661	1.29	1,721
8734	Testing laboratories	66	0	2,047	3.44	1,452
899	Administrative and auxiliary	86	0	4,892	1.42	1,439
7373	Computer-integrated systems design	128	0	2,187	2.72	1,384
8733	Noncommercial research organizations	50	0	1,823	3.17	1,247

Source: Author's calculations from 1994 and 1995 *County Business Patterns* data (Washington, DC: U.S. Department of Commerce, Bureau of the Census, 1997).

Again, the defining characteristics of the economic base approach—measurement, comparison, and extrapolation—can be combined into a relevant, powerful, analytical technique. The comparison is to similar places—geographical control groups—that did not receive the public program being evaluated. The emphasis is on measuring the difference between what actually happened with the program in place, compared to what would have happened had the program not existed. The experience of the control group, or more specifically its growth rates, are used to extrapolate the growth that would have occurred in the absence of the program.

This method and its use to measure the effectiveness of the regional planning programs of the Appalachian Regional Commission (ARC) are described in Isserman and Rephann (1995). A twin outside Appalachia was selected for each of 391 Appalachian counties on the basis of typical economic base considerations, such as industrial composition, location, income, and prior growth rates. Those twins constitute the control group. To determine whether ARC programs had any effect in stimulating economic growth and stemming population loss, the mean difference between the growth rate of each Appalachian county and its twin was calculated over all counties and tested for statistical significance for each outcome variable. The main finding is that Appalachia grew significantly faster in income, earnings, and population. The implication is that ARC's regional planning strategy succeeded in stimulating the region's growth.

More recent research provides further support for that conclusion. Congress has defined a second multistate, lagging region, the Lower Mississippi Delta , but has not funded an ARC-like regional planning program there. If the Mississippi Delta also grew faster than its twins, but without regional planning programs, the inference that regional planning was responsible for Appalachia's faster growth would be seriously undermined. Figure 19.1 summarizes geographical control group findings regarding employment and population growth in the rural portions of both regions (Isserman 1997). They are clear: Appalachia outgrew its twins, but the Delta did not. The lagging region with a sustained, comprehensive regional development program did well, and the one denied such a program fell further behind. The magnitude of the Appalachian effect is large in both relative and absolute terms. For example, the Appalachian counties grew 17 percentage points faster in private-sector employment than their twins between 1969 and 1993, a period in which rural employment grew 43 percent nationally.

The control group method of economic base analysis is relatively simple, again consisting of only comparison, extrapolation, and measurement. Yet its simplicity is its power. Comparison generates compelling information. Based in part on this research regarding outcomes and effectiveness, the Clinton administration submitted legislation in June 1998 to create the Delta Regional Commission (but neither House nor Senate took action).

ENVISIONING FUTURES

Planning is, by definition, future-oriented. A sense of the future population level and composition is essential to land-use planning, transportation

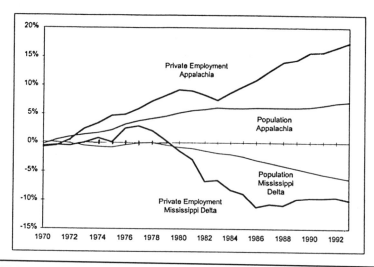

FIGURE 19.1
Growth of the rural counties of Appalachia and the Lower Mississippi Delta relative to their twins (percentage point differences, 1969-1993)

Source: Isserman 1997

planning, facilities planning, and much more. As Donald Krueckeberg and Arthur Silvers wrote in their influential textbook, *Urban Planning Analysis*, "knowledge about past populations and assumptions about future populations are fundamental to planning decisions in every aspect of community life" (1974, p. 259). Yet planners have been going about population forecasting all wrong (Isserman 1984, 1985). Planners are mechanically producing numbers that are not forecasts, using these numbers as if they were forecasts, and making plans as if the role of planning were simply to accommodate what is forecast.

The standard approaches consist of measurement and extrapolation. The most popular approach, the cohort-component method, entails measuring past fertility, mortality, and migration rates and extrapolating them into the future (Davis 1995; Isserman 1993; Klosterman 1990). Another consists of mathematical extrapolation of past trends in population change. A third extrapolates employment growth rates and then uses population–employment ratios to project population, as in Hoyt's step seven. These mechanically produced numbers usually are released to the public as projections. They are conditional statements such as, "If current birth, death, and migration rates continue, the population in 2020 will be 231,900." Unfortunately, the planning process often ignores the all-important "if" and treats the numbers as if they were forecasts of the most likely future. Planners then make land-use, transportation, and other plans to accommodate 231,000 people by the year 2020, but in most cases no one scrutinizes the critical assumptions of that unheard "if." Considerable effort has gone into testing the ability of different projection techniques to project the future accurately and to identify which techniques work best under what circumstances (Isserman 1977; Smith 1987), but all those techniques fail to engage the future in any active or creative sense. They are essentially expert-driven numerical exercises.

Economic base analysis, combined with the extrapolation techniques, offers planners the opportunity to stimulate discussion of the future, but the techniques must be used differently. Doing so is consistent with contemporary movements toward strategic planning, collaborative visioning, and other interactive, participatory forms of planning. The first analytical step is to create the kinds of economic base numbers shown in tables 19.1 to 19.3 for the entire economy. The objective is to gain an understanding of what industries constitute the economy, how the economy is specialized relative to other places, and how the economy is changing.

Charleston, West Virginia, is an interesting case in point. The economic base data helped correct an outdated image in the minds of many local officials and planners, who viewed Charleston as a declining area dependent on three stagnant industries: chemicals, mining, and state government. The data revealed a very different Charleston. In fact, it is a health services center, financial services center, communications and utilities center, regional shopping center, and wholesale trade center.

Many communities harbor outdated views of themselves and their economic bases. Using the venerable tools of economic base analysis with today's databases and computing software, a planner can radically transform public discussions about the future by presenting a reliable, detailed portrait of the present. After seeing an interesting, rich, new view of today, people can envision tomorrow far more imaginatively.

The second analytical step entails the use of conventional economic and demographic trend extrapolations in a new way. The typical practices of proffering one projection series or a high, middle, and low series (from which the middle one seems invariably to be selected) curtail public discussion in deference to the analyst's professional expertise. The opportunity for the community to engage the future is lost. No one is invited to think and participate when the planning analyst appears already to have produced the answer.

Today's computer capacity, software, and readily available machine-readable databases make it possible to generate many projection series within a week. This new development creates an opportunity to engage the public. The analyst should divulge the entire range of credible projections from numerous different techniques, grouping and explaining them in such a way that they can be comprehended and discussed by the public. The goal is to stimulate an informed consideration of the future, not the glassy-eyed acceptance of a technical exercise. The uncertainty, the options, and the technical limitations of predicting the future should all be made clear.

A good presentation will focus thought and attention on the future. In the Charleston case, a dozen credible population projection series based on reasonable economic and demographic assumptions formed a small set of scenarios, which varied by as much as 25 percent by the year 2020. The ensuing discussion focused on the implications and plausibility of the scenarios and raised key questions about the present and future nature of Charleston.

Step three is the choice of a forecast from among the many possible projections or scenarios. The need to choose creates the opportunity again to help the community engage its future. As Amy Helling (1998, 345) has written, "One of the reasons that collaborative visioning is so appealing to planners is its emphasis on citizen participation." By providing a full range of projections, explaining their underlying assumptions, and cajoling the choice out of those involved in the planning process, the analyst can stimulate a consensus-building discussion of the future in an informed, open planning process. Underlying such a process is the premise that the analyst has the skill to generate the numbers, but the public, knowing the "ground truth," is at least equally qualified to select among them.

An alternative strategy, also a departure from conventional practice, requires the planner to make that choice—at least, the initial choice. This strategy acknowledges that others involved in the planning process may lack the knowledge, time, interest, information, or ability. Forecasting requires speculation, judgment, vision, and imagination. The analyst should learn to forecast instead of avoiding the responsibility by passing it on to an untrained public or hiding behind a projection. To forecast, the analyst must bring together the economic and demographic studies into a consistent compelling view of the future. Here is another instance of why James Throgmorton (1992, 17) calls planning "persuasive storytelling about the future." After the public evaluates the persuasiveness of the story and the logic of its arguments, the story might change, as often occurs with effective public participation.

Both strategies use economic base analysis as a key starting point. They differ in where the responsibility of the planning expert stops and that of the public begins. The chief outcome in either case should be a community actively engaging its future. Used well, the old analytical techniques can be extremely effective in creating the fundamental understanding of a place that informs the entire planning process.

LESS NAÏVE IN THE INFORMATION AGE

Although this chapter has noted a persistence and continuity of fundamental approaches to economic base analysis, much has changed in terms of what the planning analyst actually does. The sheer computational power, mapping and graphing capabilities, and amount of data now available to the practitioner were unthinkable 50 years ago, or even 15 or 10 years ago. Today, one planning analyst can create more planning information, including data, graphs, and maps, in a month than an entire planning staff could have produced in a year.

No longer consumed by the task of generating the information, the analyst's main concern now should be interpreting and communicating the information. Interpretation is made easier because today's analyst can draw on the profession's now extensive quantitative experience, the availability of data series for longer time periods, and a fuller understanding of numbers and how they change. To cite one example, a CD-ROM available from the U.S. Department of Commerce (1998) for $35 now provides data on employment, population, and income for every county from 1969 through 1997. Equipped with such information, a planner is far better able to interpret and put into context recent changes and events, as well as make forecasts.

Today's planning analyst also benefits from the profession's experience with its limitations. Lloyd Rodwin (1963, 141) once defined an expert as "someone who knows what he doesn't know." Seventy years of economic base analysis have taught us that we do not know, and cannot know, certain things. Compared to the naive, optimistic scientific mind-set of the 1950s and early 1960s, planners now know that there are no fantastic formulas, no magic multipliers, and no easy answers to most planning questions. Planning is a blend of social science, art, and politics. The successful planning analyst draws on social science, but not social science alone, in creating accurate, convincing stories that we can earnestly believe and that can lead us to imagine desirable futures that we can hope to attain.

20

Changes in Theorizing and Planning Urban Economic Growth

BENNETT J. HARRISON

Within economics, geography, sociology, and political science, underlying paradigms have changed dramatically in the years since the end of World War II. As a result, some of the theories, policy prescriptions, and analytical tools currently used by urban planners have become, at best, outdated and, at worst, seriously invalid and likely to provide misleading if not downright erroneous forecasts and expectations.

More specifically, many analytical techniques and procedures in the "old" urban analysis—especially those that associate a city's growth almost uniquely with the ability of its resident firms to capture external export markets, and which support policy approaches that emphasize attracting new investments (factories, stores, offices, laboratories, and big infrastructure projects) from the outside—are being called into question. To understand how cities grow and develop, as well as how their various resident populations fare, now requires greater attention than ever before to the processes that make up what is popularly called "globalization." One of these is accelerating and remarkably universal technological change; best-practice producers can now be found at sites around the globe. Another element is the apparently growing trend toward the contracting out by firms of work formerly performed in-house, or "outsourcing." Much of the classical industrial location theory, and the associated plant-recruitment policies of local government planners, explicitly or implicitly assumed what economists call "perfectly competitive markets," including the idea that individual businesses compete with one another (if they compete at all) almost entirely at arm's length, through the impersonal mediations of supply, demand, and relative price. The new approaches emphasize the growing importance of multilocational business enterprises, networks, and strategic alliances among webs of companies and agencies that both compete *and* collaborate, with prices being only one of many relevant parameters. For example, planner-geographer Michael Storper has considerably expanded the earlier theorizing of the political scientist Charles Sabel in exploring what he and others call the "untraded interdependences" (such as trust) that keep firms and other organizations engaged with one another in repeat contracting but that are not reducible to relative prices and costs of commodities. Finally, the emerging paradigm stresses the increasing relative importance of *information*—managers' knowledge about new technologies, polyvalent capabilities of workers, local public officials' awareness of conditions in other places, the quality of local schools and community colleges—rather than (as in classic location theory) associating a locale's competitive advantages mainly with its endowment of natural resources. In this new context, some cities and regions have, in Allen Scott's well-known expression, become "new industrial spaces."

The organization of how urban development planning gets done has been transformed, too. Michael Teitz (1997) gives considerable attention to the proliferation of all manner of "public–private partnerships," special-purpose tax districts, consortia of companies and community colleges, and other institutional innovations for inducing and managing growth. Planners today are expected to demonstrate a high degree of facility with such tools as personal computer-based financial spreadsheets, without which the management and control, monitoring and evaluation of the alliances would be impossible. Planners increasingly engage in Geographic Information Systems (GIS) modeling of the changing spatial distribution of business activity within their cities and metropolitan regions, along with analyzing such diffuse processes as the interneighborhood spread of crime or the incidence of AIDS—both of which are germane to the site-selection decisions of companies. By contrast, it has become less relevant, and planners are less likely to be asked, to estimate local "economic base multipliers," a cornerstone of conventional practice in the earlier era.

Teitz also acknowledges the growing number—and arguably the political influence—of community development corporations (CDCs) and other community-based organizations (CBOs), especially in neighborhoods of color. Concerned mainly with equality, distributive justice, and power, the role of the CBOs with respect to urban growth, per se—that is, without the production and delivery of goods and services—is likely to increase. This is due to the continued trends toward "privatization"—the turning over of the production and especially the delivery of a growing number of formerly government services to the business sector—and the ongoing "downsizing" and (as explained above) outsourcing of production and service delivery from large private companies and governments to nonprofit, nongovernmental organizations. This "new view" of CBOs—as more central to urban affairs, and as increasingly engaged in collaborative partnerships with other organizations in their regions—is now widely held among such planning educators as Norman Glickman, Lisa Servon, Pierre Clavel, and Bennett Harrison, in the consulting firms and think tanks that evaluate CBO efforts, and within the private foundations that support so much of the economic development work of these entities.

The planning educator Edward Hill; former Secretary of the U.S. Department of Housing and Urban Development, Henry Cisneros; and Bruce Katz, executive director of the Center for Urban and Metropolitan Policy at the Brookings Institution, are only three of numerous experts who are reemphasizing that the rates of economic growth of cities and their suburbs are interdependent. Not all the underlying trends relating city to suburb are new; for example, jobs and power continue their century-long shift to the suburbs and beyond. However, new studies emphasize that the "suburbs" themselves have become increasingly heterogeneous: by race, ethnicity, family income, property values, and the quality of the infrastructure. An entire, new research literature and political analysis is coming into existence to make sense of the implications of the growth of black middle-class suburbanization and the deterioration of schools, public services, and physical infrastructure in many white working-class suburbs. How to more closely connect suburban and inner-city African-American populations, and the possibilities for building political alliances between inner-city and inner-suburban communities around common interests with respect to the funding of schools and the maintenance of public facilities, are problems occupying such political theorists as Theda Skocpol, John Mollenkopf, and Joel Rogers—scholars whose work has strongly influenced planning—that were scarcely imaginable two decades ago. These concerns are consonant with the "flexible new economy" writing of business strategy theorists Michael Porter and Rosabeth Moss Kanter, who emphasize both traded and untraded interdependences—webs of relationships—among economic and political actors within a metropolitan area. To reprise an earlier point, what all these scholars are doing is taking the new theory, with its associated constellation of development policy implications, further in the direction of the study of *relationship*, away from the older, sometimes almost exclusive focus of classical urban economics on resource scarcities and relative prices and costs.

Now, in any such "stages of growth" theorizing, there is always a danger in overemphasizing the sources of historical discontinuity. Many of the policy issues with which contemporary urban planners must grapple are anything but new. Moreover, for planners, it is not quite so straightforward a matter as identifying the "correct" underlying theories from economics and human geography and getting planning practices in sync. For one thing, the theories themselves are contested, and debates rage within the disciplines about which changes in how modern urban economies work are more and less salient.[1] For another, general, abstract theories can offer only frameworks for the design and evaluation of real, concrete, grounded practice. Moreover, some analytical techniques developed in earlier eras continue to be both useful and relevant to contemporary planning concerns. Indeed, such technological improvements as spreadsheets have made at least some of these older techniques, such as input-output analysis, arguably *more* useful (or, at any rate, as geographer William Breyers puts it, "easier to use"), especially when based on extensive original survey research on the purchasing practices of local actors.

While much has changed in the fabric of the urban economy and in its place in the larger, profoundly altered context of global economic and political institutions and relations, some of the most fundamental and long-standing normative issues within urban and metropolitan economics continue, rightly, to occupy the interest and energy of urban planners. Thus, for example, globalization has certainly not mitigated planners' concerns about labor market segmentation—the subjects of new books by the planner-economist Chris Tilly and by the economic geographer Jamie Peck—and, with it, who gets and does not get the "good jobs." Indeed, the urbanists Saskia Sassen and Manuel Castells both believe that the global expansion of productive and financial relations has exacerbated the tendency toward a "two-tiered economy."

Similarly, the decline of mass production and the growing importance of customization, design, product and service quality, time to market, and other determinants of profitability in this, the "age of flexibility," have in no way eliminated racial and ethnic discrimination or lessened planners' interests in how different immigrant groups are inserted differently into the spaces and life of the city. As the popular and influential writing of William Julius Wilson (and his more technical followers such as Paul Jargowsky) shows, the "new economy" continues to incorporate pockets of concentrated and persistent urban poverty, with their ability to "infect" proximate neighborhoods, stigmatize residents, and reinforce their disconnection from the larger society and region. In other words, Wilson and Jargowsky believe in the existence and importance of neighborhood effects.

Nevertheless, for all these qualifications, it does appear that many urban planning practices (and some analytical techniques) have had to undergo profound alterations in the face of broad underlying changes in the nature of urban growth processes. Most notable is the transformation from a post–

World War II "golden age" of nation–state-based corporate capitalism, in which governments deployed aggregate fiscal and monetary ("Keynesian") policies aimed at maintaining low unemployment without excessive inflation, into the more fragmented contemporary world of increasingly decentralized (but not necessarily small-scale) production. Central governments have devolved considerable power to other levels and actors; paradoxically, both the global *and* the local scales of economic and social activity have become ascendant, vis-à-vis national activity. Such urbanists as Castells, Scott, Harrison, Storper, Gordon Clark, Ash Amin, and Nigel Thrift have coined various names to capture the outlines of this emerging configuration, from a revival of "free market" ideology to "post-Fordism" to the "networked society." An even more general characterization builds on the ideas and a generative metaphor developed by Michael Piore and Charles Sabel and elaborated by David Harvey. In Harvey's words, we have entered the era of "flexible accumulation." Whatever it is called, we must examine what has changed, as well as the implications for the practice of urban planning today.

By the early 1980s, a substantial new body of urban and regional growth theory has been coming on line, and with it, a new vocabulary. Such planning educators as Ann Markusen, Doreen Massey, Susan Christopherson, AnnaLee Saxenian, Glasmeier, Scott and Storper, Harrison (in collaboration with the economist Barry Bluestone), and others were writing about business "restructuring" and increasingly complex geographic arrangements of firms, workers, residences (especially with the growth of two-earner households), industries, and occupations—what Massey calls the "spatial divisions of labor." Building on themes first developed by Piore and Sabel, planners were documenting the growth of (and engaging in the creation of policies to promote) "industrial districts." Urban planners began to make use of the (partly) new concepts of clusters, sectors, and networks. Across all the academic disciplines, influenced especially by theoretical developments in the fields of business strategy, organizational sociology, and the economics of technological change, analysts wanting to forecast and enhance local economic growth were paying less attention to inventorying the resource profiles of a place, and increasing attention to the capacity of local organizations and how relationships among these organizations were *governed*—that is, how the networks, alliances, subcontracting chains, and public–private partnerships were being managed, how they hold together, what forces threaten to pull them apart. Best-practice business development policy came to emphasize *retention* ("hold on to what you already have in place") and *entrepreneurship* (use policy to "incubate" lots of new start-ups) over (or at least along with) *recruitment* of existing businesses from elsewhere ("smokestack chasing" or, in the case of high tech, "chip chasing").

The agendas of community development corporations (CDCs) and other community-based organizations (CBOs) expanded enormously, and their methods and practices were transformed in ways that mirrored some of the most fundamental organizational principles of the new age, especially as regards the formation of alliances and collaborations across geographic and political boundaries—in a word, *turfs*—and across such functional areas as housing and jobs. In a complementary approach, Ronald Ferguson and Sarah Stoutland were replacing the old view of CBOs as largely stand-alone organizations doing "deals" with others, with models in which CBOs are embedded in complex, multilevel layers of local and regional institutional relationships.

Analytically, sector studies, case writing, spreadsheet-based financial analysis, and game-theoretic decision models were becoming as (or more) important to planners than the use of the traditional, formal urban and regional models. This was occurring even as the technological and record-keeping capabilities for vastly improving the validity and "computability" of some of the older methods (especially input–output) were actually growing.

Where do we stand today? Clearly, many contemporary urban processes and the place of the city in the regional, national, and global economies *are* different and require new theoretical and analytic tools for making sense of them. The planning journals[2] and leading academic departments[3] seem well (if unevenly) aware of these changes, and new curricula have come on line in recent years to reflect these understandings.

But some of what seems to be "new" about the theoretical bases for, and analytical tools available to, urban planners concerned with economic growth probably *is* "old wine in new bottles." Some of the more broad-brush, far-reaching claims for a regime change in urban development policy strategies may have been exaggerated, while what seemed to be so new turns out to have sometimes been mostly a matter of the changing, more variable *scales* of policy action—local, metropolitan, regional, national, global. As Teitz observes, there is still little hard empirical evidence or hypothesis-testing of the processes said by the theorists of flexible accumulation to have become dominant in economic affairs. Nor have its policy prescriptions or expectations been shown decisively to have been borne out.

Therefore, although much has changed, the openness of the new view to the future, the comparative novelty of many of its ideas, and a fundamental (and quite unprecedented) uncertainty that pervades even mainstream economic and other social scientific disciplines in the present era—all of these warrant a large dose of tentativeness and humility in making predictions about how all this is likely to turn out in the years ahead.

21

Further Notes on Changes in Theorizing

WILLIAM ALONSO

To my mind, one of our underlying concerns is the great transition in economic activity that has accelerated in the second half of the twentieth century. This transition, yet to run its course, is from an economy that was an extension of both the agricultural and the industrial revolutions, based on material production and transformation—to an economy variously characterized as being service-based, information-based, or by any number of comparable labels.

It is not that agriculture or manufacturing are less productive than services, or in any significant sense declining in their shares of national product. It is that the shares of workers in those occupations are declining, while the share of workers engaged in a formless conglomerate commonly called "services" is increasing. This quantitative dimension of economic change most of us, myself included, take to be so profound as to amount to qualitative change. It is a situation reminiscent of the late nineteenth and early twentieth centuries, when the great figures of the emergent social sciences (Marx, Weber, Durkheim, Simmel, and Park) were trying to formulate appropriate ways of understanding then emerging organizations of production and their corresponding emerging geographic correlates, the great industrial cities. The changes were extraordinary and monstrous, and these scholars tried to epitomize them in theories which, however fusty they may seem today, are still taught as the theoretical basis of sociology and political economy: alienation, class (true and false) consciousness, anomie, *Gemeinschaft* and *Gesellschaft*, and so on.

The transformation of Western societies they were trying to interpret were momentous, their efforts at interpretation were heroic and, I think, on the whole correct—if not dead-bang on, at least close enough to help one think about the social change of that period. These thinkers and observers of about a hundred years ago have become "dead white males," anachronistic whales beached and abandoned (except in the academic disciplines) in the backwaters of still ongoing social change.

I think that we are now (about a century later) undergoing, mostly blindly, comparable social and economic changes, both quantitatively and qualitatively. Theirs was from rural to urban (labels are always unsatisfactory); ours is, perhaps, from materials, from stuff, to information. As Bennett Harrison's chapter in this volume illustrates (Harrison 2000), we are trying to label this transformation at the same time we try to understand it. Hence, we are all fumbling for a new vocabulary, its terms typically having short half-lives: post-industrial, information society, service society, post-Fordism, social capital, flexible accumulation, flexible new economy, globalization, outsourcing, strategic networks, untraded interdependencies, public-private partnerships, downsizing, restructuring, and so forth.

The particular questions to be considered here have to do with how the discipline of urban planning has fared during these transformations, and what its prospects are.

The most basic transformation for urban economic planning has been the transition from the vision of Alfred Weber to that of his brother, Max. Letting Alfred stand for a host of cognate concepts and techniques, his world is one of massive resource extraction and material transformation: steel-making, large-scale manufacturing and chemical industries, a maturing goods transportation infrastructure, and so forth. Max's word (again, using him as a symbol) is one of entrepeneurship, institutions, changing social structures. Alfred is about *things*; Max is about social structures and interactions.

Even at midcentury, and for years after World War II, the techniques taught in planning schools were those of Alfred's world: the dangerous half-truths of Alfred's industrial location theory, and variants of economic base theory, from the crudest basic-service multipliers to input–output and shift-share analysis. In the practice of the discipline, the principal strategy was that of smokestack chasing, trying to attract manufacturing by tax concessions, industrial parks, and other infrastructure improvements. The practice was, for the most part, locally ineffective and probably less than a zero-sum game at the national level. It was something akin to a cargo cult: the indigenes of some South Pacific islands who, having seen American cargo planes landing in strips cleared by the Marines and unload great treasures, would clear their own strips and sit night after night, tending the fires lining them, waiting for the great silver bird to deliver its cargo of wealth.

In the late 1970s there was a sea change in attitudes, epitomized politically by Reagan and Thatcher and among academics and business gurus by the rediscovery of Schumpeter. Entrepeneurship was the key word; privatization, deregulation, and the like were (and still are) favored policies. At the local level, for economic planners, the language changed: it was not a question of attracting jobs, but one of removing the deadening hand of government and letting the magic of the market do its job. At least as far as rhetoric went, there was a shift from cargo cult language to a new one that stressed exorcising the incubus of government and allowing the spirits of entrepeneurship to dance up from the ground. Just how this was to be done was vague, amounting to fostering entrepeneurship, fostering growth, and retaining growing small enterprises. (In fact, if one checked what the thousands of enterprise, or empowerment, zones actually did, it still amounted to chasing smokestacks.)

Obviously, these changes in intellectual atmosphere had considerable consequences for intellectual premises and style of local economic planning. They also influenced it in form, as Harrison notes, in the rise of community development corporations (CDCs) and community-based organizations (CBOs). The record of these institutional initiatives is still, I gather, mostly anecdotal and hopeful. I myself am skeptical. In the first place, I have seen too many uplift programs with results that ranged from nil to dismal. Second, I sense a conflict between the notion that the source of economic dynamism is entrepeneurship, and the notion that this dynamism is available under corporatist concepts implied in the word community in the names of both these styles of organization.

Note is made how much easier it is now to do traditional economic base or input–output analysis because of powerful desktop computers and programs such as Excel. Quite true, but this leads me to the last point I want to make. The backbone of the economy of what may be called the extended nineteenth century, which carried essentially into the post–World War II period, was the extraction, transformation, and recombination of materials, from coal and ore and rubber to Model T's, and later to early plastics, prepared foods, radios, and the like. It was relatively easy to calculate how much input (steel, rubber, petroleum, glass) was needed per unit of output, and to work backward and forward to estimate the integrated whole.

The fact is, however, our economy now consists—in large, if not the most part—of activities that are much less satisfyingly material. We do not understand today's economy nearly as well as we did the earlier one. Perhaps this is as it was in the transition to the industrial age about a century ago.

As to input–output, it is difficult, if not metaphysical, to quantify the contributions to final product (and its value) of such major inputs as real estate agents, advertising agencies, corporate lawyers, and security guards. This is not to argue that they are unnecessary or unproductive; it is merely that one cannot say that product X needs $0.13 of input Y per dollar of output.

Two other factors make it much more difficult to see what large sectors of the economy are and how these sectors interact. First, the SIC categories are very badly obsolete. This was already the case at the time of the first Reagan administration, but plans to update them then were postponed for budgetary reasons (recall the gigantic boost in defense expenditures); now, nearly two decades later, they are, for many of our most dynamic economic sectors, barely in touch with reality.

Second, it is not only our conception of industrial categories that has drifted out of focus. In many cases, the very concept of the firm has become fuzzy, with doubtful boundaries. For tax and benefits considerations, employees become contractors. Principal activities are outsourced, including payroll, product design, advertising, and physical production. Major manufacturing firms, whether they make sneakers or computers, may have no productive facilities of their own. Major service firms may have only a small core staff, along with a mind-numbing set of contract relations with other, shadowy enterprises. What is done, how it is done, and who does it are dizzying processes in multidimensional international space, in cyberspace, and in a gossamer of contractual and legal constructs.

To be sure, there are still situations you can sink your teeth into: teaching school, making batteries or orange juice concentrate, or grinding lenses. But these tend to be important only in local microcosms, while in a larger context they are like the nuts and raisins floating in the matrix of a morphing fruitcake.

What, then, of the role of the city planner in local economic development? Surely there are myriad different situations, but on the whole I think that the planner cannot aspire to draw legitimacy from a mastery of hard-edged techniques (such as input–output) that might allow her or him to get a grasp of the current situation and know what to do about it in the realm of economic dangers and opportunities. I think that, on the whole, the planner cannot be a credible technician, rather that the planner must be an attentive participant, a facilitator (how easily such words come!) working with the other actors in the local public and private sectors, nurturing to local enterprise and helpful to potential new economic citizens.

Years ago, John Friedmann suggested a distinction between adaptive and developmental planning. To my mind, in today's environment, the local planner must build a solid base on the adaptive aspect, and use it where possible for developmental purposes. This planner must be a Jeeves to a world that is Bertie Wooster.

Part IV

THE PUBLIC IMAGE
AND
THE LEADERSHIP ROLE
OF THE PROFESSION

22

The Planner as Urban Designer: Reforming Planning Education in the New Millennium

ALEX KRIEGER

A quarter-of-a-century ago, planning education began to distance itself from design and spatial concerns for several primary reasons. A condemnation of urban renewal as poor, top-down problem-solving led to a growing general suspicion of master planning. A skepticism of the architect's tendency to frame society's needs primarily in physical terms gave momentum to find fuller professional autonomy from the field of architecture. A cultural inclination to seek the (presumed) more objective insights of the social sciences accelerated. And the hypothesis that studying and framing public policy was the basic task of planning gained ground. Despite such laudable reasoning about expanded professional aims, the diminished interest in design proved to be a limitation. In the transition from the "narrower" world of spatial thinking to the broader world of process and policy formulation, the work of planners became more abstract, less approachable, and, ironically, more distant from public expectations about what a plan or planners can do. Planning education is in need of reform again, now by reintroducing design thinking into the curricula.

Future historians of planning may even chart a correlation since the 1970s between the disengagement from spatial concerns (and three-dimensional visualization) and a waning public influence, even loss of professional confidence. Compare the idealism of a mid-century description of planning as "shaping the outward frame and envelope of a communal life" to a typical 1970s definition of planning as "a sociological, economical, technological, psychological, ecological science." The latter may sound all-encompassing but is, in fact, less meaningful.

Sometime after the social unrest of the 1960s, the mandate of planning shifted from a means to constructing a better world to avoiding further deterioration caused by unchecked sprawl, urban blight, rapacious developers, insensitive architects, unenlightened public officials, and, indeed, failed plans. A fear of producing more failed plans before an increasingly demanding, less patient public led to a syndrome that Alan Altshuler of Harvard refers to as the "do no harm" objective. It sounds logical enough, yet it is doubtful whether any field with such modest ambitions can achieve success, or ultimately gain respect.

Planning, in fact, has become perceived as bureaucratic. Expected to guard the status quo, planners are often seen as part of the problem: as the defenders of traditional zoning ordinances, for example, under increasing attack for perpetuating, among many things, single-use sprawl. Planning is also often accused of being reactive to real estate or political interests rather than helping guide these. Ironically, greater public involvement in the planning process has had the unanticipated consequence of diminishing regard for professional expertise. "Don't leave planning to planners" is a not uncommon refrain. Planners are expected to listen well but not often be heard. Such loss of authority in combination with a disengagement from (even disdain about) design inhibits planners from effecting—or even effectively commenting on—the stuff their constituencies wish for most frequently: improved neighborhoods, access to better places of work and commerce, and better designed environments.

Curiously, given how often planners have sought to distinguish themselves from architects, it has taken a new generation of urban-minded, sprawl-fighting architects to recapture this time-honored aim of planning—the shaping of community. Increasingly role models among planners, Andres Duany and his new urbanist colleagues have made us realize the power of *illustrating* the effects of planning: illustrating both good planning principles, in their terms, as well as the consequences of failed policies or techniques such as Euclidean zoning. It is this possibility of being able to visualize planning that is having a profound impact on citizens *and* planners themselves.

Add to the planner's educational background a grounding in urban design and you have a far more powerful professional. The DNA of my ideal planner at the dawn of the new century would consist of the following nine specifications:

1. While possessing a humanist's ethic, the best planners will have a grounding in spatial thinking and assume design to be a transformative activity. Urbanism is three-dimensional, the Internet revolution notwithstanding. Few planning processes are complete without a sophisticated ability to analyze, visualize, and orchestrate relationships in space.

2. Planners must understand the persisting importance for people of place-making and place-maintenance. Process and policies are only the means. The current national debate about "community" and "quality of life" centers on tangible things, like traffic, not notions (important though they may be) about equitable resource allocation. The best planning must be place-centered, requiring planners who can engage in a discourse about what creates and maintains good places.

3. While acknowledging the complexities of urban affairs and, thus, remaining open to insights from the parallel fields of government, economics, law, sociology, cultural geography, and history, the best planners will not hide in the shadows of other disciplines but will articulate what the art of planning itself contributes to society.

4. The best planners will value the expertise of other design professionals, including that of architects and landscape architects. This is obvious,

but interprofessional rivalries often inhibit cooperation. Landscape architecture, for example, encompasses much that is important about cities and city life, while the field's particular sensitivity to environment and place is essential to good urban thinking.

5. The best planners will understand the (nearly dominating) importance of the visual sense and of visual media in contemporary culture. Therefore, they will develop tools with which to illustrate the consequences of planning principles, not just recite them.

6. Good planners will develop an innate respect for those qualities that a society shares and for the broad public realm. They will thus seek to calibrate the needs of a group or neighborhood against those of a town or region. Though all politics may be local, wise planning cannot emerge strictly from parochial values.

7. The most effective planners must be more situationalists than ideologues. The twentieth century witnessed immense urban harm caused by those who offered a singular or universal idea of what a city is, or what urbanization should produce. That is why faith in newly offered panaceas, such as the new urbanism, should remain partial. As valuable as this discussion has been, some advocates manifest their own stubbornness to choice in settlement patterns; the sin they lay at the feet of mid-century planners.

8. The most enlightened planners will remain alert to broad demographic and economic trends. They will not be sentimentalists. They will be as interested in the ramifications of the unprecedented scale and speed of urban development in Southeast Asia as in the parallel urbanization throughout the developing world. They will distinguish among mandates, realizing that to renew the centers of cities, build new cities, restore the parts of old cities worthy of preservation, and construct equitable growth management programs on the periphery, vastly different strategies, techniques, and policies are required.

9. The best planners will *once more* be educators and advocates (though not preachers). They will not leave their constituencies confounded by overwrought theory nor helpless over the apparent insolubility of the problems at hand. They will listen closely and communicate well with multiple constituencies, and they will also lobby well on behalf of neighborhoods, cities, and the general values of good urbanism. It is pointless to train planners to be mere *absorbers* of public opinion waiting for consensus to build.

The above are the characteristics of a mature generalist. Today's world is often suspicious of generalists, considering them ill equipped at specialized skills. Yet those who can examine seemingly unrelated factors or phenomena and grasp their interrelationships—the hallmark of design education—are the most valuable professionals. The best planners should be such individuals, and as such they will be well suited to engage in the complexities of contemporary urbanism.

23

Where Have All the Planners Gone?

WITOLD RYBCZYNSKI

In August 1868, a committee of private citizens in Buffalo, New York invited Frederick Law Olmsted, already celebrated for laying out Central Park and Prospect Park, to visit the city. Buffalo had prospered because of the Erie Canal and was an important meatpacking and iron-manufacturing center, as well as a grain-handling port. The civic leaders had decided that one of the 10 largest cities in the United States should have a public park, and that Olmsted was the man to design it. He stayed in Buffalo for two days on his way to Chicago, arranging to return on his way back to address the committee at greater length.

In Buffalo a week later, Olmsted discovered that he was to address a public meeting of some 200 people, chaired by a local notable, the former President Millard Fillmore. Moreover, this august assembly expected Olmsted to describe his vision for the park. He had only two days to gather his thoughts. He and his assistant made a quick survey, walked the land, and dug test pits. There were three alternative sites, all outside the city. The largest, in an undeveloped area four miles north of downtown, consisted of 350 acres in a wooded valley. The other two were smaller: thirty-five acres beside the Niagara River, and high ground overlooking the city and Lake Erie.

Olmsted proposed that the city acquire not one but all three sites. They approximated the shape of a huge baseball diamond, with downtown Buffalo at home plate, the high ground at first base, the wooded valley at second, and the riverside site at third. The distance between the "bases" was two to three miles. He proposed parkways and tree-lined avenues to link the parks with each other and with the downtown. Despite a severe cold, he spoke for an hour "with tolerable smoothness and I should think with gratifying results,"

210

he wrote his wife Mary. "At any rate the men who started it were very much pleased and encouraged" (Schuyler and Censer 1992, 269). It was a tour de force. In two hectic days, Olmsted had conceived the outlines not of a park but of a park *system*. Indeed, he had set the parameters for a master plan that would guide the city for decades to come.

The city fathers agreed. Olmsted and his partner, Calvert Vaux, designed the three parks. They widened several of the major streets to one hundred feet to create treed avenues. They laid out a mile-long, 200-foot-wide parkway modeled on the Avenue de l'Impératrice in Paris. The parkway led to a large *rond-point* on the scale of the Place de l'Etoile; from this circle, two additional parkways radiated to two more formal squares. The longest parkway was three miles long. The Parisian influence on the plan is obvious and is at odds with Olmsted's reputation as a proponent of winding streets and picturesque planning. He was nothing if not pragmatic. He and Vaux did not produce a version of European neo-baroque planning such as would later be revived by the City Beautiful movement. Indeed, that is the strength of this plan. It is neither a geometric diagram nor a theoretical construction imposed on the city; instead, it is a complex, refined network of parks and parkways, avenues and public spaces, that represents a degree of sophistication and originality in town planning previously unknown in the United States, or, indeed, anywhere else. Olmsted and Vaux's plan received an honorable mention at the 1878 Paris Exposition. In 1879, when Edouard André, the notable French landscape architect, published his encyclopedic tome on parks and gardens, *L'Art des Jardins*, he singled out the Buffalo plan. André, who had been the assistant of the great engineer Adolphe Alphand, builder of the Bois de Boulogne, was in a good position to judge Olmsted's work.

> If ever an artist had the good fortune to design a future city and was given carte blanche, I would suggest that he study the very beautiful plans for the city of Buffalo (United States) designed by the skillful American landscape architect, Monsieur F. Law Olmsted. In his plan, different parts of the city are linked by an uninterrupted system of parks and landscaped avenues that are laid out in the grandest and most practical fashion. (André 1879, 188)

Olmsted and Vaux spent the next eight years overseeing the construction of the Buffalo park system. In the 1890s, Olmsted alone designed two more large parks for the city, and after his retirement his firm laid out a final park beside the Niagara River. Thanks to these multiple interventions, Buffalo became known as the "City of Elms."

The remarkable story of Olmsted and the Buffalo master plan is instructive in several respects. The commitment to town planning on the part of the leading citizens of Buffalo was authentic and substantial; Olmsted estimated that the total cost would be about half a million dollars (more than $15 million today), a significant sum for a city of only 50,000. The foresight of Olmsted (and the city council) is impressive. The built area of Buffalo was tiny compared to the far-reaching plan; even the closest parks were well outside the city. Olmsted warned the city council that, "after the design for a park has been fully digested, a long series of years must elapse before the ends of the design will begin to be fully realized" (*Preliminary Report* 1869, 12). Indeed, it took more than 50 years for these areas to fill in.

Equally impressive is the degree to which Olmsted concerned himself with a full range of planning issues: beautification, public health, recreation, and the urban movement. Real estate development was also addressed, since the parkways were intended to raise property values throughout the city, an early example of public planning influencing private market investment. "We should recommend that in your scheme a large park should not be the sole object in view," he advised in his preliminary report, "but should be regarded simply as the more important member of a general, largely provident, forehanded, comprehensive arrangement for securing refreshment, recreation and health to the people" (*Preliminary Report* 1869, 18). To achieve these ends, Olmsted distributed open space throughout the city, making outdoor recreation accessible to the population at large. Elsewhere, broad avenues and parkways introduced trees and greenery—and order. In Buffalo, Olmsted demonstrated how the burgeoning American industrial city could be made livable.

The plan was a radical departure from the utilitarian grid that characterized American town planning—if one can call it that—throughout most of the nineteenth century. The Buffalo park system incorporated high civic ideals. But there was nothing utopian about Olmsted's proposals; that is why he was able to explain them to the Buffalo city fathers, and that is why they adopted them with little hesitation. The parks and parkways dwarfed the city but were delicately designed to make a seamless connection with existing streets. Buffalo had been planned in 1804 by Joseph Ellicott, the brother of Andrew Ellicott, the collaborator and successor of L'Enfant in Washington. Thus, the town on Lake Erie was an early example of what John Reps has referred to as "backwoods baroque" (Reps 1965, 352). The focus of Ellicott's plan was a large square—later named Niagara Square—from which eight avenues radiated like the spokes of a wheel. Olmsted extended some of these spokes as parkways and kept Delaware Avenue as the main axis of future development. He also replanned Niagara Square to reinforce its intended role as the symbolic center of the city. He was trying to improve Buffalo, not remake it.

It is difficult to imagine a modern American city undertaking a town-planning exercise of this scale so effortlessly. First of all, it is unlikely that civic leaders, businessmen, and municipal politicians would back such an undertaking. A festival marketplace, definitely; a convention center or a sports stadium, maybe; in some cities, even a casino. Such highly visible projects are attractive because they have a financial—and political—payoff. At least, that is the argument put forward by their enthusiastic boosters. But an expensive project that does not directly generate revenue, and whose benefits will not be realized before "a long series of years"—in Olmsted's words—is less attractive.

It is equally difficult to sell such an undertaking to the modern electorate. In a recent municipal referendum, voters turned down a proposal to build Seattle Commons, an 85-acre park at the northern end of downtown Seattle. Many objections were raised, not least the cost. Buffalo built its parks and parkways on 500 acres of undeveloped rural land; Seattle needed only 85 acres, but it was expensive urban land. The cost of buying the land and developing Seattle Commons was estimated to be as much as $250 million; the relocation of two major thoroughfares added another $150 million (*Seattle Times* 1992).

The decision-making process, too, has changed. The construction of the Buffalo park system required an act of the New York state legislature to create a board of park commissioners that would acquire land for parks and streets ("not to exceed five hundred acres"), and to empower the city to issue Buffalo Park Bonds ("not exceeding five hundred thousand dollars") (*Preliminary Report* [Act of the Legislature] 1869, 31, 37). Hence, the public expressed its support for the project through its elected representatives. Today, a project of this magnitude requires lengthy public consultations. New York's Hudson River Park, a five-mile-long stretch of parkland along the river, was originally proposed a decade ago and still does not have full approval. It appears likely that Hudson River Park will be implemented one day, but many similar projects have foundered. The chief obstacles are numerous interest groups that find encouragement in a media that thrives on, and actively promotes, public controversy. Social activists and affordable housing advocates call passionately for spending the money on more pressing needs. Community groups and neighborhood associations lobby for and against the location of parks and parkways according to their parochial concerns. Environmental spokesmen voice their preoccupations. Historic preservation groups weigh in on one side, the real estate industry on another. Often the strongest voice is that of those opposed to growth and development in general. By the time the public hearings are over, it often becomes evident that the safest course of action is— inaction.

Even if, by some miracle, the opposition were silent, an interesting question remains. Where is the Olmsted who can propose how a city can and should grow, who will devise a practical and sensible solution, demonstrate how it can be implemented, and then oversee its implementation? Where are the descendants of Daniel Burnham, of John Charles Olmsted, of John Nolen? *Where are the visionary town planners?*

It is true that there are innovators in the design of large-scale physical environments. In its theme parks, and now in the town of Celebration (Florida), the Walt Disney Company has demonstrated the ability to design and manage places of public congregation. In Las Vegas, casino owners are evolving an unusual form of entertainment architecture that is gradually creating a unique and attractive urban environment. Developers have pioneered common ownership in planned communities. The popularity of regional shopping malls, whether suburban or urban, attests to the ability of the real estate industry to create commercial centers whose scale rivals the downtown of small cities.

Yet, these innovations—shopping malls, office parks, industrial campuses—exist in isolation. They lack the cohesion and interlocking synergy that is the mark of inclusive planning. With the assistance of architects who loosely group themselves under the appellation "new urbanism," developers are starting to build planned communities that integrate residential, commercial, and retail uses in a way that recalls the most successful examples of nineteenth-century town planning. The conventional critique of new urbanism, also referred to as neotraditional planning, is that "we have not yet seen widespread adoption of the idea," and that "it is too early to say" if the approach will "meet the market test" (Teitz 1996, 663). In fact, a fairly large number of neotraditional projects have been realized in the United States and Canada. The most impressive examples are in the city of Markham, outside Toronto, where 11 neighborhoods are currently under construction, representing a cumulative projected population of almost 150,000 people. Smaller projects have been realized in California, Florida, Maryland, and Oregon. There is other evidence of neotraditionalism's appeal. A 1995 attitude survey of recent and prospective home buyers found that only one-third favored conventional suburbs; the rest were attracted—in varying degrees—to neotraditional communities (American Lives 1995). A recent study found that single-family homes in one neotraditional development had a resale premium of $30,000 to $40,000 over comparable units (Tu and Eppli 1997).

If there is a latter-day Olmsted, it might be argued that it is either Andres Duany or Peter Calthorpe, both founders of the Congress for the New Urbanism. Both are effective leaders, public spokesmen, and designers. These "town planners" were trained as architects, not city planners; indeed, professional city planners are curiously absent from the debate. The most influential book on city planning published in the last 40 years is undoubtedly Jane

Jacobs' *The Death and Life of Great American Cities.* Jacobs was a journalist when she wrote that book; so is Joel Garreau, the author of *Edge City*, who offers useful insights into the contemporary metropolis. Anthony Downs, the author of the thoughtful *New Visions for Metropolitan America*, is an economist; David Rusk wrote the controversial *Cities Without Suburbs* after serving as mayor of Albuquerque; Fred Siegel, the author of *The Future Once Happened Here*, is a historian; James Howard Kunstler, who has written provocatively about American urbanism (*The Geography of Nowhere; Home From Nowhere*) is originally a novelist. The sort of person a troubled city is likely to call in for advice today is Oscar Newman (an architect), Jon Jerde (an architect and urban designer), James Q. Wilson (a political scientist), John DiIulio, Jr. (a public policy specialist), Michael Porter (a business school professor), or Robert Davis (a developer). *Where have all the planners gone?*

Alexander Garvin opens *The American City*, a historical overview of city planning, with the statement: "One thing most people share . . . is disillusionment with urban planning as a way of fixing the American city" (Garvin 1996, 1). He goes on to claim that this disillusionment is far from justified but is obliged to admit that, "despite many remarkable successes, American city planning has been plagued with continuing mistakes" (Garvin 1996, 2). The list is embarrassingly long: superblocks and megastructures, high-rise public housing, freestanding cultural, sports and government "centers," slum clearance and urban renewal, and cross-city expressways. (Expressways have destroyed much of Olmsted's Buffalo plan.) Moreover, these "mistakes" were not simply individual projects gone awry; they represent the consistent failure of fundamental planning concepts.

The two professions most heavily implicated in these failures are city planning and architecture. The experience was disillusioning, since these failed concepts were, in many ways, the backbone of the progressive and reformist modern design that had been wholeheartedly endorsed by both professions. Planners and architects reacted by withdrawing from the field. Architects ceased to talk about social improvement through design and returned to the traditional role of master builder. The art museum—not the housing project—became the formative building type. This return to formal concerns proved popular with the public (and with the media), and the most successful designers—I. M. Pei, Philip Johnson, Michael Graves, Richard Meier, Frank Gehry—were lionized. It was a hard bargain, exchanging the role of environmental designer for that of fashion maven, but it was the price of the public's absolution.

The planning profession retreated in a different direction. Unlike architects, city planners are generally not licensed to practice; so there was no sheltered field of professional activity to fall back on. Instead, the chastened profession reshaped itself in a different mold. University curricula were reconfigured to emphasize land-use regulation, public policy, and urban economics. Planners did find work—as civil servants in various governmental planning departments, and as technical consultants to a variety of interest groups such as community development corporations, historical preservation societies, environmental organizations. "The resolution of differences of interest (and the establishment of acceptable means of dealing with them) is a central problem of planning," underlines a recent planning handbook (Cullingworth 1997, 10). *Where have all the planners gone?* Into the meeting room, where they mediate, animate, negotiate, resolve conflicts, find the middle ground. It is an honorable role, but it has one drawback: it leaves the creation of an urban vision entirely to others.

In the final chapter of *The American City*, Garvin calls for a return to comprehensive planning. He cites Burnham's 1909 *Plan of Chicago*, Harland Bartholomew's 1947 plan for St. Louis, Victor Gruen's 1956 plan for Fort Worth, and Portland, Oregon's center city plan. Garvin admits that "such compelling visions of the future also require a level of boldness that is discouraged in our participatory form of government" (Garvin 1996, 428). Yet, the public's demand for participation does not contradict the need for leadership; indeed, participation without leadership produces either mealy-mouthed consensus or inaction. Exactly *who* will provide the leadership and the compelling urban visions for the future remains an open question. It may be the real estate developers, it may be the corporations, it may be the neo-traditional town planners. Most likely, it will be some combination of these three.

24

Where Are the Planners?

DENNIS FRENCHMAN

Frank Gehry, in his preface to a book entitled *The End of Architecture?*, says to the authors: "I am optimistic that all of you will get work and will make beautiful buildings and will not have to sit around and worry about the end of architecture" (Noever 1992, 13). I feel a bit like this when confronted with the question: Where are the planners?

City planning is a vital and growing profession. I can say this because I don't limit my definition of city planning to what goes on in big city planning agencies. And it's a good thing, because people in those agencies—a generation after the demise of the urban renewal program—are still paying penance for the sins of Ed Logue, Ed Bacon, Robert Moses, and the other big city planners who were once heroes and are now villains.

The profession of city planning has moved on from the urban renewal experience, and Witold Rybczynski (2000) has identified some of the ways. But I don't see city planners as being outside the process; I see them as central to reforms in the ways we think about city growth and design that have occurred over the past 25 years. During this time, planners have learned a few lessons:

> First, it is poor policy to envision the future of the city solely in terms of new real estate development. Historic and cultural resource preservation [is] of equal or greater importance. These are not only popular movements, they are also planning activities that have now taken their place in many cities as central concerns running parallel to the shaping of new development. There are now tens of thousands of historic districts in this country, each actively managed by planning processes that balance the new and the old in a way appropriate to local values. Even more important, there are hundreds of regional cultural development

217

projects involving multiple communities now being planned that are redefining the practice of regional planning. Incidentally, I do not think that preservation is driven mainly by nostalgia for old buildings, but by a demand to connect meaning to place and to heighten the identity and value of places in an information market. This vision that urban form carries messages as well as defines space has influenced the design of a lot of new development as well as preserved the old.

The second big lesson is that the natural environment really matters. We cannot have great city visions or great regions if the air and water are polluted. And these issues affect the life and form of cities in very concrete ways. As an example, Boston is now planning the reclamation of one of the great public places and amenities in the city—its incredible system of neighborhood beaches which were abandoned in the 1960s due to the poor water quality of Boston Harbor. The cleanup of Boston Harbor, now nearing completion, will allow the beaches to be restored, thus enhancing the livability of the city and the value of surrounding neighborhoods. It is already drawing people back into Boston; just look at South Boston. Now, I will admit that it took a lawsuit to start the process of cleaning Boston Harbor—but the vision to implement this was an act of traditional city planning. So the environmental movement is a popular one, but it is also an arena of city planning that is shaping urban form.

The third big lesson is that city planning is much too important to be left to city planning departments. The days are long gone when an arm of the city can envision a master scheme and implement it through eminent domain after a few public hearings. Now virtually every plan, at every scale in most places across the country, demands a full process of community involvement and consensus. This, of course, drives some architects—as well as a lot of big city planning directors—up a wall, but it at least recognizes that city building is a communal activity. And much of this planning is not motivated by city governments at all but by a variety of special-purpose organizations that are making plans that help them address the day-to-day realities of decision making and not some abstract ideal about what their community should be.

I would say that the above are huge accomplishments. Although (like urban renewal) they also represent popular movements and cultural phenomena, they have been given leadership, institutional form, and professional stature by people trained as city planners. I am convinced that, in the long run, these macro efforts will have an extremely positive impact on the quality of urban form—more than a traditional comprehensive city plan.

Another impact of this change in attitude about planning is that more city plans are being demanded to cover more situations and places than ever before: beyond the classic comprehensive plan or even project plans, there are city plans for preservation, interpretation, tourism, economic development, streetscape, bikeways, boatways, port renovations, beaches, base conversions, environmental reclamation, and so on—all of which add up to an explosion of planning that goes far beyond the purview or capability of big-city planning agencies, many of which have been mercilessly cut back in staff or do not want to take the risk. In fact, most planning—and almost all of the envisioning—is being done by private firms, much of it commissioned by nongovernment organizations.

Although there are many specialists on planning teams, a city planner who has a more comprehensive view is almost always the preferred lead—which is why big engineering, architecture, and environmental firms across the United States are adding urban planning departments to their organizations.

From a business point of view, they are right. If we look to the future, the demand for city planning and planners will only increase. Why? For two reasons already mentioned. The more information that is available to constituencies about development, the environment, and so on, the more they will demand a role in the planning for change and professionals to advise them; and the scarcer resources become—worldwide—through increases in population and everything that means, the more we will need to plan for their wise use and envision new types of sustainable communities.

While I am confident that city planners will continue to play a leading role in making these plans, I do believe that it is time to move beyond the criticism (or should I say, guilt?) about the failures of urban renewal to begin once again to envision the type of environments that fulfill the values of our profession—those that are culturally based, environmentally sensitive, and responsive to their communities. I agree with Rybczynski that envisioning is a powerful tool that we have left mainly to others, and that planners—as the professionals with a comprehensive view—are being asked, begged, cajoled to pick up once again. When I look around at what is being envisioned by others, I think we need to get on with the task.

25

Urban Design for Urban Development

LAWRENCE J. VALE

The main reason for a resurgence in interest in physical planning has been the ability of urban designers to link the issues of design to a variety of the most pressing issues of development and implementation. To suggest that architects—under the banner of *new urbanism*—have usurped the role of planners in terms of influence over the physical form of places, leaving the latter to run powerless yet meddlesome bureaucracies, is to miss half the story. Even as planning education and practice shifted toward greater engagement with policy, those architect–planners we call urban designers have not only survived as a species, they have multiplied.

At the American Planning Association national conference in Boston in 1998, for example, no fewer than 31 different sessions and 15 different "mobile workshops" had to do with themes designated in the program as "urban design." This meant that there were more sessions devoted to "urban design" than to any other topic, including such areas as "economic development," "environment," or "transportation"—subfields often thought to have taken planning away from its roots in the built environment. Even more striking than the persistence of urban design is the way topics often classified as "economic development" rely heavily on place-centered design strategies, just as urban designers increasingly have accepted the role of designers of the new institutions necessary to implement and manage place-based development. Not surprisingly, an artifact such as the APA conference program is now full of cross-listings between "urban design" and "economic development."

The renewed strength of urban design within the planning profession has come about because urban designers have made strong cases for their ideas with both business-oriented professionals and the public at large. Increasingly, urban design includes not just a concern with form but a commitment to see design as economic planning carried out by other means. Building on Kevin Lynch's early work about *The Image of the City*, urban designers are using the idea of city image more proactively—seeking innovative ways to alter the image of urban, suburban, and regional areas. This image-building process involves not only place-based and form-based visions, but also strategies for economic development and environmental stewardship.

Much of the reason for the resurgence of interest in physical planning is due to new opportunities for redevelopment of abandoned industrial landscapes, especially those located along waterfronts. Repairing these and restoring them to economic value requires both new land uses and new visions.

Increasingly, city, state, and federal leaders—at least in this country—have recognized that success in planning for economic development depends on their ability to convey a positive image of what growth looks like, as viewed by a wide range of publics. These publics include not only massively impacted neighborhood groups, but also wary city developers and bankers, disdainful suburban voters, and globally competing corporations. Public perception and image marketing of places depend on the quality of the physical environment. For example, the Herculean effort to recast the image of Cleveland in a post–Rust Belt context has taken more than the marshaling of economic statistics; it has also required the visual proof of new sports and museum facilities in formerly underused areas. The "Cleveland Tomorrow" campaign is equal parts development and public relations, and design and politics are conjoined in both parts. While part of the renewed appeal of physical planning seems due to the ease with which the entire vision-making process has been co-opted by broader municipal marketing campaigns, this process nonetheless creates genuine opportunities for urban designers.

LEARNING FROM WASHINGTON

If the broader task of this volume is to explore the entire century of planning practice, it may be worth a pause to consider two attempts at planning the future design direction of the same place, one from the beginning of the century, the other from its end. The famous Senate Parks Commission Plan (known more widely as the McMillan Plan) of 1901 attempted to resurrect, recenter, and realize the L'Enfant Plan of a century earlier, and marked a high point of the City Beautiful tradition that epitomized urban design as the twentieth century began. The new plan, prepared by the National Capital Planning Commission and released in late 1997, exhibits both clear continuities and new departures, and both the commonalities and the differences say something about the relationship between urban design and the larger political, social, and economic forces surrounding it.

In 1901, Daniel Burnham, Charles McKim, Augustus St.-Gaudens, and Frederick Law Olmsted, Jr., led a small club of other white males in a rush to Europe to visit appropriate precedents, and returned with plans to develop the Washington Mall as a place of civic pageantry and architectural order. Although they also envisioned a broad regional parks system, their main focus remained on Washington's center. Faced with no overarching system of environmental regulation and no census of potentially endangered fish and wildlife, they proposed filling in large areas of what we would now call wetlands as part of a massive waterfront redevelopment and reconfiguration effort that would be unimaginable in today's world of environmental impact statements. Instead of swamps, they envisioned the sites that would eventually become home to the temples raised to Lincoln and Jefferson. Instead of a railway line that crossed the Mall beneath the Capitol's West Front and sliced past picturesque groves of irregularly spaced mature trees, they preferred a symmetrical axiality of uninterrupted vistas. Instead of Chinatown and a red light district, they proposed the new district of government buildings now known as the Federal Triangle. This was urban design as municipal cleanser, and the results proved highly imageable and, eventually, implementable.

A century later, the National Capital Planning Commission is both directed and chaired by African Americans, and its work is subjected to public comment and review by multiple constituencies. The new group of physical planners looked not to Europe but to the needs of Washington itself. The new "Legacy Plan" focuses not on the Mall but instead attempts to recenter the image of Washington eastward and southward (NCPC 1997). It is spatially centered not on the Washington Monument, but—like L'Enfant's original vision—on the Capitol. In the new plan, urban design is explicitly linked to economic development, just as it was at the time of L'Enfant (who also sought ways to disperse key points of intensified urban development). This time, the development focuses on the Anacostia waterfront and on new ways to get there—pedestrian paths, buried freeways, and a new north–south boulevard. One overall aim—not unlike the array of Parisian *grands projets* of the Mitterand era—is to spread the largesse of the federal government, and to see public investment as a spearhead of public–private neighborhood development in impoverished areas. Moreover, like the linear public park systems proposed by Olmsted Jr. and his famous father, the new plan seeks clearance to bring parkland and open space to underserved neighborhoods. The McMillan Plan itself took several decades to realize, and most aspects of the current proposal seem even less likely to happen anytime soon.

URBAN DESIGN AS CITY IMAGING

In 1997, as in 1901, physical planning proposals carry considerable appeal because they tap into an ever-increasing reliance on image. No one would suggest the NCPC plan is a solution to the ever-mounting socioeconomic ills of Washington as a troubled and divided city, and critics will surely see the new plan as an expensive and irrelevant new exercise in municipal cosmetics. Nonetheless, it reveals important changes in physical planning practice, because it demonstrates that the pursuit of image entails more than the regularization of aesthetics. Physical planning has returned not as an alternative to economic planning but as an increasingly integrated component of urban development.

CITY IMAGING AND URBAN DEVELOPMENT

Even as urban designers begin to stake new claims on urban development practice, it must be noted that the actions of both architects and planners remain marginalized by the power of developers, lawyers, and engineers to dictate the framework of most important design decisions, especially in the United States. Wherever floor area is at a premium and site planning is driven by the need to accommodate the automobile, the result is bulkier buildings, wider roads, and—all too often—little concern for the public realm in between. Project by project, incremental change moves fitfully at best, and larger attempts to alter the images of places are never without controversy. In most cases, there are multiple contending images about what places could or should be, and corresponding conflicts over who should be empowered to shape their destiny. Efforts to reverse the seediness of Manhattan's Times Square, for example, have vacillated between images of cool corporate megatowers and family-friendly glitz. Urban designers will never be able to escape the fact that the urban built environment always serves as the flash point and symbol for larger power struggles, with roots in class, race, and gender inequalities. As urban design and urban development converge, the challenge will be to re-image development in ways that can serve multiple publics well. To gain greater influence in the future, urban designers will need to combine their visualization skills with a newfound development savvy, but at the same time do so without losing a commitment to the quality of public places.

26

The Public's Image of the Profession

Nathan Glazer

If I had taken this assignment literally, I would have had, I'm afraid, very little to say. There is no empirical evidence on the image of the profession of city planner among the general public, though perhaps the American Planning Association has commissioned a survey that tells us something about this. In the absence of such evidence, I think we would all agree that the image of the planner in the public mind is not compelling; indeed, it is rather dim. Planning itself—unless it is corporate planning—is not held in high repute generally, as we see from the rout of Marxism almost everywhere by the principles of the free market. One can plan one's personal life, one can plan for the future of one's company, defense officials are expected to plan for a future war; but planning—as we generally understand it, in professional schools of planning, that is, the arrangement of space for a variety of present and future uses in city, region, state, and nation—goes on, if at all, in a peripheral professional world that receives little attention from the mass media.

What *is* the popular image of the planner? A recent personal experience brought me in touch with professional planning in Cambridge, Massachusetts. I have been engaged in a remodeling project and have been astonished at how many restrictions there are on what I can do, though I am doing nothing exceptional. But unexceptional as is my modest project to replace a crumbling garage and connect it to my kitchen, I find I need to present a new plot plan (which happens to be identical to the plot plan I acquired with the property) which cost me $500; that I need approval from the historical commission to demolish a cinder-block garage of about the 1920s (because it is more than 50 years old); that I then need a demolition permit; that to get the demolition permit I need a statement from a pest-control service that there are no pests in the garage; that I must inform my neighbors of my plans even though the new construction will not extend beyond the restrictive envelope on my property within which I can build (and who created that envelope on my property, I am led to wonder?); that I must, of course, get a building permit; that halfway through the construction the surveyor must come back to attest that it conforms to the plans submitted; and so on. I am sure I have left out a few requirements. Cambridge may be exceptional, but I would guess, on the basis of the character of the city, that it stands high among cities in the use it makes of the services of professional planners.

I wonder—thinking about the image of the city planning profession—who the annoyed houseowner blames for all this, much of which he thinks is unnecessary. Of course, if he thinks hard about the matter, he will realize that many of these restrictions came about because of some kind of popular protest which the planner responded to as a professional rather than initiated. The planner today, in an old city like Cambridge, if he is thought of at all, is expected to protect what one has, rather than project an image of the city that ought to be. The salient characteristic of the popular image of the city and regional planner today is that he is no longer seen as a reformer. If one is feeling negative about what has happened when one comes in contact with the planner and his restrictions, he is seen as an obstruction. If one is attached to the objectives the specific requirements seem to be aiming at, he is seen as a facilitator. If one is attached to one's home and one's neighborhood, he is often seen as a threat, an ally of new development. It is clear that the dominant element in the image of the planner is no longer that of a reformer, the bringer of hope—which is what the image of the city planner used to be.

There are probably two names that best capture what the public—the thinking public—has in mind when the idea of the city planner comes up. One is Lewis Mumford; the second is Jane Jacobs. Mumford thought of himself as a planner—after all, he was a student of Patrick Geddes—though, of course, he was not a professional planner, and professional planners might think of him more as a prophet of planning than a planner. Jane Jacobs was also, of course, no planner, and had as low an opinion of them as her great antagonist, Robert Moses. Perhaps one ought to add Moses as another name that would come to the public mind when it thinks about city planning.

It is an odd trio. The first figure, Mumford, was a great critic, a reformer and prophet. He denounced, as a biblical prophet would, the city that has come to be under the shaping forces of industrialism and capitalism, and prophesied the city that should be. That city was visualized in an idyllic, pastoral section of a movie by Pare Lorentz, *The City*, made for the New York City World's Fair of 1939—a movie that was probably seen by more people than any other that has been made on the theme of city planning. We would today find it prophetic only of the contemporary American suburb, which nowadays stands in high repute with few except for those who live in it, and some neoconservative defenders of existing bourgeois tastes.

The second in our trio is the great demolisher of the image of the ideal city for our contemporary society projected by the reforming mind of Mumford and other pioneers of the sensible, the human, the humane city. Jacobs lived in Greenwich Village and applauded what the city planners of her day deplored—crowding, diversity, the unexpected, the spontaneous, the unplanned—insisting that it all came together to make a better city than any of the planners could make.

Moses's image today is shaped by the huge book on him by Robert Caro (1974), *The Power Broker*, and by our disenchantment with the city made or reshaped by the freeways, though most of us live in that city and could not possibly manage it without the freeways.

Pondering this trio, perhaps one could add others; but I can think of no one else of this level of eminence who would come to the public mind when it thinks of the planner (though as I have said, none were professional planners)—one finds that the only one who remains a contemporary hero is Jane Jacobs. That does suggest that there is a considerable problem today in constructing a positive image of the city planner.

A key moment in the transformation of the planner from admired reformer to professional came in 1961 and 1962. Perhaps I am so focused on that year or two because I was then in Washington working for the Housing and Home Finance Agency, which was soon to become the Department of Housing and Urban Development. Robert Wood, then a professor of political science on leave from MIT, was working on the reorganization of the Agency; Charles Haar was also in Washington; and many of us would soon be involved in shaping the Model Cities legislation. I have in mind two or three things that happened then or around then. One was the publication of Jane Jacobs's *The Death and Life of Great American Cities*. It dawned on many Americans that they didn't like what had been happening to their cities since World War II. A lot of good ideas—public housing, urban renewal, suburbs built according to the plats laid down by planners—seemed to be going bad. Catherine Bauer Wurster, a major advocate of public housing, which was then still seen by many as the model of reform, had just recently published her article on what had gone wrong with public housing. Public housing, recall, was the great reform of the 1930s. It was, for example, what Mayor Fiorello LaGuardia had in mind as the ideal of what reform meant for a city like New York. By the late 1950s, reformers were asking what had gone wrong with this great urban reform.

Another thing that was happening in 1961 and 1962: People who believed in the power of ideas to transform society and fix what had to be fixed had come to power. John F. Kennedy was President, and, while he did not think much about cities, some around him did. A poverty program was being launched. A big-city antidelinquency program funded by the new and self-confident Ford Foundation was underway and was being embraced by the administration as a model for the new poverty program (the brother of the President was in charge of the antidelinquency program). Federal programs to train city planners were soon to be launched, along with programs that required their use in all sorts of public planning. More and more forms of planning were instituted as prerequisites to gaining access to the scores of new programs, funded by the federal government, that were being instituted— and they required planners too.

The planner was being transformed from prophet and reformer into professional. It was an age of expansion of a professional role and self-confidence in it; but it was not to last. The idea of what the planner was supposed to be underwent kaleidoscopic changes in the urban turmoil of the late 1960s and early 1970s. Again and again, the central task of the city planner, space planning—and what really can replace it in significance?—was challenged as inadequate, incomplete, inessential. But what, after all, *could* replace it? Advocacy? Service to the political powers, whatever they were? Professionalism? The central conflicting images of what a planner in the heroic mode might be—Mumford, Jacobs, Moses—were never superseded.

Moving forward—too rapidly—to 1997, a mere 35 years or so later, one finds the professionalization has only gone further. Who can any longer follow the complexity of public housing programs? I recently received an analysis from the Citizens Housing and Planning Council of New York—a name that conjures up an earlier, simpler, more hopeful period—of the crisis confronting one of the numerous forms of publicly subsidized housing that has flowered in the wake of the crisis of the first type of public housing: the housing project. It is far too technical for anyone but a specialist to follow. This is what an organization that started out in the 1930s as an advocate of subsidized housing for the working class and of good planning now finds it necessary to do. As a corollary, today, we do not typically think of calling in the professional planner when we consider what has gone wrong with the city and suburb and what can be done about it. When we figure out what to do, we will call in the planner to help with the details.

In my search for the present contemporary image of the city planner, I looked for examples in which the image of planning and the planner had impinged on the popular mind. I recalled the cover of the *Atlantic Monthly* of September 1996. One doesn't often see the issue of cities and planning on the front page of a popular magazine, so it stood out. The *Atlantic Monthly* was featuring that month a summary of James Howard Kunstler's *Home From*

Nowhere. The cover itself reads, "Home from Nowhere: How to Make Our Cities and Towns More Livable." It portrays a patch of nondescript but pleasant, traditional northeastern or midwestern town, with a few vernacular houses, a small apartment house, a patch of green, a steeple. It must mean something that this modest, traditional image made the cover of *Atlantic Monthly*. All planners and planning students should read Kunstler's earlier (1993) book, the *Geography of Nowhere*, as well as this follow-up, *Home From Nowhere* (Kuntsler 1996). As professionals, they would find what he is saying in his passionate attack on postwar American urban building familiar and quotidian, and would know how to dispute it. But it should be read. I read it only because I recalled this cover and knew I would be writing this chapter, and, I thought, that would give me one idea of the present popular image of the planner. Kunstler excoriates what city and suburb have become. He blames traffic engineers first, but planners at least second, or perhaps tied for first:

> Does the modern profession called urban planning have anything to do with making good places anymore? Planners no longer employ the vocabulary of civic art, nor do they find the opportunity to practice it— the term civic art itself has nearly vanished in common usage. In some universities, urban planning departments have been booted out of the architecture schools and into the schools of public administration. Not surprising, planners are now chiefly preoccupied with administrative procedure: issuing permits, filling out forms, and shuffling papers—in short, bureaucracy. All the true design questions such as "How wide should Elm Street be?" and "What sort of buildings should be on it?" were long ago "solved" by civil engineers and their brethren and written into the municipal codes. These mechanistic "solutions" work only by oversimplifying problems and isolating them from the effect they have on the landscape and on people's behavior. (Kunstler 1993, 113)

It's worth thinking about these comments. The *Geography of Nowhere* is one of the few recent books about cities that one can still find in bookstores.

An even more widely read magazine, *Newsweek*, has also featured the problem of urban planning on its cover. It is an article on "the new urbanism," the new approach to making new towns and suburbs that look traditional of Elizabeth Plater-Zyberk and Andres Duany, that Kunstler admires. According to the well-informed Harold Henderson, writing for *Planning* in January 1997, it is "one of the few planning theories ever to grace the cover of *Newsweek*." One wonders when the last time a planning theory or anything like it made the cover of a major news weekly. Perhaps Buckminster Fuller was so fortunate 40 years ago. But isn't it striking that we are not surprised that 40 years ago it would have been a futurist like Buckminster Fuller or the visionary Le Corbusier who represented the new urbanism on the cover of a major news weekly, while today the representative of "new urbanism" is an advocate of the old urbanism?

It is, overall, the failure of futurism and modernism to seize the public imagination, and the failure of a world that encompasses some of the key elements advocated in that older futurist thinking—the city of skyscraper and freeway—to capture public affection, which creates the cautious environment for today's professional planner. Looking backward, it seems, has become the most popular way of going forward.

What, after all, have been some of the most powerful movements affecting and shaping the city of the last 30 years, the city after Buckminster Fuller and Le Corbusier? I can think of four, but there may be others. One is the *preservation movement*. In that stimulating period when I worked at HHFA in the early 1960s, the bankrupt Pennsylvania Railroad was preparing to tear down Pennsylvania Station in New York, a monument built to last a thousand years. And the Pennsylvania Avenue Development Corporation in Washington was proposing the demolition of the Willard Hotel, the Washington Hotel, the Old Post Office, and the creation of a square to overmatch Red Square in Moscow. It was a curator at the Smithsonian Museum of American History who started the "Don't Tear It Down!" movement that saved the Old Post Office, which now does more to bring life to Pennsylvania Avenue than anything new placed on that avenue. It was such vandalism, effected or proposed, that led to the preservation movement.

A second movement: the *new urbanism* of Plater-Zyberk and Duany and many followers and equivalents, the movement applauded and promoted with such enthusiasm by James Howard Kunstler.

A third: *environmentalism*. Here, I should mention the name of William H. Whyte, Jr., a friend of Jane Jacobs, author of the *Last Landscape*, who has some not very complimentary things to say about what planning and planners have done to cities (Whyte 1968).

And a fourth: *community advocacy*, whose main thrust, almost everywhere and always is, don't do it—don't tear down the old building, don't put in a new park, don't widen the road, simply . . . Don't.

None of these are movements that professional planners have played any great role in launching, although, in all of them, one can find professional planners involved to some degree. Planners have given the people and the developers more or less what they wanted. After the fact, it turns out that is not quite what the people wanted, after all. But that is not the planner's fault. They had to accommodate the automobile, they had to respond to economic realities, they had to adapt to governmental requirements. The role of reformer or prophet had to be left to others. In time, the changes in sentiment effected by the reformers or prophets affected the work of planners. Perhaps that is the proper relationship between the large figures who have shaped the public's views of planning and the professional planner.

Clearly, if we want to find sharp, powerfully defined images of planning and the planner, we will not go to the professional city planner. We should not be surprised by this. A profession has to routinize, systematize, and organize. It cannot take the position that only the most exceptional, the most gifted, those with the reformer's instinct or the prophet's passion, should be trained in the profession or should be able to engage in it effectively. Fair enough. Not every doctor is going to be a Pasteur, every lawyer a Brandeis, every teacher a Debbie Meyer.

Perhaps, then, the only lesson of this look backward in considering the image of the city planner is that there needs to be greater interplay between the exceptional figures who do embody the image of the planner in the public mind, and the professional practice of planning.

27

Do Americans Like City Planning?

SAM BASS WARNER, JR.

City planning, both the profession and its schools, now functions in a very different climate from the 1960s and 1970s days of popularity. Still very much in demand, planning goes forward in a contradictory atmosphere of popular acceptance and national attack.

Across the nation planners are at work in every considerable city and town. The practices of zoning and subdivision control are thoroughly established in procedure and case law. The many private institutions of real estate depend upon the predictability of these laws and the professionalism of planners for the security of their businesses. Moreover, Americans *like* planning. They like thinking about the lands, houses, stores, parks, and roads of their communities; they like imagining the future, thinking about proposals for betterment. And when there is conflict about such matters, as there often is, people turn out night after night to air their opinions and contest others.

But Americans resist regulations. My sense of this antagonism between the acceptance of planning and the animus against regulation is that it is a town-by-town clash between those with valuable properties to buy and sell who wish to trade, and those who want to keep things as they are. Often, the conflict is between the old farmer, or his heirs, and the developer on one side, and the new suburban families on the other. At other times, the conflict is between old and new residents against the municipality itself, which is in some sort of partnership with a developer. However these oppositions occur and however they play out, planners stand at the center of the fray. It is a good and useful place for them to be.

Elsewhere, beyond and above these flourishing daily exchanges, lie the obscurantists that Michael Teitz, appropriately, observes. Obscurantists today are a loose cluster of factions composed of libertarian ideologues, business interest groups and their advertisers, public relations houses and lobbyists, media moguls, and politicians who have been purchased. Is the word "purchased" too simple? Perhaps I would do well to repeat the phrase of the late, highly subsidized senator from Massachusetts, Daniel Webster: "I never took money for anything I didn't believe in." This coalition asserts the impossibility of public planning. The common statement is that planning is an exercise that government can only fail at. Governmental planning, they say, violates primordial private property rights, and it is inefficient.

It is worth spending a little more time on the free market alternative to planning than Teitz gave himself at the 1997 MIT Faculty Seminar because such a detour will help us locate the foundations on which to build a revival of planning. Planners in the United States do not operate in a setting of social democratic governments. Instead, they must do their work amid regulated private markets, and therefore they must appreciate what private markets can and cannot do.

Free markets are excellent at allocating. By means of prices, they can move what someone wants more from the hands of someone who wants the same thing less. The speed and ease of American land and housing transactions daily testify to the private market's allocating skills. Private markets, however, are good only at allocating; they possess no devices for moving toward social or economic justice, and they possess no devices for determining the scale, or limits, of the market itself. Both issues are central to the everyday business of our society, and both are central to planning.

The recent national shift toward an evermore unequal distribution of income and wealth in the midst of tax limitation and deregulation points to the behavior of open markets. The distribution of income and wealth, however, is the distribution of the very stake each person brings to the private market to bid for goods and services. The planner's daily business of review of housing and subdivision plans, and consideration of traffic alternatives, always concerns some concept of a just distribution of resources. A just distribution is never a market issue; it is always a political decision.

So, too, for the scale of the market. Left to its own devices, a private market will always reach out to whatever is scarce to begin trading. The market knows no limits. So the price rises as the fish become scarce until the last fish is caught; the demand for electricity expands, coal is mined, oil is pumped, and gas burned until the air is polluted and the atmosphere filled with carbon dioxide and the acids of sulfur and nitrogen. There is always a purchaser waiting to buy a slice of the park, to encroach on the forest. There is always someone who wants to put another noisy machine on the town lake, or place advertisements in school books and classrooms. The setting of market limits, the control of the size and reach of the private market, is very much the business of planners, and this task is always a community decision, a political decision, not a private one.

PLANNING IS POLITICS

Unlike our founders did a century ago, we do not confront a world ignorant of planning. We do not need to find another George Bernard Shaw to write a set of Fabian essays. Rather, we live in a world of planning in which a loose coalition of obscurantists tries to discredit planning as a smokescreen to cover its activities of changing laws and regulations. They do not want less government or more private enterprise; they want a government that maintains the sort of private markets that favor *their* enterprises.

In the face of this attack, Teitz does well to recall for us planning's tradition. It is, as he says, "Progressive" in its politics. He means by that a politics that both concerns itself with issues of social and economic justice and which also seeks pragmatic remedies within the established structures of democratic governments. Planning's practice, he says, is "professional"—meaning that planners feel some obligation in their work to serve the public, not just to make money. Finally, he reminds us of the idealistic bent of the profession. Planners want to make things better, a whole lot better, if possible.

With these terms, Teitz goes to the heart of the tradition. Throughout the twentieth century, planners have spoken to and for community: national community, state community, municipal and neighborhood community. Teitz points to the South Shore Bank in Chicago, and some other community development corporations, to remind us that some of the earliest social work and self-help techniques of city planning succeed as often in the 1990s as they did in the 1890s. Planning is, thus, a special profession. Planners spend a lifetime trying to identify and speak to the public interest of communities; and, in doing so, theirs must be both a technical and a political role.

By what right do planners speak for the community? Surely they are often challenged in this assertion of theirs. The answer is given in Teitz's ideology. The person most people call a "planner" is a person who makes a specialty of a concern for land, housing, and infrastructure. These are the public keys that validate the profession.

All the elements of physical planning, the very subjects and techniques that lie at the core of the profession, are now being contested. The attack of the obscurantists is but one problem; more far-reaching is the need for change brought about by new urban circumstances and new public demands. As is often the case, this necessity for change is also a wonderful opportunity.

THE NEW SETTLEMENT PATTERN

Three-quarters of the population of the United States now reside within urban regions the U.S. Census calls "metropolitan." The population and geographical extent of the old core cities may vary, but the urbanized region beyond them is both more populous and more extensive. Planners have mostly been opposed to this previous half-century of expansion. They are against sprawl, yet they have offered few alternatives. They have taken an active role in old city redesign but have had little to offer to the growing fringe except for variations on the old Neighborhood Unit.

Recently, architects have captured the public's imagination with a set of images gathered under the title "new urbanism." Their success should embarrass planners for their own neglect of the images of physical planning and lack of attention to the urban fringe. In the early twentieth century, the social and economic problems of the dense industrial city called forth such powerful ideas and images as Ebenezer Howard's village socialism and Le Corbusier's city of towers and parks. In our business-led society, a coalition of real estate dealers adapted German land-use regulation to establish the American practice of zoning. In sum, the half-century from 1890 to 1940 proved much more inventive than did the subsequent 50 years.

Perhaps the blame for lack of imagination should be placed on the continuing preoccupations of the Cold War. However it may be, I find it hard to believe that the tasteful reworking of old streetcar suburban land planning and ornamentation, the sort of thing Robert A. M. Stern is doing in Celebration, Florida, for the Disney Corporation, is the best answer we can propose to urban sprawl. The successes of the new urbanism, like those of Howard and Le Corbusier, remind us of the power of architectural and land-planning imagery as devices to stir public action. Surely, a school of planning ought to endeavor at all times to join its analyses of markets, traffic, finance, land, and the environment with representations of alternative images.

QUESTIONING ZONING

The debate about established land-use regulations is intensifying, and it is likely to get more contentious because of the ever-growing list of goals being advanced. At the outset, zoning advocates sought to stabilize real estate markets and investments by ensuring that established uses would keep their character over long periods of time. The class and racial consequences of the enacted zones have, for the past 40 years, been the object of attack by thoughtful planners concerned with social justice. Political support for mixed-class and mixed-racial communities, however, has been slow and uncertain in coming.

Now, the desire to promote active street life and reduce driving has brought a questioning of the traditional separation of uses. Many propose mixing retail and housing once more, while others talk of neighborly light manufacturing. Environmental goals put forward more severe challenges. They do so by means of the concept of carrying capacity. Any given piece of land can support only a limited human population before its streams and groundwater become polluted and its variety of flora and fauna is narrowly restricted. Zoning boards are now setting wetlands off-limits for development, and they commonly set density limits to promote particular residential styles or to make septic systems feasible. Environmentalists, however, wish to concentrate human activities and preserve large patches of open land and long corridors of green. Their visions are at odds even with the luxury of three-acre zoning. It will surely be a challenge to future planners to reconcile the traditions of American land use with the goals of social and economic justice and environmental fitness.

Parks

The setting aside of land for public parks, and their design and management, are now rich sources of conflict. Old questions of how much public parkland—and where—remain; but the goals of preserving scenery and offering some play and picnic spaces no longer suffice. In a city-region of automobiles, the range of people seeking recreation is enormous. Large crowds and heavy impacts can appear quickly at a considerable distance. On a summer weekend, Bostonians can overwhelm Cape Cod and Maine simultaneously. Meanwhile, tastes have multiplied. There are those who still want to walk and picnic quietly, and there are the hunters, fishers, and birders, as of old. Baseball, basketball, touch football, and soccer can easily be accommodated, but what about motorboats, jet skis, dirt bikes, skimobiles, and Jeeps? City dwellers go out to play with a lot of heavy equipment these days. At the very same moment, the sort of park gardening and forest tending of the past is being challenged by environmentalists as unsuitable to many nonhuman species and their settings. Moreover, old state and municipal parks often go underused because they are no longer suitable to their neighbors or fitting to modern tastes. The choices are difficult and expensive. Parkland is fixed, and urban populations are continually on the move. How might the two be tended?

Urban Water

The management of water in urban regions is now a labile subject. Even in the rainy Northeast, many municipalities are short of drinking water, while others are experiencing rapid price rises. The techniques of the nineteenth century no longer point us toward good solutions. Moreover, the habit of our predecessors in using rivers and the ground for waste disposal is coming back to haunt us. All manner of new practices are being suggested and tested. They address every scale from the household to entire watersheds. It is by no means clear just what best practice might be, but here is a field that cries out for the technical and educational skills of planners.

Schools

The provision of schools is a universal municipal function. In the United States, we have just completed a half-century of combining small schools and establishing consolidated school districts with large campuses. We are now very unhappy with the outcome. Surely it is time for planners to address the problems of raising children.

Transportation

Transportation is a core issue for planners, and for most it turns on strategies for managing the automobile. At present, the alternatives seem to be multiplying: variable pricing, traffic calming, paratransit, and varieties of regional public transportation alternatives should not be left to languish in the hands of the oil-auto-and-cement lobby.

The Family

Planning began, and begins, with considerations of the welfare of families. Land was, and should be, the servant, not the master. But what kind of family? New immigrant families and families in poverty were early concerns, and they must remain central to American practice. The two-wage-earner family now must be added to former conventional arrangements. This family's needs challenge most of our established arrangements. Who does what? What should be where? All that is clear today is that the past needs alteration.

As I explore the city-region of Boston, from Cape Cod to New Hampshire, I find everywhere a rich mix of old assets and old failures, fine towns and persistent poverty. Everywhere, even in this long-settled region, there is need for adjustment to realize new opportunities, satisfy fresh goals. Now, to successfully place their long standing of technical expertise in the issues of physical planning at the service of such communities, professional planners and their schools must both inform themselves of the new goals and conflicts and dare to be imaginative once again.

28

City Planning Since Jane Jacobs

BERNARD J. FRIEDEN

S everal commentators have suggested that city planners not only fail to play major roles in shaping the urban environment but still suffer from the image they had when Jane Jacobs launched her famous attack on the profession for the damage it inflicted on cities through the urban renewal program in the 1950s.

Yet one of the notable surprises in the recent history of U.S. cities has been the rebuilding of downtown. From the early 1960s through the late 1980s, the 30 largest metropolitan areas built as much downtown office space as they had accumulated in all the years before 1960. Most large cities doubled their downtown hotel space after 1970, 100 cities built new downtown convention centers, and more than 100 downtown retail centers took shape during the same period. Moreover, public agencies took the lead in planning and initiating these new projects, and in many cases they served as developers or co-developers with private sponsors. And city planners were prominent in these organizations: redevelopment agencies, port authorities, and specialized nonprofit corporations hired city planners as staff members or consultants and generated projects such as Pike Place Market in Seattle, Battery Park City in New York, Faneuil Hall Marketplace in Boston, the Yerba Buena Center in San Francisco, the Inner Harbor of Baltimore, the renovated Union Station in Washington, and Nicollet Mall in Minneapolis.

Some of the better-known agencies include The Port Authority of New York and New Jersey, the Pennsylvania Avenue Development Corporation, New York City's Public Development Corporation, the Boston Redevelopment Authority, and the Centre City Development Corporation in San Diego. More than 50 state and local government agencies have become directly involved in city development, with hundreds of staff members and consultants working as project planners. These agencies and their planners turned away from the kinds of projects Jane Jacobs and others had found good reasons to criticize. Most new downtown developments were responsive to public interests as well as private ones. Many included such public spaces as parks, transit stations, and places for entertainment. Some met social objectives by including special hiring agreements and creating business opportunities for city residents and minority groups.

It may be fair to fault city planners for some of the disasters of urban renewal, but fairness also requires crediting them for a remarkable turnaround in what they planned and built from the 1970s on. Unlike the typecast bureaucrat, agency heads and staff members proved eager to try new ideas, resourceful in solving problems, and willing to take the risks of trying unconventional approaches. Development strategies for city centers have come a long way since the 1950s:

- From bulldozing entire neighborhoods to the microsurgery of renovating small, strategic sites like Faneuil Hall Marketplace

- From designing single-purpose apartment or office projects for isolation from the street to featuring mixed-use centers to draw the crowds

- From compulsive modernization to preserving a sense of the past and making a feature of historic structures

- From pushing preconceived solutions on developers to planning through public–private negotiation

- From raiding federal urban-aid budgets to packaging local and private-sector funds

If city planners still suffer from the image they acquired when Jane Jacobs's critique first appeared, then public perceptions are lagging far behind the realities. Similarly, an outmoded critique of suburbia continues to feed the perception that city planners are the creators of suburbia, and that what they have created is a barren and monotonous environment foisted off on an uninformed and misled public.

As for city planners as the creators of postwar suburbia, the truth is that planners had a marginal role in the process. At that time the function of small-town and suburban planners was essentially regulatory, in contrast to the more recent emergence of big-city planners as initiators and co-developers of downtown projects. Postwar suburbia was conceived and implemented mainly by private homebuilders, subject to limited regulation by federal housing agencies and local planning authorities.

The suburban critique, however, was inaccurate not only in attributing major responsibility to city planners but also in its extreme characterization of the suburbs as a threat to the nation's culture, its environment, and the mental health of its people. A look at the journalistic treatment of suburbs in the postwar era reveals a mood verging on hysteria.

Suburbs in America were not a new phenomenon in the 1940s. In the last half of the nineteenth century, many suburbs were built along railroad lines. These early suburbs were mostly small enclaves designed to suit the tastes of a well-to-do clientele. Contemporary observers generally considered them ideal places to live. Justice Brandeis, for one, recalled the advice that wealthy Bostonians used to give their sons: "Boston holds nothing for you except heavy taxes and political misrule. When you marry, pick out a suburb to build your house in, join the Country Club, and make your life center about your club, your home, and your children." By the early twentieth century, social reformers were calling the suburbs the hope of the future for combining the best features of city and country life (Mumford 1961, 495; Donaldson 1969, 23–39).

That was while the suburbs were still for the elite. The postwar suburbs, built for a mass market, were another matter. As soon as their popularity was clear, critics began to blame them for whatever they found wrong with American society. John Keats's best-seller of 1956, *The Crack in the Picture Window*, spread the new antisuburb mythology by telling the story of two pathetic victims, John and Mary Drone. Shoddy construction and look-alike homes destroy their individuality and force them into superficial human relationships and passive conformity. A. C. Spectorsky, reviewing this polemic for the *New York Times Book Review*, pronounced it a "serious, frightening, sociological study" (Spectorsky 1957, 10). The *New York Times Magazine* ran a sober article in 1954 informing its readers that "standardized housing breeds standardized individuals, too—especially among youngsters" (Gruenberg 1954, 14).

Intellectuals and journalists carried the attack further by blaming the suburbs for creating "domineering wives, absent husbands, and spoiled children, and with it, rising marital friction, adultery, divorce, drunkenness, and mental illness." These conclusions inspired such paperback novels as *Love in Suburbia: They Spiced Their Lives with Other Men's Wives* and *The Development* ("strips bare the flimsy façade of decency concealing unbridled sensual desires of America's sprawling suburbia") (Gans 1967, xvi, xxviii). Social and architectural writers rounded out the indictment by complaining that the suburbs were politically irresponsible, culturally barren, and aesthetically objectionable, threatening to overwhelm the American landscape with "suburban sprawl."

The critics included scholars as well as journalists. Lewis Mumford described the postwar suburbs as "a multitude of uniform, unidentifiable houses, lined up inflexibly, at uniform distances, on uniform roads, in a treeless communal waste, inhabited by people of the same class, the same income, the same age group, witnessing the same television performances, eating the same tasteless prefabricated foods, from the same freezers, conforming in every outward and inward respect to a common mold" (Mumford 1961, 486).

California songwriter Malvina Reynolds set the theme to music in her song, "Little Boxes" (Reynolds 1962), performed widely in the 1960s:

> Little boxes on the hillside,
> Little boxes made of ticky-tacky,
> Little boxes on the hillside,
> Little boxes all the same.
> There's a green one and a pink one
> And a blue one and a yellow one
> And they're all made out of ticky-tacky
> And they all look just the same.

To agree with this point of view was a mark of refined taste, and to dissent was to jeopardize anyone's intellectual standing. One of the few dissenters in print was Robert Moses, who delighted in throwing stones at ivory-tower critics: "The little identical suburban boxes of average people," he wrote, "which differ only in color and planting, represent a measure of success unheard of by hundreds of millions on other continents" (Moses 1962, 57).

The attack on suburbia went further when it charged that suburban growth was a threat to American culture and society. Harrison Salisbury, a distinguished journalist writing on the front page of the *New York Times Book Review*, described the movement of middle-income families into modest suburban homes as "sponge-like population cancers spreading remorselessly along the arteries of the great motor-car routes." Citing Lewis Mumford as his authority, he explained what was happening to the cities as "unbuilding — a condition in which a more advanced form of life lost its complex character; in which there occurred not only loss of form but also loss of effective social institutions for transmitting and enlarging the cultural heritage." "One of the most chilling discoveries," according to Salisbury, was that this process was already very far advanced and that "the forces at work were doing no less than unraveling the fabric of our social organization" (Salisbury 1958).

A handful of observers who took a closer look at the new suburbs noticed weaknesses in the critique. One of the observers was urban sociologist Herbert Gans, who learned that Levitt and Sons, developers of the notorious Levittown, Long Island, were planning to build another new community near

Philadelphia in Willingboro Township, New Jersey. Gans decided to move in on opening day in 1958 in order to study the community by living in it. After two years as a resident, and two more years of follow-up visits, he reached a clear conclusion: "Most new suburbanites are pleased with the community that develops; they enjoy the house and outdoor living and take pleasure from the large supply of compatible people, without experiencing the boredom or malaise ascribed to suburban homogeneity" (Gans 1967, 409).

Similarly, other observers discovered that Levittown, Long Island, the critics' very icon of a suburban wasteland, was a great success to the people who lived there. Even the allegation that the look-alike houses would lead to mental health problems was out of touch with the facts, as residents proceeded to enlarge and remodel their homes to suit their individual needs and tastes. After a few years, the houses no longer looked alike. In 1957, when Levittown was ten years old, the residents celebrated the occasion by opening their homes to visitors and journalists, who promptly discovered that people were adapting the houses to their own needs. The *Times* reported that hardly a house could be found that was not altered in some way (Kelly 1993, 101). Barbara Kelly, who studied the evolution of Levittown, concluded that the reason for this renovation was not that the original houses had failed to satisfy the residents, but rather that the original houses gave the owners a start toward what they wanted. The early Levittowners, she noted, were short on money and long on energy and ingenuity: "Finding themselves with the rudiments of shelter on a considerable piece of land, [they] were able to build their dream from the basic framework" (Kelly 1993, 101).

By the twentieth anniversary, in 1967, the streets as well as the houses were different. "Trees that had been spindly or invisible in the aerial shots of 1947 now obscured the view. . . . The houses, once described as like 'peas in a pod,' were as varied as those in a small town of the nineteenth century. In the main, the work of changing the basic four-room cottages into individualized six- and eight-room houses had been accomplished" (Kelly 1993, 116–18). The slum that angry critics had predicted never materialized. By 1987, the basic Levitt house that had originally sold for $7,500—where it could still be found—was selling for more than $130,000, while remodeled homes went for more than $200,000 (Kelly 1993, 128).

As for the much-criticized "suburban sprawl," far from fleeing it, most Americans chose to live in it. By the early 1970s, the United States was a suburban nation, with most people both living and working in the suburbs. The developers, investors, and planners who had a hand in creating them seemed to have a better understanding of what the public wanted than the critics who sneered at them.

Part V

WHAT ABOUT THE FUTURE?

29

Planning Practice and Planning Education

LAWRENCE SUSSKIND

As a participant in the February 1997 DUSP Faculty Seminar at MIT, I was impressed with the way in which some of the speakers recounted, albeit reluctantly, what they see as a downward spiral in the importance and impact of the planning profession. They reminisced about earlier times in which, from their standpoint, planning and planners had more clout. They talked about the withering away of municipal planning departments and the irrelevancy of the planning function. They were troubled, but had few, if any, suggestions regarding what planning educators might do to help resuscitate the profession which they claim has lost its way and relinquished whatever legitimacy it once had.

Almost from the outset, it seemed to me that these seminar presenters spoke about a world of practice quite different from the one I know. They seemed to be living in a parallel universe in which the same actors and institutions exist but operate in an entirely different way. For example, they note a decline in the scope and importance of planning, while I see an increase. They see the power of planning professionals declining, while I see their influence rising. They see the ascendancy of free markets and privatization (at the expense of systems of command-and-control), while I see a growing need for governments to intervene: that is, to help us clarify our collective needs and objectives, force us to set priorities and explicate the consequences of various trade-offs, mobilize and channel the power of uncoordinated markets and motivated individuals, protect property rights, and ensure fairness in the face of unchecked self-interest—in short, protect us from ourselves and help us realize our shared ambitions.

How could we be looking in the same direction, and yet see such different things?

As it turns out, I agree with the presenters who argue that traditional city planning departments and plan-making activities are of little or no significance. Top-down, comprehensive planning at every level—from the project scale to the regional or even national level—no longer has support (if it ever did). I find this reassuring. There is finally a recognition that planning should not be the special province of technical experts (called "planners"). Instead, participatory processes that seek to empower stakeholders and acknowledge the political nature of planning are dominant. From my standpoint, that's a good thing. We now have more people involved, in more decentralized ways, in more of the decisions that affect them. This does not mean that planning and planners are less important, rather that they have different roles to play.

The real decisions about land use, economic development, environmental protection, and our collective responsibilities to each other are now made through an increasingly complex web of intergovernmental, international, and interorganizational networks. These create increasing demand, not less, for professionals who can assist in managing such complicated interconnections. Thus, there are not fewer jobs for planners, but more. Planners have not lost their leverage (I'm not sure they had much of it, anyway); they have increased it. Many of the people doing planning, however, wear no planning label. They do not work in planning departments or produce documents called plans. Instead, they work inside public–private partnerships and strategic, nonhierarchical alliances. They work as specialists (not generalists) in government departments with clearly defined regulatory responsibility. They facilitate interagency task forces and other ad hoc problem-solving arrangements. Although a lot of old-style planning still goes on, even that has been reshaped by these changes.

If I am correct, the implications for planning education are enormous. To some extent, many of our students have already realized the significance of these transformations and begun searching for new sets of skills, more specialized knowledge, and cleverer ways of entering the networks that will grant them access to the kinds of professional assignments they are seeking. That is, our students have voted with their feet—opting for courses that teach communication, negotiation, leadership, and entrepreneurship; crafting specializations that give them greater depth in a single issue area that transcends the traditional boundaries of planning departments; and internships and term-time work that allow them to make the contacts and build the personal relationships that will vault them into the positions they seek.

I want to offer five vignettes—two at the local level, two at the state level, and one at the national level—that illustrate the transitions I have noted. Each is meant to highlight a key difference between the "old" and the "new" thinking about planning. I think many have missed these transformations and are, therefore, bemoaning a kind of a planning practice that is no longer relevant. The first vignette concerns a land-use dispute, while the second is a transportation-planning problem in a rapidly growing urban area. The third focuses on a high-stakes political battle over a state-managed health care program, and the fourth considers an environmental planning problem. The fifth and final vignette looks at the national push for sustainable development.

A LAND-USE DISPUTE

My first story concerns an issue with which planners have been preoccupied for decades—the allocation of land uses (and, implicitly, the rate and pattern of development). Historically, the city I have in mind has seen its downtown deteriorate. Numerous efforts to spur new economic development in the core have failed, while growth on the periphery has increased. The construction of numerous shopping centers and commercial malls has undercut most efforts to revitalize the center of the city. The downtown has seen some reinvestment—in a sports complex and a variety of hotels aimed at the upscale visitor market.

In the past, the city planning department prepared and updated a master plan; now, though, the plan is more than a decade out of date. Even when it was timely, it did not represent a commitment to invest in infrastructure in a predictable way. Nor did the city housing agency have the funds needed to build and maintain the quality and diversity of the housing stock alluded to in the plan. The fact is, the master plan offered a long-term portrait of a city to which no one—except, perhaps the planners who made it—was truly committed. Short-term zoning decisions, capital improvements, and jaw-boning efforts by the mayor to influence private investment all moved forward in a disjointed, opportunistic way, as if the master plan did not even exist.

Now, though, a new city development task force headed by the mayor's special assistant is promoting a negotiated investment strategy to reinvigorate downtown. The 30-member task force (which includes self-selected representatives of a wide cross-section of citywide interests and is facilitated by a professional mediator) has been holding meetings in each neighborhood, trying to understand the needs and priorities of residents, business owners, and investors in each subsection of the city. Using interactive cable programming, focus groups, neighborhood surveys, storefront drop-in centers, and a home page on the Internet, they have succeeded in generating agreement on a citywide package of investment priorities (and policies to guide them). They are now asking each member of the task force to sign a letter of commitment outlining what the member will do to help realize the negotiated investment strategy. All the relevant city departments have been "at the table" throughout the conversations. Now, they too are being asked to be specific about what they will do to modify existing policies and formally commit to implement the investment strategy. The city council is being asked to commit, in writing, to a five-year implementation effort. This is front-page stuff in the newspaper, partly because the mayor's public relations people are working actively to "spin" the story.

This vignette depicts the major changes that have occurred in land-use planning practice in recent decades. The end result is not necessarily a plan; rather, it can be a negotiated investment strategy aimed at generating and coordinating public and private commitments over a five-year period. No city planning department is in charge; instead, the chief executive (the mayor) has taken the lead. Technically equipped staff (trained in planning school) represent the mayor. The public outreach effort relies on an intensive effort to communicate with various groups. The plan is built from the bottom up—piecing together the needs of each neighborhood and hammering out a package that tends to both neighborhood and citywide needs. The planner has become a mediator—seeking to build consensus while taking into account technical constraints and political opportunities.

A TRANSPORTATION DISPUTE

The second story I have in mind concerns an effort to expand the public transportation network to the outer edge of a metropolitan area. The capital investment required is substantial. The public, instead of applauding the prospect of a commitment to mass transit, is opposed—at least according to the newspapers. They object on environmental grounds, resisting all efforts to site new stations and parking facilities. They argue that the tax revenue involved ought to be used to add to highway capacity.

Where does the planning take place? Certainly engineers are involved at the state and regional levels, preparing a detailed transit system design. And, there are economic and engineering consultants playing an important role trying to generate travel demand forecasts. I would argue, however, that the most important planning activities are taking place inside the various organizations (like the Chamber of Commerce and the environmental and public transit-oriented nongovernmental organizations [NGOs]) committed to the expansion of the transit network.

Planners in this story are also central to the work of the environmental regulatory agencies, the state legislative and federal legislative committees that must allocate funds to help underwrite this investment, and the staffs of the governor, the big city mayor, and the chief executives of the smaller municipalities that must "get involved" if this project is to have a chance of winning public support. There may not even be a metropolitan planning agency or a regional transportation plan that carries any political weight in this case. There are policymakers and policymaking networks, however, who can and will be influenced by the work of transportation, economic development, land use, and environmental planners. The skills of these individuals in (1) forming and holding together a coalition in favor of this investment, (2) delivering an effective message to the public-at-large, (3) assembling sufficient technical information to win credibility in professional circles, and (4) negotiating a political victory in dozens of different venues, are what will make the difference between success and failure.

Under the "old" planning model, the preparation of a regional transportation plan by transportation planning professionals working in a regional planning agency would have been crucial to winning the DOT grant that would have made all the difference. Under the "new" planning model, a range of professionals and nonprofessionals spanning government, corporate, and nongovernmental networks, and mobilizing on behalf of a diffused set of policies in a surprising array of venues, will be key. If we find fewer transportation planners preparing fewer transportation plans, does that mean planning and planners have lost whatever influence they had? Or, should we be encouraged by the fact that more of our students are needed in a variety of settings to ensure support for expanded investment in mass transportation?

A STATE HEALTH CARE PROGRAM

My third case concerns ongoing, state-level negotiations over the settlement of tobacco claims. Billions of dollars are on the line. Most, if not all, of this money will go into state-supervised programs to improve children's health and provide medical insurance for those not presently covered. The financial value of the settlements being negotiated is staggering. If one were interested in new allocations in support of health care improvements or insurance reform, the tobacco settlement negotiations would be the place to be. There used to be federal grants in support of comprehensive state health planning. Such programs no longer exist; moreover, they were never well funded, nor did they have much impact on state policy. Planners concerned about improvements in the quality of health care now must insinuate themselves into a wide range of private and not-for-profit settings. Health policy specialists work as staff in a range of state agencies and regulatory authorities. While the tobacco settlements are being negotiated by state attorneys-general, the decisions about how to program these funds will be in the hands of elaborate coalitions of public and private actors in each state.

Should we bemoan the demise of comprehensive health planning at the state level? Or should we look to the new opportunities created by the "windfall" represented by the settlement of tobacco litigation? Does it matter that planning departments are not in the lead in deciding how these new policies will be framed? It seems to me that our job as planning educators is to prepare a set of social policy specialists capable of operating in the interstices of numerous public and private networks to build a winning coalition on behalf of those whose health care needs haven't been met by the existing "system." Here, the planning is totally opportunistic and episodic. No individual or agency has the authority or the standing to make unilateral decisions about the allocation of these funds. Technical expertise is not likely to carry the day.

Under the old model of planning practice, the essence of the professional planner's task was to do the necessary analysis, prepare technically defensible prescriptions, and step aside to let those in positions of responsibility (elected or appointed) make decisions that presumably reflected the public interest. Under the new mode, the planner's task is to identify and mobilize relevant stakeholders to help build an informed consensus on the fairest and most efficient set of policy trade-offs, to "sell" this agreement to the public, and to advocate tirelessly (over long periods of time) in a multiplicity of settings for all the small steps necessary for implementation.

ENVIRONMENTAL PLANNING: MANAGING RISK CONTROVERSIES

Environmental planning has become an increasingly popular specialization in planning schools. Some students enter this stream with a background in science or engineering, although this is not a requirement. A substantial number of environmental planning specialists expect to work internationally at some point in their careers, so they take an increasingly comparative approach to their studies. At MIT, we have more than tripled the number of environmental planning "majors" in less than 10 years.

In my fourth scenario, a recent planning graduate has been hired to help implement a state-run effort to meet the goals of the federal Clean Water Act. Plans must be prepared for each sub-watershed, spelling out how the requirements of the Clean Water Act will be met for river segments that are below standard. This is an enormously difficult task. Questions about infringement on private property rights are immediately raised in this context in the western part of the United States. Ongoing technical debates about the best way of meeting water quality standards over time dominate, especially given that states have little power to regulate non-point sources of pollution such as agricultural and urban runoff.

In this case, environmental planning does not consist of preparing an impact assessment or reviewing a permit request for consistency with easily measured performance standards. Instead, planning involves finding a delicate balance between economic development needs, public health standards, private property rights, and the rather limited powers of the state. At the heart of the question are what risks to current and future generations are acceptable, given the trade-offs involved. Facilitating the search for technically feasible but politically plausible solutions in the face of very different interpretations of acceptable levels of risk is the task of the environmental planner. This can be done from inside the local office of a state agency. It also can be done by an outside environmental consulting firm working for the state. In this case, the planners do have a responsibility for preparing plans, but the process of building consensus requires deep technical knowledge of the ecological systems and public health involved as well as elaborate risk-management skills. A general background in planning won't suffice. Specialized training is a prerequisite, along with fairly sophisticated process management skills for handling the risk controversies central to environmental planning.

SUSTAINABLE DEVELOPMENT AT THE NATIONAL LEVEL

My final vignette concerns the emergence of a planning concept like sustainability. At the federal level, a White House commission directs America's effort to implement this globally negotiated policy; no single federal agency is in charge. An ad hoc commission—involving senior corporate leaders, NGO heads, and other unofficial actors—leads the country's efforts to strive toward a level and style of development that will increase rather than diminish the options available to future generations. A small professional staff operates out of the White House. The closest parallel, historically, is the National Resources Planning Board created during the Roosevelt administration.

I find it intriguing that we should come closer to a kind of national planning than at any other time in our history during a period in which the believers in unfettered markets are at the height of their popularity. We give it other names, but that's what it is—national planning. The pressure to move in this direction is global. As a nation, we have signed a growing number of international treaties requiring us to meet certain prespecified resource management targets. The only way to meet those obligations is to coordinate public and private actions more carefully than we ever have before.

Should we be upset because the staff involved in these coordinated efforts are operating without a plan, outside of a planning context? Or, should we be pleased with the fact that the kind of intergovernmental and public–private coordination our profession has advocated for decades is finally taking hold? It is interesting to me that the staff of the President's Commission on Sustainable Development is looking to the planning profession (among others) for advice. We need to prepare our students to staff ad hoc efforts of this sort. They need the perspective and the technical agility that only planning education can provide.

As I look at the landscape of contemporary planning practice, three things stand out. First, many of the graduates of our planning program at MIT are working for a mix of public and private clients and are moving in and out of the public sector (depending on the excitement generated by particular elected administrations) during their careers. Very few will remain in the civil service for their entire professional lives. Second, many of our graduates have sacrificed breadth for depth while they are in school. Two years is hardly enough time to build the in-depth capabilities required to assume even entry-level responsibilities. Interestingly, though, these same students may switch specializations entirely as they move from their first to their second job. Finally, many of our graduates have been able to move into highly visible roles with a great deal of responsibility very soon after graduation. Their success is linked, I believe, to the strength of their entrepreneurial spirit and their innate leadership capabilities. When we admit students, we should emphasize these qualities, because I doubt that we can teach them.

We can focus on what planners are no longer able to do, or we can emphasize the expanded opportunities and emerging needs created by the shifts that have occurred. We can continue to teach the same kinds of things in the same old ways, or we can recognize the new sets of skills required of those who would plan, and make the necessary adjustments in our educational programs and practices. I say "Out with the old, in with the new"— and not a moment too soon.

30

Why Planning Theory?
Educating Citizens, Recognizing Differences,
Mediating Deliberations

JOHN FORESTER

Planning theory can be practically pitched and ethically critical, too—if and only if it takes practice seriously. It must deal with the abiding problems of politics, the ambiguities of value, and the challenges of deliberative learning that confront planners every day. At the same time, it must assess three pressing questions: (1) How can planners educate or misinform affected publics? (2) How can planners recognize or neglect citizens' particular histories and identities? and (3) How can planners mediate or fail to assist public negotiations? Any planning theory worth reading should also make us less complacent and more realistically hopeful than we have been.

Planning theory has two major concerns: planning institutions and planning practice. When we assess planning institutions, for example, not only do we face the challenges of understanding state–market relations, the subject of a vast literature, but we must also face questions of organizational and political design, something we do poorly in the planning literature as it stands. (Compare Mandelbaum et al. 1996.) When we assess planning practice, we need to do justice to the difficulties, mandates, and opportunities of planners day to day as they seek to do technical analysis, present arguments, build coalitions and empower or weaken constituencies, set agendas, define problems, negotiate, mediate, or engage in consensus-building efforts. My focus here is on the second of these two faces of planning theory.

Author's Note:
    My thanks for comments go to Dorian Fougeres, William Goldsmith, and Lloyd Rodwin.

THREE BIASES FOR PRACTICE

A decent planning theory should help us understand the possibilities of planning practice. We should not read planning theory and have to wonder, "What does this have to do with what planners actually face at work?" Thus, planning theory should take planning practice seriously in at least three ways.

First, planning theory should begin with the experiences and strategies of planners working in the face of power and inequality, with the questions, What are planners up against? and How can they respond? We can call this "the bias for recognizing planning as a political activity."

Second, we need to learn from "best practices," from the most insightful, innovative, and progressive planners we can identify, even though not all of their practice will be exemplary. In doing so, we will debate what "best" and "progressive" and even "innovative" can mean, as we should, given the lack of consensus on these terms that is to be expected. But, if we search for "best practices" and listen carefully, the skillful work of practitioners will help us refine our own research agendas in planning theory. We can call this "the bias for learning from practice."

Third, planning theory should help us to encourage the best practice we can imagine. Taking a tip from authors who show us how storytelling, literature, and drama can teach us vividly about what is at stake in real practice, we can develop critical and pragmatic planning theories enriched by powerful narrative accounts of planning practice (Forester 1995, 1999; Schön 1983). Seeking to complement vivid, even moving, description with political and ethical insight, we can call this "the bias for encouraging excellence in practice."

BEYOND THE "NEW PLANNING THEORY"

Why worry about developing a better understanding of what planners do? Why develop better planning theory? We need to worry because we have been trained to be blind to important aspects of planning. Conventional social science would have us describe or explain "what planners do"; but, as laudable (and difficult) as those goals may be, we need to do much more, as Patsy Healey and Charles Hoch have recently shown us (Healey 1997; Hoch 1994).

We would do better to think about planning theory in a new way. Planning theory is like a telescope: when it's good, it lets us focus on what's important in planning; when it's bad, it gives us headaches, eye strain, and a fuzzy and confusing picture of what we're doing. But it works over time: so insightful planning theory can help us to anticipate and respond in complex and conflictual political situations.

Even with the "new planning theory" and a new "paradigm" in the field, we are in danger of placing a misleading focus on "communication," when what we need is a better understanding of the precariousness, contingencies, and real possibilities of planning *action* (see Innes 1995; Teitz 1996). Knowing that such action is "communicative" is interesting only if it helps us understand how planning actions can be better or worse—with all the ambiguities that involves.

Whether stuck, wondering how to go on, or, in public, facing affected citizens, planners have to account for their actions in light of what they *can* do and what they *should* do. So our question should be neither, "What is planning?" nor "Why do planners do what they do?" but, rather, "How can—and how should—planners act in a precariously democratic, conflictual, highly politicized and unequal world?"

To answer those questions takes both institutional realism, for the account of actual possibilities, and careful normative thinking, too, to formulate, guide, and justify what should be done (Rorty 1988). Assessing how planners can and should act requires us to think carefully about politics, about value, and about the ways planners learn deliberatively in practice.

POLITICS

When planners must listen in the face of little time, plenty of exaggeration, relationships of distrust, and so on, they need good working theory to help them go on. Colloquially, we call this "the politics of information" or, more recently, "knowledge production." The analysis of planning should not imagine planning practice "in a vacuum"; good analysis must anticipate and help us to understand the institutional settings and pressures that actual planners must face.

VALUE

Don Schön's seminal work on problem framing (Schön 1983, 1990) left the ethics of reflective practice fairly vague. Relying on "what works" in the case at hand sounds pragmatic, but it becomes problematic whenever those with the power to define the situation are up to no good. This is the abiding problem of "situational ethics." Nevertheless, every time planners try to listen critically and not just take what they hear literally, they have to use some working planning theory to focus on, to make practical judgments about, what we can call, colloquially, "the facts that matter." To do this means learning about value, not just values—and this is a challenge of ethics that we have barely touched (Forester 1999).

DELIBERATION

When planners must justify to affected citizens what they do, they must do it articulately, soundly, and with reasons that educate a broader public (unless we reduce planners to advertising-industry image makers). Of course, we can find numerous cases in which planners justify decisions already made, prime a public for bad news, or withhold important information so that decision makers may "govern" less accountably than they might were affected publics more informed. If, however, we are interested in the possibilities of an increasingly democratic planning practice, one in which decision makers and affected publics both learn from the analysis of possible futures, from planning, then the analysis of such planning must help us to better understand the forms and possibilities of political deliberation as planners may nurture it. Recent studies of planning go some distance in this direction, and they need to be extended (Healey 1997; Hoch 1994; Throgmorton 1997).

THE CHANGING CHARACTER OF INTERDEPENDENCE

As transportation and communication systems, trade, and investments expand their reach, they knit cities and regions, towns and communities ever closer together. As this public interdependence and interdisciplinary complexity increase, so will the need for planners increase; for, as uncertainty increases, so do decision makers' needs for advice, for ways to protect investments, ways to hedge their bets.

This suggests a common corollary: the more public decision makers face uncertainty (the bigger the apparent risks they face), the more will planning analysis be sought out, and the more may planners be listened to (if not heeded). Nevertheless, as public jurisdictions, levels of government, and even regional ecologies become more interdependent, planners will continue to be caught "in between" many actors, each facing much uncertainty, each searching for good advice in the face of the prospects of investing poorly. In these positions, planners increasingly will face the demands of politicians and bureaucrats (with their personal, strategic, or structural interests), as well as their more diffuse obligations to the "public," organized and unorganized—indeed, born and not yet born.

Thus, insofar as increasing interdependence signals increasing uncertainty as well, it promises an abiding public need for planning, and with that need come complex obligations for planners who find themselves challenged to work in between the claims of multiple and conflicting parties (Forester 1989). As our understanding of interdependence becomes more sophisticated, we will come to understand correspondingly needed changes in planning methods and skills. We can see at least three recent developments here, each very different from the other.

PUBLIC EDUCATION

First, as Michael Teitz (1996) notes, we see today rapid advances in Geographic Information Systems (GIS) and modeling capacities, with implications for our capacities for exploring and reframing problems. As we become able to represent, probe, and study our ecological, physical, social, and economic interdependencies more powerfully, we come to face an entirely new set of issues involving the "public education function" that planners will increasingly serve—even if we understand it only poorly now. Not only do decision makers face increasing uncertainties, feel apparent risks, and worry about their vulnerabilities to the actions of others, so, too, do members of the public. This means, simply, that planners will increasingly play the roles of public educators, and with the advances all around us in information technologies, modeling capacities, access to the Internet, and the diffusion of personal computing technologies, the possibilities for presenting compelling public information are expanding as never before: graphically, visually, dramatically, and technologically.

THE RECOGNITION OF DIFFERENCE

Second, in the last decade, many in the planning profession have come to recognize much more clearly how race, gender, and ethnicity relate to social action. We are beginning to recognize more clearly the ambiguities and internal contradictions of "identity politics" and the "politics of difference" as they confront planners working with community diversity, with immigration, even in new ways with territorial disputes (Burayidi 1999; Sandercock 1998). In cases where continuing relationships are at stake, planners have to do much more than ask the simplistic question, "What do *they* want?" That question, of course, will often be worthwhile, but planners should not fool themselves by confusing deceptively simple answers—"money," "land," "control"—with the not-at-all simple people with whom they work.

The rationalistic presumption that historical identity reduces to economic interests—Marxist or neoclassical—too often leads planners to ask citizens to "leave their pain at the door," and this fuels anger, resentment, hostility, suspicion, anything but collaborative, productive planning. Ironically, both post-modernist theories of identity and modernist-instrumental accounts of rationality oversimplify and reduce "identity" in potentially oppressive ways, as Benhabib (1995) makes clear. These concerns lead to issues of "the politics of recognition" involving the "diplomatic recognition" that mediators often confront and that planners have a great deal to learn about (Baum 1997; Forester 1998; Sandercock 1997).

MEDIATED DELIBERATIONS

Third, we see increasing attention now to mediated negotiation strategies as ways of managing interdependence. In an account of what planners routinely do in the metropolitan Chicago area, for example, Charles Hoch finds that planners create settings for collaborative public deliberations even in adversarial contexts (Hoch 1994). In this volume, Lawrence Susskind suggests that a central role for planners involves their effective management of public deliberations. In her work on California, New Jersey, and varied cases throughout the country, Judith Innes applies Susskind's seminal work on consensus building and the broader management of public disputes (Innes 1996). In my own work, I've tried to show how public planning efforts often involve precarious processes of public deliberation—precarious because these processes of public learning, always subject to shifting political pressures (Forester 1997, 1999), can be well informed or badly manipulated. These three examples of recent work suggest that planners at all levels face the problems of encouraging participatory planning processes—far beyond the EIS processes Teitz cites—to craft good projects and avoid the traps of both participation and negotiation: the pressures toward exclusion, deal making, and prisoners' dilemma-like lose–lose outcomes, "lousy compromises."

THE NAGGING PROBLEM OF INCONVENIENCE

But a planning theory that fits practice too comfortably, an uncritical pragmatism, is not doing its job. Planning theory should help us to *improve* practice, not just describe yesterday's behavior.

"But what does 'improve' mean?" the chorus will sound. "How can we talk about 'improving' practice without making arguments about 'better and worse, good and bad, right and wrong?'" This skeptical question, of course, provides its own answer. Planning theory must embrace systematic, reasoned, careful arguments precisely about better and worse planning, good and bad planning, just and unjust planning. How could anyone with feet in the real world respect a body of "theory" that ignored questions of better and worse, good and bad, just and unjust?

"But," the skeptic will continue, "how can we have systematic, reasoned, careful discussions of such questions when they are so subjective, so relative to different people's views of the world?" This question, too, contains the seeds of its own answer, for it entangles and confuses two different claims. Yes, worldviews differ and people bring substantially different views of right and wrong; and precisely insofar as we owe each person respect, we owe them enough respect to consider their viewpoints. But we should not confuse, first, respecting a person with, second, agreeing with a viewpoint; this distinction opens up enormous room for research, study, and argument—room we can call *moral theory,* or *ethics* or *systematic, reasoned, and careful thinking about better and worse, good and bad, just and unjust.*

Thus, an inescapable part of serious thinking about planning must involve the analysis of better and worse, just and unjust—if such analysis of planning is to do anything more than describe yesterday's practice. If we wish our best thinking about planning to help improve practice, we will need that thinking to disrupt our complacency about the adequacy of yesterday's ways of doing things.

Recently, a doctoral student in planning on the West Coast noted the relative absence of divisive conflict among planning "theorists" and asked several senior colleagues who seemed to be arguing, "So, what's the problem?" The problem, simply, is complacency: a planning theory that seems to fit contemporary practice too easily, too snugly, and thus in too Panglossian a way. Can anyone begin to argue that contemporary planning practices reflect the best of all possible worlds, the best ways we can imagine to deal with widespread public distrust, with bureaucratic inefficiencies, with problems of exclusion, racism, and the marginality of weaker populations?

So one challenge faced by those in the planning academy is to nurture something more than complacent bureaucrats. To do that, we have to change the field, bring the bad news about how much more remains to be done, speak articulately to the realities of poverty and suffering, deal with race, displacement, and histories of underserved communities in ways that do not leave people's pain at the door (Krumholz and Clavel 1994).

In turn, this means building on Donald Schön's influential work to develop not only pragmatically reflective planners but historically and politically reflective planners, so that, in the pragmatism of their recognition of loss and in the pragmatism of their anticipation of politically staged argument, they are able to work critically and deliberatively, mobilizing action to meet pressing public need rather than just facilitating deal making between those already well organized. To adapt Joe Hill's words, we need to mourn *and* organize. Recognizing the history of displacement, distrust, and loss that planners in practice often face, we have to educate and encourage not therapists, but critical, politically astute pragmatists, planners able to work in the face of well-taken suspicion, all-too-real histories of loss, and no shortage of anger (see Marris 1975; Susskind and Field 1996).

Educating such planners will require that students and studies of planning encourage us to be more ambitious, to reach higher, to be ever vigilant about the political constraints we so easily accept as "realistic." That will mean, more colloquially, that we want planning theory less to congratulate us about yesterday's achievements and more to rock the boat, not just intellectually, "academically" in the protected ivory tower, but practically as well, looking at the problems of the day and our strategies for responding to them in ever more insightful, *better* ways. Hate it as we may, we need planning theory—to speak to practice situations, to learn from practice, and to encourage excellence in practice.

Facing ever greater needs to deal with social differences, public and private interdependencies, and citizens' and decision makers' needs for good information, planners themselves need critically sensitive, practically pitched planning theory to enrich their practical imaginations more, not less, than ever before.

31

Planning As Craft and As Philosophy

ANN MARKUSEN

L et me contrast the responses by the average, random transit partner to
my variously identifying myself as an economist or a planner. Whether
seated on an airplane, train, or bus, or any other site where one finds oneself
in the intimate presence of another with uncertainty as to the duration, and
regardless of whether I am in the United States or elsewhere, I find that if I
identify myself as an economist, my seatmate is apt to lean slightly away from
me and utter some noise that resembles an emphatic "Ohhhh!" This, I believe, connotes a mixture of fear and admiration but, above all, a sense that I
must be very clever but not very useful. On the other hand, if I say I am a
planner, the response is almost always friendly and interested, and after a
follow-up query on just what a planner is, accompanied by a variant of "Oh,
you should come to my town. We sure could use some of that around here."
Unless, of course, my neighbor turns out to be another economist.

Planning is a profession. It is an institutionalized activity in departments
of city planning around the country and world, with counterparts in regional,
state, even federal governments. Planning-related work takes place in both
private-sector and not-for-profit organizations as well. For the foreseeable
future, I believe that we will face continued demand for the skills and training
of planners in the complex built environments in which we live. It is hard to
imagine any other profession usurping or supplanting our role, albeit the
arenas in which we practice may shrink or expand, depending on competition from other ideologies and professions.

The objects of planning's activities are the form and function of cities
and regions, from the urban design of neighborhoods and city centers to transportation planning, from housing provision to social services, from economic

261

development to environmental planning. Planning still has a full plate, and it is not threatened with technological obsolescence, the clever coinage of "planning without planners" notwithstanding. I predict that we will be able to continually rely on demand for our skills and that we will continue to attract good young people because the arenas in which we work are challenging, often exciting, at least to the imagination, if not in daily practice.

Planning, however, could be much more than it is, and therein lies the opportunity. In two articles on the state of planning for *Urban Studies,* Michael Teitz makes two troubling statements about planning. He argues that planning has not succeeded in engaging the great social issues of our times— poverty, health, education and the declining quality, security, and compensation for work. Second, he points out that over the past two decades, planning has had less and less to do with cities and has become chiefly a suburban profession. In other words, planning follows development (Teitz 1996, 1997). The corollary is that planning has faltered on the downside, on the disinvestment front.

I would like to hold out the possibility that planners can expand their frontiers and make major contributions to poverty, health, employment, and inner-city issues. Planners' skills and habits of thinking are particularly adaptable to these issues for reasons I would like to explore at greater length. Let me start with the record. What can we learn from the planning profession's record of service, its impact on the real world?

PLANNING AS A CRAFT AND A PHILOSOPHY

Profession is a lovely word. It suggests commitment, competence, community. Besides a profession's institutional forms—the organizations where it is practiced and the associations to which its members belong—each profession possesses a reservoir of craft and a (hopefully) coherent philosophy with which it pursues its work.

I want to argue here that planning *as a craft* has been quite successful, but that planning *as a philosophy* has become less and less so. Planning possesses a synthetic, communitarian, forward-looking philosophy—and, in my view, a superior one. But, over the past few decades, it has lost ground to the utilitarian philosophy of neoclassical economics.

PLANNING AS A CRAFT

Planners practice a set of skills that draw variously from the physical and social sciences, as well as the arts. They work in "shops" with apprenticeship systems where younger, recently trained planners work alongside more experienced ones. Let me begin by enumerating several accomplishments in American urban and regional planning that suggest we have been relatively successful in our craft.

Recent studies suggest that the Tennessee Regional Authority and Appalachian Regional Commission regional planning experiments, designed to reverse regional underdevelopment, were relatively successful (Isserman and Rephann 1995; Hargrove and Conkin 1986), even though their intent and achievement were largely to integrate the target regions into the greater American capitalist development mainstream.

Land-use planning is another area of considerable achievement (Kaiser and Godschalk 1995; Teitz 1996). Although it has had its ups and downs and its critics, land-use planning remains a robust area that has met the challenges of explosive centrifugal development with growth management and of critiques of "large-grained" segregation of urban development with innovations in mixed-use development.

On the third front, researchers have argued that community development corporations, often staffed by individuals trained in planning, have made a dramatic difference in stabilizing inner-city and even rural communities and reversing rural decline (Briggs, Mueller, and Sullivan 1996; Fainstein 1996; Harrison and Weiss 1998; Harrison, Weiss, and Gant 1995). Similarly, community-based financial institutions have helped revitalize urban neighborhoods where conventional banks have stopped lending. An example is South Shore Bank's work in Chicago (Parzen and Keischnick 1994).

The fourth arena is that of manufacturing extension programs, designed as a response to plant closings and large-scale urban decline in mature cities and regions (Shapira 1996). By the mid-1990s, these innovations of a decade earlier, many of them fashioned by economic development planners, had become among the few to emerge and survive as a part of the Clinton administration's technology policy initiatives.

These examples are but some among many and are, of course, skewed toward the regional and economic development portion of the planning spectrum I know best. Each draws on skills sets, a common understanding of the urban/regional planning context, an exposure to social and economic theory, familiarity with institution building, an appreciation for political complexity, and a willingness to experiment that are fused only, I would argue, in the planning profession.

But, of course, the limits to planning achievement are set by larger social, economic, and ideological forces. In the current era, the greatest vulnerability of planning lies in the fact that its basic philosophy has been successfully contested by the economics profession. All the craft in the world will not prevail if the rationale for planning is eroded, as it appears it may be in the future.

PLANNING AS A PHILOSOPHY

Planning philosophy has four features that distinguish it from its aggressive competitor: foresight, the notion of the commons, an emphasis on equity, and an appreciation for the quality of life as a social outcome.

The Exercise of Foresight

In the task of planning, a planner must actively envision the future. Often setting in place physical structures, spatial patterns, and organizational structures designed to persist, planners anticipate the future, including changes in context that may affect the use or durability of their results. Planners incorporate the experience of future generations in their plans when weighing options, without discounting them as economists might. Few professions or organizations, the exception being the Pentagon, have as long a time horizon as we do, certainly not doctors or lawyers or even college professors. This habit of foresight, often simply implicit, is central to planning practice and a major hallmark of planning philosophy.

The Notion of the Commons

Central to planners' understanding of our domain is the idea of the commons—that considerable human experience takes place in arenas that are shared and thus cannot be allocated by market means. Urban space bears many of the features of commons. It is impossible to exclude any particular group from enjoying many of its pleasures; still, overuse can undermine the quality of the experience. Planners' efforts often are aimed at shaping urban land and space uses in ways that work with the principle of the commons. Planners are, even when not using the language, strong believers in collective action and in legitimate and important roles for the public sector.

Equity as a Normative Criterion

Planning can be practiced solely as an exercise in efficiency—say, maximizing the social welfare function in the presence of market failures. But few professions are as explicit about the equity dimensions of their choices and actions. Planners go beyond simply thinking about and assessing equity consequences. We often put in place processes of participation and representation that help ensure greater equity. This does not mean, necessarily, that we succeed. The corrosive effects of a lopsided wealth-and-income distribution on politics or private practice generate perverse outcomes. Almost no planner, however, would argue publicly that equity is not a legitimate and important concern in the design and evaluation of planning practice.

Quality of Life

Planners are more environmental than materialistic in that we generally work with a multifaceted sense of what the "good life" is. In designing neighborhoods, communities, social programs, even economic development initiatives, planners generally address the anticipated outcome for the quality of life, in both its aesthetic and its integrative dimensions. Streets that encourage conversation and safety, for instance, can be valued as much as those that facilitate rapid pass-through of vehicles. Growth controls are another example. Accepting a broad quality-of-life goal invites more conflict among interested parties and citizens, but that is par for the course for planners. The point is that quality of life, not simply tax take or land values, is the preferred outcome. Strategies for the "highest and best" use of land or the generation of jobs generally are held to this more demanding criterion.

PLANNING'S GREAT COMPETITOR: NEOCLASSICAL ECONOMICS

Planning as a public philosophy has a great competitor in neoclassical economics. Unfortunately for planners, economists have, over the past 20 years, aggressively moved their rather narrow ideas of human behavior and social systems into secondary schools and the media, and there they have found fertile ground. Economists have provided the major ideological tools for discrediting and dismantling the public sector, ushering in privatization and rolling back regulation.

How does the philosophy of neoclassical economics vary from that of planners?—Profoundly, on each of the dimensions laid out above. First, economists, as a group, disparage foresight. Theirs is a marginalist philosophy that focuses on short-term adjustments. The discount rate employed by economists to evaluate the present value of future benefits is very high and more or less minimizes any effects more than seven years into the future. Economists use forecasting techniques that extrapolate recent trends into the future—a "more of the same" practice that works well in times of stability or growth but that performs terribly in periods of downturn or crisis. In a clever device known as "option demand," parents and citizens may "opt" for strategies vis-à-vis the environment or social programs that ensure that things are not worse for their children and grandchildren; but, in economic theory, the latter have no status at all, since they are not present to register their demand themselves.

Second, economists respond to the "tragedy of the commons" by recommending as much privatization as possible, even if the equity consequences are negative. Further, economists have been chiefly responsible for new bu-reaucratic theories of behavior that portray public employees as "satisficers" and empire builders rather than public servants. (Oddly enough, corporate CEOs are not similarly disparaged, although these public choice theories origi-nally were based on theories about the behavior of corporate executives un-der monopolistic conditions.) The savaging of the public sector and the popu-larity of privatization are, in part, products of the success of public choice theory relative to planning philosophy, especially over the past two decades.

Third, neoclassical economics, in evaluating the outcomes of economic and government behavior, has narrowed its normative criteria to efficiency alone. Up through the mid-1970s, the standard economics textbook offered three main criteria—efficiency, equity, and stability—with none taking pre-cedence over the others. More recently, concern with stability has evaporated with the rise of the "microeconomic foundations of macroeconomics." Worse, economists now consider equity and the distribution of income to be the domain of the sociologist. This frees economists from having to trade off efficiency and equity goals. The prospect that a capital gains tax reduction, purported to raise investment and therefore efficiency in the future, would also be highly inequitable is something economists need not be concerned about today. If you don't like the income distribution, they would say, do something about it, but not as a part of economic policymaking.

This means that considerations of poverty and quality of life are close to inadmissible in contemporary economic reasoning and evaluation. Since eco-nomics has been making inroads into so many applied areas of the academy and social practice, mainly as an ideology, market remedies increasingly are prescribed without concern for adverse impacts on the quality of life or a worsening in the distribution of wealth or income.

Economists as a group are not often found engaging in institutional design, rule making, or program design. Those outside the university build models, interpret data, and make prescriptions—but on the narrow criteria just discussed. They have, however, done a magnificent job propagating their philosophy. As I suggest below, this ideological battle has not been adequately joined by planners, to our detriment.

THE SCORECARD: PLANNING'S LOSSES TO NEOCLASSICAL ECONOMICS

I would like to illustrate my contention that planning has lost ground in the philosophical struggle for the public mind by listing a number of cases in which planning's approach has succumbed to neoclassically inspired competitors.

First, let us reflect on the great centrifugal force of suburban decentrali-zation. In the United States, this process has proceeded with much greater force than elsewhere, and its consequences for urban life have been more debilitating. Traditionally, planners argued that the proliferation of independent local governments in a metropolitan area violates the principle of commons and imposes negative externalities—that the public good would best be served by continuing to incorporate outlying jurisdictions in the same body politic. This argument was based, in turn, on the notions that it would be important for suburbanites to pay for central-city amenities provided by the latter, that economies of scale in service provision argued for a single public provider (in at least some cases), and that equity goals would be more easily attained in a single jurisdiction.

However, in a provocative piece in 1956, the economist Charles Tiebout argued that individual citizens would be better served by being able to select a residence among competing jurisdictions, each of which would strive to provide the best public service package at the lowest public cost. Tiebout's article was hailed even though considerable effort was being made to overcome suburban fragmentation, for example, in the Minneapolis–St. Paul tax-base–sharing plan and in the Dade County, Florida, metropolitan consolidation. Tiebout's argument, along with its famous "voting with your feet" metaphor, were powerful ideological counterparts to suburban resistance to incorporation and helped roll back the consolidation tide.

Another powerful conflict has been played out over public investments. In the past decade, the legitimacy of public investment, especially investment that increases the public quality of life and/or overall economic performance, rather than activities that can generate appropriable revenue streams, has been undermined. This is especially true in the antideficit-spending philosophy that achieved national consensus in the 1990s. The federal government has no capital account, so that investments in education and infrastructure—despite their longer-term payoffs in terms of productivity, income, and tax revenues—must be funded completely out of current revenue sources (Eisner 1994). (Think of the average household, in contrast, which frequently chooses to borrow to finance housing purchases and college educations, knowing that these will pay off in the future.) Although academic studies clearly have documented the economic payoffs to infrastructure and education investments (Aschauer 1990; Baker and Schafer 1995), public spending in both areas has been declining because economists' rhetoric has been more powerful than that of planners. Foresight has fallen to the more powerful logic of balanced budgets.

A third, critical arena of philosophical contention concerns public education. Here, economists' arguments about efficiency—that competition among schools, driven by parental choice, will better allocate scarce educational resources—are gaining ground over those of planners and educators worried about the profoundly negative equity consequences of privatization.

Economists probably are not correct in their claim for the superiority of private-sector schooling, given the temptation for corporate operators to put profits above quality in the longer run. Although citizens are still voting (as in Milwaukee, recently) to preserve public schooling, the ideological attraction of the private schooling model is proving very powerful.

My final example is drawn from an area of planning where I have been working myself for five years—the conversion of defense plants and military bases to other productive uses. Although few accounts have been written on previous periods of defense downsizing, it turns out that disparate public- and private-sector actors aggressively pursued the transfer of people and facilities from military to civilian uses. Government planners began as early as 1942 to plan for post–World War II conversion (Ballard 1983). Businesses sponsored competitions and awards for the best record at conversion and across the nation joined newly formed business roundtables for mutual support at the local level. Many local governments created conversion assistance programs. The GI Bill was passed, providing four-year income and tuition support for veterans returning to college; and the Marshall Plan, by speeding reconstruction in Europe, generated vigorous orders for American capital equipment. Foreseeing post-Vietnam cuts, President Johnson included an entire section in his annual President's Economic Report on conversion strategies. President Nixon and his Democratic Congress, in cutting defense spending, devoted most of that peace dividend to social spending.

In the post–Cold War era, despite deep and rapid cuts—a diminution in procurement spending of 70 percent in real terms in less than a decade—little conversion action has been initiated in either the private or the public sector. A modest Congressional program grew a bit larger under President Clinton, only to be slashed by the 104th Congress. No GI Bill has been offered to either soldiers or defense plant workers. Although defense contractors were offered short-lived opportunities to compete for a few billion dollars in Technology Reinvestment Program funds and were encouraged to diversify by new "dual use" procurement policies, the Pentagon refused to envision or evaluate what the appropriate post–Cold War defense industrial base might be (Markusen 1998).

Instead, the Pentagon followed private industry's lead in allowing competition-eroding mergers among the largest contractors, and worse, reimbursing them for the costs of consolidation in what some have called "payoffs for layoffs." The result is a highly defense-dependent and more heavily monopolized contracting sector led by highly profitable, chiefly "pure play" (that is, nondiversified) defense companies that have little incentive to move people or technologies into civilian markets (Oden 1999). Their influence has made it difficult to lower the defense budget another $100 billion to levels most analysts agree is adequate for security. In this drama, neoclassical economists like Murray Weidenbaum, who disparage the ability of contractors to convert while arguing that any government intervention would be a distortion of the market, have played a facilitating role (Weidenbaum 1992).

THE CHALLENGE: PUBLIC DISCOURSE AND NEW FRONTIERS

The ascendancy of neoclassical economics in public discourse has created an environment that is relatively hostile to planning philosophy and practice. The neoclassical predilection for prescribing market solutions for everything, while championing the private sector above the public, is consonant, of course, with the interests of those sectors invested in free trade, global economic integration, an accelerating rate of change, and the rise of short-term financial returns over other criteria in allocating investment and human capital. This regime heightens economic insecurity, accelerates the rate of displacement, and, because it is associated with bringing poor Third World non-unionized workers into competition with American workers, worsens the income distribution. When government attempts to perform its traditional role as provider of the safety net and guarantor of employment and public investment, the cost of government rises—ergo, the attack on public-sector deficits and the disparagement of government competence. The public sector also becomes the target of private-sector efforts to "cream off" assets and programs that can be run profitably by restricting benefits and/or clientele (Lynch and Markusen 1995).

I believe that the planners' philosophy is closer to the heart of American concerns than is that of free markets; but we will have to do a better job of airing it before a larger public, while also defending our record of achievements. There are three things, in particular, that we could do as a profession to regain the stage: (1) engage in the public discourse, (2) showcase planning "best practice," and (3) diversify into new fields.

ENGAGING THE DISCOURSE

At this juncture, planners have little choice but to join more forcefully in the public debate, articulating the significance of foresight, husbandry of the commons, equity, and the quality of life. We must join the battle for the public imagination. This means choosing battles carefully and using conflicts at hand to illustrate and educate. I'll use here a recent example that involved a public employees union rather than planners, but I think it serves as a model of what planners could do as well. In August 1996, a group of women home health aides organized by AFSCME walked off the job in an Illinois veterans home in a conservative town downstate. Built recently, the home was designed to be operated by an outside contractor, in this case, a Tennessee firm that paid workers little more than the minimum wage and about 40 percent less than comparable workers at other state veterans homes. In walking out, the women made privatization a major issue in their campaign. They made a bid for, and won, the support of their community and of families of veterans served in the home. Within the month, the Republican governor, who at first claimed this was a simply a matter between contractor and employees, was forced by Republican legislators from the area to put pressure on the contractor to settle. Within two months, they did, offering wage hikes that more or less eliminated all differentials between the two sets of nursing homes.

Planners could do the same with many of the issues—public investment, land use, transportation, social services, economic development—in which they find themselves embroiled. Successful mobilization means not only offering a strong argument on the grounds of foresight, equity, and so on, but doing one's homework in combating truisms offered by the other side. Most public-sector and antiplanning naysayers rely on anecdotes rather than solid research results in decrying public-sector intervention and planning. On conversion, for instance, planners working in regions with closing military bases or at-risk defense plants could showcase research showing that, on average, converted bases host more civilian jobs than they did as bases. Similarly, they could oppose the recent strategy communities have followed in pouring millions of dollars into fighting base closings and refusing to plan for alternative uses on the basis that this might encourage the Base Closing Commission to think they are less needy of the base. Planners could demonstrate that advance planning has made a big difference to success elsewhere.

In cities facing defense plant closings, planners could contradict the rhetoric of the naysayers who contend that big defense contractors are congenitally unable to compete in civilian markets by showing that defense companies have been highly successful in shifting people and resources into new product lines, especially when the public sector has helped with finance and technical assistance for the transition. The same well-worn anecdotes about the failure of Grumman in buses, or Boeing-Vertol in trolley cars, can be swamped with allusion to Hughes's success in communications satellites and TRW's success with airbags, not to mention research results from two different survey teams showing a remarkable ability to diversify on the part of firms of all sizes (Kelley and Watkins 1995; Feldman 1996).

Planners must be more strategic in taking up this debate. Few planners write op-ed pieces in local newspapers defending planning principles or airing successful cases. We have to learn to write in different ways to do so—

short, argumentative pieces work best in this format. And planners should more actively seek forums in which to debate the privateers, whether it be television or before local community groups.

I can think of a couple of examples recently in which the dedicated few working through the media and/or a well-orchestrated campaign at the community level made a real difference in the outcome. One is the recent success of doctors, nurses, and healthcare workers in developing countries mobilized against the manufacture, trade, and use of land mines. By publicizing the horrific effects of land mines, which remain lethal for years after wars and blow up in the faces of farmers and children, they were able to use a chiefly media-targeted campaign to win public support for a global ban, despite the opposition of the industry poised to lose sales.

Another example is the living-wage campaigns mounted in several American cities, such as Baltimore, by coalitions of trade unions and community groups. By taking their issue to the larger public, dramatizing wage erosion over the past decade, and citing academic studies concluding that higher minimum wages do not endanger jobs, they have been able to win locally passed legislation establishing a minimum wage above the national floor.

Planners are used to talking locally, but mainly among ourselves and those constituents most active in the workplace. We need to reach a larger audience if we are to counter the corrosive effect of neoclassical economics thinking. (An AFSCME district found to their amazement that their own workers, all of them supported by tax dollars, were as prone as any other citizens to believe antigovernment rhetoric and vote for tax cuts and against higher public spending; they had to mount an educational campaign within their own ranks to counter such thinking.) It takes time and energy to do this, but every planners group should devote part of its time to this project. Not to engage is to acquiesce in the further delegitimation of our field.

DISSEMINATION OF BEST PRACTICE

A complementary activity for planning is the showcasing of achievements and "best practice," frequently and to a broad audience. We live in an era of marketing; often the public's view of what works and does not work is heavily influenced by their limited encounters with specific cases, usually via newspapers and television. Often contemporary truisms, such as "government can't do things as well as the private sector," are flatly contradicted by daily experience; but, unless this is pointed out to people, they can easily accept the popular rhetoric. Newspapers and nightly TV news are prone to profile failures rather than successes, scandals rather than routine work well done. But there are ways to turn planners' successes into heartwarming stories that can be presented to the media and policymakers alike.

I can think of several instances in recent years in which successful innovations have been acclaimed, developed into more ambitious proposals, and promulgated into nationwide or at least multiurban programs. These are drawn mainly from economic development practice, which I know best; but I trust that similar examples could be found in almost any area of planning practice.

One is the remarkable success of manufacturing extension services first proposed by planners in declining industrial states (Luria and Russell 1981; Bluestone and Harrison 1982). Pioneered in states such as Massachusetts, Michigan, and New York, to help small and medium-size companies cope with the disappearance of customers and/or stiffer competition from abroad, news of successful programs was actively disseminated, resulting in the diffusion of activities across the country. In the 1990s, first Congress and then the Clinton administration developed and funded programs based on partnerships with the states, which subsequently were consolidated in the U.S. Department of Commerce and were able to withstand an attack by the Republican Congress in 1996.

A second example is the proliferation of self-help credit unions for the working poor, remarkable for their Third World origins. Credit pooling by poor working women's groups in India and Bangladesh in the 1980s was evaluated positively (Noponen 1992) and underwritten by international aid groups and foundations. Subsequently, similar microcredit programs were implemented in a number of American cities as a means of not only overcoming financial constraints but enabling information sharing and peer group formation among inner-city residents attempting to start their own businesses. Although not a substitute for broader economic development initiatives, these programs are likely to become much more widespread as a result of active academic and practitioner showcasing (Servon 1997).

Defense conversion is another arena where successful conversion experiences, evaluated and disseminated, have encouraged local groups in disparate communities to replicate the effort. Working with local groups and networks of conversion activists across the United States, several of our studies on precocious efforts early in the post–Cold War era, in defense-dependent locales such as St. Louis, Long Island, and Los Alamos/Santa Fe, helped other groups across the country fashion strategies and select among government programs in mounting a regionwide effort (Oden et al. 1993; Oden et al. 1994; Markusen et al. 1995). Similarly, good research on past defense downturns and what seemed to have worked then—after World War II, the Korean and Vietnam wars—has helped contemporary planners prepare for the closing of bases or defense plants (Ballard 1983; Hill and Raffel 1993; Hill et al. 1991; Hill 1997).

Planners who have been involved with or who know of a successful local experience would be doing the larger community a great service by setting aside time to write up the process and results. Too often in planning, because success tends to be local news only, practitioners in other locales replicate each other's efforts without the benefit of results from experiments elsewhere. For that matter, even failures or mixed results deserve public airing and analysis, because they tell us much about mistakes to be avoided and/or likely are countervailing forces to good planning ideas.

DIVERSIFICATION INTO NEW FIELDS

Just where the boundaries of our field lie is always a contentious issue in planning. Some argue forcefully that planners should stick to traditional strengths in land-use transportation and urban design, while others contend for (and practice) social, environmental, and economic development planning. A number of contemporary problems seem to be ideally suited to planners' craft and philosophy, and they are not being handled that well by other professions. They represent an opportunity for us as a field, a chance to expand our horizons, diversify our portfolios, and integrate our work across urban and regional space.

One such area is poverty policy. Planners already have contributed much to the analysis of and prescriptions for urban poverty, especially in the area of housing. The recent scholarship on poverty, however, has been conducted largely by social scientists with impressive research skills but less than impressive ideas about how to fix the system. In 1996, Congress passed a welfare bill that acknowledges that the "system is broken" (although not everyone would agree) and that we are changing it but we don't know what we are changing it to. In my view, this is largely the result of entrusting welfare reform to policy wonks from sociology and policy schools who have studied in minute detail how welfare mothers and other recipients respond to different variations in programs, but who are less adept at understanding how institutional and community structures affect the economic and life chances of the poor.

Planners, in contrast, are grounded in communities where the intersections between poverty and urban structure and programs are evident. Now that responsibility for welfare has devolved upon the states, planners will have greater opportunity (and greater necessity) to offer designs, ideas, and insights linked to land use, housing, economic development, and transportation planning. Successes such as community development corporations and self-help credit collectives may be harbingers of a fuller menu of organizational and institutional ways of combating poverty, which planners are ideally suited to design and propagate.

Healthcare is another arena where, it seems to me, community-based planning is positioned to make a great contribution. The excesses of the medical model, the consolidation of healthcare delivery into HMOs, and the growing crisis in coverage—all have created an opening for planners to innovate new, community-based, preventive and home healthcare delivery systems that are integrated more thoroughly into community networks and neighborhoods.

A third arena is employment training and job creation. The minimum-wage challenge reviewed above is an example of how local initiatives that target employers can improve residents' income materially. Another outstanding example is the pioneering Wisconsin Training Partnership in the Milwaukee area, where employers and unions together are investing in skills assessment and training systems designed to ensure lifetime skills enhancement, a quality labor force, and high-wage work for the region—an experiment now being replicated by the U.S. Department of Labor around the country. Even more generally, planners can help to integrate social and economic policy in ways few other professionals are trained to think (Fainstein and Markusen 1993).

PLANNING'S POTENTIAL

Planning as a craft has a solid clientele, one that could be expanded in ways that would strengthen existing areas of expertise and enlarge planners' sphere of influence. We could continue on the present course, although this risks becoming less influential as public policy schools proliferate and expand. Planners, I would argue, do a better job on several social and economic policy fronts than do professionals trained in public policy schools; the latter are immersed in applied neoclassical economics (cost–benefit analysis and so on), with little social theory or institutional analysis that might better equip them to understand the complexity of the real world and how to craft a new program or policy. Why shouldn't planners challenge those in public policy and showcase our considerable achievements? Why shouldn't we ply our craft, based on multidisciplinary understandings of urban and regional structures and processes, on the pressing issues of our times—be they poverty, continued urban decentralization, the deterioration of employment and the environment, or the need to invest in infrastructure and education?

To thrive in the twenty-first century, planning will have to assume the burden of defending the public sector and the commons, while keeping equity on the national and local agendas and stressing the critical role of foresight, and of envisioning and planning for the future. No other profession is likely to do so, although we can count on allies among public health practitioners, environmentalists, trade union activists, community groups, and some groups of lawyers. Personally, I cannot imagine a more exciting or demanding arena in which to be teaching, researching, and practicing.

32

Reflections and Research on the U.S. Experience

MICHAEL B. TEITZ

Some future observer may well look back at the 30 years from 1965 to 1995 as a golden age of American planning.[1] Despite the failure of some federal planning efforts, continuing decline in the central cities, and denunciations by critics of the quality of the suburban built environment, this period saw the greatest expansion of operational power on the part of urban planners since the profession emerged in the late nineteenth century. That this occurred is not simply the result of the growth of income and population, with its concomitant urbanization and infrastructure development after World War II, although those are certainly critical influences. For planning as an activity recognized and supported by public funds, we must also look to two important trends.

The first trend was the increase of environmental concerns and public awareness, which gave rise in the 1960s to key national and state legislation for environmental protection. These laws lent status to groups formerly excluded from legally challenging development, thereby changing the planning process profoundly. They also required extensive data gathering and analysis for the purpose of assessing the environmental impacts of proposed developments, leading to the formation of new planning-related organizations. In short, the environmental revolution empowered citizens and organized environmental groups, as well as created new demand for planners, both those working for public agencies and those working for nongovernmental organizations. By the late 1980s, the process of development was, in many respects, so transformed as to be unrecognizable from that of the 1960s.

Author's Acknowledgment

I am indebted to Karen Chapple for her valuable assistance in preparing this chapter.

This chapter is adapted from material previously published by Carfax Publishing Ltd., (a member of the Taylor & Francis Group), Abingdon, Oxfordshire, United Kingdom, in its journal, *URBAN STUDIES*. It is reprinted with permission of the publisher.

M. Teitz, 1996. American planning in the 1990s: evolution, debate, and challenge. *Urban Studies* 33, 4–5: 649–71

M. Teitz, 1997. American planning in the 1990s, Part II: the dilemma of the cities. *Urban Studies* 34, 5–6: 775–95

A second, closely related trend was a shift in relative power between local citizens, on one hand, and developers and local governments, on the other. Many factors have contributed to this change. Among them are the widely publicized negative effects of urban renewal, a federally supported program in the 1950s that generated huge opposition; the efforts at empowerment by the War on Poverty of President Lyndon Johnson in the 1960s; and the widespread growth in local environmental awareness and opposition to growth and change at the local level. Although the level of power of the organized citizenry varied widely from place to place, their role in planning decisions had increased substantially by the 1980s, especially in their capacity to stall or prevent development. Paradoxically, this shift increased both the demand for and influence of local planners, who often found new allies in local planning disputes and who began to develop new roles in intermediation and consensus building in complex, conflictual situations. Planning and development became a complex process throughout the United States, and planning emerged as a key profession in managing this shift in power. Indeed, the term *growth management* has emerged as a conventional usage with real substance. Whereas planning generally did not become more deeply institutionalized, in the sense of increasing its professional strength through such means as registration or professional exclusivity in public appointments, the growth in demand was reflected in the increased number of openings in the field and the expansion of planning education and the roles that planning program graduates took on in the field.[2]

Behind these movements in planning are profound economic and social changes in American society. Beginning in the 1970s, these shifts have given rise to major debates, both about the scale and the significance of the changes, as well as appropriate social responses to them. Arguably the most important of the changes has been the decline in the rate of growth of productivity that has occurred over the past 20 years. By this point, there is little debate among economists that the decline is real and that it has reduced the rate of income growth overall. The "growth dividend" that fueled the social programs and public infrastructure investments in the postwar period has disappeared. Fiscal stringency has become endemic at all levels of government. Population growth, however, has not ceased—which implies that the social task of housing and providing infrastructure became much more complex.[3]

With such changes, it is not surprising that the accepted political orthodoxies have been called into question. The liberal agenda of the Democratic Party that has dominated national politics since the Great Depression has been aggressively challenged by a conservative Republican message. Although the reality of politics makes all ideological programs imperfect, there can be little doubt that voters have become profoundly unwilling to accept increases in taxation, and that there is substantial hostility to the interventionist and regulatory styles that marked the postwar years, whichever party was in power. In this context, planning finds itself in a paradoxical situation. In the simplest sense, its regulatory style is distinctly out of step with what appear to be powerful trends in a society, and its precepts are therefore disputed. Yet, a case can be made that, in the context of increasing anxiety, uncertainty, and hostility to a distant federal government, people will attempt to increase their sense of security within the range of an environment they can politically control—namely, the local community.

At the same time, the restructuring of the industrial system—in part, a response to global competition—has altered the life chances and employment expectations of American workers. Low-skilled, unionized manufacturing jobs have been eliminated in great numbers while nonunionized, low-wage employment in the service sectors has grown substantially; and the premium to high-skill employment in all sectors has increased. With large firms permanently shedding jobs at all levels, a sense of uncertainty and anxiety has become a staple of media reports. There are some grounds for anxiety. Behind the static median real income, substantial shifts in income distribution have seen the economic status of the lowest 25 percent of the population decline absolutely, while the middle remains stagnant, and the upper quartile has increased its relative advantage. To some extent, the impacts of these shifts have been muted by the boom of the 1990s and growth in the number of two-earner households, but, at the same time, the nature of the family unit itself has changed with large increases in employment of women and in female-headed, single-parent families. Added to these social and economic changes, the demography of the country has been affected by the aging of the baby boom generation of the 1950s and the influx of immigrants that has raised the proportion of foreign-born inhabitants to the highest level in 90 years. Especially in growth states such as California, the racial and ethnic mix of the population has been transformed, with major impact on politics, social relations, and public services.

Changes in the American economy and society have powerful implications for planning. Despite slowing productivity, income gains and a widening income distribution have permitted continuing suburban development. The impact of this development, both in older metropolitan peripheries and in newer regions of growth, has been to generate environmental pressure and demands for planning. At the same time, the larger changes have had critical effects on older metropolitan areas and their inner-city cores.

Metropolitan core cities are a traditional focus for planning, and their fate is closely tied to the field. Immigration, technological change, and competition have created a mixed picture for the central cities in the 1990s (Glickman et al. 1996; Stegman and Turner 1996). Some have been prospering; for others, their long-term population decline appears to have slowed, and new sectors have emerged; for still others, conditions are worse than ever. The 1980s decade saw continuing population decline of as much as 10 to 15 percent in many older cities in the Northeast, Midwest, and South, even as their metropolitan areas grew, while newer central cities in the West and Southwest were still gaining population (Glickman et al. 1996). Clearly, when we speak of the central or inner cities of the United States, we must now distinguish carefully between those newer cities still able to annex land or able to attract population, and those either declining or in a condition of stability or slow growth.

A new wave of immigration, both legal and illegal, has reshaped the populations of many cities to a degree not seen since the early part of this century. Although the issue is controversial, there can be little doubt that this influx of cheap labor has affected the prospects of earlier migrants to the cities, particularly African Americans who came in great numbers from the rural South to the cities during World War II and succeeding decades. By the 1980s, those and their descendants who had not been able to move out of the cycle of poverty were in desperate straits.

Reflecting the structural shifts that have occurred, the proportion of employment in producer services grew substantially during the decade, even among the most depressed cities. Other service sectors showed modestly rising shares, except for the public sector, where the share generally declined. Business services generally pay well, but the other sectors are mixed, with the result that incomes have continued to polarize. With the long-term fall in the rate of productivity growth after 1973, and the growing inequality of incomes, low-skill populations have done poorly in the U.S. labor market. Insofar as these populations also are more than proportionately minority and located in the cities, the result has been catastrophic. Unemployment and poverty rates for the cities generally are close to twice those of the suburbs, no matter at what point in the business cycle. For African American and Hispanic populations, poverty rates were more than 25 percent, typically four to five times the average suburban rate. This situation has led directly to a continuing debate about the "underclass."

In summary, the condition of the inner cities reflects their position within the larger economic environment. For those able to participate effectively in the sectors of growth over the past two decades, the picture is relatively positive. In this, cities resemble the suburbs of almost all areas in the United States. For those cities unable to participate, the result has been much more problematic. Many of them have found themselves attempting to cope simultaneously with loss of manufacturing employment, rapid immigration, and the increasing isolation of the poorest groups within the population. That dilemma has attracted a resurgence of research and policy interest about questions of poverty. These debates have influenced decision makers and provided the context of much that planners have thought and done in relation to inner-city problems. The direct contribution of planning as a field to the research and debate has been surprisingly small, however. This is ironic because the strand of planning that is rooted in the reformist and progressive responses to the problems of the nineteenth-century capitalist city clearly saw its mission to respond to inadequate housing, poverty, congestion, and transportation, and planners sought to address those problems directly within the urban context.[4]

EVOLUTION AND DEBATE: LAND-USE PLANNING AND LOCAL ECONOMIC DEVELOPMENT

The fortunes of planning have long been associated closely with those of development. This is evidenced by the continued importance of the traditional core of the field, local land-use planning, and the new focus within the field on local economic development.

LAND-USE PLANNING

It is now a quarter of a century since the suburbs exceeded the aggregate population of central cities in U.S. metropolitan areas. With that development has come, in Downs's (1994, 5–7) term, a "dominant vision" among ordinary people of the appropriate form of settlement comprising geographically unconstrained low-density development, detached single-family housing, widespread ownership of automobiles, low-rise workplaces with automobile access, small communities that are politically autonomous to a substantial degree, and an absence of visible poverty, brought about by the concentration of the poor in older, central-city areas. America is a suburban country, at least in terms of the environment inhabited by most of its people. The planning profession has never entirely come to terms with this fundamental change, despite the reality that most planners now deal with problems and issues in a suburban context. We may attribute this, in part, to the grievous problems of the older central cities, which deservedly continue to attract much attention from planners; but there are also serious differences among planners and urban analysts in their views of the automobile and its role in the future structuring of American cities.

THE EVOLUTION OF PRACTICE AND METHOD

Effective professions continue to evolve in response to social changes that bring new demands, as well as technological developments that may increase professions' technical capacity. Typically, both social and technological change are recognized by innovators, but the adoption of innovations may be relatively calm or it may be marked by substantial debate over differences.

Land-use planning is an example where innovation has been notable but not fiercely resisted.

Despite challenges and debates, land-use planning remains at the core of planning practice in the United States, as it has for the past 60 years (Kaiser and Godschalk 1995). Many critics of land-use planning have seen it as, at best, unresponsive to social issues, and, at worst, reinforcing discriminatory and exclusionary practices (Friedmann 1993). In the 1960s and 1970s, when planning was enmeshed in the social conflicts in American cities, and its intellectual basis was being challenged by the adoption of social science and political economy perspectives in the schools, land-use planning was often seen as uninteresting or irrelevant. Indeed, by that time, the comprehensive or general plan, a guiding document for long-range physical development, was often a routine exercise undistinguished by technical or substantive innovation. That this was so is a tribute to such people as Alfred Bettman, Edward M. Bassett, and, later, T. J. Kent and F. Stuart Chapin—all of them innovators, disseminators, and teachers of this approach to local planning, which dominated practice (Bassett 1938; Chapin 1963; Kent 1964).

Land-use planning has proved more durable than its critics; more important, it has shown a new burst of creative energy in the past decades. This development has been stimulated by the larger contextual changes described above, but it has also come from the innovative work of practitioners and decision makers in American communities. The phenomenon reflects the legal basis of American planning. Unlike many countries, the United States has no national legislation that prescribes local land use and management in the general sense (Cullingworth 1993, 1994). Specific national laws, especially those dealing with environmental issues, constrain or mandate state and local actions; but they are not the legal basis of state and local land-use planning.[5] That basis rests in the constitutions of the United States and its individual states, as well as in state and local legislation. Public activity must meet the requirement of constitutionality at both the federal and the state levels, the key historic judicial test of which was the finding by the U.S. Supreme Court in the *Euclid* case (1926) that zoning without compensation for property owners is constitutional. The judicial basis for planning from that time has been the police power, which permits governments to regulate land use in the interest of public health and safety without compensation to owners unless there is a judicial finding of a "taking" of property. This is a complex question that will be discussed further. The important point here is to note that it leaves the construction of planning legislation and institutions to the state and local levels of government, thereby creating the potential for great diversity in styles and purposes of planning. In fact, that diversity has been limited by the tendency of state and local governments to adopt variations on model legislation, the prototype of which was the Standard City

Planning Enabling Act of 1928, drafted under the aegis of the U.S. Secretary of Commerce at the time, Herbert Hoover, and widely distributed as a model to follow. The fairly uniform character of the master plan approach was very much a result of these origins, but the potential for diverse innovations, always there, has borne fruit in recent years.

In their survey of developments in land-use planning, Kaiser and Godschalk (1995, 371ff) focus on the evolution of the general plan into four prototypes and hybrid forms that fit the contemporary situations of communities: the land-use design plan, the land classification plan, the verbal policy plan, and the development management plan. Reflecting the growing importance of the natural environment and fiscal realities, Kaiser and Godschalk see the emergence of a design–policy–management hybrid of all these, incorporating long-range land-use planning in a framework of policy, standards, and implementation. This format embodies both the traditional tools of zoning and subdivision control with newer tools associated with growth management, including state standards, phased-growth programs, geographic development boundaries, and controls on the rate of development (Kelly 1993). Such plans are likely to be the product of much more interactive and participatory processes, owing to the use of new technology and the increased interest and participation by citizen groups. They are continually being created and redesigned at the local level, thanks to the ingenuity of professional planners and citizens.

The changes in process, which stem from the rising awareness of the environmental and fiscal impacts of growth, have been especially important at the state level, where there have been several efforts to go beyond individual community efforts to control development in ways that lead to mutually adverse outcomes. Two aspects of this trend are especially important—substance and process. Substantively, states as different as Florida, New Jersey, Oregon, and Vermont have sought to manage growth and development to a degree far exceeding anything seen in the traditional enabling act approach (DeGrove 1992; Gale 1992; Knaap and Nelson 1992). Their success has been mixed, but the very fact of the effort marks an important evolution of planning in the United States, in which there is a substantial restructuring of governance (Bollens 1992) and some evidence of an improvement in the quality of local plans (Berke and French 1994).

The improvement in quality of land-use planning has, in part, been facilitated by the rapid adoption of Geographic Information Systems (GIS) as a planning tool. Planners have responded enthusiastically to this technological advance—and for good reason. That GIS has the potential to improve operational effectiveness in relation to such things as data accuracy, availability, and access seems evident to planners in their day-to-day work. Perhaps the most intriguing aspect of GIS is its potential to change the character of analysis for decision making (Harris and Batty 1993). From the outset of the use of computers in planning in the United States, researchers and practitioners have envisioned their capacity to provide information rapidly, to model and simulate the urban environment, and to permit the construction of real-time alternatives in the course of the planning process. The first round of this effort, in the 1960s, produced basic advances in understanding but did not live up to its promise (Lee 1973). Nonetheless, in the succeeding two decades, a quiet development of models continued, especially in metropolitan transportation planning. The rapid improvement of computing speed and memory capacity in microcomputers, an astonishing decline in the cost of hardware, together with the creation of rapidly improving GIS software, has changed the situation to a remarkable degree. Not only have large-scale models enjoyed a modest revival (Wegener 1994), but the possibilities created by imaginative use of GIS have begun to permit new types of urban models that can incorporate constraints at a level of detail that begins to approximate that needed by planners and decision makers in practice (Landis 1994a, 1994b).

A further aspect of the evolution of land-use planning concerns process. The increasing complexity of land-use decisions and the growing number of players in the decision process have led to new forms of planning, particularly through negotiation (Dorius 1993; Forester 1987; Susskind and McCreary 1985) and consensus building (Innes 1992; Innes et al. 1994). Explicit processes for building consensus have emerged from experience in negotiation (Godschalk 1992) and through ideas from many sources. For example, from corporate strategic planning, we see the importance of the identification and commitment of stakeholders (Bryson 1988), and from the field of dispute resolution, new forms of conflict management that seek to bypass the traditional political and judicial systems (Susskind and Cruikshank 1987). Given the high stakes and strong concern among parties over land-use decisions, this seems a natural tendency that is now beginning to make itself felt. The evidence for the value of consensus-building processes for land-use planning certainly is not complete, but there are good arguments for its serious consideration in the field coming from what historically have been vastly different positions.

One source of support comes from planning theory, which also has been evolving. Theorists such as Forester (1989) and Innes (1995) are advocating the idea of communicative action, based on Habermas's concept of communicative rationality (Habermas 1984). For planning theory, the key element of communicative rationality is its focus on practice as the source of knowledge. From the perspective of communicative action, to understand a field of practice, it is first necessary to study it closely, listen to the language of its practitioners and those who are affected by it, and take seriously what they have learned from experience. Prescriptively, good practice carries this further through utilization of this knowledge in planning processes that draw on and respect this knowledge, principally in the search for consensus through structured but open and participatory dialogue.

Attractive as the ideological content of communicative action may be, especially to academics and students who do not have to deal with the realities of planning in a capitalist market economy, one may doubt that this is the only reason for its quiet advance. Radical theories and the support of advocacy and equity as primary concerns in planning have been a forceful presence in the field since the 1960s, particularly in a few planning schools. Although they have been influential in many ways, these views have never come to dominate either teaching or practice. Academics and practitioners alike recognized that such an outcome would most likely have further marginalized the field. Despite its appeal in terms of widely held values (Innes 1995), as well as the misgivings of critics, communicative action is not the stealth radicalism of the 1990s. Rather, its appeal is much broader and rooted in attention to practice and to the methodology of building agreement on complex issues.

The political and legal attack on land-use planning in the 1990s is discussed later in this chapter. Yet the activity, itself, appears to be better grounded now than it has been in years. As Beatley's work on ethical land use shows, this is a time of growing sensitivity to the complex impacts of regulation (Beatley 1991, 1994). And a new wave of interest in sustainability is motivating imaginative ways to innovate in land-use planning (Beatley 1995), albeit with the usual complement of trendiness that the field seems to indulge. Whether this will turn out to have substance remains to be seen, but the fact is that land-use planning has a new lease on life that is based on advances in practice.

DEBATES OVER LAND-USE PLANNING

The evolutionary trends in urban planning already discussed are accompanied by powerful, sometimes conflictual debates over some critical questions. No dynamic professional field is without such issues; they mark the boundary of what is known and believed about practice in relation to the changing world in which it is carried on. In this section, we take up two of these issues—first, metropolitan growth and transportation, and, second, urban design. Although they are closely linked in practice, it is convenient to treat them separately in order to bring out the character of the debate involved. These are two among many possible issues, but they are of great importance to the future of planning in America.

Most planners probably are close to a "balanced-growth" perspective on metropolitan growth. Essentially, this view accepts the reality of low density, with the automobile as the dominant means of transportation; but it seeks alternatives. One reason is that the suburban metropolis is seen as inefficient in terms of transportation, as evidenced by complaints over suburban traffic congestion and commute times; the other is that the suburban metropolis is environmentally problematic, especially because of air pollution.

Higher-density centers consisting of employment and commercial clusters are now emerging within the low-density metropolis as employment decentralization follows population. Popularly identified as "edge cities" (Cervero 1989b; Garreau 1991), these concentrations are found almost universally in American metropolitan areas. It is argued that they represent a new form of development that means higher density and a more urban character in suburban environments. In an automobile-dominated system, the growth of suburban, concentrated employment has powerful implications for transportation effectiveness. Traffic congestion has appeared in places where it was never previously experienced, with strong political repercussions. Efforts to reshape the behavior of drivers who commute alone have included the construction of high-occupancy-vehicle (HOV) lanes on suburban freeways, which offer incentives to car and van pools. Companies have come under regulatory pressure to have a certain proportion of their employees commute to work by means other than driving alone. Among planners, spatial imbalance between jobs and housing (Cervero 1989a) is widely regarded as a critical contributor to traffic congestion in the suburbs and as a source of inaccessibility to employment for those segments of the population, especially the urban poor, who do not drive to work. Although relatively few metropolitan areas have attempted to formally regulate the relationship between development of employment opportunities and housing, the notion of jobs–housing balance has become a standard element of planners' assessment of problems in metropolitan development. The possibility that traffic problems may be mitigated by land-use change appeals to those opposed to low-density development for other reasons.

The second perception critical to the balanced-growth view is linked to suburban employment growth but is driven heavily by natural and social environmental concerns. It emphasizes the effects on environmental quality of metropolitan development that is very large in scale and auto dominated. Both federal and state legislation has sought to improve air quality by a variety of means (for example, the creation of air quality management districts for critical air basins). After the obvious measures to control point-source pollution have been taken, it rapidly becomes evident that auto emissions are a major contributing factor. Among the ways to curb such pollution is the possibility that a different, denser, urban form might yield lower levels of auto travel, either through proximity of origins and destinations or through increased feasibility of alternative means of transportation. Planners tend to see such arguments in a positive light. Traditionally, they have favored the qualities of urbanism associated with density, namely liveliness and choice; they are often concerned about the environment; and they see automobiles as subsidized (Hanson 1992). For many planners, the perceived wastefulness of urban sprawl and the threat to open space, farmland, and environmentally sensitive environments posed by uncontrolled, low-density development are givens. Energy waste in an auto-dominated system has also been seen by environmentalists and planners as a powerful reason to question low-density development. These views have come together in the movement against "sprawl" and for higher densities and sustainable development that has recently gained much attention in planning and environmental policy circles (Newman and Kenworthy 1991).

These views are not held solely by urban planners; they have been widely reflected in research, in political debates, and in legislation, to the point of becoming the conventional wisdom. They are visible in much of the federal legislation affecting metropolitan development in recent years. Both the 1991 Intermodal Surface Transportation Efficiency Act (ISTEA) and the Clean Air Act Amendments of 1990 require that land-use considerations be taken into account in planning transportation investments. Although there are always many reasons for the adoption of specific programs in the American political system, there can be little doubt that the decentralization of metropolitan employment, declining air quality, suburban traffic congestion, and energy consumption have all been important arguments in the passage of legislation that has directed huge public investments in new heavy and light rail systems.

Not everyone agrees with this version of the future of urban development. For years, urban analysts have studied the link between land use and transportation (Kelly 1994) but have tended to say little about policy. A few critics, notably Peter Gordon and Harry Richardson (Gordon et al. 1989), argue that the automobile-based metropolitan area is both efficient and desirable, and that public investment in fixed-rail systems is particularly unjustified. By and large, the planning profession and federal, state, and local legislatures took little notice, although such a view evidently has been the basis of the real politics of suburban development since the 1950s. Recently, however, there has been a burst of work, both by planners (Audirac et al. 1990) and by economists linked to planning and urban analysis, which challenges the basic assumptions about higher-density development and raises serious questions about urban development and transportation strategy. This work is receiving increased attention because of the changing political environment and budgetary stringency that is afflicting all levels of government, but that is not the only reason for its impact. It reflects a body of serious research now at the point where its findings cannot easily be ignored.

Although this research indicates that the emergence of growth centers may make possible changes in transportation modes, the fundamental dominance of the automobile for commuting probably will continue or even increase. As Giuliano (1995a, 1995b) points out, the metropolitan structure is already in place; thus, the leverage for change through land use and density is minimal.[6] The implications for policy are to shift the incentives for driving much more directly, for example, by addressing the large, untaxed fringe benefit that is given in the form of "free" parking by suburban employers (Shoup 1993; Shoup and Pickrell 1980).[7] A similar argument can be made that technological solutions to automobile emissions are likely to be much more effective than policies intended to reduce vehicle miles traveled, whether through land-use regulation, promotion of transit, or transportation management (Bae 1993).

Needless to say, this assault on the mainstream view has not gone unanswered. Anthony Downs (1994) appears to favor policies intended to shape metropolitan structure in a direction that would increase densities and limit development. His reasons have to do with his long-term concern for the poor and racial minorities, arguing that the single-family house and automobile-dominated city have been major factors in the widening divisions of American society. Robert Cervero (1996), who has been examining the question of the effect of jobs–housing balance and density on commuting in the San Francisco Bay area, joins Downs in concluding that restriction of higher-density housing development through zoning and other NIMBY methods is the major planning failure in this realm and that direct regulation of jobs–housing balance probably is not necessary. As we will see in the next section, Cervero remains convinced that higher-density development in suburban settings has value, in good part because transportation will remain a serious metropolitan problem, for which the critics' solution, namely, achieving transportation pricing that is close to true marginal social cost, is even less likely than the implementation of other means.

At this point, there can be little doubt that the mainstream of planning is unconvinced by the critics. With some thoughtful exceptions, the two sides mostly run on parallel tracks. However, in the current political environment, this is a problematic situation for the mainstream. Their opponents have a ready audience in Washington, where the message is welcome in a market-favoring, antiregulation, budget-cutting era. Nonetheless, planning policy in America is worked out ultimately at the state and local levels. There, the struggle is by no means decided.

DEBATES OVER URBAN DESIGN

The debate over the form of the emerging metropolitan areas and their transportation needs has been echoed in the realm of physical design. Dissatisfaction with suburban environments has long been expressed from many quarters, the most recent probably being the feminist critique of the single-family house and suburban neighborhood as isolating and inappropriate for women in this era (Hayden 1981). In the past decade, however, a new school of design for suburban development has emerged, harking back to much older roots in the idea of community and the virtues of density. This approach, known as "neotraditional" or "new urbanist" planning and design, has been created largely by architects, notably Duany and Plater-Zyberk (1991) and Calthorpe (1993). Its hallmark is the design of housing complexes intended to recover a mixture of small-town and urban values seen as having been lost in the low-density suburb (Christoforidis 1994). In its exemplar—Seaside, Florida, designed by Plater-Zyberk and Duany—the style involves a self-conscious choice of historic forms, both in housing and subdivision layout that is reminiscent of the romantic designs sometimes seen in older suburbs. However, there is an underlying logic that uses the single-family house, grid street pattern, and relatively dense layout of the late–nineteenth-century American small town to attempt to recapture perceived benefits of density. Increased social inter-action and "neighborhood" quality asserted to come with higher density are the primary benefits intended. The ghosts of Ebenezer Howard (1898) and Clarence Perry (1929) are abroad, albeit in an inverted form with respect to density. In order to realize such an environment, not only are higher densities required, but the automobile's impact on pedestrian movement and interac-tion must be curbed. For this purpose, the traditional grid layout of streets is preferred to the cul-de-sacs and curves of conventional, suburban subdivi-sion design, and garages are relegated to alleys behind the houses, thereby creating a continuous frontage and promoting the use of porches and pedes-trian interaction on the street.

Whether new urbanism works on its own terms, and whether it can meet the test of the market, have yet to be determined fully. If Seaside and its few imitators were all that comprises neotraditionalism, there would be little point in viewing it as anything other than another design fad. But there is an interesting link to the question of planning for metropolitan development discussed in the previous section. That connection appears in the work of Calthorpe and others who have connected the idea of redesigning for density with changes in transportation structure (Beimborn et al. 1991; Calthorpe 1993; Calthorpe and Mack 1989; Newman and Kenworthy 1991; Rabinowitz et al. 1991). Calthorpe's notion of "pedestrian pockets" aims to insert is-lands of higher-density housing into the suburban landscape in a way that meets the new urbanist objectives of a pedestrian environment and reduced automobile dependence. An important means of achieving this is to link such developments with transit nodes and create substantial communities that are both suburban and transit oriented.

Evidence from studies of the impacts of new transit systems in major metropolitan areas suggests that densification does indeed occur around stations, as would be expected in a market environment, but that its appearance depends upon local political attitudes to development and may not occur in close proximity. To what extent that development will permit or encourage pedestrian, or nonautomobile, travel remains uncertain (Cervero 1995), but Cervero's recent work suggests that with appropriate planning, transit villages may be part of the future as well as the past.

LOCAL ECONOMIC DEVELOPMENT

In the past decades, local economic development has quietly emerged as a second major sphere of interest and activity in urban policy. Although states and cities in the United States have engaged in efforts to promote and expand their economies since the beginning of the republic, this activity was generally not undertaken explicitly by government. Instead, dominant local economic business interests were able to secure their objectives through coalitions that could shape political outcomes. Of course, during periods of crisis such as the Great Depression, public intervention did occur; but it was not until after World War II that systematic local intervention through the mechanism of urban renewal became institutionalized. Even then, it was done in the name of slum clearance rather than economic development per se. Eisinger (1988) makes a good case that there was a significant change after the mid-1970s, largely as a result of the new competitive pressures on local economies that accompanied the opening of American markets to imports and the long-term slackening in growth of productivity. The localized collapse of manufacturing employment stimulated a search for alternatives, sometimes at any cost. At the same time, the federal government, which had intervened extensively through the War on Poverty in the 1960s, was withdrawing from major budgetary commitments to the cities and states in favor of expanding individual entitlement programs.[8]

The Emergence of Local Economic Strategies

These strategies have emerged in the past two decades as a major function of states and cities in the United States in response to broad changes in the economy. It is an important phenomenon in its own right, and, for the cities, is especially critical for the development of the central business districts. Community development focuses much more on populations in poverty and is more closely connected with the inner cities. Each of these activities is more or less uneasily related to planning and has captured the attention of planners.

Three features of the emergent state and local economic development activity should concern us here. First, it was ushered in under the banner of a new conceptual basis that was appealing to planning. Second, it explicitly sought to engage local governments as active participants in development through partnership arrangements. Third, it was accompanied, for the first time, by the creation of institutional structures that sought to professionalize local economic development activity. All three features were visible in the central cities.

The traditional approach to local economic development in the United States has relied on the idea that growth requires inward capital investment to develop local resources, utilize local labor, and create sales to nonlocal markets. Analysis of the local economic base was, in fact, a simple pre-Keynesian export multiplier developed in planning practice. The stimulation of, and support for, inward investment was seen primarily as a function of local business organizations, such as Chambers of Commerce and real estate interests. The role of government was to provide the infrastructure for development, especially residential, and to maintain a favorable local "business climate" by keeping taxes low. When necessary, incentives for the attraction of a new firm could be offered by providing various property tax abatements. Notwithstanding a long series of efforts by regional economists to discredit the use of tax incentives, this view of local development continued to dominate local political perceptions of appropriate policy. In the 1980s, the business-attraction strategy did not disappear; if anything, competition among localities for new branch plants rose to higher levels, stimulating new interest (Loveridge 1996). Some incentives have even gained intellectual support (Bartik 1991). However, the traditional view was challenged by a set of ideas that might be called the "new local economic development" (Blakely 1989; Eisinger 1988; Teitz 1994).

In essence, the new conceptual structure argues that localities faced with economic difficulties had to turn to their own resources, that viable economic activity needed to be based in the creation of new local enterprises, and that the key to such development lay in the active participation of local governments in partnership with the private sector. This endogenous growth (or, in Eisinger's [1988] terminology, "demand side") message was attractive to planners, reinforcing their tradition of local action. It also appealed to those states and localities, particularly the inner cities, where there seemed to be little prospect of attracting major investments, for example, Japanese auto assembly plants that were being located on greenbelt sites in nontraditional manufacturing locations such as Tennessee. Whether the new framework would actually lead to economic development was undemonstrated, but the arguments of Eisinger (1988), Blakely (1989), and others were widely read and discussed. Relatively few studies have actually attempted to measure the extent to which cities have adopted these ideas, but there are clear indications that they have penetrated practice (Reese and Fasenfest 1996).

Especially appealing was the notion of partnership between local governments and business in the process of local economic development. This idea had been given currency by the federal Urban Development Action Grant (UDAG) program, put in place during the Carter administration of the late 1970s. Under the UDAG program, the federal government provided funds for local economic development projects that were to be leveraged by private investment in partnership with local governments.[9] Rich (1992, 168-169) argues that, despite its termination, the UDAG program was important in moving urban economic development into a partnership mode and away from simple tax incentives. However, as Mollenkopf (1983) has shown, the idea that local governments should become active participants in the process of development, in what he called the "pro-growth coalition," had already emerged from the changing economic circumstances and evolving politics of the cities in the 1970s. But not all planners were sanguine about the idea (Fulton 1989; Peiser 1990).

The third element of the evolution of local economic development is its institutionalization and professionalization within government and in non-governmental organizations (Blakely 1996; Visser and Wright 1996). As economic development became more widely recognized as a part of local government activity, so the question of its placement within the governmental structure arose, and its participants began to form quasi-professional organizations. For planning, this has raised a number of issues, particularly over what the functional and organizational relationship of planning and economic development should be within government. The outcome is by no means clear. Functionally, the two are often in conflict, as citizens use the planning process to slow down or block development, or developers seek to override planning constraints. Organizationally, in some cities, economic development and planning are separate departments; in others, economic development resides in the mayor's office, reflecting the importance of high-level interaction in the pro-growth coalition politics; in still others, planning and economic development have been subsumed into larger departments, often also including urban redevelopment agencies. What is evident is that planning and economic development in the 1990s are intimately related in tension as well as in mutual support.

This is apparent as well in the professionalization of economic development. Although there is, as yet, no formal profession, its practitioners are being formally trained in planning, business administration, and public policy schools, among others (Visser and Wright 1996). Planning schools, in particular, have developed curricular and teaching positions in the area, often supplementing and extending what was traditionally seen as regional development. Texts and handbooks have been written (Blair 1995; Blakely 1989; Lyons and Hamlin 1991). Professionally, economic development practice is supported by what has become a significant journal, *Economic Development Quarterly*, which offers both theoretical and practice-oriented papers from a range of disciplines.[10] Organizations of state and local economic development practitioners have been expanding in a fashion that is a familiar feature of emergent professions in the United States. In short, this is now an important professional element both within and outside planning, comparable in its development to the emergence of environmental planning.

For the older central cities, local economic development is especially important. Faced with serious economic problems, they have grasped at nostrums of all kinds, often with disappointing results.[11] The challenge of economic development is complex, however. Elected officials are striving to overcome the dominant images of poverty and its associated ills, which leads them to seek development that will "turn the city around," a euphemism for bringing back the middle-class population. To do this, they have emphasized the development of advanced sectors and the renewal of central business districts. They must also respond to the needs and political demands of impoverished groups who clamor for equitable outcomes, especially through community development. Trying to square this circle is not easy. Both thrusts have generated highly conflictual responses in planning, epitomized by central business district and community development. In practice, cities have channeled resources into two different types of local development: the redevelopment of the central business district, and community development in inner-city neighborhoods. Within each approach, there is some debate over the efficacy of policy, although research is generally not conclusive. Perhaps the most interesting issue not explicitly spelled out in the literature concerns whether the two approaches are complementary or conflicting in their development goals.

Planning and Central Business District Development

In the 1980s, the pattern of inner-city public involvement with economic development described by Mollenkopf (1983) continued and intensified to a remarkable degree. The boom of the 1980s produced a huge amount of new office construction. Although the largest amount of office development actually took place in suburban metropolitan locations, a substantial quantity went into older central-city cores. Along with offices, there were new hotels, retail complexes, convention centers, and cultural facilities, even in some of the most depressed cities.

This intense growth was accompanied by several types of planning analysis and some debate about the role of planning (Peiser 1990; Robertson 1995). At the large theoretical scale, planning researchers such as Castells (1989) and Sassen (1991) sought to understand the sources of growth in the informational mode of development and growing spatial integration and specialization of production. Their work was accompanied by an eruption of research cutting across planning and geography, by those such as Scott (1993a, 1993b) and Storper and Walker (1989), who attempted to make sense of the complex changes in urban functioning that were under way, linking change to larger forces at work.

At the level of urban development processes, writers such as Fainstein (1994), Frieden and Sagalyn (1989), and Pagano and Bowman (1995) have been trying to unravel the complexities of the public–private relationships in development. Their work, too, has generally aimed to analyze the character of the new processes that were appearing in cities all over the world. At the level of economic development policy, the growth spurt also induced new debate about the equity issues involved in central business district growth (Keating and Krumholz 1991; Krumholz and Forester 1990), which are discussed below. Downtown development's effectiveness as a strategy for public investment also saw considerable debate, both at the broad policy level (Frieden 1990; Frieden and Sagalyn 1989; Sagalyn 1990) and for specific types of investment (Fenich 1994). Finally, at the level of practice, are the planning issues of urban design and infrastructure investment, among others (Robertson 1993). Within planning, this activity has created new employment opportunities calling for real estate and project development skills and training (Dowall 1990).

In the late 1980s, most of this large-scale central-city development simply stopped. Faced with serious fiscal problems, cities did their best to cope; but, in fact, they were able to do little. Nonetheless, cities have continued to put forward initiatives. Many of them appear to have taken on symbolic importance, notably public support for the expansion or construction of sports stadiums, as cities try to prevent professional sports teams from moving away.[12] However, not all are turning to these measures, which have dubious economic efficacy (Shropshire 1995). Reporting on a survey of local officials (Clarke and Gaile 1990), Clarke (1991) found that entering the 1990s, most of them were broadening their strategies and looking for more indigenous growth and smaller, lower-cost projects. It suggests that the new economic development conceptions are beginning to take hold. Even though the cities are, in many respects, on their own, the sense has not disappeared that the central city is a critical component of metropolitan development. The debate has grown concerning relations between central cities and their metropolitan areas, spurred partly by David Rusk's (1993) analysis of "elastic" cities, those able to expand their boundaries, which appear to coincide with better metropolitan performance in general.

In retrospect, central business district economic development planning in the inner cities seems to have been more a function of the building boom than anything else. As a result, planners are now more savvy about development, with the scars to show how they have learned. Cities are still looking for investment but are finding little. Much of the literature, however, seems rather detached. Even such powerful studies as Fainstein's (1994) do not seem to lead to convincing policy conclusions. Studies by scholars with a more explicitly professional outlook, such as Robertson's (1995), seem rather remote from the economic realities of development. We know a lot more about how the process worked in the boom of the 1980s. During the 1990s recovery, cities continued attempting to reinforce their downtowns for all the reasons they have traditionally done so; but in the future they will face increasing opposition from other claimants on local resources.

PLANNING AND COMMUNITY DEVELOPMENT

There has been a long stream of work in planning devoted to the issues of the poor and community development. Much of the engagement since the War on Poverty has focused on neighborhood or community development, largely through the medium of local organizations and community development corporations (CDCs) (Boothroyd and Davis 1993; Vidal 1995). That work continues. However, the past two decades have seen the growth of a community development perspective, generally known as "equity planning," which incorporates a larger view that extends to the city and the region.

Equity planning has its roots in the 1960s, with the rediscovery among planners of advocacy for the disadvantaged, most closely associated with Paul Davidoff (1965) and Chester Hartman (Metzger 1996).[13] That advocacy, however, with its strong redistributive intent and talk of "guerrillas in the bureaucracy," was generally seen as being in opposition to the organized and institutionalized forces of government and planning, and therefore requiring separate community-based institutions for its legitimacy. Often it was substantially Marxist in tenor. In 1969, however, the appointment of Norman Krumholz as planning director for Cleveland by its first African American mayor, Carl Stokes, led to the definition of an institutionalized form of planning practice that focused on the poor and worked explicitly with community organizations. This effort culminated in the Cleveland Policy Planning Report (Cleveland City Planning Commission 1975), which was widely discussed. Subsequently, Krumholz, who became an academic, has worked with other planning scholars and advocates actively pursuing the idea of engaging government in a planning mission that recognizes the necessity of serving the poor and disadvantaged. Though redistributionist in aim, this effort was politically and ideologically pragmatic, reflecting much more the American Progressive tradition, though many of its participants were further leftward on the ideological spectrum (Clavel 1994; Krumholz 1994; Krumholz and Clavel 1994; Krumholz and Forester 1990; Mier 1993). From their work have emerged most of the ideas associated with equity planning, or, in a slightly different variation, progressive planning.

From the perspective of economic development and the aggressive pursuit of employment opportunities for minorities and the poor, the equity planning experience of Chicago during the brief administration of Mayor Harold Washington from 1983 to his untimely death in 1987 is critical. Washington appointed Robert Mier as economic development commissioner (Giloth and Wiewel 1996). Mier, whose death has cost planning one of its most influential and productive scholar-practitioners, led a group seeking to reorient the city's economic development strategy away from downtown and large projects and toward the needs of the poor and neighborhood residents (Mier 1993). The Chicago Development Plan (1984) embodied this conception, placing job opportunities as one of its four central goals. Under Mier's guidance, the city created industry task forces to focus on local business development and retention, and worked closely with community development corporations to develop local business opportunities (Clavel and Wiewel, 1991). Given that this occurred during the period of huge downtown office expansion, the redirection of policy was remarkable, although, perhaps, it was made fiscally possible by that growth. With the death of Mayor Washington, Chicago politics reverted to a more conventional form, but a considerable legacy has been left, both for the theory and the practice of equity planning, as other cities, such as Berkeley, California; Boston, Massachusetts; and Burlington, Vermont, moved in that direction.

Research on equity planning has been extensive, but it mostly takes the form of case studies and it is difficult to draw aggregate conclusions (Clavel 1986; Krumholz and Clavel 1994; Simmons 1996). By the early 1990s, many of the equity planners had moved on from their cities, and the idea's future is now hard to gauge. Although it is firmly established in planning education and is influencing practice (Metzger 1996, 115), there are considerable problems for equity planners in practice (Krumholz 1994; Simmons 1996). However, two events in this decade have refocused the attention of planning on community development in the central cities. The first was the Los Angeles riots; the second was the return of the federal government to community development.

The riots in Los Angeles in April 1992 gave new prominence to the black underclass. It reminded people that racial black–white tensions in U.S. cities continued to be critical and awakened them to interethnic hostility as an important element in the inner city (Baldassare 1994, 3–5; Pastor 1995). In their suddenness, and in the extent of property destruction far beyond ghetto boundaries, the riots generated renewed attention to their underlying causes as well as ideological debate about their meaning and appropriate nomenclature (Johnson et al. 1992, 1994).[14] A flurry of measures followed the riots, notably the formation of Rebuild L.A., an organization intended to bring the private sector deeply into the process. It was largely unsuccessful, but considerable new capital, both public and private, found its way into the troubled area. Whether the city's government has shown an effective response is debatable (Regalado 1994), but the riots certainly influenced the federal government.

The return of the federal government to inner-city community development was undoubtedly accelerated by the riots, but it was more directly associated with the election of President Clinton, the first Democrat in the White House since Jimmy Carter's departure in 1981. It was clear from the beginning of the administration that concern with the budget deficit and fiscal austerity would permit no large-scale urban initiatives. What emerged in 1993 was a new program calling for "empowerment zones" (Snow 1995), which combined some aspects of the idea of the enterprise zone concept (Green 1990), favored by conservatives, with a community development approach favoring nonprofit organizations and local decision making. The aim of the program was to return to place targeting of the poorest cities and neighborhoods. In accord with the tougher rhetoric of the Clinton administration, however, localities would have to compete for a small number of awards by demonstrating how bad their problems were and how effective their networks of local organizations. As it turned out, politics played its normal role of diluting programs intended to concentrate resources geographically.[15]

Important as the Empowerment Zone program is as an indicator of federal reengagement with the cities, its underlying conceptual framework, in what usually is called community development, may be even more important (Bendick and Egan 1993; Dreier 1996; Vidal 1995). Over the decades since World War II, inner-city policy has had a curious on-again, off-again relationship with the idea of community. During the War on Poverty, it was a key concept for urban policy, resulting in the formation of numerous local community development corporations, many of which still exist. Under subsequent Republican administrations, a combination of belief in individual initiative and blaming the poor reduced federal involvement and place-based programs. Neighborhood planning organizations and CDCs survived through hard times, albeit with an ambiguous message about development, since they had been service delivery organizations, and local control frequently means opposition to any change (Marquez 1993; Wenocur 1991).[16] Since the 1980s, the idea of community, both in a larger sense and as a part of urban policy, has seen a rejuvenation with key works by Castells (1983), Bellah et al. (1985, 1992), and Etzioni (1993), while the related concept of social capital has been widely discussed through the work of Putnam (1992).[17] It appears that this idea is generating new interest among numerous influential groups in American society.

The question of whether community development can make a significant, long-term difference to populations in deep poverty is complex and difficult. Vidal (1992) gives a guardedly optimistic assessment. Others such as Marquez (1993) are less sanguine; he points out that, although individual CDCs may be effective, in the absence of continued subsidy, they are forced to adapt to a survival mode, which diminishes their impact on community problems.

It is unlikely that community development could survive on public-sector support alone in this era; thus, support from foundations is critical. Among the major foundations, such as Ford and Annie E. Casey, there is a resurgence of interest in promoting a new round of support for what Giloth (1995) calls "targeted economic development." Although incorporating community development as a key element, its proponents see this as focusing on employment and income for the disadvantaged. Thus, it combines ". . . employment training, human services, and enterprise development to enhance access to and creation of jobs, careers, and self-sufficiency for the disadvantaged" (Giloth 1995, 280). Clearly, this approach has much in common with the new economic development, while also representing an expansion of community economic development as it has been done by CDCs. At the same time, there is increasing attention being paid to the potential power of networking among CDCs (Harrison and Weiss 1998), developing out of research on such networks in regional development (Indergaard 1996; Putnam 1992; Saxenian 1994, 1996). Whether networking is simply another hoped-for nostrum to produce effective community-based involvement remains to be seen.

In many ways, the recent resurgence of federal interest in community development is encouraging. Although tempered by hard experience and limited by fiscal stringency, it shows that some attention is being paid to the dire situation of the populations of the older inner cities. Whether the effort will succeed remains uncertain.

CHALLENGES TO PLANNING

No matter how heated the debates within a professional field, the existence of the activity itself is rarely called into question. However, a combination of legal decisions, policy transformations, and ideological shifts pose a serious challenge to planning. Forces now at work in society beyond the field itself have the potential to threaten some of its most basic foundations. The legitimacy of planning is further challenged by another uncomfortable development: among the urban policy fields, planning has been slow to enter the debate on inner-city poverty policy. While equity planning does address distributional issues, few planners have responded to the debate on the structural and cultural causes of poverty. Interestingly, both dilemmas reveal a fundamental weakness of planning: as a development-driven phenomenon, it seems unable either to counter the political force of property rights proponents or to respond to a critical policy debate that engages most of the other social sciences and policy fields.

DEREGULATION AND TAKINGS: THE LEGAL CHALLENGE

Since the early 1970s, there have been two contradictory trends in American policy toward government intervention in the market and private behavior. First, we have seen the greatest expansion of federal, state, and local intervention since the Great Depression in the name of environmental protection, consumer protection, and concern for special groups such as the disabled. In particular, the National Environmental Protection Act (NEPA) of 1970 marked the beginning of a major stream of legislation, policy, and public and private action that continues today, generating debate and conflict. This was the largest expansion of peacetime regulatory power in the United States. Yet, the same two decades witnessed the emergence of a powerful movement against regulation—in many instances, directed precisely against the regulations established in the 1930s to meet the economic crisis. Among the sectors where price and other regulations have been eliminated or significantly reduced are airlines, trucking, telecommunications, broadcasting, and financial services. The deregulation movement has strong ideological overtones, but it is also based on powerful arguments for economic efficiency and growth, which emerged from a long stream of research in economics and a new set of legal theories.

For planning, both tendencies have been important. The rapid growth of environmental awareness generated whole new realms of work for planners (the designation "environmental planner" scarcely existed before 1970), together with major new regulatory tools and powers, for example, the environmental impact statement. However, this change simultaneously increased the regulatory burden on the business sector most closely associated with planning—namely, development. By nature unsympathetic to anything that prevents growth, developers and builders see other realms being deregulated and feel unfairly penalized. The growing role of local residents in the development decision process, and the emergence of growth control in its various forms, simply reinforced this trend. That a backlash has followed is scarcely surprising.

The discussion of land use pointed out that the ability to regulate land use through zoning without compensation has been critically important to local governments and planning in the United States (Fischel 1995). Constitutional law in this area seemed settled for many years, permitting a high level of regulation so long as some value remained in the zoned property and no physical "invasion" of the property occurred. In the 1980s, however, the U.S. Supreme Court handed down a number of decisions that appeared to challenge the capacity of local governments to regulate in the way to which they had become accustomed (Callies 1993; Fischel 1995). Three cases, in particular, have raised serious questions—*First English*, *Nollan*, and *Lucas*— apparently setting tighter limits to regulation than had previously been acceptable to state courts.[18] There is some debate over the significance of the decisions for land-use planning (Callies 1993; Carlson 1995; Fischel 1995; Merriam 1994). Nonetheless, the threat appears disturbing, particularly in light of the larger political shifts in the country. Since 1991, legislatures in 23 states have introduced legislation that would compensate landowners when their property value is diminished by regulation by more than a specific proportion. None has passed, but the issue is alive and open to citizen initiatives in some states. The effect on the behavior of land-use regulators must be inhibiting.

It may seem inconsistent that this chapter identifies land-use planning as an area of evolutionary advance in planning at the same time that its legal basis may be threatened. However, much of the progress in land-use planning may be attributed to the growth of a positive environmental regulatory environment over the past 20 years. The uncertain legal situation casts doubt on the continuation of that professional movement, but the outcome is still unclear. In the immediate future, the larger ideological and political shifts going on in the country are likely to be more important.

IDEOLOGY: STEPPING TO THE RIGHT

The American political spectrum has shifted to the right in the past decades, but planning did not experience a major negative impact. This was partly because so much of its work is conducted and legislated at the state and local levels, where local interests are likely to be stronger, and partly because that shift was still accompanied by major federal legislation on the environment and transportation that called for planning. It seems likely, however, that continuing pressure on government action due to budgetary constraints, and ideological hostility to government intervention in general, may be felt—nationally and locally.

The Republican congressional victory in 1994 brought about a situation in which the possibility of undoing or radically restructuring more than 50 years of liberal legislation became a real possibility.[19] For planning, this means debate about issues in at least three realms. Environmental regulation, which has been governed since 1970 by the National Environmental Policy Act, faces both regulatory relaxation and stringent cuts in resources. Mass transit subsidies, especially for new rail transit construction, have been under attack, and, although favored by the current economic boom, still face serious opposition. The substitution of block grants to the states for many federal categorical programs is likely to affect central cities, with their poor populations, more than other places. For the cities, this is not a new experience; they have lost much political power as their relative population has fallen.

What is undebatable is that the terms of discussion have changed profoundly. It can no longer be taken for granted that government intervention will be seen as the appropriate response to urban issues. The ideological presumption may be just the reverse.

While the tumult and shouting occur at the national level, some observers have begun to call attention to the effect of changing ideologies and behavior at regional and local levels. These take many forms—from fringe organizations seeking to deny the validity of any government above the local level, to coalitions of economic interests that oppose environmental policy and attempt to wrest control of land and resources away from the federal government, to suburban enclaves that are literally privatizing government itself. The latter represent, as it were, the option of exit, as opposed to voice, and loyalty, in Hirschman's famous trilogy (Hirschman 1970). Since the 1970s, there has been a substantial increase in common interest developments, or CIDs, in which the owners of homes also share in the ownership and management of common space. In its simplest form, a CID may be nothing more than a condominium apartment complex that has a swimming pool for the use of its residents; at its most complex, it may be a "gated community" with controlled access, its own security force, and stringent controls on the appearance of homes and the behavior of residents.[20] Management of CIDs is carried out through homeowner associations whose powers are defined by restrictive covenants within the deeds of ownership of individual properties. Such covenants may legally bind the property owners in ways that far exceed anything that could be enforced by formal local governments.

A case can be made that gated communities represent a physical manifestation of a deep ideological shift against government itself. Driven in part by fear of crime and the desire for security, decreasingly accepting of a common responsibility for poorer segments of the population, and increasingly hostile to taxation, those who have the financial means are opting out of local government, as it has been known in America (Blakely and Snyder 1997). The irony, of course, is that in so doing, they are part of a long planning tradition of ideal and utopian communities, and of a parallel tradition of small-scale community life. In accord with both traditions, they experience a good deal of internal conflict (Barton and Silverman 1994). In many respects, the gated community represents the logical culmination of a form of suburbanization that created small, fragmented political units that benefited their residents but consciously attempted to exclude others. Such separation is the paradoxical concomitant of ever-greater global communications and electronic interconnections. Some observers fear that it is part of a growing separation of the population into rich and poor that will ultimately threaten social stability.

PLANNING AND THE DEBATE OVER INNER-CITY POVERTY

Inner cities, poverty policy, and planning in the United States have been intertwined throughout this century—from the reform and progressive movements of the late nineteenth and early twentieth centuries to the War on Poverty of the Johnson administration in the 1960s, the issue of concentrations of poor and, later, minority populations in the inner cities. The debate over the incidence and causes of poverty focused increasingly on the state of populations within the inner cities, where concentrations of poor, largely African American minorities were accompanied by rising crime, drug use, welfare dependency, family dissolution, out-of-wedlock births, school dropout, and other behavioral characteristics perceived as social pathologies. Arguments about causation polarized around the importance of culture and social reinforcement of behavior that impeded upward mobility within the poverty population, versus structural forces that were preventing the poor from realizing their aspirations to gain access to the economic benefits enjoyed by the rest of the population. Foremost among these structural impediments were racism, discrimination, segregation, and lack of access to employment opportunities. By and large, the structural view prevailed as cultural models were discredited. Policy proposals also polarized between those aimed at increasing individuals' ability to improve their economic situation ("people" policies), as opposed to those that asserted the need to deal with poverty within the context of the communities within which the poor were living ("place" policies).

William Julius Wilson (1987) was especially influential in his argument for the "spatial mismatch" hypothesis, which, in his view, was reinforced by the weakening of the social fabric that occurred as those residents able to move out of declining neighborhoods did so.[21] Ironically, that they could leave was due in large part to the success of those aspects of the War on Poverty that had reduced racial discriminatory barriers to employment, particularly in the public sector, while opening better residential opportunities, both within the cities and to a modest extent in the suburbs. Wilson, in what amounted to a partial return to a cultural theory of poverty, argued that economic forces had reduced the employability of inner-city minorities, both through reduction of opportunities and reinforcement of behaviors antithetical to effective competition in the labor market.

This idea fell on fertile ground. In the early 1980s, there was a resurgence, in new form, of cultural arguments about poverty, especially in conservative critiques of welfare dependency, as creating incentives that ran counter to individual economic advancement (Gilder 1981; Mead 1986; Murray 1984). Despite powerful, well-grounded counterarguments, these ideas deeply affected both federal policy and public opinion, laying the groundwork for the attack on welfare programs in the 1990s. More immediately, however, they were connected to the emergence of a debate over what was called the "underclass."[22] Whether explained as due to rural origins, family structure and self-reinforcing behaviors (Auletta 1982; Lemann 1991), or through isolation and entrapment for structural reasons, especially racism (Glasgow 1980), the underclass notion of poverty in the 1980s and 1990s focused on the existence of a part of the population that is out of the economic mainstream. Living in areas that are isolated, segregated, and crime-ridden, this population is characterized by low labor market attachment, low educational achievement, and a wide range of socially reproved behaviors, such as welfare dependency, drug use, single-parent households, and engagement in the underground economy. This idea is familiar to anyone who has read the writings of late-nineteenth-century reformers, whose mixture of concern and disapproval is so reminiscent of current views. There are differences, however. One is the existence of welfare support as an option, albeit under heavy pressure with the welfare reform legislation passed in 1996. The second difference is the existence of strong critical voices against the underclass idea.

In this critical debate, not just about national poverty policy but also centrally about the inner cities, it might have been expected that researchers and practitioners in planning would have played a considerable role. Since its emergence, the underclass concept has attracted enormous attention, both in support and in opposition. The history of planning, both early on and during the period of the War on Poverty, would suggest that many planners find the idea ideologically unacceptable—and, indeed, they have. However, the work of the field largely ignored the debate altogether. Virtually no major planning journal gave the underclass much attention, and there has been remarkably little published research on the issues it raises, despite their relevance to the future of the older inner cities. The work has been carried out primarily by sociologists, economists, political scientists, and others.

There has been an avalanche of criticism of the underclass idea. Gans (1990) was one of the first to discuss the idea critically in the planning literature, arguing that, once again, it is a way to stigmatize and blame the poor. This theme was taken up at greater length by Goldsmith and Blakely (1992) in their book, which argues a structuralist position, and in a set of invited editorials in the *Journal of the American Planning Association* (Cordova 1994; Grigsby 1994; Hartman 1994; Mier 1994). Nonetheless, substantial research on the issue in planning is thin.[23] Criticism of the underclass idea was made most effectively by a sociologist, Katz (1989, 1993), drawing on a line of thought that manifested itself very strongly in the 1970s. Apart from Goldsmith and Blakely (1992), Galster and Hills's (1992) collection of pieces on the issue provides the broadest look at the idea from a planning perspective, arguing that segregation into poorer schools reduces employment opportunities and contributes to a vicious circle of inadequate performance and reinforcement of underclass behaviors that, in turn, reinforce the discriminatory attitudes of the majority.

Alternatives to the underclass idea tend to focus on two main themes. The first is the cluster of ideas around the structural economic explanation for inner-city concentrations of deep poverty, exemplified by Wilson's (1987) spatial mismatch hypothesis. Wilson, building on earlier work by Kain (1968), argued that underclass African American youth, especially, were cut off from employment opportunities by continuing housing market discrimination and the suburbanization of new employment. Kasarda (1985, 1989, 1993) was a major contributor to this argument through his extensive empirical research. The spatial mismatch view has not been universally accepted. However, Kain (1992), in a masterly review of the issue, generally finds empirical support for the idea despite the passage of 30 years. The structural economic explanation of inner-city poverty, which sees the underclass phenomenon as the result of profound changes in access to employment, seems now to be dominant, with a concomitant view of associated behavioral traits.

Wilson's response is to call for a massive program to retrack ghetto youth toward education and the labor market (Wilson 1996). Despite the fact that he is seen as a conservative by those on the left, this approach does not appeal to conservatives, who increasingly are focused on morality and deviant behavior. Thus, the spatial mismatch argument is rejected by both ends of the spectrum.

Beyond the economic explanations are those that seem to turn back toward the radical, structural arguments of the 1960s and 1970s that insisted on the primacy of race as a factor in the perpetuation of inequality in the United States. In planning, this is the theme of Goldsmith and Blakely (1992), but it is more powerfully argued by sociologists, such as Massey and Denton (1993), who argue from a substantial empirical analysis that discrimination and resultant racial segregation remain the single most powerful factor generating inner-city urban poverty. Their analysis countered Wilson's assertion of the importance of the loss of role models for black youth because of a major outmigration of middle-class African American households from the ghettos. Furthermore, they found that the manufacturing job losses led to increased poverty only in the context of racial segregation. Efforts to sort out the effect of race, let alone discrimination, on the conditions of urban poverty have not been as frequent in planning as one might expect from the importance of the problem.

At this point, it seems that the issue of inner-city poverty reflects larger ideological tensions in American life. For the left, the suggestion that social pathology exists, and that it may contribute to the manifest problems of inner-city neighborhoods, continues to be fiercely resisted as labeling and "blaming the victims" of systemic forces of capitalism and racial discrimination (Cordova 1994). For the right, the same problems are blamed on long-term welfare dependency and a self-reinforcing culture that can be changed only by draconian measures. Added to this is the recent return of what looks like early-twentieth-century racial eugenics in writers such as Herrnstein and Murray (1994). The center has undoubtedly shifted rightward over the past decade, as evidenced by a Democratic president's endorsement of welfare reform despite the vehement opposition of liberals within his own party. Nonetheless, it is probably fair to say that policy analysts in this area are closer to Wilson's view of the world than to most others, with perhaps some convergence. Kasarda and Ting's (1996) careful empirical analysis indicates that both structural and cultural-political factors are operating together. As Galster (1995, 59ff) notes, however, as the 1990s wind down, ideologues are faced with some difficult demographic facts. Urban poverty is increasingly spatially concentrated, and it is growing among children in single-parent, female-headed households. "Tough" welfare policies may have long-term beneficial effects, but their outcome is uncertain and the negative impact on children very real. Recent national policy decisions curbing welfare suggest that the mainstream is willing to take that risk, but it is not likely to bear the cost. In any event, planning has contributed little to the debate.

AN INTELLECTUAL PRESENCE

Though small in comparison to other professions, city planning has a lively intellectual presence in the universities and a genuine set of tasks in practice. Its academics and practitioners maintain a tradition of questioning and discontent with the ability and willingness of the profession to meet the standards and levels of performance that they would like, but the field progresses nonetheless. Its character reflects major trends in American political, economic, and social life; but it also has its own blend of idealism and professionalism that sets it apart from other groups in the urban policy world. At this point, the field is challenged by serious issues that range from debates over the nature of the city itself to the ideological acceptability of public intervention and regulation of development. Among the most significant for the long term are the questions of the future of the central cities and the gulf between the races in American urban life.

Overall, planning has seen growing sophistication, in both practice and research, in the fields of land-use planning and economic development. But the record of planning has been little better than that of any other profession in addressing inner-city issues. In some respects, notably the disasters of public housing and urban renewal in the 1950s and 1960s, it is worse, clearly contributing to the process of deterioration. It may be fair to say, however, that planners did learn from those errors. Planners also learned much from rethinking local economic development and from the community development efforts of the 1960s through the 1980s. Although they did not discover how to make community economic development effective, there can be no doubt that local communities, even of the poor, now have a stronger voice in the planning and development process. Ironically, though, the emergence of new voices also presents a major threat to planning, as evidenced by the increasingly antiregulatory stance of property owners.

At the beginning of the twenty-first century, modern professional planning in the United States is about 100 years old. It is a unique endeavor, both in its focus on the urban environment and in its idealism about improving the quality of life for people. As we might expect, the record of achievement is mixed. Nonetheless, the idealistic strain, rooted in the American Progressive tradition, remains evident within the field, although, as noted above, paying less attention to the inner cities and the poor. The next hundred years will bring new challenges to planning, both from the global economic transformation that is occurring and from the growing domination of social life by market forces. Planning as a profession has built the technical capacity to engage those changes in a way that supports its traditional values. Whether it can continue to be viable as a field and have a significant impact will depend on the next generation of planners.

33

Implications for Planners of Race, Inequality, and a Persistent "Color Line"

LAWRENCE D. BOBO

There is no such thing as race-neutral policy or planning in the United States. To eliminate racial inequality, especially in the form of distinctly black urban ghettos, we must have an explicit policy and planning goal of addressing the black–white divide.

Structural and cultural dimensions in the United States uniquely disadvantage African Americans. They experience the highest levels of hypersegregation among all minority groups. "Hypersegregation" means blacks are unevenly distributed across physical space and isolated from other races. Roughly two-thirds of the black population would have to change their current physical location to achieve a random distribution in living space. African Americans are the most segregated racial group in the United States. Most neighbors of black people are black, and blacks live in central cities in a small geographic space. Higher income buys less spatial mobility—the ability to leave black ghettos—for African Americans than for Asians and Hispanics. The mobility that higher income does buy for African Americans is immediately constrained by residential proximity to declining inner-city neighborhoods. There is something deeply structural about black segregation.

Seventy-four percent of whites live in the suburbs, and a clear majority of blacks and Latinos live in the cities. This is especially troubling because political strength is moving from the cities to the suburbs, taking with it government resources. The increasing overlap of race, physical space, and political boundaries should be on the table for greater discussion by planners.

Data from auditing studies show how residential segregation is reproduced through prejudice and discrimination. In an auditing study, matched pairs of individuals or couples are sent to buy a house to examine the type of treatment they receive. In roughly 50 percent of the visits, African Americans receive worse treatment than whites: they are shown fewer places, told that an apartment listed as available is no longer available, told an apartment is renting for more than that told a white couple, and so on. Since a housing search usually involves seeing multiple listings, almost every housing search by blacks is likely to encounter some racial bias.

In the absence of powerful racial barriers in the housing market, the degree of concentrated poverty in black ghettos would be much less. Blacks would have been better able to follow the movement of low-skill and manufacturing jobs to the suburbs.

Data show persistent racial disparities in labor markets and wealth. For example, whites are more likely to be economically comfortable and less likely to be very poor than blacks: the percentage of whites economically very comfortable is almost 20 percent, whereas the percentage of blacks is less than 10 percent; the percentage of whites economically very poor is less than 5 percent, while the percent of blacks is roughly 20 percent. Although there is a growing black middle class, the tale since 1973 is mostly one of stagnation, even deterioration. In urban areas, the black–white ratio of unemployment is not the typical two-to-one; it is a five-to-one disadvantage for blacks.

Wealth is the fundamental structural difference between blacks and whites. The white-to-black wealth ratio is 11.5 to 1. Black wealth is mostly in houses and cars, which are not usable assets, whereas white wealth is in liquid assets, savings, and business investments. The divergence of wealth is so great that black households making $45,000 per year have roughly the same wealth as white households making $15,000 to $20,000 per year.

On the positive side, there has been a transformation in the attitudes most whites hold toward African Americans. Positions openly endorsed by whites in the 1940s and 1950s—such as being against an integrated society and having a black family live on the block or next door—are no longer endorsed by most whites in survey polls. The percentage of blacks, however, *does* matter. Small proportions of blacks, generally less than 5 percent, are tolerated. The only cities with sharp declines in residential segregation are those where the proportion of blacks remains small, usually 5 percent or less.

Whites are also more supportive of racial intermarriage, with 80 percent opposing laws that prevent racial intermarriage. Only 60 percent, however, personally support intermarriage. White–Asian and white–Hispanic marriages are much more common than white–black marriages.

Another positive trend is recent Census data showing a rapid expansion in the number of multiracial communities—communities with blacks, Latinos,

Asians, and whites. But it is not clear whether this development is stable or a moment of transition.

Because the problems are structural, neither the economy nor public policy is race-neutral. For example, the federal educational policy switch in 1978 from grants to loans had a devastating impact on blacks. In 1978, there was no difference in the odds that a black high school graduate would attend college, in comparison to a white graduate. By 1985, 10 percent fewer blacks were attending college, and the gap has continued to widen. This was a race-neutral policy, but it had a huge impact on African Americans. To redress these problems requires race-specific policies.

There are seven actions planners of good will should take.

1. When facing resource-allocation decisions, planners should ask: What are the effects on the racial divide? Does the decision diminish the reproduction of racial segregation? Does it decrease gaps in access to employment? Does it increase job access for those in ghettos? Always pose an explicit race question.

2. Planners should push for local efforts against housing discrimination and encourage the regular conduct of auditing studies.

3. Planners should advocate for more low-income housing developments and access to suburbs for poor city residents through rental vouchers, tax incentives, and restrictions on large-lot zoning.

4. Planners should monitor real estate brokers and agents, and their lenders, for discriminatory practices like advertising that signals "this community is white."

5. Planners should support affirmative action programs and the employment of poor people in government.

6. Planners should support regional and metropolitan planning initiatives and incorporate inner-city minorities in them.

7. Planners should expand the role of human relations commissions in governance by institutionalizing human relations impact reports, which would be similar to an environmental impact report, for any large-scale government project. We care about how governmental decisions affect smog, congestion, and other aspects of the physical environment; we ought to care just as much about how governmental decisions affect black access to employment, education, and the development of integrated living spaces.

34

Racism and Deliberative Democracy

ERNESTO J. CORTÉS, JR.

In thinking about urban planning from an organizing perspective, it is important to recognize that there is an enormous amount of racism and oppression that needs to be dealt with and overcome; but, that is not the only thing I believe. I am not that cynical about America. Yes, America has always been racist, but there has always been this opportunity. Notwithstanding the racism, notwithstanding the oppression, notwithstanding the sustained class bias, what is intriguing about the U.S. experience is that there also has been another side to it.

De Tocqueville wrote about this complication, this contradiction of the human experience, which he called the "Augustinian soul." One way to interpret de Tocqueville's use of "Augustinian soul" is that, throughout history and as part of human nature, we encounter an inclination to be oppressors, a sort of human sickness. But de Tocqueville also said that there is an antidote for this illness, namely family and religion, and that these things are the building blocks of civil society.

There is a hopefulness that comes from the language and traditions of families, congregations, and the language of representative democracy— *deliberative democracy*. These traditions, and the struggle to live up to the language of democracy, have always created an interesting contradiction and dialectic that creates a space for people to move in. If organizers and planners fail to take advantage of these opportunities, if discussions on the state of planning and racism are kept among the realm of academic experts, then we fail not only as organizers and planners, we fail as Americans. Yes, the notion of the commons must be part of planners' understanding, as Ann Markusen suggests (Markusen 2000)—the addendum to which may be to say that this notion of the commons also must be part of planners' practice and craft. If we do not, as Markusen asserts, "join the battle for the public imagination" by extending the conversations beyond the realm of experts, then we risk losing our birthright.

Sheldon Wolin wrote an intriguing chapter titled "Contract and Birthright" in his book, *Presence of the Past* (Wolin 1989). Wolin articulates that we have this birthright—this burden, if you will. And this birthright is our politicalness. It is this obligation and responsibility to forge the space, the public space, which enables us to create institutions that allow for the possibility of changing the parameters of race and class structure. And at times it has been done successfully. It has been a long and difficult struggle. It happened with the abolitionist movement, it happened with the Civil War, notwithstanding the fact that we lost the battle for reconstruction. There have been glimmers, some moments of hopefulness. Pessimism naturally flows from an analysis of race relations in the United States, but American history is filled with these antinomies. Within these contradicting truths, there are opportunities being created. I am fearful, however, that these opportunities are going to be lost if we are overcome by the analysis. Analysis that is not connected to some kind of action can lead to an intellectual dead end.

In a sense, the birthright that organizers and planners have is very similar. Part of the responsibility of being a planner entails as Markusen suggests, looking at the profession of planning as a craft. It takes what James Scott calls *metis*, which refers to cunning and craft (Scott 1998). Not cunning as it is negatively associated; rather, it is associated with a local knowledge, a specialized knowledge gained from practice until it becomes second nature. For planners, as for organizers, this means taking time to know the community not through blueprints and policy, not just through communication with public officials, but through deliberate face-to-face conversations with citizens about the interests of citizens.

In the experience of the Industrial Areas Foundation (IAF) organizations, the most significant conversations and dialogues between African Americans, Latinos, and Anglos have taken place after they have built coalitions around issues. First, they may struggle together on issues such as after-school initiatives and job-training programs that cut across racial lines. After trust emerges and people have built solidarity because they have worked together, only then can they have serious, profound, tension-filled conversations about race. But it is difficult, maybe impossible, to have honest conversations about racial questions without that trust—without those coalitions. If improving the situation for minorities is the objective, be it for Latinos, Asians, Native Americans or African Americans, then the way to best do that is to create these kind of coalitions.

Race matters. Race matters with respect to income and with respect to wealth. But if you really want to do something about poor families, if you really want to do something about the situation facing many of the African American and Latino families, the way to organize is not along racial lines or ethnic lines. The way to organize people is in the broadest possible coalitions.

If the energy is focused on race-specific strategies, the greater payoff may be forgone, not just for African Americans and Latinos but for everyone. The most successful IAF strategies have affected not just African Americans, not just Latinos, not just Asians, but have cut across ethnic, racial, and gender lines. Organizing interracially and interfaith around strategies to improve the lives of poor people is sure to get broader support.

In San Antonio, the IAF organizations are now challenging the fact that the city has been giving significant subsidies in the form of tax abatements to hotels that employ people at poverty wages—primarily Latinos and African Americans. In a captive market, San Antonio has chosen to subsidize vast hotel chains like the Marriott and Hyatt. Now Latinos, Anglos, and African Americans are going to the city together and saying, "This makes no economic sense at all. If you are going to do that, you are going to have to pay people a living wage." It is because the strategy includes leaders from all parts of San Antonio that they are able to negotiate with the city with some energy and power.

A broad-based approach is a necessary part of strategies to improve income, to improve wealth, to improve asset formation, and, more important, to create possibilities for effective civic engagement. The success of these efforts is closely tied to the extent that we organize across racial, class, and ethnic lines—to the extent that we recognize that what poor people need most, whether they be African Americans, Latinos, or Asian Americans, is some kind of connection or intermediary institutions. Unfortunately, our schools, churches, and many other institutions have been bombarded, and adults among these institutions no longer have the relationships needed to help mediate between families and the market.

When I grew up in San Antonio in the 1950s, I lived in a very tight, very segregated neighborhood—what we called a *barrio*. My *barrio* was all Mexican, but for me that was not such a bad thing because there were more than 250 adults who organized around me—250 adults who felt that they could intrude on my life, 250 adults who felt that they could give me advice, tell me what to do, and tell me where to go to college. Everyone from the bus driver in the morning when I got up, to the school cafeteria people, to my neighbors, to my aunts and uncles, to my *compadres*, and my *comadres*—all these people felt they had the right to tell me what to do, what to wear, what to eat, and what to study.

When I began to organize in Los Angeles, I found the opposite situation. Instead of 250 adults organized against one kid, it was 70 kids organized against one adult. The adults were under house arrest: afraid to go to church, afraid to attend festivals, even intimidated by their own children. Adults were fearful of participating in the activities that are requisite for a civil society.

That was 20 years ago. Today, I find this situation almost everywhere I go, whether it is New Orleans, Houston, or Dallas.

Planners, as do organizers, need to take part in rebuilding the existing intermediary institutions and creating new ones that enable organized adults across a number of community institutions to conspire and collaborate with one another about the future for their families. One of the largest problems people without wealth and connections will continue to face is how to negotiate a career ladder for themselves. The career ladders of the past no longer exist for most Americans because the nature of work has been reorganized. We're told that an eighteen-year-old can expect to change jobs seven times in his lifetime. The realities of our changing economy require parents, teachers, local businesses, planners, and other adults to toil at how we enable schools and communities to prepare tomorrow's workforce.

Cities need planners that have local knowledge and that understand the need for intermediary institutions. When people participate only as disconnected, isolated individuals, incredible struggles and fights ensue, and ultimately, permanent hostility exists among those who ought to have been collaborating. Effective planners are familiar with the local customs to the extent that the mechanisms set up to implement public policy and allocate resources are organically connected to all kinds of formal and informal networks of relationships that exist in the community. It takes the *metis* that Jane Jacobs modeled in her ability to engage in deliberations with the community about education, the raising of children, the pressures on families, and what happens to property. It requires focused face-to-face conversations to develop effective participation of citizens and time to gain the local knowledge and customs to get to a place where people have built the social capital necessary to mobilize consent across race and economic lines.

To begin addressing issues of poverty and race requires recognizing the grave inequalities. Race matters to the extent that it helps us meet the challenge of rebuilding and reconnecting institutions that allow families to thrive. Race matters as we develop *metis* and learn how to generate public policy and urban planning that does no harm—and ideally that enables communities to figure out collaborative strategies that will develop the capability and competence of intermediary institutions. In the midst of these considerations, institutions need to develop some thickness, some stability, and some power, through a culture of conversation that includes all parts of the community. Once adults across institutions can be relational, and can agitate one another and struggle with one another, only then can they pull together the fragments of the intermediary institutions that used to exist. Congregations and schools can then begin to use this network and structure to enable people to negotiate with those who have power, and thereby begin to transform their communities.

35

Planning's Three Challenges

BISHWAPRIYA SANYAL

W hen Lloyd Rodwin and I decided to hold a faculty colloquium on the
planning profession, one of our objectives was to determine whether
planning curricula need alteration in order to respond to new challenges facing the profession. As Rodwin describes in chapter 1, we began by looking
externally at four other disciplines—economics, political science, philosophy, and literature—to better understand the extent to which the field of city
and regional planning (CRP) was experiencing similar or different problems.
We thought this comparison would be useful for at least two reasons. First, in
learning about the mistakes of these relatively older disciplines, CRP could
avoid repeating them. Second, CRP, which has been marked by self-flagella-
tion since the mid-1960s, could perhaps become less self-critical and somewhat more confident intellectually, if one could demonstrate that the problems it has faced as an intellectual discipline are not unique.

In making comparisons with other disciplines, Rodwin identifies three
criteria, based on the discussion of transformation in American academic
culture in the winter 1997 issue of *Daedalus*. Without repeating Rodwin's
analysis, I want simply to remind the reader that the three criteria are (1)
methodological rigor or social relevance, which seems to be the central concern of economists; (2) the service function of a discipline, which seems to be
somewhat deficient for economics as well as philosophy, notwithstanding John
Rawls's (1971) heroic effort in writing *A Theory of Justice*; and, finally, (3) the
struggle over values, which seems to mark literature. A fourth criterion, which
signifies the strength of any discipline, is its intellectual capital formation, or
lack thereof. Rodwin quotes Charles Lindblom (1959) to demonstrate that none
of the social science disciplines—and that includes economics—can demonstrate that the new knowledges created "have been either unarguably or demonstrably necessary."

How does CRP score on an assessment of these four criteria? And what are the implications of such an assessment for restructuring planning education? I want to focus on these questions in this concluding chapter. I begin by arguing that CRP as a discipline fares quite well in meeting the four general criteria. Perhaps that is why there were no loud cries for major restructuring of planning education by participants at the 1997 MIT Faculty Seminar, barring those of Witold Rybczynski and Alex Krieger, who argue for the forceful return of CRP to physical planning. I then argue against complacency by laying out what I consider three specific challenges facing CRP: (1) the need for a new synthesis of physical and social planning; (2) the need for new procedural theories about how to be effective in planning practice; and (3) the need for new normative theories to justify government involvement in shaping the destinies of cities and regions. In focusing on these three challenges, I do not contest Rodwin's assessment that CRP has grown out of the adolescent stage and is now poised to approach adult life, cognizant of all its limitations and complexities. My intention is to caution planners against complacency by reminding them that CRP faces three specific challenges which, if not addressed, eventually will fracture the fragile intellectual coherence of the profession.

"SATISFICING" THE FOUR CRITERIA

CRP seems to have performed reasonably well when judged according to the four general criteria of analytical rigor and social relevance, service function, consensus on core professional values, and intellectual capital formation. In Herbert Simon's (1965) words, the field may not have achieved the "optimum" level of performance, but it has met the requirements for "satisficing" performance.[1]

First, CRP transcended the dichotomy between analytical rigor and social relevance nearly 30 years ago. True, there was a time in the early 1950s when CRP was mesmerized by the power of analytical techniques. As Melville C. Branch noted in his classic piece (1959), many had hoped that major advances in analytical techniques, such as operations research and game theory, would contribute to more precise ways of constructing comprehensive master plans for American cities. The planners who focused not on cities but on larger spatial entities like regions also had much faith in the power of analytical techniques. Armed with a variety of techniques and formal models, regional scientists had thought that they could lead CRP from its preoccupation with intuitively analyzed and hand-drawn master plans to rigorously examined and scientifically derived solutions to the problems of cities and regions (for a good review of this effort, see Isserman 1995). As Rodwin points out, however, this claim faltered within a few years, as many American cities erupted in violence in the mid-1960s and civil rights movements politicized the interpretation of urban problems. The positive result of this outcome was that CRP matured intellectually, outgrowing what some have lightheartedly called "physics envy." The negative result was that, in incorporating politics into planning, some lost the ability to differentiate between the two. On the whole, the issue of whether to choose rigor over relevance was put to rest. There was a general understanding that CRP faces, in Rittel and Webber's (1973) words, "wicked problems" that do not lend themselves to formal modeling of the kind embraced by economists. In other words, unlike economics and philosophy, which chose rigor over relevance, CRP opted for the latter at least 30 years ago. The choice was not free of problems, however. In stressing relevance, CRP sometimes overemphasized political understanding over technical knowledge. John Dyckman (1978) had foreseen this danger when he noted that just because all planning has political consequences does not mean planning and politics are the same. Fortunately, as the political passion of the 1960s began to subside, CRP came to recognize that good practice requires both rigor of technical knowledge and political astuteness to understand social relevance.[2] In this regard, CRP seems to have reached maturity ahead of some other disciplines.

Second, CRP also seems to have performed its service function reasonably well, if the employment of graduates is considered an indicator of success. As Susskind, Frenchman, Frieden, and Baxter argue in this volume, CRP graduates are working at the community, national, and even international levels, and in various domains ranging from private, nonprofit activities to quasi-public and public-sector institutions. In other words, a broad-based professional education has served the profession well by enabling it to adapt to changing circumstances in which planning activities are no longer confined to traditional city planning offices but have become decentralized over a varied set of organizations ranging from community development corporations to regional planning councils. To my knowledge, no one in the colloquium systematically probed the cause of this success. Some, like Susskind and Frenchman, merely pointed out that the evidence indicates that the CRP graduates are gainfully employed and engaged in various socially important activities ranging from negotiations to reconstruction of declining cities and regions. Why the profession was able to respond to these varied demands and how well the graduates performed their tasks are issues that did not receive much attention, partly because there seemed to be a consensus among the participants that the profession has performed reasonably well. This consensus would have pleased Harvey Perloff, who voiced concern about these issues in the 1970s (Perloff and Klett 1974). Perloff argued then that the profession had responded well when planning jobs increased exponentially during the 1960s, primarily due to sharp increases in federal spending on urban problems. But he was concerned as well whether, in the process of producing more and more planners, the profession had compromised on the quality of training. Yet, as we gathered for the colloquium in 1997, no one raised the concern that planning graduates have not been rigorously trained. On the contrary, there was a general feeling that planners have performed reasonably well, despite the reversal of trend in federal spending for cities as compared with the 1960s.

The third criterion is a consensus on core professional values, the kind the field of literature seems to lack at the moment. It seems to me that, notwithstanding the protests from Chester Hartman, CRP has unambiguously accepted that social, economic, and racial equalities are central to good planning practices. This is evident in the charters of both the American Planning Association (APA) and the Association of Collegiate Schools of Planning (ACSP). (See the mission statement of APA on the web page for the American Institute of Certified Planners {at www.planning.org. For ACSP, see www.uwm.edu/~frankn/acsp/mission-html}.) It is also evident in Israel Stollman's chapter in this volume (chapter 11), where he forcefully argues that there is no such thing as "equity planning" as a subfield within CRP, because the concern for equity is at the heart of the profession. As past president of the APA, Stollman presents a view widely shared by planning professionals across the country. Similarly, issues of ethics and social representation are prominent on the agendas of CRP annual conferences. In fact, these concerns are so strong and pervasive that they sometimes impede analytical rigor and deeper understanding of these issues.

Some may disagree with this congratulatory tone about CRP's stance on equality. These critics point out that CRP retreated on its principles in the face of an ideological attack against planning in the 1980s (for example, Marcuse 1984). This is probably true, but any assessment of this kind needs to take into account a longer time period covering not only the 1980s but, say, the past 50 years. Such an assessment would demonstrate, unquestionably, that at the core of CRP's values is a belief that inequality is detrimental to social cohesion, and that equality of opportunities enhances the quality of life. In this regard, CRP is much ahead of both economics and literature: unlike economics, CRP is deeply engaged with issues of social values; unlike literature, within CRP there seems to be a consensus—perhaps not absolute, but predominant, on the appropriate professional values to pursue (Hoffman 1989).

Finally, if the increase in the number of doctoral programs is an indicator of effort at intellectual capital formation, Rodwin's fourth criterion, then

CRP stands out for its achievement over the past 40 years. The first doctoral program in CRP was launched by Harvard University in 1942; since then, the number of schools offering doctoral degrees in planning steadily increased—to 30 by 1998 (ACSP 1993, 4). One could, of course, argue (as Lindblom does) that doctoral programs alone do not guarantee that new and useful knowledge is being produced.[3] The most one can say by looking at the growing number of doctoral programs is that increasingly an effort is being made to produce new knowledge. To counteract this argument, one needs to provide examples of new knowledge that has influenced professional practice. CRP is not devoid of such examples. As early as 1974, Perloff and Klett noted that CRP had contributed significantly in demonstrating the importance that urban problems should be treated in a broad regional context, rather than in the narrowly defined jurisdictional framework that characterized federal programs up to that time (Perloff and Klett 1974, 169). During the 1970s, this understanding of urban problems was broadened further through excellent research on globalization, industrial restructuring, and deindustrialization. Among the faculty from planning programs who led this research are Bennett Harrison, Manuel Castells, Ann Markusen, Saskia Sassen, and Michael Storper. The Deindustrialization of America, by Barry Bluestone and Bennett Harrison (1982), was one of the first pieces of research in this topic area. These issues are now central to the effort of many cities and regions struggling to attract industries and investment. True, our understanding of the causal relationships between the global and urban economies are still far from precise (a point raised by William Alonso, in responding to Bennett Harrison's chapter in this volume). Nevertheless, one cannot deny that the sensitivity of policymakers to the issue of deindustrialization was heightened as a result of research performed primarily by CRP academics.

Similarly, CRP has contributed much to the better understanding of environmental issues, at both the urban and the regional levels. Michael Teitz mentions numerous examples in chapter 32 in this volume. CRP cannot take sole credit for generating these insights, but it deserves some credit for perfecting the art of environmental impact assessment, environmental dispute resolution, and so on (for a good review, see Susskind and Cruikshank 1987). Yet another example of CRP's contribution to intellectual capital formation is found in the domain of real estate planning. Prior to 1980, real estate issues were addressed only tangentially by a handful of faculty in business schools who focused on financial issues. Now, thanks to a growing body of research on real estate markets and finance within planning programs, planners are less likely to be caught off guard in the face of adverse market outcomes.[4] This new knowledge has also helped planners devise various innovative partnerships involving private, public, and nongovernmental institutions in delivering housing and facilitating economic development (for good examples, see Frieden and Sagalyn 1989). These are no small achievements. They confirm that intellectual capital formation within CRP has been relevant for practice, which is more than political scientists or philosophers can claim.

AGAINST PROFESSIONAL COMPLACENCY

I have argued so far that, as assessed by Rodwin's four general criteria, CRP has performed reasonably well. In his analogy, CRP, as a field, seems to have outgrown the adolescent stage: its earlier grandiose expectations and equally large frustrations have given way to a sense of limits and maturity that one associates with experience in life. Does that imply that CRP now needs simply to stay on course, go into more depth in a few areas it has carved out for itself, and begin to enjoy the benefits of the intellectual harvest reaped from hard work in earlier years? Rodwin does not answer this question directly, although he mentions in passing a few issues CRP needs to address in the near future as it consolidates its position as a distinctive profession.

One issue CRP needs to address is how to integrate spatial with socioeconomic planning approaches in the search for solutions to urban and regional problems. Vale articulates this challenge but does not specify what it will take to achieve such an intellectual synthesis between two planning approaches that differ considerably in their epistemological orientation. A second issue is that CRP still lacks theories of planning practice, both descriptive and normative, that practicing planners can rely on, a sentiment voiced by Stollman at this colloquium and shared by European planners (Albrechts 1998). A third issue is that CRP, as a primarily government-centered activity,[5] must acknowledge and help counteract the growing distrust and dislike of government among ordinary citizens. These three issues pose significant challenges for CRP; if unaddressed, they may gradually undermine the importance of the profession. On hindsight, it is surprising that only the first of these three issues received attention at the colloquium. The second and third issues were largely ignored. I raise them in this concluding chapter in the hope that whoever may be planning the next colloquium on CRP will consider probing these challenges in greater depth.

CHALLENGE ONE:
INTEGRATE SPATIAL AND SOCIOECONOMIC PLANNING

The 1997 MIT Faculty Seminar generated one conclusion: architect-planners, whose ideas were somewhat overshadowed by those of the social scientists who entered the field of CRP in the 1960s, are regaining their voice. Among the contributors to this volume, Alex Krieger, chair of the Department of Urban Planning and Design at Harvard's Graduate School of Design, articulated this new voice most persuasively. His argument goes as follows: CRP, in its quest for better understanding of social, economic, and political aspects of cities and regions, has moved too far away from its original concern and area of expertise—namely, how to design livable and enjoyable communities and cities. However, this conscious move away from traditional urban design and land-use planning has not generated innovative solutions to urban problems. On the contrary, planning has been reduced to mere "process management" to arrive at decisions that, in the name of consensus building, generate suboptimal solutions. Others who supported Krieger's (1997) call for the primacy of spatial planning were Allan Jacobs and Witold Rybczynski. Dennis Frenchman, Terry Szold, and Lawrence Vale were sympathetic to Krieger's appeal but are less critical of socioeconomic planning. Rybczynski argues that consensus building has stripped planners of their authoritative role to propose solutions to urban problems. Now, planners are more eager to forge consensus than to present solutions, which leads to outcomes that are not opposed by anyone but that lack professional distinction.

It is important to recognize that physical planners are returning with new confidence in their ability because they have generated the most compelling new idea in CRP: new urbanism. Krieger argued that HUD's allocation of considerable federal resources to propagate new urbanism in central cities is a significant step in a new direction, away from the last 30 years of socioeconomic policies geared to low-income, inner-city neighborhoods. HUD's embrace of new urbanism is clear recognition that socioeconomic planning has failed to deliver on its promise, that the only hope for the future is to return to "spatial determinism," which has been berated by the social scientists since the 1960s (Broady 1968).

Can the physical planners resurrect urban design by ignoring the critiques of policy planners over the past 40 years? Have their theories and techniques evolved to a new height that justifies the kind of intellectual assertiveness Krieger represented? As an architect-planner myself, I wish I could answer this question affirmatively. Unfortunately, the colloquium did not demonstrate a new and heightened level of competence on the part of physical planners. It did demonstrate that medium and small-sized cities still use master plans, despite all their shortcomings (see chapter 5 by Philip Herr in this volume). New information technologies such as GIS and Orthobrowser now allow planners to store varied land-use data more precisely in digital maps. And, physical planners did invent new urbanism, the only new "big idea" in the field. (Alan Altshuler argued at the 1997 Faculty Seminar that one reason for the relatively poor image of the profession is its lack of ideas.)

Though significant, whether these achievements add up to a new conceptual approach for enhancing the quality of life of urban areas is questionable.

Colloquium participants did not directly address this issue, in part because they were generally skeptical that physical planning alone can adequately address America's deepening urban problems. This is not to say that they dismissed physical planning as a sort of cosmetic device superficially applied to a decaying and disintegrating social fabric. Clearly, the level of antidesign sentiment that marked the profession for a time in the 1960s has subsided. Now, even the staunchest advocate of socioeconomic planning grudgingly admits that physical planning, if done with adequate appreciation of socioeconomic factors, provides a useful approach to addressing urban problems. But new urbanism, which Krieger holds up as a model of new thinking, does not integrate physical and socioeconomic planning well (see Landecker 1996). Krieger himself agrees to this criticism of new urbanism but argues that it is the only proposal that embodies a concrete vision. According to him, although one can find numerous faults with this vision, that does not diminish its importance as the only tangible solution to urban problems to emerge since the invention of suburbia after World War II.

Although Krieger is correct in proposing new urbanism as the only new model available to planners, it is not an example of how physical planners can address urban problems on their own, free of socioeconomic criticism. If good quality of life is to remain the key objective of CRP, physical planners simply cannot ignore social scientists—in particular, economists, psychologists, sociologists, and historians, who have contributed immensely over the past 40 years in understanding quality of life. The physical planner's intuitive understanding of the economy, society, and polity is not an adequate substitute for specialized knowledge in these areas.

When subjected to close scrutiny, new urbanism, which claims to have a social understanding of contemporary America, falls apart as a new type of utopia, marked not by futuristic hopes but, rather, by nostalgic memories of a homogeneous, urban America that no longer exists (Kelbauch 1997). Also, new urbanism does not take into account such crucial social trends as growing income inequality, growing opposition to taxes of every kind, and growing job insecurity in a volatile and globalized economy. I recognize that no model could address all these issues at once; however, that does not mean these issues can simply be ignored by designing friendly neighborhoods of houses with front porches, broad sidewalks, and set-back garages. Thanks to research over the past 40 years, we know the limits of spatial determinism well enough to be skeptical of proposals such as new urbanism. I, for one, am unable to disregard that informed skepticism and return to the drawing board, animated by the prospects of a new era in urban design.

It is equally true, however, that we cannot throw out the drawing boards and concentrate our intellectual energy only on socioeconomic analysis. As Rodwin rightly points out in this volume, CRP cannot ignore spatiality and the three-dimensional understanding of cities and regions if it is to retain a sense of professional identity. As a field, CRP is more than the sum of urban economics, urban sociology, and urban anthropology; without an explicit recognition that space and place are central elements of CRP, it is difficult to argue that CRP has a unique, specialized knowledge that no one else can offer. This has been recognized by both the APA and the ACSP in their professional statements. It is a lesson CRP, as a field, has learned at considerable cost.

Starting with the collapse of the University of Chicago's planning program in 1957, up to the incorporation of UCLA's planning program in a school of public policy in 1996, there have been clear indications that CRP cannot justify itself as a distinctly defined professional activity if it deviates too far from its early concern with the urban built form and physical planning. Both the University of Chicago and UCLA's programs were designed on the explicit assumption that good planning requires a general multidisciplinary education, one that can help students transcend the naive idea that spatial planning is the answer to America's urban problems. Although both programs had a significant impact on the field by producing outstanding scholars, these scholars could find institutional homes only in traditionally structured CRP programs. In other words, both programs helped broaden the definition of planning to the point where it became "application of knowledge to action" (Friedmann 1987), but this very broad definition did not serve them well. Lacking its original connection to both the built and the unbuilt environments, the term *planning* lost its power to convey a sense of special expertise. This, in turn, reduced the power of claims these planning programs could make to university administrators of providing specialized knowledge that no other department could provide.

The benefit of incorporating a spatial sensibility within CRP is that it not only helps institutionally, it also increases the intellectual power of the discipline's conceptual framework. This was implicitly acknowledged by most of the Seminar's participants, barring one or two who argue for more specialized knowledge of design skills. This is a sign of intellectual maturity, by demonstrating an understanding that it is necessary for good planning to comprise both spatial and socioeconomic components. Neither alone can address urban problems adequately. Having acknowledged that, we must ask ourselves what it will take to synthesize the two. Who could do it? What will it take to educate such versatile individuals? These are difficult questions that need further discussion.

As a planning educator, my immediate concern is the duration of professional educational programs in CRP. As it is, a master's degree in CRP requires two years of coursework, which many students find difficult to pay for. In a survey of 99 master's degree students in the Department of Urban Studies and Planning at MIT, the average debt at graduation was $37,000 (Seidman 1999). What would happen if the coursework were extended to cultivate both spatial and socioeconomic sensibilities among the graduates? Also, since the planning educators themselves are specialized into one or the other form of planning, how can they be expected to assist students in intellectually bridging the two approaches? The colloquium generated no response to these questions. The closest it came to articulating a solution was to propose that studio exercises, of the kind central to planning education in the 1950s, return to the curriculum. To borrow a statement from Webber and Collignon (1998), the drawing boards replaced by cubicles in planning schools in the 1960s must return. The new studios, however, will be different from those of the 1950s; there is even some hope that new information technology and new multimedia facilities can provide the students and faculty a new range of possibilities for analysis, representation, and communication (see Shiffer 1999). Aided by these new techniques, could planning students and educators become more skilled at seeking holistic solutions, blending physical and social planning?

Needless to say, technique is no substitute for a conceptual framework, although technique does help in the conceptualization and analysis of problems. The challenge facing CRP is to devise a new conceptual framework (and an accompanying methodology) that would blend spatial and socioeconomic analyses. The search for solutions in a studio setting is only a beginning toward that ultimate end; it is a step forward from strictly socioeconomic problem analyses that reveal "contradictions" and result in "deconstructing interpretations" but that, in themselves, do not generate a new conceptual framework.

The key is to focus on a set of problems that require the blending of spatial and other sensibilities. In this regard, the relatively new category of problems considered by environmental designers seems promising. These problems require expertise in physical design and site planning, along with a deep appreciation of environmental issues. Also, they are amenable to visual analysis, which can now be done fairly elegantly, using advanced information technology. This kind of problem, addressed in a studio setting by a group of faculty with different specializations, may begin to produce the conceptual building blocks for a new, synthetic approach in CRP, a possibility Perloff pointed out as early as 1974, when he described environmental design as combining traditional design approaches with social science and systems analysis (Perloff and Kreff 1974, 170).

A second type of problem that requires a synthesis of knowledge of the built environment with socioeconomic understanding is that of declining cities.

Efforts by declining cities to reverse the trend by investing in large-scale physical projects to alter the popular perception of their future potential have been documented (see Farbstein and Wener 1996). These efforts—some successful, others less so—range from the construction of new baseball stadiums to riverfront developments to cultural and historic preservation of old industries as museums for tourists. Such efforts must be physical in nature, in part because they are intended to alter the physical appearance of decline, and in part because cities have no control over national or global economic trends that adversely affect them. Physical projects provide declining cities with the only mechanism by which they can attempt to influence their own destiny; as the evidence suggests, some have been successful in doing so. These successful efforts can become conceptual building blocks for a new synthetic approach in CRP if they are studied, in studio settings, by faculty members who can converse intellectually across their respective areas of expertise.

CHALLENGE TWO:
CONSTRUCT PLANNING THEORIES TO MEET THE NEEDS OF
PLANNING PRACTITIONERS

There is a consensus among planning academics and practicing planners that one of the core competencies necessary to obtain the professional degree is an understanding of how to be an effective practitioner. The Planning Accreditation Board (1998) requires all accredited planning schools to offer at least one course for master's-level students on this topic. Usually titled "Planning Theory," this course, a second course on statistics, and a third on microeconomics constitute the core curriculum for master's students in most planning programs. Also, almost all planning schools require doctoral students to take one or two courses on planning theory, as well as a qualifying examination on this topic area, as part of the requirement for doctoral candidacy.[6] At ACSP's annual conference, there is a special track of paper presentations and roundtable discussions on planning theory. Also, an official conference is held every two years or so on planning theory. There is now a special journal, *Planning Theory*, devoted entirely to this topic area, published by the Departmento Scienze del Territorio in Milan. Its editorial board is headed by Luigi Mazza from Italy, but the majority of the board members are U.S. planning academics. And there are at least five textbooks on planning theory, some edited and others written by sole authors: Faludi 1973; Burchell and Sternlieb 1978; Healey et al. 1982; Campbell and Fainstein 1996; Mandelbaum et al. 1996.

To look at the growth in the volume of literature and the extent of academic discourse on planning theory, one would think there must be increasing demand from the professional community of practicing planners for better education on this topic area. Yet, none of the practicing planners who participated in the colloquium considered it important enough for serious deliberations. On the contrary, Israel Stollman, APA's ex-president, remarks in this volume that planning theory in its current form is not at all useful for practicing planners. In arriving at this pessimistic conclusion, Stollman reviewed what some consider the cutting edge in contemporary planning theory—namely, "communicative planning theory." In this volume, Judith Innes summarizes the essence of "communicative planning theory," and John Forester elaborates on the theory. Note that both Innes and Forester are academic planners, although both have studied empirically the nature of planning practice. None of the practicing planners who contributed to this volume—Cortés, Frenchman, Herr, Howe, Stollman, and Szold—refer to communicative planning theory or any other planning theory in discussing how to be effective in practice!

What explains this mismatch between the growing interest in planning theory among academic planners and the dramatically opposite lack of interest among practicing planners? And what kind of challenge does this pose for the profession and planning academia? To answer these questions, one has to look back to the early 1960s, when planning theory was emerging as an intellectual area of concern. Until then, there had been no need for a discussion of how planners could be effective in practice. The rational comprehensive model of planning practice, which guided the preparation of master plans, reigned as the sole paradigm of practice.

In the late 1950s, the rational comprehensive model first came under attack from political scientists and organizational theorists such as Charles Lindblom, Herbert Simon, and others (Dahl and Lindblom 1953; March and Simon 1958; Lindblom 1959). Rodwin refers to Lindblom's critique—that planners do not seek "optimum solutions," as claimed in the rational comprehensive paradigm, but rather adopt "satisficing solutions" that planning institutions can derive under severe constraints of time, knowledge, and other resources. Unfortunately, in the mid-1960s, this kind of institutional criticism of planning practice was submerged in more political and ideological criticism by the planners themselves (Dahl 1961; Davidoff 1965; Rabinowitz 1969). For example, Lindblom was criticized for proposing only incremental changes when, according to the critics, what was required to solve the 1960s crisis was a major structural transformation (Friedmann 1973). Similarly, Simon was criticized for arguing that there are institutional limits to whether problems can be understood comprehensively, taking into account all aspects. The critics dismissed Simon as a conservative unwilling to explore radical solutions to social problems (Crozier 1964; Michael 1968).

For the sake of brevity, I will not recapitulate the various strands of the criticism of the rational comprehensive model except to point out one of its consequences: institutional criticisms of planning set aside and argued against in the search for a planning theory that was explicitly political and normative. The overall impact of this trend was that it discredited rational planning style as futile, technocratic exercise and dismissed institutional analysis as being driven by the interests protecting the status quo; but it could not create an alternative theory of problem solving that practicing planners could utilize (Innes 1983). True, advocacy planning provided an alternative model of practice, but only for certain types of problems; and it was not a theory of practice for traditional land-use planners within established institutions. These traditional planners searched for a theory of action that was sensitive to politics but also acknowledged institutional constraints and contingencies (see Vasu 1979). Unfortunately, by the late 1960s, there was no such theory of action, although planning theory as a topic area for teaching and research had grown significantly by then (for a survey of the key articles on planning theory up to that time, see Faludi 1973).

Some may argue that the criticism of rational comprehensive planning was beneficial in that it helped the profession outgrow its naive technocratic self-image. The loss of hegemony of the rational model also led to the sprouting of many alternative models, ranging from Amitai Etzioni's "mixed scanning" (1967) to Paul Davidoff's "advocacy planning" (1965) to John Friedmann's "transactive planning models" (1973). But none of these models, including those that appeared fairly recently under the banner of "communicative planning theory," could re-create a new, broad-based professional consensus about what planning is, why it is needed, how it is performed, and how it ought to be performed amid constraints and contingencies in advanced capitalist democracies (Hall 1989). Consequently, nearly 30 years after the collapse of the rational planning model, we are left with the "regime theory of planning" on the far left (Lauria 1997), equity planning somewhat closer to the center (Krumholz and Forester 1990), and consensus planning even closer to the middle of the ideological spectrum (Ozawa 1991).

Some planning theorists claim that they have a new insight about what "post-modern planning" should be (Harper and Stein 1996). Judith Innes, for example, argues in this volume that "post-modern planning is about making connections among ideas and among people and that this connection process sets in motion a whole series of changes." In describing planning that way, she draws on the research of John Forester, who, in turn, was influenced by Jürgen Habermas's theory of communicative action (1984). For those planning theorists who consider Habermas somewhat insensitive to issues of power inequalities, Michel Foucault has been a source of inspiration. These theorists have focused on "the dark side of planning," hoping such focus would inject a sense of realism into an otherwise utopian planning discourse (Yiftachel 1998).

It is startling that practicing planners such as Szold, Frenchman, Stollman, and Herr, who contributed to this volume, retain a sense of purpose and optimism about planning despite the chaos among planning theorists. One reason practitioners can carry on with their day-to-day tasks is that they never relied on any "planning theory." This, however, is no indication that planning, as a profession, can perform and prosper without a theory. Neither does it mean that practicing planners perform their tasks with *no* theory. As Donald Schön notes in his seminal work (1983), effective practitioners rely on implicit theories of action, learning from past actions about why certain types of interventions work, while others do not. Schön called these planners "the reflective practitioners," a term that has gained popularity among academic planners, in part because it lends itself to multiple interpretations. If one were to ask a practicing planner, however, if he or she is a reflective practitioner, or what it would take to become one, one would be likely to evoke an ambiguous response (Baum 1983).

A key challenge for the profession, I propose, is to refine Schön's somewhat normative description of planning practice and ground it in concrete institutional analysis of the kind Lindblom, Simon, March, and (my favorite) Albert Hirschman have cultivated over the past 30 years (for a good review of Hirshman's work, see Rodwin and Schön 1996). There is already a move in that direction in the research by the "new planning theorists" who focus on the day-to-day practice of professional planners to understand how planners respond to different interest groups, negotiate consensual solutions, and inject their own preferences and values in the process (for example, Schön 1986; Forester 1993; and Hoch 1994). This research, however, is focused more on individuals—or *agency*, as sociologists would say—than on institutional structures. There is also excessive concern about political power and how its unequal distribution affects policy outcomes. This normative concern is important for the field of CRP. As I mentioned, there seems to be a professional consensus that issues of equity, social justice, and so on lie at the heart of the profession; but, this normative concern needs to be pursued with explicit recognition of institutional constraints and opportunities. This is not a new insight (see Wildavsky 1964; Beneviste 1970; and Mandelbaum 1986), but one that deserves more attention than it currently draws in research on planning theory.

There are numerous institutional questions that planning theorists need to address if their theories are to be of any use to practicing planners. Foremost among these are questions about the institutional autonomy necessary for planning. The word *planning* assumes that planners have relative autonomy from market as well as social forces to plan.[7] How is this autonomy created? What are the limits of this autonomy? Is there a relationship between the extent of planners' autonomy and the style of planning they pursue? In other words, do planners choose a particular planning style—be it rational, comprehensive, incremental, advocacy, or social learning—or is the style planners adopt an outcome of the nature and extent of their autonomy to plan at a particular moment? These are important questions because the current literature on planning theory, best exemplified by John Friedmann's book *Planning in the Public Domain* (1987), assumes that individual planners choose their styles according to ideological preferences. Thus, one may decide to be a radical planner because one believes in radical planning; others may choose advocacy planning, a social learning approach, and so on. To what extent does this analysis accurately reflect why planners prefer one style over another, and why do the same planners choose different styles for different problems? These are questions regarding descriptive, not normative, planning theory. We first need to better understand why planners act as they do. Only then can we prescribe how they should plan. This has been the preoccupation of planning theorists.

Again, I do not underestimate the need for normative theories; but they must be grounded in a deep understanding of institutional reality, provided by scholars like Lindblom, March, and Hirschman (see March and Simon 1958; Hirschman 1967; March and Olsen 1989). In this effort, the relatively recent research by new institutional economists is useful because it focuses on the transaction cost, which is a major factor for all institutions. Planning theorists should build on such explanations of institutional behavior rather than allow themselves to become bogged down in their deep concern for structural imbalances in power relationships or other, equally difficult systemic causes. This is not to say that good planning theory can ignore the shortcomings of capitalist, democratic societies. It should address these issues only as they reveal themselves to the practicing planners in their institutional setting as they struggle to gain the autonomy to plan.

To summarize, then, current planning theory falls far short of what is useful for practicing planners. Much effort is needed to bridge this gulf. Failure to do so would further reduce communication between academic and practicing planners. The former would continue to consider the latter as conservative and beholden to powerful interests, while the latter would continue to ignore the former as liberal utopians whose theories are irrelevant to planning practice.

CHALLENGE THREE:

REJUSTIFY GOVERNMENT INTERVENTION

In his 1996 *Urban Studies* article, and in his chapter in this volume, "Reflections and Research on the U.S. Experience" (Teitz 2000), Michael

Teitz argues that planning, defined broadly as government intervention, has been under attack since the 1970s, although, despite this attack, environmental planning flourished during the same period. He provides some examples of the intellectual attack on planning, arguing that the recent attack on "taking" as an illegal activity can hurt the rationale for land-use planning in a fundamental way. He also argues that the attack on the welfare state and redistributive social policies since the 1980s does not speak well for planning, which seems to be in retreat, except in the domain of environmental concerns. Teitz, however, does not suggest how these intellectual attacks on planning are to be counteracted.

Lloyd Rodwin and I circulated a version of Teitz's 1996 paper to the 1997 Seminar participants at the beginning of our deliberations. Our purpose was to utilize the paper as a springboard to generate debate. Surprisingly, no one responded to Teitz's warning in a systematic way. Some participants, such as Nathan Glazer and Bill Wheaton, argued, indirectly, that the attack on planning was legitimate. Glazer, for example, argued that planning has lost the reputation it once had as a force for progressive reform, and is now preoccupied with creating various types of restrictions, which are at best a nuisance for citizens (see chapter 26 of this volume). Wheaton, a faculty member in the Department of Urban Studies and Planning and head of the Real Estate Center at MIT, raised the issue that urban planning is ineffective because small political jurisdictions do not permit planners to act on problems that usually cut across several jurisdictions.

On the positive side, Susskind and Frenchman argued that planning cannot be considered in retreat because planning graduates are gainfully employed in various types of jobs at various institutional levels. They argued that the old version of planning, institutionally located in city planning offices, has been successfully decentralized and transformed, and that the new version is effective in responding to the concerns of our times. Neither Susskind nor Frenchman, however, provided a reason why the profession has been able to transform itself. Sam Bass Warner also brushed off the criticism of planning, arguing that such criticism was generated by "libertarian ideologues, business interest groups and their advisors, public relations houses and lobbyists, media moguls, and politicians who have been bought" (chapter 27 of this volume). Warner called this group "obscurantists" and predicted that ultimately the obscurantists will be swept away on the tide of popular support for planning at the local level.

The only one who elaborates Teitz's warning is Ann Markusen (chapter 31). Although she did not present the paper in the colloquium, we decided to include it in this volume precisely because of the important issues it raises. Markusen proposes an explanation as to why planning, which has been relatively successful at the micro level, is under severe attack at the macro level.

She argues that planners' most formidable enemies are neoclassical economists, who have delegitimized four concepts central to planning—namely, the exercise of foresight, the notion of the commons, equity as a normative criterion, and quality of life. On the basis of this analysis, she proposes that the resurrection of planning's popularity requires a three-pronged approach: planners must engage in public discourse to influence public opinion; they must showcase planning's "best practices"; and they must diversify into new fields.

Although I agree with the thrust of Markusen's argument, I do not think we should simply blame the neoclassical economists for planning's loss of popularity. We need to ask: Why did neoclassical economists succeed in influencing public opinion when the planners did not? Markusen's plausible answer to this question is reflected in her prescriptions: planners did not engage in public discourse to influence public opinion, and they did not showcase sufficiently planning's best practices. I am not convinced, however, that these are the reasons why neoclassical economists have been successful in diminishing the role of planning.

First, the neoclassical economists did not showcase their best practices either. On the contrary, there seems to be a growing skepticism about their interpretation of how markets work (see Thurow 1998; Stiglitz 1998). Second, there is evidence that planners at the local level are more engaged now than ever before in influencing public opinion about the benefits of public participation in planning (McClendon and Catanese 1996). And, finally, Markusen does not explain why the anti-planning attitude seems especially pronounced in the United States compared to Western European countries, although neoclassical economists are actively propagating their ideas all over the world.

To fully appreciate Markusen's concern, one needs to take a historical approach. Sam Warner asserts, in chapter 27, that, historically, Americans like planning but resist regulations. If regulatory activities are a key part of planning, how can one reconcile the fact that Americans like planning but not regulations? Warner does not see this contradiction because he does not consider planning a primarily governmental activity. He sees planning as a collective process of local-level decision making about local resources. To quote: "[Americans] like thinking about the lands, houses, stores, parks, and roads of their communities; they like imagining the future, thinking about proposals for betterment. And when there is conflict about such matters, as there often is, people turn out night after night to air their opinions and context others."

Is Markusen wrong, then? Do Americans like planning despite the propaganda against it by the neoclassical economists? The answer depends on how one defines *planning*. What Warner describes as a fondness for planning, some would say, is an example of how Americans deeply distrust planning when it is initiated by government. In other words, popular participation in planning activities is not an affirmation of government-initiated planning. Quite the opposite; it is an indication that Americans are willing to challenge planning as a professional activity requiring specialized technical knowledge, which Americans see as a top-down idea that hurts local autonomy. It is also an indication that, although Americans care deeply about their communities, they are deeply skeptical about government-initiated planning, which they consider bureaucratic, coercive, and controlled by the dictates of individuals and institutions far removed from themselves. Perloff (1974) has noted this popular anti-planning attitude: "We are dealing with a field where our own uncertainties and weaknesses reflect the reluctant, almost schizophrenic, view of planning held by society at large" (p. 128). John Dyckman (1983) raised the same concern when he noted that Americans are, at best, ambivalent about public planning itself. He argues that, "unlike planners in some countries, where planning is honored ideologically, if not in execution, American planners are unsure of the degree of national commitment to their work" (p. 279). More recently, President Clinton confirmed this view in his public interviews while visiting China, commenting that, "In America, we tend to view freedom as the freedom from government abuse or from government control. This is our heritage" (1998, A8).

This distrust of planning and government was somewhat subdued and neutralized in the first half of this century, primarily because of successful government intervention during the Great Depression and during World War II (Bordo et al. 1998). Even after World War II, planning was accepted as a technical, rational exercise necessary for rapid urbanization and economic growth. True, there were some dissenters, such as Fredrick Hayek (1944) and Karl Popper (1945), who warned that state-initiated planning was contrary to personal freedom. As a result, some planning initiatives were withdrawn. For example, the National Resources Planning Board, in which Rexford Tugwell played a key role as a planner, was abolished near the end of World War II. Nevertheless, there was hardly any popular reaction at the time against CRP. Drawing professional legitimacy from close association with civil and sanitary engineering and architecture, CRP was successful in presenting itself as a technical and rational exercise necessary for the protection of public interest and enhancement of the overall quality of urban life (Branch 1966).

The 1960s ushered in a new phase in planning history marked by popular protest against not only planning efforts such as urban renewal, but also government activities in general. Much has been written about this historical period (Farber 1994; Surge 1998), so I do not want to repeat the old arguments except to point out that planning came under attack by planners themselves and also by urban sociologists, urban political scientists, and anthropologists who,

collectively, dismissed the efficacy of rational, comprehensive planning as political manipulation by dominant social groups controlling the government
apparatus (two books that spearheaded the critique were Gans {1962} and
Glazer {1988}). The arguments against planning cover a wide ideological
spectrum. On the left are the neo-Marxists who argue that planning by the
capitalist state was intended not to serve the people but to save capitalism
from the crisis it had created (Harvey 1985). On the right is the argument
that planning is, at best, ineffective and, at worst, counterproductive (for a
review, see Hirschman 1991). In the center are the post-modernists who
argue that planning is part and parcel of the modernization project and, hence,
should be rejected as yet another form of social control to implement a hege-
monic vision of progress (for a review, see Dear 1986).

The neoclassical economists' attack on planning, which Markusen describes so well, emerged from the right of the ideological spectrum simultaneously with the attacks from these other quarters. What instigated the neoclassical economists, however, was not their dislike of modernization. On the
contrary, they argued that the pace of economic modernization had slowed
because of inefficient and excessive government intervention in capital, commodities, and labor markets. In justifying this attack, neoclassical economists
pointed out the sharp decline in the economic growth rate, which was accompanied at the time by a surprisingly high rate of inflation (the term
stagflation was created to describe this paradox; see Killick 1989). Neoclassical economists blamed this outcome on Keynesian economic management,
which had guided government policies, both economic and social, since the
1930s. They pointed out, time and again, how such policies led to the steadily
increasing federal budget deficits (Friedman et al. 1970). Social programs,
supported by federal and state governments, also came under attack as critics
demonstrated that these programs were not self-sustaining and, worse, had
been counterproductive in increasing demands on the welfare state (for a
review, see Katz 1989).

The convergence of attacks by the neoclassical economists, neo-Marxists,
post-modernists, and disillusioned planners themselves led to the outcome
Markusen outlines in her chapter 31 in this volume. These attacks severely
damaged the conceptual foundation of one idea at the heart of the planning
profession, the notion of public interest.[8] The neo-Marxists argued that the
term *public interest* hides the reality that the interests of dominant classes drive
planning efforts. The post-modernists argue that there is no such thing as
public interest, because there is no such thing as the public. They argue that,
in the name of public interest, the government and dominant social groups in
control of government coerce other social groups with different identities
and allegiances into following the modernization paradigm. They also argue

that there is no such thing as the truth, least of all, a truth propagated by the government, and urge a deconstruction of social reality to uncover the motives of dominant groups who provide a falsely coherent social logic to support their self-serving arguments. Hence, the planners had no special claim to the understanding of urban reality; if anything, their interpretation was tainted by the government's need for social control and economic coercion (see Friedmann 1992).

The neoclassical economists' argument against the notion of public interest was couched in the form of rational choice theory, which gained immense popularity in the mid-1970s. According to this theory, no one cares about the public interest. Ultimately, all individuals and groups are interested in pursuing their own interests. This is true for market agents, as well as such state actors as planners. This kind of argument discredits well-intentioned social policies geared toward reducing inequality of access to social resources. Such policies are dismissed as ultimately benefiting policymakers and planners by either increasing their budgets or providing new opportunities for "rent extraction" from prospective beneficiaries (Buchanan et al. 1980). In other words, issues such as equity, which are central to planning, are not under attack directly, because no one can argue against equity; rather, the attack is indirect but more convincing—that government programs which claim to reduce inequities are meant to benefit primarily the bureaucrats. The logical conclusion of this argument is to reduce government intervention and planning and rely on either the market or nongovernmental sector to respond to social problems.

The neoclassical economists' attack on planning was, of course, not limited to the attack on the notion of public interest. As Markusen rightly points out, the attack on planning took a variety of forms. One such attack, which she does not highlight but I consider central to planning ideas, is the accusation that planning, which in the past was considered necessary to rectify market failure, is actually contributing to "state failure." Some argue that state failure is ultimately more harmful than failed market outcomes because it benefits state actors and thwarts state reforms (Sklar 1979; Weiner and Huntington 1987). This argument gained credence with the collapse of the former Soviet Union and East European countries, even though the evidence indicates that state reforms in these countries were, at times, initiated by state actors themselves (Cohen and Hammel 1980). The discredited state argument is also used to explain the slow pace of economic development in Africa, although the African examples demonstrate that state intervention can both fail and succeed, depending on many other factors that are usually not taken into account by neoclassical economists (Nelson 1990; Przeworksi 1991).

Responding effectively to these attacks on planning is a major challenge for both planning academia and the profession. It is a battle for the hearts and minds of ordinary citizens who must be convinced that government can and should play a key role in enhancing the quality of life of all citizens. Some would rely on the pendulum theory, which assumes that public opinion constantly fluctuates between two poles, one signifying affinity for the market and the other for government; and that the pendulum swings every 10 years or so, as it becomes apparent to citizens that neither the government nor the market can consistently satisfy them (Hirschman 1992). According to this line of thinking, planners need not worry too much about the current tide against government and planning. The available evidence, however, does not support this argument. As Michael Sandel (1996) has documented well, people's distrust of government has increased steadily since the mid-1960s; and, in many cases, social policies, once dismantled, fail to be reinstated, as the pendulum theory would predict.

Markusen proposes another approach—namely, that planners concentrate on publicizing their best practices rather than obsessively discussing their failures. This argument has some merit. It is true that much more has been written about great planning disasters than great planning successes. We know that there have been some significant planning achievements in the face of adversity (Osborne and Gaebler 1992; Tendler 1998). But success stories are not sufficient to reconstruct a public philosophy that justifies planning. Hence, some have called for a new, reinvigorated liberalism (Brinkley 1998; Matusow 1998).

The main argument for a reinvigorated liberalism is that the persuasive power of old liberalism, which justified government intervention in economy and society, has declined because of the crisis of the welfare state, which compromised liberal principles on many fronts (for a good review, see Sandel 1984 and Fraser and Gerstle 1989). Hence, what is required is the reconstruction of a normative argument for government intervention in the economy and society. Such a philosophical reconstruction should take into account past mistakes made by government and planning and should deliberately avoid an uncritical statism of the kind that would make planners cheerleaders for government. However, a reinvigorated liberalism would also require strong commitment to social progress and a worldview that government, market, and civil society must complement each other in moving forward toward that goal. How to create such a mind-set, not only among planners but among all citizens, remains the single most important challenge for the planning profession.

CONCLUSION

I began this analysis by discussing how the profession of city and regional planning has performed according to four criteria: methodological rigor, service function to society, consensus on core professional values, and intellectual capital formation. I argued that, according to these four *general* criteria, CRP has performed reasonably well. I also argued that this modest success should not tempt us to underestimate the gravity of three *specific* challenges facing the profession:

1. Physical and social planning still need to be integrated rigorously into a truly holistic analytical approach.

2. CRP still lacks theories of planning processes that practicing planners can rely upon.

3. There is need for a new, reinvigorated liberalism that would reconstruct ordinary citizens' respect for government and planning.

APPENDICES

Chapter Endnotes

CHAPTER ONE. LLOYD RODWIN

1. This section on identity issues and the next one on thematic and paradigm change are revised from Rodwin, *Cities and City Planning* (New York and London: Plenum Press, 1984, pp. 262–70).

2. For example, foundation staffs, university administrations, and young professionals in the field.

3. Kuhn used the term *paradigm* in several ways in his book, and this provoked controversy. He tried to clarify the definition in the second edition of his publication. The two meanings he ascribes to the term *paradigm* are (1) "the entire constellation of beliefs, values and techniques shared by the members of a given community"; (2) "one sort of element in that constellation, the concrete puzzle solutions which, employed as models or examples, can replace explicit rules as a basis for the solution of the remaining puzzles of normal science"; Kuhn 1970, p. 170. Holton, on the other hand, uses the notion of themata or theme to refer to the "dimension of fundamental presuppositions, notions, terms, methodological judgments and decisions."

4. Kuhn has provided three telling instances from the field of physics. Thus, commenting on the state of astronomical studies, Copernicus once observed: "It is as though an artist were to gather the hands, feet, head and other members for his images from diverse models, each part excellently drawn, but not related to a single body, and since they in no way match each other, the result would be a monster rather than man." And Wolfgang Pauli, in the months before Heisenberg's paper on matrix mechanics pointed the way to a new quantum theory, wrote to a friend: "At the moment physics is again terribly confused. In any case, it is too difficult for me and I wish I had been a movie comedian or something of the sort and had never heard of physics." Einstein even wrote: "It was as if the ground has been pulled out

from under one, with no firm foundation to be seen anywhere, upon which one could have built"; Kuhn, pp. 83–87.

5. Indeed, for many decades the profession's growth owed much to the prevalence of this view. As Israel Stollman, the former director of the American Institute of Planners, reminds us, "The key to the profession's growth was the acquisition of official responsibilities: zoning and subdivision regulations in the 1920s in accordance with a comprehensive plan; public works programs in the 1930s in accordance with a comprehensive plan; urban renewal in the 1950s in accordance with a comprehensive plan. The planning became 'whatever there are grants-in-aid of' in accordance with a comprehensive plan. The expansion of responsibilities was paralleled by closer ties with political decision makers. When federal planning supports contracted in the early 1980s, planning staff scrambled to keep programs going, and many agencies found strong local support for their emphases on growth management and environmental protection" (see Stollman, chapter 11 in this volume).

6. These courses dealt with ways of: (a) making an inventory of the physical characteristics of the city as well as the characteristics of the population and households and major activities in the city (industrial, commercial, civic, residential, recreational, etc.); (b) projecting the likely changes and trends; (c) analyzing theories and problems involved in the location of these activities and in preparing area, neighborhood, urban, and regional land-use plans to accommodate these activities, taking account of alternative goals and policies for such development; and (d) learning how to use subdivision, zoning, and other relevant land-use control techniques and policies to achieve these ends. For a leading text in the field, see Chapin 1979.

7. MIT's lack of success in sustaining the Urban Systems Laboratory (established mainly to involve engineering, management, and other departments in urban problems) points up the same lesson: that urban and regional questions have only a minor bearing on the central concerns of the other programs.

8. The Ford Foundation, somewhat disappointed by the results of its efforts and skeptical as to future possibilities, withdrew from the field, perhaps a little prematurely. See Pendleton, *Urban Studies*, 1974.

9. Indeed, the paradigm was dominant for nearly a half-century if one traces it back to the period before the professional schools were established. For example, in 1938, E. M. Bassett's book, *The Master Plan,* summed up the standard ideas on this subject; and the idea of the master plan was already in vogue in the 1920s. See also Scott, *American City Planning,* 1969.

10. This comment was made during the MIT seminar discussion on February 11, 1997, following a presentation by Rybczynski.

CHAPTER THREE. JUDITH E. INNES

1. Glasmeier (Glasmeier and Kahn 1989), in a survey of graduates of U.S. planning schools, found that a high proportion of graduates were employed in jobs that had not existed at the time of their education.

2. Elizabeth Morris has developed this idea in her dissertation at the University of California, Berkeley, which used the cases of San Francisco and Baltimore.

3. Some of these are documented in Innes et al. (1994).

4. Innes (1995) has argued that many planning theorists are doing this today and provides a number of examples.

5. Theorists and researchers on practice, such as Healey (1992, 1993) and Forester (1989) have not only been studying practice but also arguing that it is centrally about communication.

CHAPTER EIGHT. DONALD A. SCHÖN

1. This summary of the history of the city planning profession is taken in large part from Mel Scott, *American City Planning Since 1890* (Berkeley, CA: University of California Press, 1969).

2. See, for example, Herbert Gans, *Urban Villagers* (New York: The Free Press, 1962).

3. The case study presented here is derived from videotapes and interview notes originally collected by William Ronco, then a graduate student in the Department of Urban Studies and Planning at MIT. I am grateful to Dr. Ronco for his help in generating this material and for his contributions to earlier versions of its analysis. The material presented in this article is substantially different from earlier treatments of it, however, and the responsibility for it is entirely my own.

4. See Chris Argyris and Donald A. Schön, *Theory in Practice* (San Francisco: Jossey-Bass, 1974).

CHAPTER TEN. CHRISTIE I. BAXTER

1. The Independent Sector estimated 1990 revenues from 391,000 charitable and religious organizations to be $458.1 billion—$416.4 billion from 133,357 charitable organizations and $41.7 billion from 257,648 religious congregations. In the same year, the federal government raised $482.6 billion in personal income taxes; state and local governments raised $539 billion from all taxes (Federal Reserve Board 1993). The Independent Sector's survey covered less than 30 percent of all nonprofit organizations, estimated to total 1.4 million as of 1990. In addition to 501(c)(3)

organizations, the IRS exempts from taxation social advocacy organizations, veterans' groups, labor unions, mutual insurance companies, and other such entities.

2. The Urban Institute study team sought to track the financial fortunes of nonprofits over a three-year period beginning in 1981. At that time, federal funding to nonprofits in the study exceeded private giving by more than half.

3. Analyses of shifts in nonprofit revenues suggest that these organizations have achieved a financial life independent of government support. For example, as the Reagan administration implemented cuts in federal funding to nonprofits, Salamon expected to see them shrink in size and that social service, community development, and environmental improvement organizations would be the hardest hit. He found the reverse. Between 1981 and 1983, nonprofits operating in the areas of mental health, housing and community development, institutional and residential care, health education and research, and culture and the arts grew, replacing lost government revenues with fees (Salamon et al. 1986). Ten years later, the Independent Sector reported that, as of 1991, only 8.7 percent of nonprofit revenues came from government grants or fees paid by government agencies (Hodgkinson et al. 1993b). Other surveys suggest that government funds account for closer to 29 percent of nonprofit revenues.

4. Using a medical metaphor, urban renewal planners held that if the most "blighted" uses were removed and the land redeveloped into "sound" uses, decaying cities would return to health. The U.S. Supreme Court relied on this metaphor when it upheld public land takings for urban renewal.

5. In another instance, DSNI found itself in competition with the Boston Parks Department; both were applying for state grant funds for park development. In both cases, DSNI prevailed.

6. In a two-sector economy in which the public sector plans and designs programs, and private entities implement, getting the private market to respond appropriately has long been a problem. See Bardach (1977) and Pressman and Wildavsky (1973).

CHAPTER SEVENTEEN. LEONARD ORTOLANO

Author's Acknowledgment

I have many people to thank for their comments on the early drafts of this chapter: Greg Browder, Alnoor Ebrahim, Stephanie Ohshita, Lloyd Rodwin, Ernesto Sanchez-Triana, Bish Sanyal, and Anne Shepherd, for the many helpful comments they provided. In addition, I owe thanks to Greg Lindsey and his associates at Indiana University for providing me with copies of syllabi for courses in environmental planning taught at U.S. and Canadian universities. Finally, I would like to acknowledge the helpful comments I received from the following persons in response to my presentation of a draft of this paper at the Annual Mid-winter Symposium of the Ph.D. Program of Urban Design and Planning of the University of Washington, Seattle, WA (March 5 and 6, 1998): Marina Alberti, Timothy Beatley, Hilda Blanco and Robert Lee.

1. My definition incorporates concepts that others have included in definitions of environmental planning and management. For example, Marsh (1983, 3) defined *environmental planning* as "a 'catchall' sort of title applied to planning and management activities in which environmental (as opposed to social, cultural, or political, for example) factors are central considerations. . . . Landscape planning [a new title for land-use planning] represents one of the major areas of environmental planning that addresses both relatively new topics associated with development and land use, such as toxic waste disposal and urban microclimate, as well as traditional ones, such as watershed management and site planning" (Marsh 1983, 3). As another example, Faludi (1987, 139) offers the following definition: "In discussing environmental planning I am ignoring distinctions between urban and rural planning, land-use planning and environmental protection. . . . As an umbrella term, environmental planning is preferable to 'land-use planning,' which often refers to the making of statutory schemes. . . . Many aspects are not touched upon [by land-use planning], such as performance standards for the emission of pollutants, management plans for public facilities like parks, forest, coastlines or water catchments, and assessments of economic, social, and environmental impacts" (Faludi 1987, 139). Note also Petulla's view that "*environmental management* and ancillary specialists are responsible for managing land, water resources, the air environment, and solid or hazardous wastes under the administrative mandates of federal, state and local regulations" (Petulla 1987, 129; emphasis added).

2. In corporate settings, environmental professionals who work on the following tasks are frequently called *environmental managers*: environmental impact assessment, environmental auditing, compliance with environmental regulations, environmental monitoring, emergency response to environmental accidents, health and safety, relations with citizens groups, and lobbying of public officials. Clearly, some of these activities fall under what I will call environmental planning. The distinctions that I gloss over by using only the term *environmental planner* wouldn't exist if the field were called *environmental planning and management*. Unfortunately, that long name is too cumbersome to use.

3. My information about the content of courses in environmental planning came from Professor Greg Lindsey (School of Public and Environmental Affairs, Indiana University). He and his colleagues recently gathered syllabi of graduate environmental planning courses being taught at U.S. and Canadian universities. Professor Lindsey

graciously sent me all the many syllabi he and his associates had collected for their own purposes.

4. Efforts to protect the environment by controlling the disposal of pollutants date back to the sewer systems constructed during the third millennium B.C. Thomas (1972, 1) describes a sewer system constructed in this period for Mohendjodaro, a city of perhaps 40,000 people located near the Indus River in the Indian subcontinent.

5. Examples of these environmental conditions include the presence of backyard privies and cesspools that contaminated groundwater used as a supply of drinking water. Shattuck was the principal author of the *Report of the Sanitary Commission of Massachusetts* (1850), which was influenced by the pioneering sanitary survey conducted in Great Britain by Edwin Chadwick and his associates in 1842 (Fair and Geyer 1954, 7–8).

6. The "designers of sewer systems became known [as sanitary engineers] in the decade following the civil war" (Peterson 1983, 21). During the 1970s, sanitary engineers started calling themselves environmental engineers, a name that is still used. By the 1970s, the subject matter treated by environmental engineers included air pollution, solid and hazardous waste, and noise pollution, in addition to water supply and wastewater disposal.

7. Facts in this paragraph are from Hey and Waggy (1979, 128).

8. A few federal water pollution control laws existed before the mid-1950s, but the Federal Water Pollution Control Act of 1956 marks the beginning of the federal government as a major player in regulating water pollution. For an account of federal regulations to control water pollution, see Ortolano (1997, chapter 12).

9. For examples of such conflicts, see Novotny and Olem (1994, 723–27).

10. See, for example, Primack, Moldal and Hilton (1995, 177) for information on the U.S. Environmental Protection Agency's attempts to promote "watershed restoration" as a strategy for meeting water quality management goals.

11. For more on non-point sources of water pollution from cities, see Novotny and Olem (1994).

12. Public health issues did not seem to play a major role in motivating early programs to regulate air quality. As late as the 1930s, the prevailing view of public health experts was that "the air in itself is not dangerous and is not a true vehicle of disease" (Prescott and Horwood 1935, 70). The health effects of air pollution became clear in 1948, when an air pollution episode in Donora, Pennsylvania, caused 20 people to die and several thousand people to become ill.

13. See Elsom (1992) for an introduction to contemporary air quality problems.

14. For examples of market-based air quality management systems, see Kosobud and Zimmerman (1997).

15. For more on the numerous effects of automobile dependence in Silicon Valley and elsewhere, see Garreau (1991) and Jackson (1985).

16. Some of the SCAQMD's regulatory programs are analyzed in National Academy of Public Administration (1994).

17. For an account of what was known about groundwater contamination from landfills before 1970, see Colten and Skinner (1996, chapter 2).

18. See Percival et al. (1992) for details on the federal regulation of hazardous waste.

19. Although many hazardous substances are not solid, hazardous and solid waste are discussed together here because RCRA (in Section C) defines "solid waste" to include hazardous substances in solid, liquid, and gaseous forms.

20. For evidence of the way poor and minority communities have been disproportionately exposed to hazardous substances, see Lazarus (1993). He also cites studies indicating that enforcement of environmental laws is more lax in poor and minority communities (relative to middle-class white communities).

21. For documentation on the extent of the brownfields issue and what is being done about it, see Davis and Margolis (1997).

22. Marsh was an important contributor to policy debates on irrigation and forestry in the nineteenth century. He authored *Man and Nature*, which was reprinted in the 1960s; see Marsh (1864).

23. While NEPA requires assessments for proposed laws, regulations, and policies in addition to decisions affecting projects, the influence of NEPA on projects is most widely discussed.

24. For an introduction to NEPA and its influence on organizations, see Clark and Canter (1997) and Ortolano (1997, chapter 15).

25. For evidence of how wide a portion of the U.S. population embraced environmental values, see Kempton, Boster, and Hartley (1997).

26. *The Limits To Growth* was written by Meadows et al. (1972); *Small Is Beautiful* was written by Schumacher (1973).

27. For examples of such programs, see Santa Clara Valley Water District (1997, chapter 6).

28. Citations for these studies from the 1950s are given by Platt (1991, 238).

29. The surge of state activism in this period became known as the "quiet revolution" after the title of a report prepared by Bosselman and Callies (1971) for the U.S. Council on Environmental Quality.

30. For details on statewide growth management programs, see Stein (1993).

31. For an introduction to the "regulatory taking issue," and ways that courts and legislatures have responded to it, see Rose (1997).

32. For more on this shift from large urban parks to neighborhood-scale parks and playgrounds, see Cranz (1982, chapter 2).

33. Information in this paragraph is from Hays (1987, 89).

34. See Platt (1991, 281–84) for information on studies and programs mentioned in this paragraph.

35. Private efforts to preserve open space date back to 1891, when the Massachusetts legislature created a tax-exempt corporation, Trustees of Reservations, to engage in land conservation activities.

36. Similar organizations exist at the national level; for example, The Trust for Public Lands.

37. These estimates of the number of local and regional land trusts are from Hocker (1996, 248).

38. Many contemporary ecosystem restoration efforts have precedents in work carried out by two organizations from the New Deal era: the Works Progress Administration (WPA) and the Civilian Conservation Corps (CCC). For examples of the restoration work carried out by the WPA and the CCC, see Mcdonald (1995).

39. The history of ecologically based landscape design is summarized by Steiner (1994).

40. The analysis approach sketched here had been used long before publication of *Design with Nature* (see, for example, Glickson 1956). Although McHarg did not invent the approach, his presentation of this planning method in *Design with Nature* helped popularize it. An indication of McHarg's influence is given by Stewart Udall (in the foreword to McHarg's autobiography): McHarg's "gifts as a master teacher enabled him to 'reproduce himself' by creating a small army of devoted professors and planners who are busy here and abroad carrying their own 'McHarg approach' to new levels of creativity" (Udall, in McHarg 1996, xii).

41. For examples, see the references cited by Twiss (1973).

42. All figures in this paragraph are from Kenworthy and Laube (1996, 282); see that source for information on cities used in computing average figures.

43. For an introduction to the many definitions of sustainable development, see Lelé (1991).

44. This widely cited phrase is from *Our Common Future,* the report of the World Commission on Environment and Development (1987, 43) that popularized the concept of sustainable development.

45. The term "sustainable cities" does not yet have a standard definition, and other terms are sometimes used as synonyms. Consider, for example, Roseland's characterization of the *eco-city concept*: "Streets for people, not cars. Destinations easily accessible by foot, bike, and public transit. Health as wellness rather than as absence of disease. Restoration of damaged wetlands and other habitats. Affordable housing for all. Food produced and consumed locally. Renewable sources of energy. Less pollution and more recycling. A vibrant local economy that does not harm the environment. Public awareness and involvement in decision-making. Social justice for women, people of color and the disabled. Consideration of future generations." (Roseland 1997, 1)

46. The work of Rees and Wackernagel (1996a, 1996b) builds on earlier studies by Odum (1963), Wolman (1965), and others who analyzed how cities rely on hinterlands. For information on tools and procedures to help create sustainable cities, see Beatley and Manning (1997) and the special issue of *Environmental Impact Assessment Review* edited by Alberti and Susskind (1996).

CHAPTER EIGHTEEN. LAWRENCE SUSSKIND

1. See *Globalizing North American Planning Education Final Report*, ACSP Commission of Global Approaches to Planning Education, April 1994.

2. See M. Alberti and L. Susskind, eds., "Managing Urban Sustainability," *Environmental Impact Assessment Review* 16, 4–6 (July–November 1996).

CHAPTER TWENTY. BENNETT J. HARRISON

Author's Acknowledgment

This paper not only draws on many sources but is itself, in part, a reworking of things I have written recently with other partners. I particularly wish to acknowledge Amy Glasmeier and Karen Polenske, my co-authors of a long review paper written in 1996 for the U.S. Economic Development Administration.

1. Two examples are the disagreements about the relative importance of "agglomeration" and "neighborhood effects." Urban and regional economics defines

"agglomeration" as the tendency of economic activity to cluster together in space (to massify), beyond what might be expected, knowing only the size of a local population and the level of local income. It is likely to be created and sustained by different types of "externalities." One of these is associated with higher-than-average specialization of a place in one or a tightly interconnected set of producers and support services in the same sector; these are called "localization" economies and constitute the theoretical foundation for "industrial districts." Localization, or specialization, externalities are usually named after the father of neoclassical microeconomic theory, Alfred Marshall.

By contrast, agglomeration may be due to more general, cross-sector constellations of mutually supportive but diverse activities, such as a critical mass of schools, laboratories, cultural organizations, and a deep pool of skilled labor that can be employed by many different kinds of firms and agencies. Originally called "urbanization" economies by Edgar M. Hoover, this second type of externality is now commonly called (even by such mathematical economists as Edward Glaeser and J. Vernon Henderson) "Jacobs" economies, after the planner Jane Jacobs.

Which force dominates, and whether indeed there even is a pervasive tendency toward agglomeration or whether (as Amy Glasmeier argues) such externalities become apparent only beyond some critical minimum city size threshold, are all subjects for debate within the field. In any case, these are actually rather old ideas in planning that have recently been revived and become the subject of great attention and a flurry of publications in economics.

An analytically related question is whether the disproportionate concentration of a particular population in a small geographic space—stigmatized welfare recipients, a high concentration of youth with criminal records, poor housing stock—actually reinforces concentrated and persistent urban poverty. This can happen through "contagion" effects, the relative absence of well-connected workers and other role models, or generally the low quantity and poor quality of information about jobs, political options, and housing opportunities. The quest for reliable measurement of such "neighborhood effects" is presently a major research interest within the field, especially among urban economists and public policy analysts.

2. Teitz mentions *Economic Development Quarterly*. Papers on urban and community economic growth and development now appear regularly in many other journals, as well, including Fannie Mae's journal *Housing Policy Debate*, the *Journal of Planning Education and Research*, the *International Journal of Urban and Regional Research*, *Regional Studies*, the several sub-species of *Environment and Planning*, the *Journal of Policy Analysis and Management*, *Urban Affairs Quarterly*, HUD's house journal, *Cityscape*, the *Journal of Urban Economics*, *Land Economics*, the *Journal of Regional*

Science, Regional Science and Urban Economics, the *International Regional Science Review,* and, of course, the journal that contains Teitz's 1996 and 1997 essays, *Urban Studies*.

3. The field of urban (and especially community-level) economic development was more or less invented as an academic area by planning departments. Field examinations and named degrees first appeared in the 1970s, initially in the planning schools of MIT and the University of North Carolina, then at Cornell, the University of California–Berkeley, UCLA, and, more recently, Rutgers and the University of Illinois–Chicago. These remain the leading departments teaching economic development in the United States.

CHAPTER THIRTY-TWO. MICHAEL B. TEITZ

1. The focus of this paper is on the United States, rather than on the whole of North America. Although there is much in common between U.S. and Canadian planning, to incorporate both would be beyond the scope of this account. To include Mexico would be even more difficult. Following common usage, the paper uses "U.S." and "American" interchangeably unless otherwise noted.

The evidence for the paper is drawn primarily from the American planning literature, together with the author's discussions with people in the field.

2. American planning has long differed from that in the United Kingdom or in European countries in its looser professional identity and greater detachment from older professions, especially architecture and engineering. As a result, it has enjoyed greater autonomy, albeit at the price of professional insecurity.

3. The long boom of the 1990s has tempered this trend and has even led to assertions that the productivity decline has been reversed by new technology. Whether this is so remains to be seen.

4. It should be noted that this early reform impulse in planning did not dominate the field's development and agenda in the succeeding decades. Nonetheless, it has remained an important part of planning's ethos and self-image, rising and receding at different periods (Hall 1988).

5. For land-use planning, among the most important have been the 1954 Housing Act, Section 701, which required communities to adopt long-range general plans as a condition for receiving funds under certain federal programs; the Environmental Protection Act, which established the critical role of environmental concerns in development; and the 1991 Intermodal Surface Transportation Efficiency Act, which reshaped federal requirements on local transportation management.

6. The point is reinforced by the continuing trend toward exurbanization (Davis et al. 1994; Nelson and Dueker 1990). Such areas, beyond the conventionally defined suburbs but clearly linked to metropolitan areas, now house more than 60 million people and are the fastest-growing type of settlement in the United States.

7. This argument was originated by Shoup, who was far ahead of his time.

8. Through changes such as linkage of Social Security to inflation and support of health care for the elderly through Medicare, federal expenditures shifted decisively toward individual entitlements. When budgetary pressures grew, these could not be restrained politically.

9. It is interesting to note that a version of this program was adopted by Britain shortly thereafter and remained in place long after its abandonment in the United States.

10. Planners appear to be increasingly turning to specialized publications such as *Economic Development Quarterly* or *Housing Policy Debate* when writing about inner-city issues.

11. Over the past three decades, for example, the city of Oakland has failed in attempts to subsidize a downtown shopping center, a historic district, a major hotel, and, most recently, an ice rink.

12. The attraction of professional sports teams is an enduring topic that continues to mesmerize city officials despite negative analyses (Baade and Dye 1988). Recent discussions have noted that even regional franchises are attracting attention with, perhaps, even less economic basis than national franchises (Johnson 1991; Rosentraub and Swindell 1991), but the issue remains in some dispute (Blair 1992).

13. Metzger (1996) provides an excellent and comprehensive review of equity planning.

14. Among different groups, terms used to describe the Los Angeles events include "riots," "uprising," "rebellion," and "civil unrest." Given the complex nature of the occurrence, the diverse participants, and their varied motives, all might be invoked.

15. This is a historic feature of federal place-based programs for economic development since at least the efforts of the Area Redevelopment Administration to create growth poles in the 1960s.

16. Their public nadir may have been the publication in the *New York Times* of a widely cited critique of the whole concept (Lemann 1994), but the tide was already turning.

17. Putnam's work dealt with Italy, but subsequently he has written extensively about what he perceives as the decline in social capital in the United States (Putnam 1995, 1996).

18. *First English Evangelical Lutheran Church* v. *County of Los Angeles* (1987); *Nollan* v. *California Coastal Commission* (1987); *Lucas* v. *South Carolina Coastal Council* (1992).

19. The reelection of President Clinton certainly inhibited this process but has by no means reversed it, as is clear from the passage of welfare reform.

20. Stories about such regulations abound, including specification of permissible house colors, prohibitions on parking anything other than cars in front of houses, and similar constraints on behavior that would be fiercely resisted as unconstitutional in other circumstances.

21. Wilson was, in fact, resurrecting an idea originally developed by Kain (1968, 1992).

22. Most writers on the topic attribute the original usage to Myrdal (1944), whose work remains central to discussions of race in America.

23. Planners have long been opposed to racism, and some have written about it very effectively, for example Mier (1994), Goldsmith and Blakely (1992), and Blakely's (1992, 1994) superb but pessimistic review articles. In many respects, Blakely, Mier, and Krumholz have been the conscience of the field. However, in recent years, some planners' research has focused more narrowly on the profession, for example, Hoch (1993).

CHAPTER THIRTY-FIVE. BISHWAPRIYA SANYAL

1. Simon argued that organizations do not strive for the best or optimum solution but instead opt for solutions that meet the basic threshold of good performance. He termed these suboptimal but workable solutions "satisficing."

2. John Friedmann acknowledged this dual demand of good practice in his speech accepting the Distinguished Planning Educator award of ACSP in Buffalo, New York, on October 28, 1988. See J. Friedmann (1989), "Planning in the Public Domain: Discourse and Praxis," *Journal of Planning Education and Research* 8,2: 128–30.

3. L. Rodwin cites C. Lindblom (1997) in chapter 1 of this volume. See C. Lindblom (1997), "Political Science in the 1940s and 1950s," *Daedalus* (Winter): 225–52.

4. The creation of special centers for studies of real estate within planning schools started in 1984 at MIT. Prior to that, research on real estate was conducted by a handful of academics in a few business schools, such as the University of Wisconsin and the University of Pennsylvania. In general, business schools do not consider real

estate to be a legitimate and rigorous subfield of planning studies. The establishment of real estate centers has provided a new impetus, legitimacy, and visibility to research on real estate issues. (For a review of the literature, see Ratcliffe and Stubbs 1996.)

5. I realize that CRP graduates do not all work for government agencies, but, on the whole, planning is strongly linked to the notion of government intervention to rectify market failures. Also, more than 60 percent of APA members work in government agencies.

6. The Department of Urban Studies and Planning at MIT is one of the exceptional programs that do not offer any course on planning theory and do not require any qualifying examination on that topic area. The University of California at Berkeley has discontinued the requirement for a planning theory examination for doctoral students.

7. Dyckman (1983) wrote: "A good planning theory would be one that places in perspective the nature of the society and the state that delegates the planning powers, sets the planning tasks, and limits the exercise of technical discretion. It would also be a theory that analyzes and exposes the social forces and cultural traditions that give rise to the idea of planning and that limit its uses."

8. For a full review of the attack on the notion of public interest, see R. Marshall and H. Campbell (1998), "Is There a Need to Reinvent Planning? A Review of Changing Conceptualizations of the Public Interest in British Planning," paper presented at AESOP Annual Congress, Aveiro, Portugal.

Bibliography

Abrams, M. H. 1997. The transformation of English studies: 1930–1995. *Daedalus:* 105–32.

Alberti, M., and L. Susskind, eds. 1996. Managing urban sustainability. *Environmental Impact Assessment Review* 16: 4–6 (special issue).

Albrechts, L. 1998. Learning from experience. Paper presented at the annual conference of the Association of European Schools of Planning, Aveiro, Portugal. July 22–25.

Alexander, J. 1954. The basic–nonbasic concept of urban economic functions. *Economic Geography* 20: 246–61.

Alonso, W. B. 1971. Beyond the interdisciplinary approach to planning. *Journal of the American Institute of Planners* 37: 171–72.

Altshuler, A. 1965a. *The city planning process*. Ithaca, NY: Cornell University Press.

Altshuler, A. 1965b. The goals of comprehensive planning. *Journal of the American Institute of Planners* 31: 186–95.

Altshuler, A. 1970. Decision making and the trend toward pluralistic planning. In E. Erber, ed., *Urban planning in transition*. New York, NY: Grossman.

Altshuler, A. 1997. Remarks presented at MIT Faculty Seminar, "The Profession of City Planning," MIT, Cambridge, Massachusetts. February.

American Lives. 1995. New urbanism study: revitalizing suburban communities. Unpublished report. San Francisco, CA: American Lives.

American Planning Association (APA). 1996. *1995 APA salary survey*. American Planning Association, Chicago, Illinois.

André, E. 1879. *L'art des jardins: traité général de la composition des parcs et jardins*. Paris: Masson. Translation by Witold Rybczynski.

Andrews, R. B. 1953. Mechanics of the urban economic base: historical development of the base concept. *Land Economics* (May): 161–67.

Andrews, R. B. 1958. Comments regarding criticisms of the economic base theory. *Journal of the American Institute of Planners* 24, 1: 37–40.

Argyris, C., and D. Schön. 1974. *Theory in practice*. San Francisco, CA: Jossey-Bass.

351

Aschauer, D. 1990. *Public investment and private sector growth.* Washington, DC: Economic Policy Institute.

Association of Collegiate Schools of Planning (ACSP).1993. Report of the Commission on the Doctorate in Planning to ACSP.

Audirac, I., A. H. Shermyen, and M. T. Smith. 1990. Ideal urban form and visions of the good life: Florida's urban growth management dilemma. *Journal of the American Planning Association* 56: 470–82.

Auletta, K. 1982. *The underclass.* New York, NY: Random House.

Baade, R. A., and R. F. Dye. 1988. Sports stadiums and area development: a critical review. *Economic Development Quarterly* 2: 265–75.

Bae, C-H. C. 1993. Air quality and travel behavior: untying the knot. *Journal of the American Planning Association* 59: 65–74.

Baker, D., and T. Schafer. 1995. *The case for public investment.* Washington, DC: Economic Policy Institute.

Baldassare, M., ed. 1994. *The Los Angeles riots: lessons for the future.* Boulder, CO: Westview Press.

Ballard, J. 1983. *The shock of peace.* Washington, DC: University Press of America.

Banfield, E. C., and J. Q. Wilson. 1963. In *City politics.* Cambridge, MA: Harvard University Press and MIT Press. ch. 14.

Barber, W. J. 1997. Reconfigurations in American academic economics: a general practitioner's perspective. *Daedalus (Journal of the American Academy of Arts and Sciences).* Winter.

Bardach, E. 1977. *The implementation game.* Cambridge, MA: MIT Press.

Bartik, T. 1991. *Who benefits from state and local economic development policies?* Kalamazoo, MI: W. E. Upjohn Institute for Employment Research.

Barton, S. E., and C. J. Silverman. 1994. *Common interest communities: private governments and the public interest.* Berkeley, CA: Institute of Governmental Studies Press.

Bassett, E. M. 1938. *The master plan.* New York, NY: Russell Sage Foundation.

Baum, H. 1997. *The organization of hope.* Albany, NY: State University of New York Press.

Baum, H. S. 1983. Politics and ambivalence in planners' practice. *Journal of Planning Education and Research* 3: 13–22.

Baxter, C. 1996. Canals where rivers used to run. *Economic Development Quarterly* 10.

Baxter, C. 1997. Nonprofits: new settings for city planners. Paper presented at MIT Faculty Seminar, "The Profession of City Planning," MIT, Cambridge, Massachusetts. February.

Baxter, C., J. Weiser, and J. Culler. 1991. *Philanthropic practice: a case study of the Hyams Foundation.* Cambridge, MA: MIT Project on Social Investing.

Beatley, T. 1991. A set of ethical principles to guide land use policy. *Land Use Policy* 8: 3–8.

Beatley, T. 1994. *Ethical land use: principles of policy and planning*. Baltimore, MD: Johns Hopkins University Press.

Beatley, T. 1995. Planning and sustainability: the elements of a new (improved?) paradigm. *Journal of Planning Literature* 9,4: 383–95.

Beatley, T., and K. Manning. 1997. *The ecology of place: planning for environment, economy, and community*. Washington, DC: Island Press.

Beauregard, R. 1989. Between modernity and post-modernity: the ambiguous position of U.S. planning. *Environment and Planning D: Society and Space* 7: 381–95. Reprinted in S. Campbell and S. Fainstein, eds., 1996, *Readings in planning theory*. Cambridge, MA: Blackwell.

Beimborn, E., and H. Rabinowitz, with P. Gugliotta, C. Mrotek, and S. Yan. 1991. *Guidelines for transit-sensitive suburban land use design*. Washington, DC: U.S. Department of Transportation.

Bellah, R., R. Madsen, W. Sullivan, A. Swidler, and S. Tipton. 1985. *Habits of the heart: individualism and commitment in American life*. Berkeley, CA: University of California Press.

Bellah, R., R. Madsen, W. Sullivan, A. Swidler, and S. Tipton. 1992. *The good society*. Berkeley, CA: University of California Press.

Bendick, M. Jr., and M. L. Egan. 1993. Linking business development and community development in inner cities. *Journal of Planning Literature* 8: 3–19.

Beneviste, G. 1970. *Bureaucracy and national planning: a sociological case study*. New York, NY: Praeger.

Benhabib, S. 1995. Global complexity, moral interdependence, and the global dialogical community. In Martha Nussbaum and Jonathan Glover, eds., *Women, culture, and development: a study of human capabilities*. Oxford, UK: Clarendon Press. pp. 235–55.

Berke, P. R., and S. P. French. 1994. The influence of state planning mandates on local plan quality. *Journal of Planning Education and Research* 13: 237–50.

Bernick, R., and R. Cervero. 1996. *Transit villages for the 21st century*. New York, NY: McGraw-Hill.

Blair, J. P. 1992. Benefits from a baseball franchise: an alternative methodology. *Economic Development Quarterly* 6: 91–5.

Blair, J. P. 1995. *Local economic development: analysis and practice*. Thousand Oaks, CA: Sage Publications.

Blakely, E. J. 1989. *Planning local economic development*. Thousand Oaks, CA: Sage Publications.

Blakely, E. J. 1992. Villains and victims: poverty and public policy. *Journal of the American Planning Association* 58: 248–52.

Blakely, E. J. 1994. Review of D. Massey and N. A. Denton (1993), American apartheid: segregation and the making of the underclass, in *Journal of the American Planning Association* 60: 547–48.

Blakely, E. J. 1996. Response—Economic development as a profession: a response to Visser and Wright (1996), *Economic Development Quarterly* 10: 21–7.

Blakely, E. J., and M. G. Snyder. 1997. *Fortress America: gated communities in the United States*. Washington, DC: Brookings.

Bloom, H. 1994. *The Western canon*. New York, NY: Harcourt Brace. Cited in Abrams 1997, p. 127.

Bluestone, B., and B. Harrison. 1982. *The deindustrialization of America: plant closings, community abandonment, and the dismantling of basic industry*. New York, NY: Basic Books.

Blumenfeld, H. 1955. The economic base of the metropolis: critical remarks on the "basic–nonbasic" concept. *Journal of the American Institute of Planners* 21, 4: 114–32.

Bolan, R. S. 1974. Mapping the planning theory terrain. In D. R. Godschalk, ed., *Planning in America: learning from turbulence*. Washington, DC: American Institute of Planners.

Bollens, S. 1992. State growth management: intergovernmental frameworks and policy objectives. *Journal of the American Planning Association* 58: 454–67.

Boothroyd, P., and H. C. Davis. 1993. Community economic development: three approaches. *Journal of Planning Education and Research* 12: 230–40.

Bordo, M., C. Goldin, and E. N. White. 1998. *The defining moment: the Great Depression and the American economy in the twentieth century*. Chicago, IL: University of Chicago Press.

Bosselman, F., and D. Callies. 1971. *The quiet revolution in land use control*. Washington, DC: U.S. Government Printing Office.

Branch, M. C. Jr. 1959. Comprehensive planning: a new field of study. *Journal of the American Planning Association* 25,3: 115–19.

Branch, M. C. Jr. 1966. *Planning: aspects and applications*. New York, NY: John Wiley & Sons.

Briggs, X., E. Mueller, and M. Sullivan. 1996. *From neighborhood to community: evidence on the social effects of community development*. New York, NY: Community Development Research Center, New School for Social Research.

Brinkley, A. 1998. *Liberalism and its discontents*. Cambridge, MA: Harvard University Press.

Broady, M. 1968. *Planning for people: essays on the social context of planning*. London, UK: Bedford Square Press.

Bryson, J. 1988. *Strategic planning for public and nonprofit organizations*. San Francisco, CA: Jossey-Bass.

Buchanan, J. M. et al., eds. 1980. *Toward a theory of the rent-seeking society*. College Station, TX: A&M University Press.

Burayidi, M., ed. 1999. *Urban planning in a multicultural society*. Westport, CT: Greenwood Press.

Burchell, R. W., and G. Sternlieb, eds. 1978. *Planning theory in the 1980s: a search for future directions*. New Brunswick, NJ: Center for Urban Policy Research (CUPR Press).

Byrd, A. 1990. *Philanthropy and the black church*. Washington, DC: Council on Foundations.

Callies, D. L., ed. 1993. *After **Lucas**: land use regulation and the taking of property without compensation*. Chicago, IL: American Bar Association.

Calthorpe, P. 1989. The pedestrian pocket. In D. Kelbaugh, ed., *The pedestrian pocket book*. Princeton, NJ: Princeton Architectural Press.

Calthorpe, P. 1993. *The next American metropolis: ecology, community, and the American dream*. Princeton, NJ: Princeton Architectural Press.

Calthorpe, P., and M. Mack. 1989. Pedestrian pockets: new strategies for suburban growth. In *The pedestrian pocket book: a new suburban design strategy*. Princeton, NJ: Princeton Architectural Press.

Campbell, S., and S. Fainstein, eds. 1996. *Readings in planning theory*. Malden, MA: Blackwell.

Carlson, W. E. 1995. To take or not to take: what exactly is the *Lucas* question? *Journal of Planning Literature* 10: 92–103.

Caro, R. A. 1974. *The power broker: Robert Moses and the fall of New York*. New York: Knopf.

Castells, M. 1983. *The city and the grassroots*. Berkeley, CA: University of California Press.

Castells, M. 1989. *The informational city*. Oxford, UK: Blackwell.

Cervero, R. 1989a. Jobs–housing balance and regional mobility. *Journal of the American Planning Association* 55: 136–50.

Cervero, R. 1989b. *America's suburban centers: the land-use–transportation link*. Boston, MA: Unwin Hyman.

Cervero, R. 1995. California's transit village movement. *Journal of Public Transportation*.

Cervero, R. 1996. Jobs–housing balance revisited: trends and impacts in the San Francisco Bay Area. *Journal of the American Planning Association* 62,4: 492–511.

Chapin, F. S. 1954. Employment forecasts for city planning. *Journal of the American Institute of Planners* 20: 60–73.

Chapin, F. S. Jr. 1963. *Urban land use planning*. 2d ed. Urbana, IL: University of Illinois Press.

Chapin, F. S. 1979. *Urban land use planning*. 3rd ed. Urbana, IL: University of Illinois Press.

Christoforidis, A. 1994. New alternatives to the suburb: neo-traditional developments. *Journal of Planning Literature* 8: 428–40.

Cisneros, H. G. 1989. Have planners taken their eye off the ball? *Journal of the American Planning Association* 55: 78–9.

City of Chicago. 1984. *Chicago works together: 1984 Chicago development plan.* Chicago, IL: City of Chicago.

Clark, R., and L. Canter. 1997. *Environmental policy and NEPA: past, present and future.* Boca Raton, FL: St. Lucie Press.

Clarke, S. E. 1991. Rebuilding city economies. *Economic Development Quarterly* 5: 175–83.

Clarke, S. E., and G. S. Gaile. 1990. *Assessing the characteristics and effectiveness of market-based urban economic development strategies.* Washington, DC: U.S. Economic Development Administration.

Clavel, P. 1986. *The progressive city: planning and participation, 1969–1984.* New Brunswick, NJ: Rutgers University Press.

Clavel, P. 1994. The evolution of advocacy planning. *Journal of the American Planning Association* 60: 146–49.

Clavel, P., and W. Wiewel, eds. 1991. *Harold Washington and the neighborhoods: progressive city government in Chicago, 1983–1987.* New Brunswick, NJ: Rutgers Unversity Press.

Cleveland City Planning Commission. 1975. *Cleveland policy planning report.* Cleveland, OH: Cleveland City Planning Commission.

Cohen, S. F., and K. V. Hammel. 1980. *Voices of Glasnost: interviews with Gorbachev's reformers.* New York, NY: W. W. Norton.

Colten, C. E., and P. N. Skinner. 1996. *The road to Love Canal: managing industrial waste before EPA.* Austin, TX: University of Texas Press.

Community form plan, summary paper: vision, guiding principles, and form districts. 1996. Cornerstone 2020, Louisville and Jefferson County, Kentucky, Comprehensive Plan.

Cordova, T. 1994. Refusing to appropriate: the emerging discourse on planning and race. *Journal of the American Planning Association* 60: 242–43.

Cranz, G. 1982. *The politics of park design: a history of urban parks in America.* Cambridge, MA: MIT Press.

Crozier, M. 1964. *The bureaucratic practitioner.* Chicago, IL: University of Chicago Press.

Cullingworth, J. B. 1993. *The political culture of planning: American land use planning in comparative perspective.* New York, NY: Routledge.

Cullingworth, J. B. 1994. Alternate planning systems: Is there anything to learn from abroad? *Journal of the American Planning Association* 60: 162–72.

Cullingworth, J. B. 1997. *Planning in the USA: policies, issues, and processes.* New York, NY: Routledge.

Dahl, R. A. 1961. *Who governs? Democracy and power in an American city.* New Haven, CT: Yale University Press.

Dahl, R. A., and C. E. Lindblom. 1953. *Politics, economics, and welfare*. New York, NY: Harper.

Davidoff, P. 1965. Advocacy and pluralism in planning. *Journal of the American Institute of Planners* 31.

Davis, H. C. 1995. *Demographic projection techniques for regions and smaller areas: a primer.* Vancouver, BC: University of British Columbia Press.

Davis, J. S., A. C. Nelson, and K. J. Dueker. 1994. The new 'burbs: the exurbs and their implications for planning policy. *Journal of the American Planning Association* 60: 45–59.

Davis, T. S., and K. D. Margolis, eds. 1997. *Brownfields: a comprehensive guide to redeveloping contaminated property*. Chicago, IL: American Bar Association.

Dear, M. 1986. Post-modernism and planning. *Environment and Planning D: Society and Space* 4: 367–89.

DeGrove, J. M., with D. Miness. 1992. *The new frontier for land policy: planning and growth management in the states.* Cambridge, MA: Lincoln Institute of Land Policy.

Dickens, C. 1843. *A Christmas carol in prose, being a ghost story of Christmas*. London, UK: Chapman & Hall.

Dodge, W. R. 1996. *Regional excellence: governing together to compete globally and flourish locally*. Washington, DC: National League of Cities.

Donaldson, S. 1969. *The suburban myth*. New York, NY: Columbia University Press.

Dorius, N. 1993. Land use negotiation: reducing conflict and creating wanted land uses. *Journal of the American Planning Association* 59,1.

Dowall, D. E. 1990. The public real estate development process. *Journal of the American Institute of Planners* 56.

Downs, A. 1994. *New visions for metropolitan America*. Washington, DC: Brookings Institution, and Cambridge, MA: Lincoln Institute of Land Policy.

Dreier, P. 1996. Community empowerment strategies: the limits and potential of community organizing in urban neighborhoods. *Cityscape: a Journal of Policy Development and Research* 2.

Duany, A., and E. Plater-Zyberk. 1991. *Towns and town-making principles*. New York, NY: Rizzoli International Publications.

Duerksen, C. 1996. Form, character, and context: new directions in land use regulations. In *Proceedings of the American Planning Association Annual Conference*, pp. 1–5.

Dyckman, J. W. 1978. Three crises of American planning. In R. W. Burchell and G. Sternlieb, eds., *Planning theory in the 1980s: a search for future directions*. New Brunswick, NJ: Center for Urban Policy Research (CUPR Press).

Dyckman, J. W. 1983. Planning practice in an age of reaction. *Journal of Planning Education and Research* 3: 5–12.

Eisinger, P. K. 1988. *The rise of the entrepreneurial state: state and local economic development policy in the United States*. Madison, WI: University of Wisconsin Press.

Eisner, R. 1994. *The misunderstood economy: what counts and how to count it.* Cambridge, MA: Harvard University Press.

Elsom, D. M. 1992. *Atmospheric pollution: a global perspective.* 2d ed. Oxford, UK: Blackwell.

Erikson, E. H. 1968. *Identity: youth and crisis.* New York, NY: W. W. Norton.

Etzioni, A. 1967. Mixed-scanning: a "third" approach to decision-making. *Public Administration Review* (December).

Etzioni, A. 1993. *The spirit of community: rights, responsibilities, and the communitarian agenda.* New York, NY: Crown.

Fainstein, S. 1994. *The city builders: property, politics, and planning in London and New York.* Oxford, UK: Blackwell.

Fainstein, S. 1996. Developing success stories. In Willem van Vliet, ed., *Affordable housing and urban redevelopment.* Thousand Oaks, CA: Sage.

Fainstein, S., and A. Markusen. 1995. Urban policy: bridging the social and economic development gap. In J. Boger and J. Wegner, eds., *Race, poverty and American cities.* Chapel Hill, NC: University of North Carolina Press.

Fair, G. M., and J. C. Geyer. 1954. *Water supply and waste-water disposal.* New York, NY: John Wiley & Sons.

Faludi, A. 1987. *A decision-centred view of environmental planning.* New York, NY: Pergamon Press.

Faludi, A., ed. 1973. *A reader in planning theory.* Oxford, UK: Pergamon Press.

Farber, D. 1994. *The age of great dreams: America in the 1960s.* New York: Hill & Wang.

Farbstein, J., and R. Wener. 1996. *Building coalitions for urban excellence.* Cambridge, MA: Bruner Foundation.

Federal Reserve Board. 1993. *Flow of funds accounts: flows and outstandings, fourth quarter 1992.* Washington, DC: Federal Reserve Board.

Feldman, J. 1996. *Success and failure in diversification after the Cold War: results of the national defense economy survey.* CUPR Working Paper No. 112. New Brunswick, NJ: Rutgers University, Project on Regional and Industrial Economics.

Fenich, G. G. 1994. An assessment of whether the convention center in New York is successful as a tool for economic development. *Economic Development Quarterly* 8: 245–55.

Fischel, W. A. 1995. *Regulatory takings: law, economics, and politics.* Cambridge, MA: Harvard University Press.

Forester, J. 1987. Planning in the face of conflict: negotiation and mediation strategies in local land use regulation. *Journal of the American Planning Association* 53.

Forester, J. 1989. *Planning in the face of power.* Berkeley, CA: University of California Press.

Forester, J. 1993. Learning from practice stories: the priority of practical judgment. In F. Fischer and J. Forester, eds., *The argumentative turn in policy analysis and planning*. Durham, NC: Duke University Press.

Forester, J. 1995. The rationality of listening, emotional sensitivity, and moral vision. In S. Mandelbaum, L. Mazza, and R. Burchell, eds., *Planning theory in the 1990s*. New Brunswick, NJ: Center for Urban Policy Research (CUPR Press).

Forester, J. 1997. *Democratic deliberation and the promise of planning*. 1995 Lefrak Lecture. Monograph published by the University of Maryland, Department of Urban Studies and Planning, College Park, MD.

Forester, J. 1998. Rationality, dialogue, and learning: what community and environmental mediators can teach us about the practice of civil society. In John Friedmann and Michael Douglass, eds., *Cities for citizens*. New York, NY: John Wiley & Sons.

Forester, J. 1999. *The deliberative practitioner: encouraging participatory planning processes*. Cambridge, MA: MIT Press.

Fraser, S., and G. Gerstle, eds. 1989. *The rise and fall of the New Deal order*. Princeton, NJ: Princeton University Press.

Frieden, B. J. 1990. Center city transformed: planners as developers. *Journal of the American Planning Association* 56: 423–28.

Frieden, B. J. 1997. City planning since Jane Jacobs. Paper presented at MIT Faculty Seminar, "The Profession of City Planning," MIT, Cambridge, Massachusetts. February. Revised for L. Rodwin and B. Sanyal 2000, *The Profession of City Planning: Changes, Images, and Challenges, 1950–2000* (ch. 28).

Frieden, B. J., and L. B. Sagalyn. 1989. *Downtown, Inc.: how America rebuilds cities*. Cambridge, MA: MIT Press.

Friedman, M., et al., eds. 1970. *Milton Friedman's monetary framework: a debate with his critics*. Chicago, IL: University of Chicago Press.

Friedmann, J. 1973. *Retracking America*. Garden City, NY: Anchor Press.

Friedmann, J. 1987. *Planning in the public domain: from knowledge to action*. Princeton, NJ: Princeton University Press.

Friedmann, J. 1989. Planning in the public domain: discourse and praxis. *Journal of Planning Education and Research* 8, 2: 128–30.

Friedmann, J. 1992. *Empowerment: politics of alternative development*. Cambridge, MA: Blackwell.

Friedmann, J. 1993. Toward a non-Euclidean mode of planning. *Journal of the American Planning Association* 59.

Fulton, W. 1989. Visionaries, deal makers, incrementalists: the divided world of urban planning. *Governing* 2.

Gale, D. E. 1992. Eight state-sponsored growth management programs. *Journal of the American Planning Association* 58.

Gallagher, C. 1997. The history of literary criticism. *Daedalus* (Winter).

Galster, G. 1995. *Reality and research: social science and U.S. urban policy since 1960.* Washington, DC: Urban Institute Press.

Galster, G., and E. Hill, eds. 1992. *The metropolis in black and white: place, power, and polarization.* New Brunswick, NJ: Center for Urban Policy Research (CUPR Press).

Gans, H. 1962. *The urban villagers.* New York, NY: Free Press.

Gans, H. 1967. *The Levittowners.* New York, NY: Pantheon Books.

Gans, H. 1990. Deconstructing the underclass: the term's dangers as a planning concept. *Journal of the American Planning Association* 56.

Garreau, J. 1991. *Edge city: life on the new frontier.* New York, NY: Doubleday.

Garvin, A. 1996. *The American city: what works, what doesn't.* New York, NY: McGraw-Hill.

Gilder, G. F. 1981. *Wealth and poverty.* New York, NY: Basic Books.

Gilles, J., and W. Grigsby. 1956. Classification errors in the base-ratio analysis. *Journal of the American Institute of Planners* 22: 17–23.

Giloth, R. 1995. Social investment in jobs: foundation perspectives on targeted economic development during the 1990s. *Economic Development Quarterly* 9: 279–89.

Giloth, R., and W. Wiewel. 1996. Equity development in Chicago: Robert Mier's ideas and practice. *Economic Development Quarterly* 10: 204–16.

Giuliano, G. 1995a. The weakening transportation–land use connection. *Access* 6: 3–11.

Giuliano, G. 1995b. Transportation and land use: theories, evidence, and policy dilemmas. Unpublished paper.

Glaeser, E., H. Kallal, J. Scheinkman, and A. Shleifer. 1992. Growth in cities. *Journal of Political Economy* 100: 1126–52.

Glasgow, D. G. 1980. *The black underclass: poverty, unemployment and entrapment of ghetto youth.* San Francisco, CA: Jossey-Bass.

Glasmeier, A., and T. Kahn. 1989. Planners in the 80's: who we are, where we work. *Journal of Planning Education and Research* 9, 1: 5–17.

Glazer, N. 1988. *The limits of social policy.* Cambridge, MA: Harvard University Press.

Glickman, N. J., M. J. Lahr, and E. K. Wyly. 1996. *State of the nation's cities.* Washington, DC: U.S. Department of Housing and Urban Development.

Glickson, A. 1956. Recreational land use. In W. L. Thomas, Jr., ed. *Man's role in changing the face of the earth.* Chicago, IL: University of Chicago Press.

Godschalk, D. R. 1992. Negotiating intergovernmental development policy conflicts: practice-based guidelines. *Journal of the American Planning Association* 58: 368–78.

Goldsmith, W. W., and E .J. Blakely. 1992. *Separate societies: poverty and inequality in U.S. cities.* Philadelphia, PA: Temple University Press.

Goodman, W. I., and E. C. Freund. 1968. *Principles and practice of urban planning.* Washington, DC: International City Managers' Association.

Gordon, P., A. Kumar, and H. W. Richardson. 1989. Congestion, changing metropolitan structure, and city size in the U.S. *International Regional Science Review* 12: 45–56.

Green, R. E., ed. 1990. *Enterprise Zones: new directions in economic development.* Newbury Park, CA: Sage Publications.

Grigsby, J. E. 1994. In planning there is no such thing as a race-neutral policy. *Journal of the American Planning Association* 60: 240–41.

Gruenberg, S. M. 1954. Homogenized children of new suburbia. *New York Times Magazine* (September 19).

Haar, C. M. 1953. The master plan: an impermanent constitution. *Law and Contemporary Problems* 20: 353–418.

Habermas, J. 1973. *Legitimation crisis.* Boston, MA: Beacon Press.

Habermas, J. 1984. *The theory of communicative action: reason and the rationalization of society.* Translated by T. McCarthy. Boston, MA: Beacon Press.

Haig, R. M. 1928. Major economic factors in metropolitan growth and arrangement. Vol. 1 of *Regional Survey of New York and Environs.* New York, NY: Committee on Regional Plan of New York and Its Environs.

Hall, P. 1988. *Cities of tomorrow.* Oxford, UK: Basis Blackwell.

Hall, P. 1989. The turbulent eighth decade: challenges to American city planning. *Journal of the American Planning Association* 55,3(Summer): 275–82.

Hanson, M. E. 1992. Automobile subsidies and land use: estimates and policy responses. *Journal of the American Planning Association* 58: 60–71.

Hargrove, E., and P. Conkin, eds. 1986. *TVA: fifty years of grassroots bureaucracy.* Urbana, IL: University of Illinois Press.

Harper, T. L., and S. M. Stein. 1996. Post-modernist planning theory: the incommensurability premise. In S. J. Mandelbaum, L. Mazza, and R. W. Burchell, eds., *Explorations in planning theory.* New Brunswick, NJ: Center for Urban Policy Research (CUPR Press).

Harris, B. 1958. Comments on Pfout's test of the base theory. *Journal of the American Institute of Planners* 24, 4: 233–37.

Harris, B., and M. Batty. 1993. Locational models, geographic information, and planning support systems. *Journal of Planning Education and Research* 12: 184–98.

Harrison, B. 2000. Changes in theorizing and planning urban economic growth. In L. Rodwin and B. Sanyal, *The profession of city planning: changes, images, and challenges, 1950–2000.* New Brunswick, NJ: Center for Urban Policy Research (CUPR Press). ch. 20.

Harrison, B., and M. Weiss. 1998. *Workforce development networks: community-based organizations and regional alliances.* Thousand Oaks, CA: Sage.

Harrison, B., M. Weiss, and J. Gant.1995. *Building bridges: CDCs and the world of employment training.* New York, NY: Ford Foundation.

Hartman, C. 1994. On poverty and racism, we have had little to say. *Journal of the American Planning Association* 60: 158–9.

Hartman, C. 1997. The planning profession and reform. Paper presented at MIT Faculty Seminar, "The Profession of City Planning," MIT, Cambridge, Massachusetts. February.

Harvey, D. 1985. On planning the ideology of planning. In David Harvey, *The urbanization of capital: studies in the history and theory of capitalist urbanization*. Baltimore, MD: Johns Hopkins University Press.

Hayden, D. 1981. *The grand domestic revolution: a history of feminist designs for American homes, neighborhoods, and cities*. Cambridge, MA: MIT Press.

Hayek, F. A. 1944. *The road to serfdom*. New York, NY: George Routledge & Sons.

Hays, S. P. 1987. *Beauty, health and permanence: environmental politics in the United States, 1955–1985*. Cambridge, UK: Cambridge University Press.

Healey, P. 1992. A planner's day: knowledge and action in a communicative perspective. *Journal of the American Planning Association* 58, 1: 9–20.

Healey, P. 1993. Planning through debate: the communicative turn in planning theory. In F. Fischer and J. Forester, eds., *The argumentative turn in policy analysis and planning*. Durham, NC: Duke University.

Healey, P. 1997. *Collaborative planning: making frameworks in fragmented societies*. London, UK: Macmillan.

Healey, P., and G. McDougall, eds. 1982. *Planning theory: prospects for the 1980s. Selected papers from a conference held in Oxford, UK, 2–4 April 1981*. Oxford, UK: Pergamon Press.

Helling, A. 1998. Collaborative visioning: proceed with caution! *Journal of the American Planning Association* 64, 3: 335–49.

Herrnstein, R., and C. Murray. 1994. *The bell curve: intelligence and class structure in American life*. New York, NY: Free Press.

Hey, D. L., and N. H. Waggy. 1979. Planning for water quality: 1776-1976. *Proceedings of the American Society of Civil Engineers, Journal of the Water Resources Planning and Management Division* 105, WR1 (March): 121–131.

Hildebrand, G. H., and A. Mace. 1950. The employment multiplier in an expanding industrial market: Los Angeles County, 1940–47. *Review of Economics and Statistics* 32, 3: 241–49.

Hill, C. 1997. *Re-use of former military bases: an evaluation of four converted naval bases*. Doctoral dissertation, Rutgers University, New Brunswick, NJ.

Hill, C., and J. Raffel. 1993. *Military base closures in the 1990s: lessons for redevelopment*. Briefing Paper 15. Washington, DC: National Commission for Economic Conversion and Disarmament. March.

Hill, C., S. Deitrick, and A. Markusen. 1991. Converting the military industrial economy: the experience at six facilities. *Journal of Planning Education and Research* 11: 101–118.

Hirschman, A. O. 1967. *Development projects observed*. Washington, DC: Brookings Institution.

Hirschman, A. O. 1970. *Exit, voice, and loyalty: responses to decline in firms, organizations, and states*. Cambridge, MA: Harvard University Press.

Hirschman, A. O. 1992. *Rival views of market society and other essays*. Cambridge, MA: Harvard University Press.

Hoch, C. 1993. Racism and planning. *Journal of the American Planning Association* 59: 451–60.

Hoch, C. 1994. *What planners do*. Chicago, IL: APA Planners Press.

Hocker, J. W. 1996. Patience, problem solving and private initiative: local groups chart a new course for land conservation. In H. L. Diamond and P. F. Noonan, eds., *Land use in America*. Washington, DC: Island Press. pp. 245–59.

Hodgkinson, V., M. Weitzman, S. Noga, and H. Gorshi. 1993a. *A portrait of the independent sector*. San Francisco, CA: Jossey-Bass.

Hodgkinson, V., M. Weitzman, C. Toppe, and A. Noga. 1993b. *Nonprofit almanac*. Washington, DC: Independent Sector.

Hoffman, L. 1989. *The politics of knowledge: activist movements in medicine and planning*. Albany, NY: State University of New York Press.

Holland, J. H. 1995. *Hidden order: how adaptation builds complexity*. Reading, MA: Addison-Wesley.

Holmes, O. W. 1920. *Collected legal papers*. New York, NY: Harcourt Brace and Co.

Holton, G. 1974. *Thematic origins of scientific thought: Kepler to Einstein*. Cambridge, MA: Harvard University Press.

Howard, E. (1898) 1947. *Garden cities of tomorrow*, ed. F. J. Osborn. London: Faber and Faber.

Howe, E. 1994. *Acting on ethics in city planning*. New Brunswick, NJ: Center for Urban Policy Research (CUPR Press).

Hoyt, H. 1945. The importance of the economic background in city planning. *Journal of the American Institute of Planners* 11, 1: 16–19.

Indergaard, M. 1996. Making networks: remaking the city. *Economic Development Quarterly* 10: 172–87.

Innes, J. 1983. Usable planning theory: an agenda for research and education. *Journal of Planning Education and Research* 3: 36–45.

Innes, J. 1992. Group processes and the social construction of growth management: Florida, Vermont and New Jersey. *Journal of the American Planning Association* 58: 440–53.

Innes, J. 1994. Planning institutions in crisis. *Planning Theory* 10-11: 81–96.

Innes, J. 1995. Planning theory's emerging paradigm: communicative action and interactive practice. *Journal of Planning Education and Research* 14, 3: 183–89.

Innes, J. 1996. Planning through consensus building: a new view of the comprehensive ideal. *Journal of the American Planning Association* 62,4: 460–72.

Innes, J., J. Gruber, M. Neuman, and R. Thompson. 1994. *Coordinating growth and environmental management through consensus building.* CPS Report: A Policy Research Program Report. University of California, Berkeley, California Policy Seminar.

Isard, W., D. F. Bramhall, G. A. Carrothers, P. J. H. Cumberland, L. N. Moses, D. O. Price, and E. W. Schooler. 1960. *Methods of regional analysis.* Cambridge, MA: MIT Press.

Isserman, A. 1980. Estimating export activity in a regional economy: a theoretical and empirical analysis of alternative methods. *International Regional Science Review* 5,2: 155–84.

Isserman, A. 1984. Projection, forecast, and plan: on the future of population forecasting. *Journal of the American Planning Association* 50,2: 208–21.

Isserman, A. 1993. The right people, the right rates: making population estimates and forecasts with an interregional cohort-component model. *Journal of the American Planning Association* 59, 1: 45–64.

Isserman, A. 1995. The history, status, and future of regional science: an American perspective. *International Regional Science Review* 17, 3: 249–96.

Isserman, A. 1996. It's obvious, it's wrong, and anyway they said it years ago? Paul Krugman on large cities. *International Regional Science Review* 19,1-2: 37–48.

Isserman, A. 1997. The federal role in rural economic development: some empirical evidence with implications for current policy debates. In B. Harrison and M. Weiss, eds., *Rethinking national economic development policy.* Boston, MA: Economic Development Assistance Consortium.

Isserman, A., and T. Rephann. 1995. The economic effects of the Appalachian Regional Commission: an empirical assessment of 26 years of regional development planning. *Journal of the American Planning Association* 61, 3: 345–64.

Jackson, K. T. 1985. *Crabgrass frontiers: the suburbanization of the United States.* New York, NY: Oxford University Press.

Johnson, A. T. 1991. Local government, minor league baseball, and economic development strategies. *Economic Development Quarterly* 5: 313–24.

Johnson, J. H. Jr., C. K. Jones, W. C. Farrell, Jr., and M. L. Oliver. 1992. The Los Angeles rebellion: a retrospective view. *Economic Development Quarterly* 6: 356–72.

Johnson, J. H. Jr., W. C. Farrell, Jr., and M. R. Jackson. 1994. Los Angeles one year later: a prospective assessment of responses to the 1992 civil unrest. *Economic Development Quarterly* 8: 19–27.

Joint Center for Urban Studies of MIT and Harvard University. 1971. *The role of university-based urban centers.* Cambridge, MA: Joint Center. pp. 6, 108–9.

Kain, J. F. 1968. Housing segregation, Negro employment, and metropolitan decentralization. *Quarterly Journal of Economics* 82: 175–98.

Kain, J. F. 1992. The spatial mismatch hypothesis: three decades later. *Housing Policy Debate* 3: 371–460.

Kaiser, E., and D. Godschalk. 1995. Twentieth-century land use planning: a stalwart family tree. *Journal of the American Planning Association* 61,3: 365–84.

Kaiser, E., D. Godschalk, and F. Chapin, Jr. 1995. *Urban land use planning.* 4th ed. Urbana, IL: University of Illinois Press.

Kasarda, J. 1985. Urban change and minority opportunities. In P. E. Peterson (1985), *The new urban reality.* Washington, DC: Brookings Institution.

Kasarda, J. 1989. Urban industrial transition and the underclass. *Annals of the American Academy of Political and Social Science* 501: 26–47.

Kasarda, J. 1993 Inner-city concentrated poverty and neighborhood distress: 1970–1990. *Housing Policy Debate* 4: 253–302.

Kasarda, J., and K. Ting. 1996. Joblessness and poverty in America's central cities: causes and policy prescriptions. *Housing Policy Debate* 7: 387–419.

Katz, M. 1989. *The undeserving poor: from the war on poverty to the war on welfare.* New York, NY: Pantheon Books.

Katz, M., ed. 1993. *The "underclass" debate.* Princeton, NJ: Princeton University Press.

Keating, W. D., and N. Krumholz. 1991. Downtown plans of the 1980s: the case for more equity in the 1990s. *Journal of the American Planning Association* 57: 136–52.

Kelbauch, D. 1997. The new urbanism. *Journal of Architectural Education* 51,2: 142–44.

Kelley, M., and T. Watkins. 1995. The myth of the specialized military contractor. *Technology Review* 98,3 (April): 52–8.

Kelly, B. M. 1993. *Expanding the American dream.* Albany, NY: State University of New York Press.

Kelly, E. D. 1993. *Managing community growth: policies, techniques and impacts.* Westport, CT: Praeger.

Kelly, E. D. 1994. The transportation–land-use link. *Journal of Planning Literature* 9: 129–45.

Kempton, W., J. S. Boster, and J. A. Hartley. 1997. *Environmental values in American culture.* Cambridge, MA: MIT Press.

Kent, T. J. 1964. *The urban general plan.* San Francisco, CA: Chandler Press.

Kenworthy, J. R., and F. B. Laube. 1996. Automobile dependence in cities: an international comparison of urban transport and land use patterns with implications for sustainability. *Environmental Impact Assessment Review* 16,4–6: 279–308.

Killick, T. 1989. *A reaction too far.* London, UK: Overseas Development Institute.

Klosterman, R. E. 1990. *Community analysis and planning techniques.* Savage, MD: Rowman & Littlefield.

Knaap, G., and A. C. Nelson. 1992. *The regulated landscape: lessons on state land use planning from Oregon.* Cambridge, MA: Lincoln Institute of Land Policy.

Kosobud, R. F., and J. M. Zimmerman, eds. 1997. *Market-based approaches to environmental policy: regulatory innovations to the fore.* New York, NY: Van Nostrand Reinhold.

Kreps, D. M. 1997. The current position. *Daedalus* (Winter).

Krieger, A. 1997. Remarks presented at MIT Faculty Seminar, "The Profession of City Planning," MIT, Cambridge, Massachusetts. February.

Krieger, A. 2000. The architect as urbanist. In L. Rodwin and B. Sanyal, eds., *The profession of city planning: changes, images, and challenges, 1950–2000.* New Brunswick, NJ: Center for Urban Policy Research (CUPR Press). ch. 22.

Krueckeberg, D. A., and A. L. Silvers. 1974. *Urban planning analysis: methods and models.* New York: John Wiley & Sons.

Krugman, P. 1991. *Geography and trade.* Cambridge, MA: MIT Press.

Krumholz, N. 1994. Advocacy planning: Can it move to the center? *Journal of the American Planning Association* 60: 150–1.

Krumholz, N., and P. Clavel. 1994. *Reinventing cities: equity planners tell their stories.* Philadelphia, PA: Temple University Press.

Krumholz, N., and J. Forester. 1990. *Making equity planning work: leadership in the public sector.* Philadelphia, PA: Temple University Press.

Kuhn, T. 1970. *The structure of scientific revolutions.* 2nd ed. Chicago, IL: University of Chicago Press.

Kunstler, J. H. 1993. *The geography of nowhere: the rise and decline of America's man-made landscape.* New York: Simon & Schuster.

Kunstler, J. H. 1996. *Home from nowhere: remaking our everyday world for the twenty-first century.* New York, NY: Simon & Schuster.

Lakatos, I., and Musgrave, A., eds. 1970. *Criticism and the growth of knowledge.* New York, NY: Cambridge University Press.

Landecker, H. 1996. Is new urbanism good for America? *Architecture* 85, 4: 67–77.

Landis, J. D. 1994a. The California urban futures model: a new generation of metropolitan simulation models. *Environment and Planning B: Planning and Design* 21: 399–420.

Landis, J. D. 1994b. A new tool for land use and transportation planning. *Access* 5: 15–20.

Lauria, M., ed. 1997. *Reconstructing urban regime theory: regulating urban politics in a global economy.* Newbury Park, CA: Sage.

Lawrence, B. 1998. Interview by Robert Yaro of the Regional Plan Association with Barbara Lawrence, vice president of the National Growth Management Leadership Project (NGMLP). March 27.

Lazarus, R. J. 1993. Pursuing environmental justice: the distributional effects of environmental protection. *Northwestern University Law Review* 87,3: 787–857.

Le Gates, R. T., and F. Stout, eds. 1996. *The city reader.* London, UK: Routledge.

Lee, D. B. Jr. 1973. Requiem for large-scale models. *Journal of the American Institute of Planners* 39: 163–78.

Lelé, S. M. 1991. Sustainable development: a critical review. *World Development* 19,6: 607–21.

Lemann, N. 1991. The promised land: the great migration and how it changed America. New York, NY: Alfred A. Knopf.

Lemann, N. 1994. The myth of community development. *New York Times Magazine* (January 9): 26–31, 50, 54, 60.

Levy, J. M. 1997. *Contemporary urban planning.* 4th ed. Englewood Cliffs, NJ: Prentice-Hall.

Liberty, R. 1998. Interview by Robert Yaro of the Regional Plan Association with Robert Liberty, president of the NGMLP. March 27.

Lindblom, C. E. 1959. The science of muddling through. *Public Administration Review* 19: 79–88.

Lindblom, C. E. 1997. Political science in the 1940s and 1950s. *Daedalus* (Winter).

Long, N. E. 1975. Another view of responsible planning. *Journal of the American Institute of Planners* 41: 311–16.

Loveridge, S. 1996. On the continuing popularity of industrial recruitment. *Economic Development Quarterly* 10: 151–58.

Lowry, I. S. 1964. *A model of a metropolis.* Santa Monica, CA: Rand Corporation.

Lupo, A. 1997. Planners visualize Boston at 400; Mayor Menino launches a series on planning, development. *The Boston Globe.* March 30.

Luria, D., and J. Russell. 1981. *Rational reindustrialization.* Detroit, MI: Widgetripper Press.

Lynch, R., and A. Markusen. 1994. Can markets govern? *The American Prospect* (Winter): 125–34.

Lyons, T. S., and R. E. Hamlin. 1991. *Creating an economic development action plan: a guide for development professionals.* New York, NY: Praeger.

Mandelbaum, S. J. 1986. The institutional focus of planning theory. In B. Checkoway, ed., *Strategic perspectives on planning practice.* Lexington, MA: Lexington Books.

Mandelbaum, S. J., L. Mazza, and R. W. Burchell. 1996. *Explorations in planning theory.* New Brunswick, NJ: Center for Urban Policy Research (CUPR Press).

March, J., and H. A. Simon. 1958. *Organizations*. New York, NY: Wiley.

March, J., and J. P. Olsen. 1989. *Rediscovering institutions*. New York, NY: The Free Press.

Marcuse, P. 1984. Professional ethics and beyond: values in planning. In M. Wachs, ed., *Ethics in planning*. New Brunswick, NJ: Center for Urban Policy Research (CUPR Press).

Markusen, A. 1998. The post–Cold War American defense industry: options, policies and probable outcomes. In Efraim Inbar and Ben-Zion Zilberfarb, eds., *Politics and economics of defense industries in a changing world*. London, UK: Frank Cass & Co.

Markusen, A. 2000. Planning as craft and as philosophy. In L. Rodwin and B. Sanyal, *The profession of city planning: changes, images, and challenges, 1950–2000*. New Brunswick, NJ: Center for Urban Policy Research (CUPR Press). ch. 31.

Markusen, A., J. Raffel, M. Oden, and M. Llanes. 1995. *Coming in from the cold: the future of Los Alamos and Sandia National Laboratories*. New Brunswick, NJ: Rutgers University, Project on Regional and Industrial Economics.

Marquez, B. 1993. Mexican-American community development corporations and the limits of directed capitalism. *Economic Development Quarterly* 7: 287–95.

Marris, P. 1975. *Loss and change*. New York, NY: Anchor (reprinted RKP, 1986).

Marris, P. 1996. *The politics of uncertainty: attachment in private and public life*. London, UK: Routledge.

Marsh, G. P. 1864. *Man and nature; or physical geography as modified by human action*. New York, NY: Charles Scribner. Reprint 1965, D. Lowenthal, ed. Cambridge, MA: Belknap Press of the Harvard University Press.

Marsh, W. M. 1983. *Landscape planning: environmental applications*. New York, NY: John Wiley & Sons.

Massey, D. B. 1973. The basic-service categorization in planning. *Regional Studies* 7, 1: 1–15.

Massey, D., and N. Denton. 1993. *American apartheid: segregation and the making of the underclass*. Cambridge, MA: Harvard University Press.

Matusow, A. J. 1984. *The unraveling of America: a history of liberalism in the sixties*. New York, NY: Harper & Row.

McClendon, B. W., and A. J. Catanese, eds. 1996. *Planners on planning: leading planners offer real-life lessons on what works, what doesn't, and why*. San Francisco, CA: Jossey-Bass.

Mcdonald, M. 1995. The coalition to restore urban waters. *Restoration & Management Water* 13,1: 98–103.

McHarg, I. L. 1969. *Design with nature*. Garden City, NY: Doubleday/Natural History Press.

McHarg, I. L. 1996. *A quest for life: an autobiography*. New York, NY: John Wiley & Sons.

McKnight, J. n.d. *The future of low-income neighborhoods and the people who reside there: a capacity-oriented strategy for neighborhood development*. Evanston, IL: Center for Urban Affairs and Policy Research, Northwestern University.

McLean, M. L., and K. P. Voytek. 1992. *Understanding your economy*. Chicago, IL: American Planning Association.

Mead, L. 1986. *Beyond entitlement: the social obligations of citizenship*. New York, NY: Free Press.

Meadows, D. H., D. L. Meadows, J. Randers, and W. W. Behrens III. 1972. *The limits to growth: a report for the Club of Rome's project on the predicament of mankind*. New York, NY: New American Library.

Medoff, P., and H. Sklar. 1994. *Streets of hope*. Boston, MA: South End Press.

Merriam, D. H. 1994. The taking issue. *Journal of the American Planning Association* 60: 402–4.

Metzger, J. T. 1996. The theory and practice of equity planning: an annotated bibliography. *Journal of Planning Literature* 11: 112–26.

Michael, D. N. 1968. On coping with complexity: planning and politics. *Daedalus* 47,4: 179–93.

Mier, R., ed. 1993. *Social justice and local development policy*. Newbury Park, CA: Sage Publications.

Mier, R. 1994. Some observations on race in planning. *Journal of the American Planning Association* 60: 184–202.

Modernizing state planning statutes. 1996. "Growing Smart" Working Papers. Planners Advisory Service, Report No. 462/463. Chicago, IL: American Planning Association.

Mollenkopf, J. H. 1983. *The contested city*. Princeton, NJ: Princeton University Press.

Moses, Robert. 1962. Are cities dead? *Atlantic* 209 (January).

Moyerman, S. S., and B. Harris. 1955. The economies of the base study. *Journal of the American Institute of Planners* 21: 88–93.

Mumford, Lewis. 1961. *The city in history: its origins, its transformations, and its prospects*. New York, NY: Harcourt Brace Jovanovich.

Murray, C. 1984. *Losing ground: American social policy 1950–1980*. New York, NY: Basic Books.

Myrdal, G. 1944. *The American dilemma: the Negro problem and modern democracy*. New York, NY: Harper and Row.

National Academy of Public Administration. 1994. *The environment goes to market: the implementation of economic incentives for pollution control*. Washington, D.C.

National Capital Planning Commission (NCPC). 1997. *Extending the legacy: planning America's capital for the 21st century*. Washington, DC: NCPC.

Nehemas, A. 1997. Trends in recent American philosophy. *Daedalus* (Winter).

Nelson, A. C., and K. J. Dueker. 1990. The exurbanization of America and its planning policy implications. *Journal of Planning Education and Research* 9: 91–100.

Nelson, J. M. 1990. *Economic crisis and policy choice: the politics of adjustment in the Third World.* Princeton, NJ: Princeton University Press.

New York Times. 1998. *Questions for the President: give and take with China's students.* p.A8. June 30.

Newman, P. W. G., and J. R. Kenworthy. 1991. *Towards a more sustainable Canberra: an assessment of Canberra's transport, energy, and land use.* Perth, Australia: Institute for Science and Technology Policy, Murdoch University.

Nisbet, R. 1962. *Community and power.* New York, NY: Oxford University Press.

Noever, P., ed. 1992. *The end of architecture?* Munich, Germany: Prestel-Verlag.

Noponen, H. 1992. Loans to the working poor: a longitudinal study of credit, gender, and the household economy. *International Journal of Urban and Regional Research* 16,2: 234–59.

North, D. C. 1955. Location theory and regional economic growth. *Journal of Political Economy* 63: 243–58.

North, D. C. 1956. A reply. *Journal of Political Economy* 64: 165–68.

Novotny, V., and H. Olem. 1994. *Water quality: prevention, identification and management of diffuse pollution.* New York, NY: Van Nostrand Reinhold.

Nussbaum, M. 1990. *Love's knowledge.* New York, NY: Oxford University Press.

Oden, M. 1999. Cashing in, cashing out, and converting: restructuring of the defense industrial base in the 1990s. In Ann Markusen and Sean Costigan, eds., *Arming the future: a defense industry for the twenty-first century.* New York, NY: Council on Foreign Relations.

Oden, M., C. Hill, E. Mueller, J. Feldman, and A. Markusen. 1993. *Changing the future: converting the St. Louis economy.* New Brunswick, NJ: Rutgers University, Project on Regional and Industrial Economics.

Oden, M., E. Mueller, and J. Goldberg. 1994. *Life after defense: conversion and economic adjustment on Long Island.* New Brunswick, NJ: Rutgers University, Project on Regional and Industrial Economics.

Odum, E. P. 1963. *Ecology.* New York, NY: Holt Rinehart and Winston.

Ordorica, R. 1995. Telephone interview by Christie I. Baxter with Curtis Meadows.

Ortolano, L. 1997. *Environmental regulation and impact assessment.* New York: John Wiley & Sons.

Osborne, D., and T. Gaebler. 1992. *Reinventing government: how the entrepreneurial spirit is transforming the public sector.* Reading, MA: Addison-Wesley.

Ozawa, C. 1991. *Recasting science: consensual procedures in public policy making.* Boulder, CO: Westview Press.

Pagano, M. A., and A. O'M. Bowman. 1995. *Cityscapes and capital.* Baltimore, MD: Johns Hopkins University Press.

Parzen, J., and M. Kieschnick. 1994. *Credit where it's due.* Philadelphia, PA: Temple University Press.

Pastor, M. Jr. 1995. Economic inequality, Latino poverty, and the civil unrest in Los Angeles. *Economic Development Quarterly* 9: 238–58.

Peiser, R. 1990. Who plans America—planners or developers? *Journal of the American Planning Association* 56: 496–503.

Pendleton, W. 1974. *Urban studies and the university: the Ford Foundation experience.* New York, NY: The Ford Foundation.

Percival, R. V., A. S. Miller, C. H. Schroeder, and J. P. Leape. 1992. *Environmental regulation.* Boston, MA: Little, Brown.

Perloff, H. 1957. *Education for planning: city, state, and regional.* Baltimore, MD: Johns Hopkins University Press.

Perloff, H. S., and F. Klett. 1974. The evolution of planning education. In D. Godschalk, ed., *Planning in America: learning from turbulence.* American Institute of Planners.

Perry, C. A. 1929. *The neighborhood unit. Neighborhood and community planning regional survey, Volume VII, Regional Plan of New York.* New York, NY: Regional Planning Association.

Peterson, J. A. 1983. The impact of sanitary reform upon American planning, 1840-1890. In D. A. Krueckeberg, ed., *Introduction to planning history in the United States.* New Brunswick, NJ: Center for Urban Policy Research. pp. 13–39.

Petulla, J. M. 1987. *Environmental protection in the United States.* San Francisco, CA: San Francisco Study Center.

Pfouts, R. W. 1957. An empirical testing of the economic base theory. *Journal of the American Institute of Planners* 23, 2: 64–69.

Pfouts, R. W. 1960. *The techniques of urban economic analysis.* West Trenton, NJ: Chandler-Davis Publishing Company.

Piore, M. J., and C. F. Sabel. 1984. *The second industrial divide: possibilities for prosperity.* New York, NY: Basic Books.

Piven, F. F. 1975. Planning and class interests. *Journal of the American Institute of Planners* 41: 308.

Planning Accreditation Board. 1998. *Guidelines for program administration for the preparation of self-study.* Planning Accreditation Board.

Platt, R. H. 1991. *Land use control: geography, law and public policy.* Englewood Cliffs, NJ: Prentice-Hall.

Popper, K. R. 1945. *The open society and its enemies.* New York, NY: Routledge and Kegan Paul.

Porter, M. E. 1990. *The competitive advantage of nations.* New York, NY: Free Press.

Preliminary report respecting a public park in Buffalo and a copy of the act of the Legislature authorizing its establishment. 1869. Buffalo, NY: Matthews and Warren.

Prescott, S. C., and M. P. Horwood. 1935. *Sedgwick's principles of sanitary science and public health.* New York, NY: Macmillan.

Pressman, J., and A. Wildavsky. 1973. *Implementation.* Berkeley, CA: University of California Press.

Primack, A., D. R. Moldal, and M. D. Hilton. 1995. Restoration for clean water. *Restoration and Management Notes* 13,2: 176–78.

Przeworski, A. 1991. *Democracy and the market: political and economic reforms in Eastern Europe and Latin America.* New York, NY: Cambridge University Press.

Putnam, H. 1997. A half century of philosophy, viewed from within. *Daedalus* (Winter).

Putnam, R. D. 1992. *Making democracy work: civic traditions in modern Italy.* Princeton, NJ: Princeton University Press.

Putnam, R. D. 1995. Bowling alone: America's declining social capital. *Journal of Democracy* 6: 65–78.

Putnam, R. D. 1996. The strange disappearance of civic America. *The American Prospect* 24: 34–48.

Rabinowitz, F. 1969. *City politics and planning.* New York, NY: Atherton Press.

Rabinowitz, H., E. Beimborn, C. Mrotek, S. Yan, and P. Gugliotta. 1991. *The new suburb.* Washington, DC: U.S. Department of Transportation.

Ransom, J. C. 1972. Criticism, Inc. Reprinted in D. Lodge, ed. (1972), *Twentieth century literary criticism: a reader.* London, UK: Longman. p. 232.

Ratcliffe, J., and M. Stubbs. 1996. *Urban planning and real estate development.* London, UK: UCL Press.

Rawls, J. 1971. *A theory of justice.* Cambridge, MA: Harvard University Press.

Rees, R., and M. Wackernagel. 1996a. Urban ecological footprints: why cities cannot be sustainable—and why they are a key to sustainability. *Environmental Impact Assessment Review* 16,4–6: 223–48.

Rees, R., and M. Wackernagel. 1996b. *Our ecological footprint: reducing human impact on the earth.* Gabriola Island, British Columbia, Canada: New Society Publishers.

Reese, L. A., and D. Fasenfest. 1996. More of the same: a research note on local economic development policies over time. *Economic Development Quarterly* 10: 280–89.

Regalado, J. A. 1994. Community coalition building. In M. Baldassare, ed. (1994), *The Los Angeles riots: lessons for the future.* Boulder, CO: Westview Press.

Reps, J. W. 1965. *The making of urban America: a history of city planning in the United States.* Princeton, NJ: Princeton University Press.

Reynolds, M. 1962. *Little boxes* (sound recording). *Pete Seeger's greatest hits* (Columbia).

Rich, M. J. 1992. UDAG, economic development, and the death and life of American cities. *Economic Development Quarterly* 6: 150–72.

Rittel, H. W., and M. M. Webber. 1973. Dilemmas in a general theory of planning. *Policy Science* 4: 155–69.

Robertson, K. A. 1993. Pedestrian strategies for downtown planners: skywalks v. pedestrian malls. *Journal of the American Planning Association* 59: 361–70.

Robertson, K. A. 1995. Downtown redevelopment strategies in the United States: an end-of-the-century assessment. *Journal of the American Planning Association* 61: 429–37.

Rodwin, L. 1963. Choosing regions for development. In C. J. Friedrich and S. E. Harris, eds., *Public policy*. vol. 12. Cambridge, MA: Harvard University Press.

Rodwin, L. 1972. Innovations for urban studies. *Planning* 38: 182–86.

Rodwin, L., and D. Schön, eds. 1996. *Rethinking the development experience: essays provoked by the work of A. O. Hirschman*. Washington, DC: The Brookings Institution; Cambridge, MA: Lincoln Institute of Land Policy.

Rorty, A. 1988. *Mind in action: essays in the philosophy of mind*. Boston, MA: Beacon Press.

Rose, C. M. 1997. Property rights and responsibilities. In M. R. Chertow and D. C. Esty, eds., *Thinking ecologically: the next generation of environmental problems*. New Haven, CT: Yale University Press.

Roseland, M. 1997. Dimensions of the future and eco-city overview. In M. Roseland, ed., *Eco-city dimensions: healthy communities*. Gabriola Island, British Columbia, Canada: Healthy Planet New Society Publishers.

Rosentraub, M. S., and D. Swindell. 1991. "Just say no?" The economic and political realities of a small city's investment in minor league baseball. *Economic Development Quarterly* 5: 152–67.

Rusk, D. 1993. *Cities without suburbs*. Washington, DC: Woodrow Wilson Center Press.

Rybczynksi, W. 1997. Remarks presented at MIT Faculty Seminar, "The Profession of City Planning," MIT, Cambridge, Massachusetts. February.

Rybczynski, W. 2000. Where have all the planners gone? In L. Rodwin and B. Sanyal, eds., *The profession of city planning: changes, images, and challenges, 1950–2000*. New Brunswick, NJ: Center for Urban Policy Research (CUPR Press). ch. 23.

Sagalyn, L. B. 1990. Explaining the improbable: local redevelopment in the wake of federal cutbacks. *Journal of the American Planning Association* 56: 429–41.

Salamon, L., and A. Abramson. 1982. *The federal budget and the nonprofit sector*. Washington, DC: The Urban Institute.

Salamon, L., J. Musselwhite, and C. DeVita. 1986. Partners in public service: government and the nonprofit sector in the American welfare state. Prepared for delivery at the Independent Sector Spring Research Forum. Washington, DC: The Urban Institute.

Salisbury, H. E. 1958. Cities in the grip of revolution. Review of *The exploding metropolis* by the editors of *Fortune*. *New York Times Book Review* (October 5).

Sandel, M. J. 1984. *Liberalism and its critics*. London, UK: Basil Blackwell.

Sandel, M. J. 1996. *Democracy's discontent: America in search of a public philosophy*. Cambridge, MA: Harvard University Press.

Sandercock, L. 1997. *Towards cosmopolis*. New York, NY: John Wiley & Sons.

Sandercock, L. 1998. *Making the invisible visible: a multicultural planning history*. Berkeley, CA: University of California Press.

Santa Clara Valley Water District (SCVWD). 1997. *Integrated water resources plan: final report*. San Jose, CA: SCVWD.

Sanyal, B. 1997. Remarks presented at MIT Faculty Seminar, "The Profession of City Planning," MIT, Cambridge, Massachusetts. February.

Sanyal, B. 2000. Planning's three challenges. In L. Rodwin and B. Sanyal, eds., *The profession of city planning: changes, images, and challenges, 1950–2000*. New Brunswick, NJ: Center for Urban Policy Research (CUPR Press), ch. 35.

Sassen, S. 1991. *The global city: New York, London, Tokyo*. Princeton, NJ: Princeton University Press.

Saxenian, A. 1994. *Regional advantage: culture and competition in Silicon Valley and Route 128*. Cambridge, MA: Harvard University Press.

Saxenian, A. 1996. Inside-out: regional networks and industrial adaptation in Silicon Valley and Route 128. *Cityscape: A Journal of Policy Development and Research* 2: 41–60.

Schön, D. 1983. *The reflective practitioner: how professionals think in action*. New York, NY: Basic Books.

Schön, D. 1986. Towards a new epistemology of practice. In B. Checkoway, ed., *Strategic perspectives on planning practice*. Lexington, MA: Lexington Books.

Schön, D. 1990. *The reflective turn: case studies in and on educational practice*. New York, NY: Teacher's College Press.

Schumacher, W. F. 1973. *Small is beautiful: economics as if people mattered*. New York, NY: Harper and Row.

Schuyler, D., and J. T. Censer, eds. 1992. *The papers of Frederick Law Olmsted. Volume vi: The years of Olmsted, Vaux & Company, 1865–1874*. Baltimore, MD: Johns Hopkins University Press.

Scott, A. J. 1993a. *Technopolis: high-technology industry and regional development in Southern California*. Berkeley and Los Angeles, CA: University of California Press.

Scott, A. J. 1993b. The new Southern Californian economy: pathways to industrial resurgence. *Economic Development Quarterly* 7: 296–309.

Scott, James C. 1998. *Seeing like a state: how certain schemes to improve the human condition have failed*. New Haven, CT: Yale University Press.

Scott, M. 1969. *American city planning since 1890.* Berkeley, CA: University of California Press.

Seattle Times. December 17, 1992.

Seedco. 1998. Partnerships for the future, a Seedco/HBCU conference report. Baltimore, MD.

Seidman, K. 1999. Proposal for a loan forgiveness program. Mimeo, Massachusetts Institute of Technology, Cambridge, MA.

Servon, L. 1997. *Credit and social capital: the community development potential of U.S. microenterprise programs.* CUPR Working Paper No. 122. New Brunswick, NJ: Rutgers University, Center for Urban Policy Research.

Shah, Praful. 1979. Economic base studies: forecasting, fiscal impact, evaluation. In F. S. So, I. Stollman, F. Beal, and D. S. Arnold, eds., *The practice of local government planning.* Washington, DC: International City Management Association.

Shapira, P. 1990. Modern times: learning from state initiatives in industrial extension and technology transfer. *Economic Development Quarterly* 4,3: 186–202.

Shapira, P., and J. Youtie. 1996. *Coordinating industrial modernization services: impacts and insights from the U.S. Manufacturing Extension Partnership.* Atlanta, GA: Georgia Tech Economic Development Institute, Georgia Institute of Technology.

Shiffer, M. J. 1999. Planning support systems for low-income communities. In D. Schön et al., eds., *High technology and low-income communities.* Cambridge, MA: MIT Press.

Shiffman, R. 1992. Neighborhoods as an entry point for change. *Conference report: building strong communities.* Cleveland, OH: Annie E. Casey Foundation.

Shoup, D. C. 1993. Cashing out employer-paid parking. *Access* 2: 3–9.

Shoup, D. C., and D. Pickrell. 1980. *Free parking as a transportation problem.* Washington, DC: U.S. Department of Transportation.

Shropshire, K. L. 1995. *The sports franchise game: cities in pursuit of sports franchises, events, stadiums, and arenas.* Philadelphia, PA: University of Pennsylvania Press.

Simon, H. 1965. *The shape of automation for men and management.* New York, NY: Harper & Row.

Simmons, L. 1996. Dilemmas of progressives in government: playing Solomon in an age of austerity. *Economic Development Quarterly* 10: 159–71.

Sklar, R. L.1979. The nature of class domination in Africa. *Journal of Modern African Studies* 17,4: 531–52.

Smith, S. K. 1987. Tests of forecast accuracy and bias for county population projections. *Journal of the American Statistical Association* 82, 400: 991–1012.

Snow, L. 1995. Economic development breaks the mold: community-building, place-targeting, and empowerment zones. *Economic Development Quarterly* 9: 185–98.

So, F. S.; I. Hand; and B. D. McDowell. 1986. *The practice of state and regional planning.* Chicago: American Planning Association.

So, F. S., I. Stollman, F. Beal, and D. S. Arnold, eds. 1979. *The practice of local government planning.* Washington, DC: International City Management Association.

Solow, R. 1997. How did economics get that way and what way did it get? *Daedalus* (Winter).

Spectorsky, A. C. 1957. Nothing down and a lifetime to pay. *New York Times Book Review* (January 20).

Stegman, M. A., and M. A. Turner. 1996. The future of urban America in the global economy. *Journal of the American Planning Association* 62: 157–64.

Stein, J. M., ed. 1993. *Growth management: the planning challenge of the 1990s.* Newbury Park, CA: Sage Publications.

Steiner, F. 1994. Landscapes through time. In T. J. Bartuska and G. L. Young, eds., *The built environment: a creative inquiry into design and planning.* Menlo Park, CA: Crisp Publishers, Inc.

Stiglitz, J. E. 1998. Towards a new paradigm for development: strategies, policies, and process. Prebisch lecture delivered at UNCTAD, Geneva, Switzerland, October 19.

Stollman, I. 2000. Looking back, looking forward. In L. Rodwin and B. Sanyal, eds., *The profession of city planning: changes, images, and challenges, 1950–2000.* New Brunswick, NJ: Center for Urban Policy Research (CUPR Press). ch. 11.

Storper, M., and R. Walker. 1989. *The capitalist imperative: territory, technology, and industrial growth.* Oxford, UK: Blackwell.

Surge, T. J. 1998. *The origins of the urban crisis: race and inequality in post-War Detroit.* Princeton, NJ: Princeton University Press.

Susskind, L. 1973. The future of planning education. In D. R. Godschalk, ed., *Planning in America: learning from turbulence.* Washington, DC: American Institute of Planners.

Susskind, L., and A. McCreary. 1985. Techniques for resolving coastal resource management disputes through negotiation. *Journal of the American Planning Association* 51: 365–74.

Susskind, L., and J. Cruikshank. 1987. *Breaking the impasse: consensual approaches to resolving policy disputes.* New York, NY: Basic Books.

Susskind, L., and P. Field. 1996. *Dealing with an angry public.* New York, NY: The Free Press.

Teitz, M. B. 1994. Changes in economic development theory and practice. *International Regional Science Review* 16: 101–6.

Teitz, M. 1996. American planning in the 1990s: evolution, debate, and challenge. *Urban Studies* 33, 4–5: 649–71.

Teitz, M. 1997. American planning in the 1990s, Part II: the dilemma of the cities. *Urban Studies* 34, 5–6: 775–95.

Teitz, M. 2000. Reflections and research on the U.S. experience. In L. Rodwin and B. Sanyal, eds., *The profession of city planning: changes, images, and challenges, 1950–2000.* New Brunswick, NJ: Center for Urban Policy Research (CUPR Press). ch. 32.

Tendler, J. 1998. *Good government in the tropics.* Baltimore, MD: Johns Hopkins University Press.

Thomas, H. A. Jr. 1972. Waste disposal in natural waterways. In R. Dorfman, H. D. Jacoby, and H. A. Thomas, Jr., eds., *Models for managing regional water quality.* Cambridge, MA: Harvard University Press.

Thomas, M. D. 1957. The "economic base" and a region's economy. *Journal of the American Institute of Planners* 23, 2: 86–92.

Throgmorton, J. 1992. Planning as persuasive storytelling about the future: negotiating an electric power rate settlement in Illinois. *Journal of Planning Education and Research* 12: 17–31.

Throgmorton, J. 1996. *Planning as persuasive storytelling: the rhetorical construction of Chicago's electric future.* Chicago, IL: University of Chicago Press.

Thurow, L. 1998. Asia: the collapse and the cure. *New York Review of Books.* February 5.

Tiebout, C. 1956. A pure theory of local expenditures. *Journal of Political Economy* 64: 416–24.

Tiebout, C. 1957. Input–output and foreign trade multiplier models in urban research. *Journal of the American Institute of Planners* 23: 126–30.

Tiebout, C. 1962. *The community economic base study.* New York, NY: Committee for Economic Development.

Tu, C. C., and M. J. Eppli. 1997. Valuing the new urbanism: the case of Kentlands. Unpublished paper, Department of Finance, George Washington University.

Twiss, R. H. 1973. Planning for areas of significant environmental and amenity value. In P. M. McAllister, ed., *Environment: a new focus for land-use planning.* Report No. NSF/RA/E-74-001. Washington, DC: National Science Foundation.

U.S. Department of Commerce. 1998. Regional economic information system, 1969–1996. CD-ROM. Washington, DC: U.S. Department of Commerce, Bureau of Economic Analysis.

U.S. Environmental Protection Agency. 1992. *Environmental equity: reducing risk for all communities.* Report No. EPA 230-R-92-008. Washington, DC: U.S. EPA.

Vale, L. 2000. Urban design for urban development. In L. Rodwin and B. Sanyal, eds., *The profession of city planning: changes, images, and challenges, 1950–2000.* New Brunswick, NJ: Center for Urban Policy Research (CUPR Press). ch.25

Vasu, M. L. 1979. *Politics and planning: a national study of American planners.* Durham, NC: University of North Carolina Press.

Vidal, A. C. 1992. *Rebuilding communities: a national study of urban community development corporations.* New York, NY: Community Development Research Center, Graduate School of Management and Urban Policy, New School for Social Research.

Vidal, A. C. 1995. Reintegrating disadvantaged communities into the fabric of urban life: the role of community development. *Housing Policy Debate* 6: 169–230.

Vining, R. 1949. The region as an economic entity and certain variations to be observed in the study of systems of regions. *American Economic Review* (May): 89–104.

Visser, J. A., and B. E. Wright. 1996. Professional education in economic development: conflicting expectations for college programs in the Great Lakes region. *Economic Development Quarterly* 10: 3–20.

Webber, M. M. 1963. The prospects for policies planning. In L. J. Duhl, ed., *The urban condition*. New York, NY: Basic Books.

Webber, M. M., and F. C. Collignon. 1998. Ideas that drove DCRP. *Berkeley Planning Journal* 12: 1–19.

Wegener, M. 1994. Operational urban models: state of the art. *Journal of the American Planning Association* 60: 17–29.

Weidenbaum, M. 1992. *Small wars, big defense*. New York, NY: Oxford University Press.

Weiner, A. M., and H. Hoyt. 1939. *Principles in real estate*. New York, NY: Roland Press.

Weiner, M., and S. Huntington, eds. 1987. *Understanding political development*. Boston, MA: Little, Brown.

Wenocur, S. 1991. Community organizing and urban planning: Whose interests do professions serve? *Journal of the American Planning Association* 57: 497–501.

Whitehead, A. N. 1906. *Introduction to mathematics*. London, UK: Williams and Norgate.

Whyte, W. H. 1968. *The last landscape*. New York, NY: Doubleday.

Wildavsky, A. 1964. *The politics of budgetary process*. Boston, MA: Little, Brown.

Wilson, J. H. 1975. *Herbert Hoover: forgotten progressive*. Boston, MA: Little, Brown.

Wilson, W. J. 1987. *The truly disadvantaged: the inner city, the underclass, and public policy*. Chicago, IL: University of Chicago Press.

Wilson, W. J. 1996. *When work disappears: the world of the new urban poor*. New York, NY: Alfred A. Knopf.

Wolin, S. S. 1989. *Presence of the past: essays on the state and Constitution*. Series in Constitutional Thought. Baltimore, MD: Johns Hopkins University Press.

Wolman, A. 1965. The metabolism of cities. *Scientific American* 213, 3: 179–88.

Wood, R. C. 1958. *Suburbia*. New York, NY: Arno Press.

World Commission on Environment and Development. 1987. *Our common future*. New York, NY: Oxford University Press.

Yaro, R. D., and T. Hiss. 1996. *A region at risk*. Washington, DC: Island Press.

Yiftachel, O. 1998. Planning and social control: exploring the dark side. *Journal of Planning Literature* 12,4.

Contributors

WILLIAM ALONSO, former director of the Center for Population Studies at Harvard University and Richard Saltonstall Professor of Population Policy, taught at Yale University, the University of California–Berkeley, and Stanford University during his academic career. He served as adviser to the U.S. departments of Agriculture, Commerce, and HUD; the World Bank; the United Nations Fund for Population Activities; and the Ford Foundation. Dr. Alonso died in February 1999.

CHRISTIE I. BAXTER is Principal Research Scientist and Lecturer in the Department of Urban Studies and Planning at MIT. Director of the MIT Project on Social Investing, Dr. Baxter is also Associate Director of MIT's Project on Military Base Redevelopment. In her work on private-entity investments in social-purpose ventures, she has designed and conducted educational programs to help foundations, urban nonprofits, and their partners invest in public projects.

LAWRENCE D. BOBO is Professor of Sociology and Afro-American Studies at Harvard University. He is coauthor of *Racial Attitudes in America: Trends and Interpretations* (Harvard University Press, 1997) and *Racialized Politics: The Debate on Racism in America* (University of Chicago Press, 2000).

PHILLIP L. CLAY, Associate Provost and Professor of City Planning at MIT, formerly served as chair of the Department of Urban Studies and Planning at MIT and assistant director of the MIT–Harvard Joint Center for Urban Studies. His research concentration is on national urban policy, low-income housing, and community-based development organizations.

ERNESTO J. CORTÉS, JR. is Southwest Regional Director of the Industrial Areas Foundation (IAF). In 1974, Dr. Cortés founded the San Antonio-based Communities Organized for Public Service (COPS), the local IAF affiliate. Dr. Cortés is the recipient of a MacArthur "Genius" award for his outstanding work in grassroots community organizing.

ANTHONY DOWNS is Senior Fellow at The Brookings Institution. Formerly chairman of the Real Estate Research Corporation, in 1967 Dr. Downs was appointed by President Lyndon Johnson to the National Commission on Urban Problems. He later served an appointment by former HUD Secretary Jack Kemp to HUD's Advisory Commission on Regulatory Barriers to Affordable Housing.

JOHN FORESTER is Professor and Chair of the Department of City and Regional Planning at Cornell University. Author of the widely cited *Planning in the Face of Power* (University of California Press, 1989), Dr. Forester's research focuses on the dynamics of power, rationality, and consensus building in the planning process. His latest book, *The Deliberative Practitioner: Encouraging Participatory Planning Processes,* was published by MIT Press in 1999.

DENNIS FRENCHMAN is Professor of the Practice of Urban Design and head of the City Design and Development Program at MIT. A registered architect, he is founding principal and vice president of ICON Architecture, Inc., a Boston-based architecture, urban design, planning, and landscape architecture firm with an international practice.

BERNARD J. FRIEDEN is Ford Professor of Urban Development and Associate Dean of the School of Architecture and Planning at MIT. A former director of the MIT–Harvard Joint Center for Urban Studies and former chair of the MIT Faculty, Dr. Frieden has focused his research on the politics of urban development, on public–private relations in city-building, and on the redevelopment of city centers.

RALPH GAKENHEIMER, Professor of Urban Planning at MIT, is a participant in the Cooperative Mobility Program at the MIT Center for Technology, Policy, and Industrial Development. His work focuses on infrastructure and transportation planning in metropolitan areas of developing countries.

NATHAN GLAZER, Professor Emeritus of Sociology and Education at Harvard University, is the author or editor of books on American ethnicity, race relations, and social and urban policy. The distinguished social scientist's most recent book, *We Are All Multiculturalists Now,* was published by Harvard University Press in 1997.

BENNETT J. HARRISON was Professor of Urban Political Economy in the Milano Graduate School of Management and Urban Policy at the New School for Social Research in New York before his death in 1999. During his career, he taught at Harvard University's Kennedy School of Government, at Carnegie Mellon University, and at MIT. His important work, *The Deindustrialization of America: Plant Closings, Community Abandonment, and the Dismantling of Basic Industry,* was coauthored with colleague Barry Bluestone in 1984.

CHESTER HARTMAN, founder and former chair of the Planners Network, is President and Executive Director of the Poverty and Race Research Action Council in Washington, D.C. Dr. Hartman has served as a consultant to numerous public and private agencies, including HUD, the U.S. Civil Rights Commission, the Urban Coalition, and the Legal Aid Society of New York.

PHILIP B. HERR is founder and principal of Herr & Associates, Planning Consultants, in Newton Corner, Massachusetts, and a retired Adjunct Professor in the Department of Urban Studies and Planning at MIT. His practice and teaching focus on community planning and growth management issues. Herr has authored numerous publications, including many for the National Trust for Historic Preservation.

CON HOWE has been Director of Planning for the City of Los Angeles since 1992. In New York City, he served as executive director of the Planning Department in the late 1980s and directed the Lower Manhattan Project, a public–private partnership that planned and promoted improvements in Lower Manhattan, including the first comprehensive plan for that area in 25 years. Howe earlier directed the Massachusetts Land Bank and served in the Massachusetts Governor's Office.

JUDITH E. INNES is Professor of City and Regional Planning and Director of the Institute of Urban and Regional Development at the University of California, Berkeley. She also directs the University–Oakland Metropolitan Forum, a partnership that aims to bring together the resources of the university and the city. Her research is on planning processes, currently focusing on consensus building in land use, environmental, and transportation planning.

ANDREW M. ISSERMAN is Professor of Rural Economic Policy and Planning in the departments of Urban and Regional Planning and Agricultural and Consumer Economics at the University of Illinois, Urbana-Champaign. He headed the Regional Research Institute of West Virginia University for 12 years and is editor of *International Regional Science Review.*

ALLAN B. JACOBS, an architect and city planner, is a Professor of City and Regional Planning at the University of California, Berkeley. During his extensive professional career, he worked in cities as diverse as Boston, Cleveland, Calcutta, Pittsburgh, and San Francisco (where he directed the Department of City Planning). His most recent book, *Great Streets* (MIT Press, 1993), is a major reference for architects and urban designers.

ALEX KRIEGER, FAIA, is Professor in Practice of Urban Design and Chair of the Department of Urban Planning and Design in the Harvard Graduate School of Design at Harvard University. A founding principal of Chan Krieger & Associates in Cambridge, Massachusetts, Mr. Krieger's design firm has received eight national design awards as well as prizes from the American Institute of Architects and *Progressive Architecture*.

ANN MARKUSEN is Professor of Planning and Public Affairs at the Hubert Humphrey Institute at the University of Minnesota. She is a Senior Fellow of the Council on Foreign Relations and has advised government at all levels on high technology, industrial and regional policy, and economic development. She is coauthor or coeditor of *Second Tier Cities: Rapid Growth Beyond the Metropolis* (University of Minnesota Press, 1999); *Trading Industries, Trading Regions* (Guilford Press, 1993); and *The Rise of the Gunbelt* (Oxford University Press, 1991).

LEONARD ORTOLANO is UPS Foundation Professor of Civil Engineering and director of the Program on Urban Studies at Stanford University. A specialist in water resources and environmental planning, Dr. Ortolano has served as an environmental engineer for the U.S. Environmental Protection Agency and as a consultant to environmental management firms and agencies in this country and abroad.

WITOLD RYBCZYNSKI holds the Martin and Margy Meyerson Chair in Urbanism at The University of Pennsylvania, where he is Professor of Real Estate and director of the Urban Design Program. An Honorary Fellow of the American Institute of Architects and a regular contributor to such publications as the *New Yorker, New York Review of Books,* and the *Atlantic*, Professor Rybczynski's latest book is *A Clearing in the Distance: Frederick Law Olmsted and America in the Nineteenth Century*.

DONALD A. SCHÖN, who died in 1997, was Ford Professor of Urban Studies and Education at MIT. Author of the influential 1983 work, *The Reflective Practitioner*, Dr. Schön studied the dynamics of public and organizational learning, professional education, and professional effectiveness. He directed the

Institute for Applied Technology at the National Bureau of Standards and served as president of the Organization for Social and Technological Innovation.

ISRAEL STOLLMAN has taught and practiced planning for the last 50 years. In 1957 he founded and served as chair of the graduate program in City and Regional Planning at Ohio State University. Now Executive Director Emeritus of the American Planning Association, he directed the APA from its establishment in 1978 as a consolidation of the American Institute of Planners and the American Society of Planning Officials.

LAWRENCE SUSSKIND is Ford Professor of Urban and Environmental Planning and head of the Environmental Policy Group at MIT. He is president of the Consensus Building Institute, a Cambridge, Massachusetts–based not-for-profit organization. His book with Patrick Field, *Dealing With An Angry Public* (Free Press), won the 1996 award for Best Book in the Dispute Resolution Field.

TERRY S. SZOLD is Lecturer in the Department of Urban Studies and Planning at MIT and principal of Community Planning Solutions, a land-use planning consulting firm. She has served on the Board of Directors of the Massachusetts chapter of the American Planning Association and received the chapter's 1996 Faye Seigfriedt Award. Her work in promoting economic development in the North Suburban Boston Region was recognized by the Outstanding Community Leadership Award from that area's chamber of commerce.

MICHAEL B. TEITZ is Director of Research at the Public Policy Institute of California and Professor Emeritus of City and Regional Planning at the University of California, Berkeley, where he taught from 1963 until 1998. He has written and consulted widely on economic development and housing economics and policy. Dr. Teitz has served as consultant or adviser to the U.S. Department of Housing and Urban Development; the municipal governments of New York City, Los Angeles, and Berkeley, California; and numerous other public- and private-sector clients.

LAWRENCE J. VALE is Associate Professor and Associate Head of the Department of Urban Studies and Planning at MIT, where he is also a Margaret MacVicar Fellow. His 1992 book, *Architecture, Power, and National Identity* (Yale University Press), received the Spiro Kostof Book Award from the Society of Architectural Historians. His forthcoming book, *From the Puritans to the Projects: Public Housing and Public Neighbors,* will be published by Harvard University Press.

MARTIN WACHS is Director of the Institute of Transportation Studies at the University of California, Berkeley, where he is also Professor of City and Regional Planning and Professor of Civil and Environmental Engineering. Before moving to Berkeley, he was a faculty member in Urban Planning at UCLA for 25 years, where he served three terms as department chair. Dr. Wachs, who has published widely in the field of transportation planning and policy as well as ethics in planning, is the current chairman of the Transportation Research Board.

SAM BASS WARNER, Jr., an urban historian, is currently a visiting professor in the Department of Urban Studies and Planning at MIT. Author of the highly regarded book, *The Urban Wilderness,* he is best known in the Boston and Philadelphia areas for his histories of those cities. He is at work with other scholars writing about contemporary American city-regions.

ROBERT D. YARO is Executive Director of the Regional Plan Association (RPA), an independent metropolitan research and advocacy organization that works in the tri-state New York–New Jersey–Connecticut metropolitan region. Yaro's 1996 book, *A Region At Risk* (with T. Hiss), sets forth RPA's Third Regional Plan for the New York-New Jersey-Connecticut Metropolitan Area, with strategies to sustain the competitiveness of the region.

Acknowledgments

I t was Bishwapriya Sanyal's idea that Lloyd Rodwin should conduct, once again, the Department of Urban Studies Faculty Seminar. Lloyd then proposed the focus: The Profession of City Planning. Not surprisingly, Lloyd and Bish ended up planning and organizing the February 1997 seminar (with some helpful initial suggestions from Lawrence Susskind). Lloyd Rodwin performed most of the editing chores; Mark Rossi provided first drafts of the seminar discussions; and Bish Sanyal raised the funds for the seminar, with major support from William Mitchell, Dean of the School of Architecture and Urban Planning at MIT.

The main seminar participants were the MIT faculty contributors to this volume. Other full- or part-time participants were Aixa Cintron, Lawrence Bacow, Charles Boyce, John de Monchaux, Aaron Fleisher, Joseph Fereirra, Langley Keyes, Paul Levy, Louis H. Orzack, Lisa Peattie, Karen Polenske, Martin Rein, Mark Schuster, Qing Shen, Meenu Tewari, and William C. Wheaton.

Six of the chapters were added to the volume by the editors to supplement the papers presented at the seminar. These are "Challenge and Creativity in Post-Modern Planning," by Judith E. Innes; "How City Planning Practices Affect Metropolitan-Area Housing Markets, and Vice Versa" by Anthony Downs; "Planning As Craft and As Philosophy," by Ann Markusen; "Limits to Reflection-in-Action," by our recently deceased colleague, Donald A. Schön; and the editors' contributions, "Images and Paths of Change in Economics, Political Science, Philosophy, Literature, and City Planning: 1950–2000" (Lloyd Rodwin), and "Planning's Three Challenges" (Bishwapriya Sanyal).

We are particularly indebted to Brenda Blais and Maddy Arnstein for extremely patient and indispensable assistance for the typing and other tasks involved in getting the manuscript to the publisher; and, as usual, Rolf R. Engler provided indefatigable and indispensable administrative assistance.

One final observation: To keep the price of this book reasonable, discussions from the sessions devoted to the activities of the profession in Europe and the developing countries, as well as the resume of the discussions at the seminar, were omitted. These discussions may be published in a future volume.

Lloyd Rodwin
Bishwapriya Sanyal

Index

A

Abrams, M. H., 8, 11
Abramson, A., 90
accessibility, 137, 143
Adams, Thomas, 45
Adams Township, Pennsylvania, 39
advocacy
  community, 229, 293
  groups, 20, 64, 84
  planning, 56, 64, 83, 86, 113, 324
African-American institutions, 94-95, 97
African Americans, 293, 310
  and National Capital Planning Commission,
    222
  inflows to central cities, 110
  in inner cities, 196, 300-303
  mobility, 305
  poverty rates, 278
agglomeration, 374n 1
air quality
  management, 146-147
  national regulations, 167-168
Albuquerque, New Mexico, 215
Alexander, John, 178
Allen African Methodist Episcopal Church,
  94-95, 97
Alonso, William, 20-21, 316
Alphand, Adolphe, 211
Althusser, Louis, 11, 23
Altshuler, Alan, 97, 207, 318
American City Planning Institute, 106
American City, The (Garvin), 215, 216
American Economic Review, 178
American Economics Association, 5
American Institute of Certified Planners
  (AICP), 87, 101, 105
American Institute of Planners, 103, 105
American Philosophical Association, 7
American Planning Association, 220, 323
  and planning practice, 179
  APA Journal, 113
  charter, 315
  Form-Based Planning approach, 39

Growing Smart initiative, 37, 44, 102
  Planning and Community Equity, 104
  professional statement, 320
  specialized technical divisions, 101
  surveys of professional planners, 85, 224
  Understanding Your Economy, 181
American Social Science Association, 155
American Society of Planning Officials
  (ASPO), 106
Amin, Ash, 198
André, Edouard, 211
Andrews, Richard, 179, 180
Appalachian Regional Commission (ARC),
  107, 189, 263
Argyris, Chris, 77, 80
Arkansas, 94
Arnold, Mathew, 8
Arrow, Kenneth, 5
Asia, 158, 209
Asians, 110, 309
Association of Collegiate Schools of Planning
  (ACSP), 315, 320, 322
Association of Research on Non-profit
  Organizations and Voluntary Action, 91
Atlantic Monthly, 227-228
Australia, 158
automation, 135
automobile dependency, 158

B

Bacon, Ed, 99, 217
Baltimore, Maryland, 94, 157, 237, 271
Bangladesh, 272
Bartholomew, Harland, 216
Base Closing Commission, 270
Bassett, Edward H., 280
Battery Park City (New York), 22, 237
Baxter, Christie I., 314
Beatley, T., 159, 283
Bedford Stuyvesant Restoration Corporation,
  91
Bellah, R., 296

387